C000200562

STREET ATLAS

Bedfordshire

Bedford, Biggleswade, Dunstable, Leighton Buzzard, Luton

**.philips-maps.co.uk

First published in 2001 by

Philip's, a division of
Octopus Publishing Group Ltd
www.octopusbooks.co.uk
2-4 Heron Quays, London E14 4JP
An Hachette Livre UK Company
www.hachettelivre.co.uk

Third edition 2009
First impression 2009
BEDCA

ISBN 978-0-540-09209-3 (spiral)

© Philip's 2009

Ordnance Survey®

This product includes mapping data licensed
from Ordnance Survey®, with the permission of
the Controller of Her Majesty's Stationery Office.

© Crown copyright 2009. All rights reserved.
Licence number 100011710

Data for the speed cameras provided by
PocketGPSWorld.com Ltd.

Ordnance Survey and the OS symbol are
registered trademarks of Ordnance Survey, the
national mapping agency of Great Britain

Printed and bound in China by Toppan

Contents

II **Mobile safety cameras**

III **Key to map symbols**

IV **Key to map pages**

VI **Route planning**

VIII **Administrative and Postcode boundaries**

1 **Street maps** at 3½ inches to 1 mile

133 **Index** of towns, villages, streets, hospitals, industrial estates, railway stations, schools, shopping centres universities and places of interest

Digital Data

The exceptionally high-quality mapping found in this atlas is available as digital data in TIFF format, which is easily convertible to other bitmapped (raster) image formats.

The index is also available in digital form as a standard database table. It contains all the details found in the printed index together with the National Grid reference for the map square in which each entry is named.

For further information and to discuss your requirements, please contact
victoria.dawbarn@philips-maps.co.uk

Mobile safety cameras

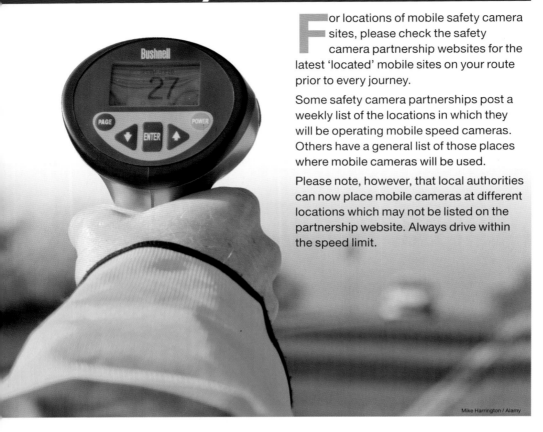

Mike Harrington / Alamy

For locations of mobile safety camera sites, please check the safety camera partnership websites for the latest 'located' mobile sites on your route prior to every journey.

Some safety camera partnerships post a weekly list of the locations in which they will be operating mobile speed cameras. Others have a general list of those places where mobile cameras will be used.

Please note, however, that local authorities can now place mobile cameras at different locations which may not be listed on the partnership website. Always drive within the speed limit.

Useful websites

Bedfordshire and Luton Casualty Reduction Partnership
www.drivesafely.org

Bedfordshire Police Online
www.bedfordshire.police.uk

Luton Borough Council
www.luton.gov.uk

Bedfordshore County Council
www.bedscc.gov.uk

Further information
www.dft.gov.uk
www.dvla.gov.uk
www.highways.gov.uk
www.road-safe.org
www.thinkroadsafety.gov.uk

Motorway with junction number	
Primary route – dual/single carriageway	
A road – dual/single carriageway	
B road – dual/single carriageway	
Minor road – dual/single carriageway	
Other minor road – dual/single carriageway	
Road under construction	
Tunnel, covered road	
Speed cameras - single, multiple	
Rural track, private road or narrow road in urban area	
Gate or obstruction to traffic (restrictions may not apply at all times or to all vehicles)	
Path, bridleway, byway open to all traffic, restricted byway	
Pedestrianised area	
Postcode boundaries	
County and unitary authority boundaries	
Railway, tunnel, railway under construction	
Tramway, tramway under construction	
Miniature railway	
Railway station	
Private railway station	
Metro station	
Tram stop, tram stop under construction	
Bus, coach station	

Acad	Academy	Inst	Institute	Recn Gd	Recreation Ground
Allot Gdns	Allotments	Ct	Law Court		
Cemy	Cemetery	L Ctr	Leisure Centre	Resr	Reservoir
C Ctr	Civic Centre	LC	Level Crossing	Ret Pk	Retail Park
CH	Club House	Liby	Library	Sch	School
Coll	College	Mkt	Market	Sh Ctr	Shopping Centre
Crem	Crematorium	Meml	Memorial	TH	Town Hall/House
Ent	Enterprise	Mon	Monument	Trad Est	Trading Estate
Ex H	Exhibition Hall	Mus	Museum	Univ	University
Ind Est	Industrial Estate	Obsy	Observatory	W Twr	Water Tower
IRB Sta	Inshore Rescue Boat Station	Pal	Royal Palace	Wks	Works
		PH	Public House	YH	Youth Hostel

Ambulance station	
Coastguard station	
Fire station	
Police station	
Accident and Emergency entrance to hospital	
Hospital	
Place of worship	
Information Centre (open all year)	
Shopping Centre	
Parking	
Park and Ride	
Post Office	
Camping site	
Caravan site	
Golf course	
Picnic site	
Important buildings, schools, colleges, universities and hospitals	
Built up area	
Woods	
Water name	
River, weir, stream	
Canal, lock, tunnel	
Water	
Tidal water	
Non-Roman antiquity	
Roman antiquity	
Adjoining page indicators	

■ The small numbers around the edges of the maps identify the 1 kilometre National Grid lines

■ The dark grey border on the inside edge of some pages indicates that the mapping does not continue onto the adjacent page

The scale of the maps on the pages numbered in blue is 5.52 cm to 1 km • 3½ inches to 1 mile • 1: 18103

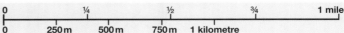

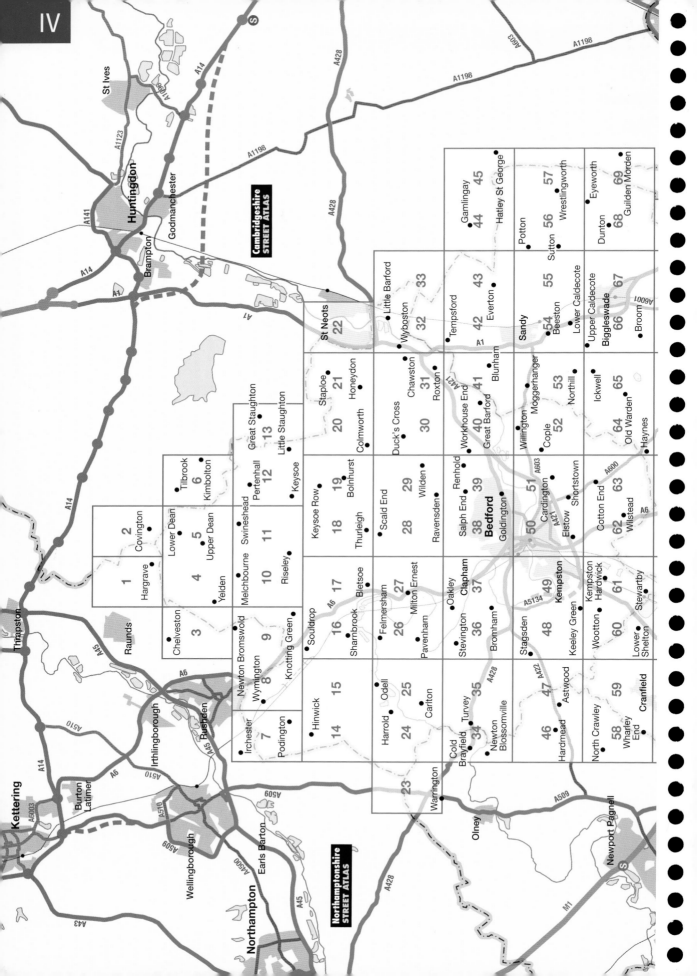

St Ives

Huntingdon

Brampton

Godmanchester

Cambridgeshire STREET ATLAS

Kettering

Burton Latimer

Wellingborough

Northampton

Northamptonshire STREET ATLAS

Thrapston

Raunds

Irthlingborough

Rushden

Olney

Newport Pagnell

St Neots 22

Little Barford

Wyboston 32 33

Staploe 21
Honeydon

Colmworth 20

Chawston 31
Duck's Cross
Roxton
30

Tempsford 42
Everton
Blunham

Workhouse End 41
Great Barford 40

Gamlingay 44 45
Hatley St George

Potton 56 57
Sutton Wrestlingworth

Eyeworth
Dunton 68 69
Guilden Morden

Sandy 54 55
Beeston
Lower Caldecote
Upper Caldecote
Biggleswade 66 67
Broom

Willington 53
Moggerhanger
Northill 65
Cople 52
Ickwell
Old Warden 64
Haynes

Keysoe Row 18 19
Bolhurst
Thurleigh

Scald End 28 29
Wilden
Ravensden

Salph End 39
Renhold
Goldington 38

Bedford
Cardington 51
Shortstown
Elstow
Cotton End 63
Wilstead 62
A6

Great Staughton 13
Little Staughton
Keysoe

Tilbrook 6
Kimbolton
Pertenhall 12
Swineshead 11

Lower Dean 5
Upper Dean
Melchbourne 10
Riseley

Covington 2
Hargrave 1
Yelden 4

Chelveston 3
Newton Bromswold 9
Wymington 8
Knotting Green

Souldrop 16 17
Sharnbrook
Bletsoe
Felmersham 26 27
Milton Ernest
Pavenham

Oakley 36 37
Clapham
Stevington
Bromham

Stagsden 48 49
Kempston
Keeley Green
Kempston Hardwick 61
Wootton 60
Stewartby
Lower Shelton

Hinwick 14 15
Odell
Harrold 24 25
Carlton

Cold Brayfield 34 35
Turvey
Newton Blossomville

Hardmead 46 47
Astwood
North Crawley

Cranfield 58 59
Wharley End

Warrington 23

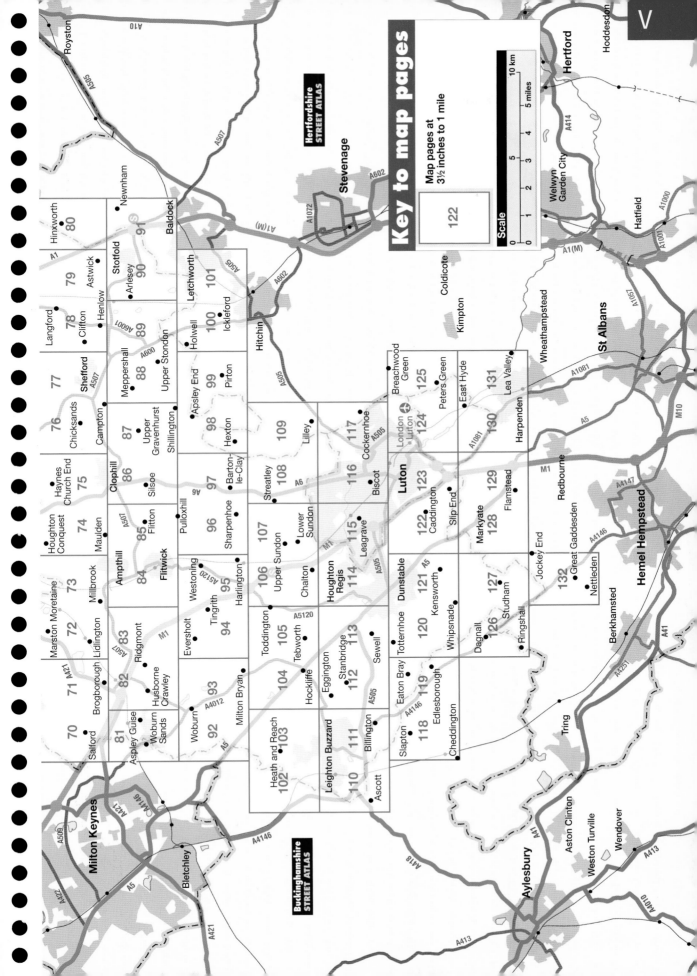

Key to map pages

V

Map pages at 3½ inches to 1 mile

122

Scale

0   1   2   3   4   5 miles
0   5   10 km

Hertfordshire STREET ATLAS

Buckinghamshire STREET ATLAS

Hoddesdon
Hertford
Welwyn Garden City
Hatfield
St Albans
Wheathampstead
Harpenden
Redbourne
Great Gaddesden
Nettleden
Hemel Hempstead
Berkhamsted
Tring
Aston Clinton
Weston Turville
Wendover
Aylesbury

Royston
Newnham
Hinxworth **80**
Astwick **79**
Langford **78**
Baldock **91**
Stotfold **90**
Arlesey
Henlow
Clifton
Shefford **77**
Meppershall **88**
Upper Stondon **89**
Letchworth **101**
Ickleford
Holwell **100**
Pirton **99**
Hitchin
Stevenage
Breachwood Green **125**
Peters Green
East Hyde
Lea Valley **131**
Kimpton
Coldicote
London Luton **124**
130
Chicksands **76**
Campton
Upper Gravenhurst **87**
Shillington
Apsley End **98**
Hexton
Lilley
Cockernhoe **117**
Caddington **122**
Slip End **123**
Flamstead **129**
Markyate **128**
Haynes Church End **75**
Clophill **86**
Silsoe
Barton-le-Clay **97**
Streatley **108**
Biscot **116**
Luton
Jockey End
132
Houghton Conquest **74**
Maulden
Flitton **85**
Pulloxhill
Sharpenhoe **96**
Lower Sundon **107**
Leagrave **115**
Dunstable
Kensworth **121**
Whipsnade **120**
Studham **127**
Ringshall
Dagnall **126**
Ampthill
Flitwick **84**
Westoning **95**
Harlington
Tingrith
Upper Sundon **106**
Chalton
Houghton Regis **114**
Totternhoe
Eaton Bray
Marston Moretaine **72**
Lidlington
Ridgmont **83**
Husborne Crawley **82**
Brogborough **71**
Eversholt **94**
Toddington **105**
Tebworth
Hockliffe **104**
Eggington
Stanbridge **112**
Sewell **113**
Edlesborough **119**
Cheddington
Slapton **118**
Salford **70**
Aspley Guise **81**
Woburn Sands
Woburn **92**
Milton Bryan **93**
Heath and Reach **102**
103
Leighton Buzzard **110**
Billington **111**
Ascott
Milton Keynes
Bletchley

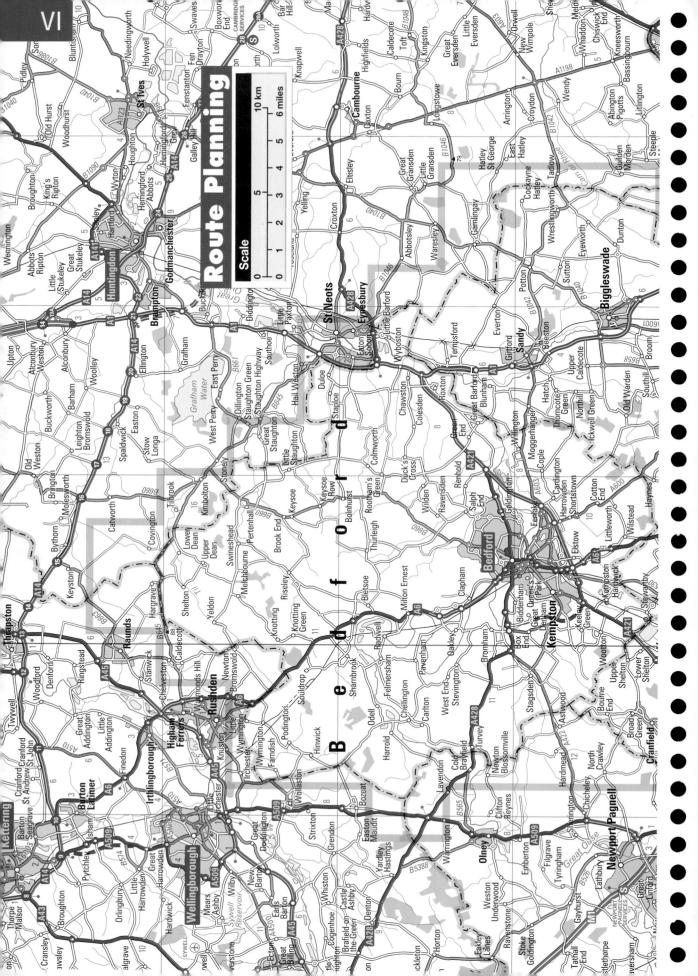

Route Planning

Scale

```
0        1    2    3    4    5        10 km
0             1    2    3    4    5    6 miles
```

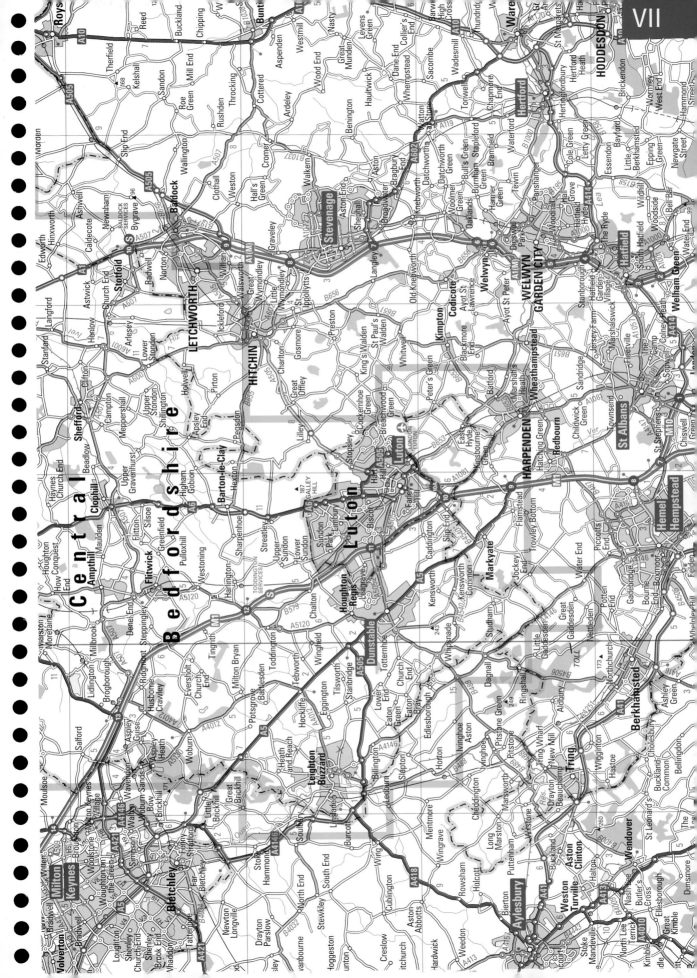

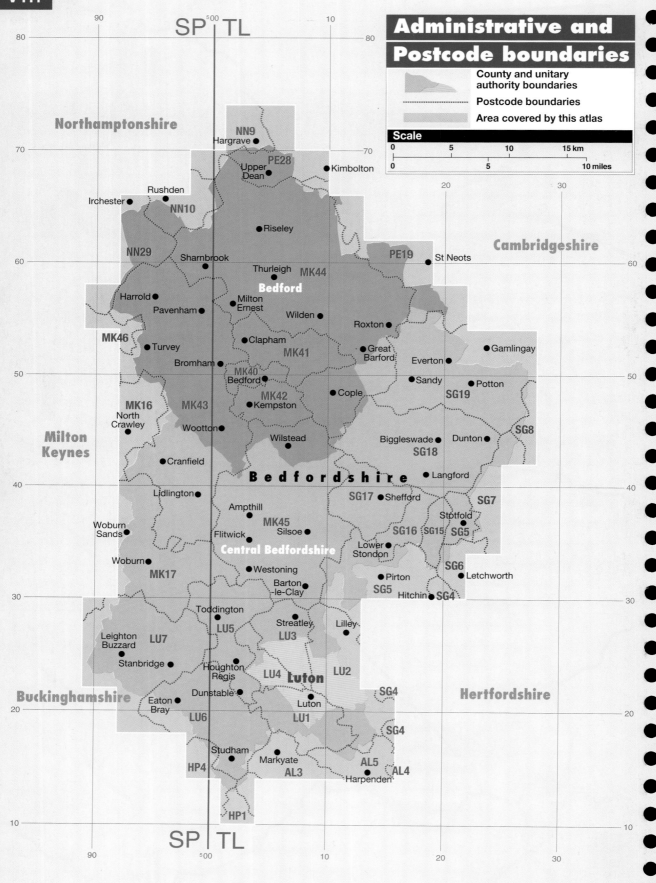

Administrative and Postcode boundaries

County and unitary authority boundaries
Postcode boundaries
Area covered by this atlas

Scale
0   5   10   15 km
0   5   10 miles

Northamptonshire

Cambridgeshire

Milton Keynes

Buckinghamshire

Hertfordshire

Bedford

B e d f o r d s h i r e

Central Bedfordshire

Luton

NN9
PE28
NN10
NN29
MK44
MK46
MK41
MK40
MK16
MK43
MK42
PE19
SG19
SG8
SG18
SG17
SG7
MK45
SG16
SG15
SG5
SG6
SG5
SG4
MK17
LU5
LU7
LU3
LU4
LU2
LU6
LU1
SG4
SG4
HP4
AL5
AL4
AL3
HP1

Hargrave
Upper Dean
Kimbolton
Rushden
Irchester
Riseley
Sharnbrook
Thurleigh
St Neots
Harrold
Milton Ernest
Wilden
Roxton
Gamlingay
Pavenham
Turvey
Clapham
Great Barford
Everton
Bromham
Bedford
Cople
Sandy
Potton
Kempston
North Crawley
Wootton
Wilstead
Biggleswade
Dunton
Cranfield
Langford
Lidlington
Shefford
Ampthill
Stotfold
Woburn Sands
Flitwick
Silsoe
Lower Stondon
Letchworth
Woburn
Westoning
Pirton
Barton-le-Clay
Hitchin
Toddington
Streatley
Lilley
Leighton Buzzard
Stanbridge
Houghton Regis
Dunstable
Luton
Eaton Bray
Studham
Markyate
Harpenden

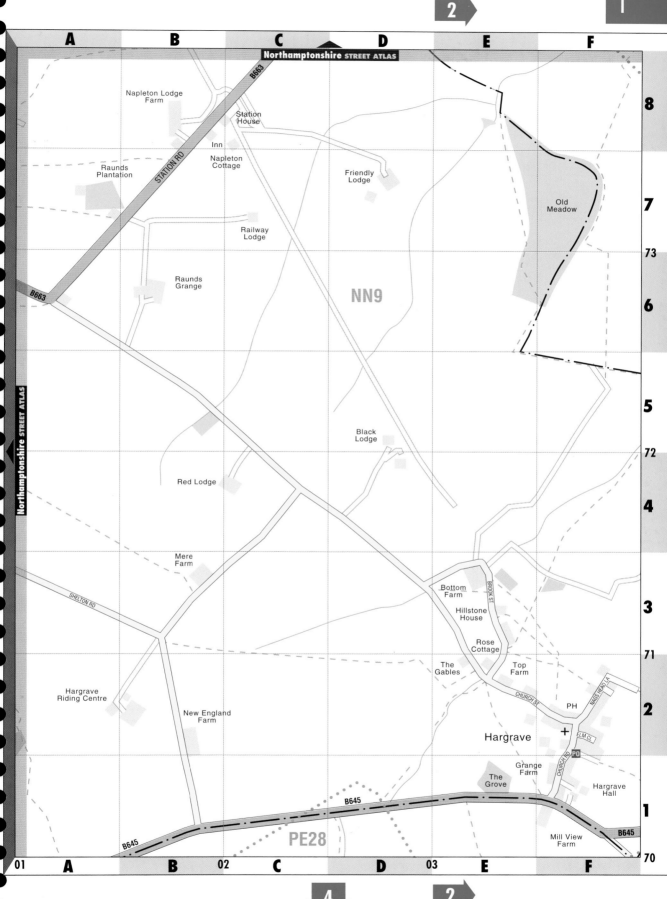

A B C D E F

8

7

73

6

5

72

4

3

71

2

1

70

Napleton Lodge Farm

Station House

Inn

Napleton Cottage

Raunds Plantation

STATION RD

B663

Friendly Lodge

Old Meadow

Railway Lodge

Raunds Grange

NN9

B663

Black Lodge

Red Lodge

Mere Farm

SHELTON RD

Bottom Farm

BROOK ST

Hillstone House

Rose Cottage

The Gables

Top Farm

Hargrave Riding Centre

New England Farm

CHURCH ST

PH

NAGS HEAD LA

Hargrave

+

ELM CL

PO

CHURCH RD

Grange Farm

The Grove

Hargrave Hall

B645

B645

PE28

B645

Mill View Farm

B645

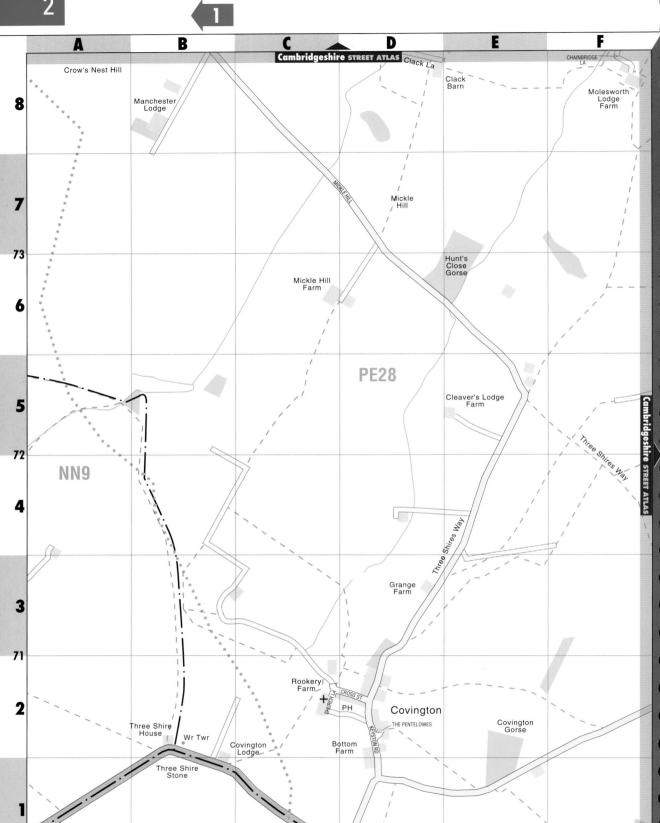

Crow's Nest Hill

Manchester Lodge

Clack La

Clack Barn

CHAINBRIDGE LA

Molesworth Lodge Farm

MICKLE HILL

Mickle Hill

Hunt's Close Gorse

Mickle Hill Farm

PE28

Cleaver's Lodge Farm

Three Shires Way

NN9

Three Shires Way

Grange Farm

Rookery Farm

CROSS ST

CHURCH LA

PH

Covington

THE PENTELOWES

KEYSTON RD

Covington Gorse

Three Shire House

Wr Twr

Covington Lodge

Bottom Farm

Three Shire Stone

B645

04   A   B   05   C   D   06   E   F   70

Cambridgeshire STREET ATLAS

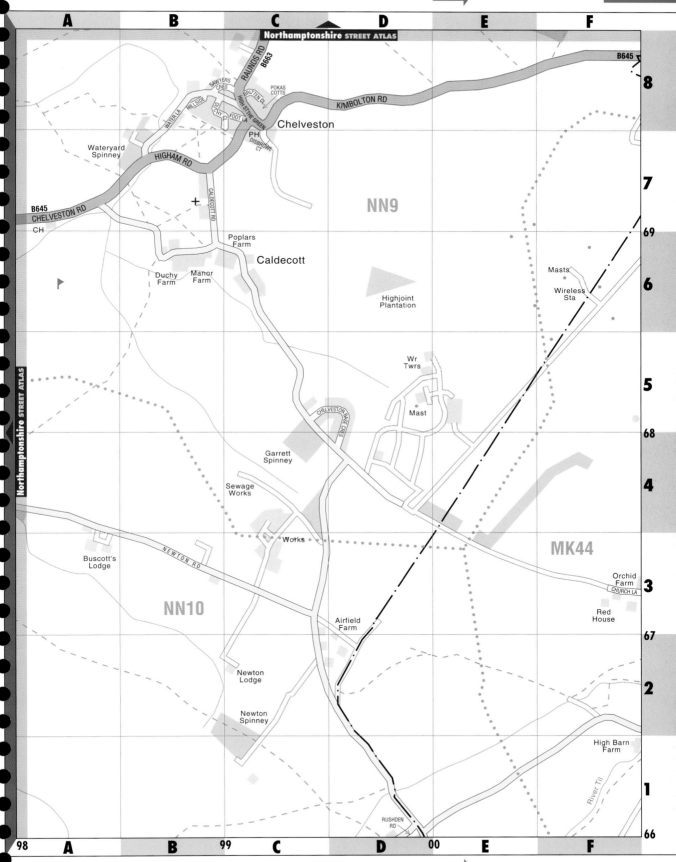

Northamptonshire STREET ATLAS

B645

B663
RAUNDS RD

SAWYERS
CRES

POKAS
COTTS

KIMBOLTON RD

BRITTEN CL

HIGH STNE GREEN

WATER LA
HILLSIDE
DUCHY CT
FOOT LA

Chelveston

PH
DISBROWE
CT

Wateryard
Spinney

HIGHAM RD

NN9

8

B645
CHELVESTON RD

CALDECOTT RD

7

CH

69

Poplars
Farm

Masts

Caldecott

Wireless
Sta

6

Duchy
Farm

Manor
Farm

Highjoint
Plantation

Wr
Twrs

5

CHELVESTON RISE CRES

Mast

68

Garrett
Spinney

4

Sewage
Works

MK44

Works

NEWTON RD

Buscott's
Lodge

Orchid
Farm
CHURCH LA

3

NN10

Red
House

67

Airfield
Farm

2

Newton
Lodge

High Barn
Farm

Newton
Spinney

River Til

1

RUSHDEN
RD

66

Northamptonshire STREET ATLAS

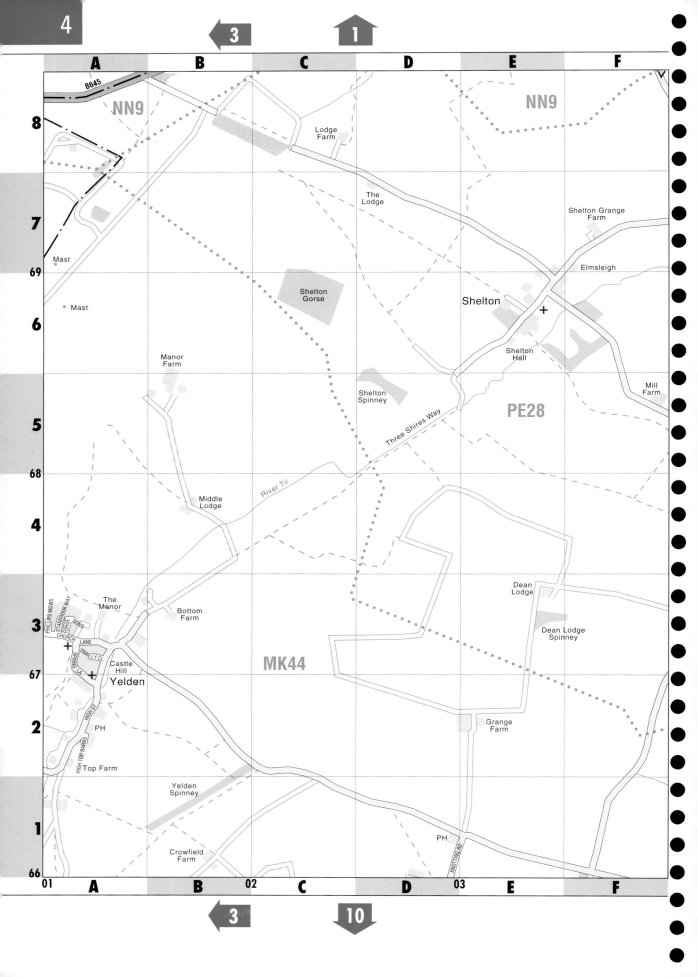

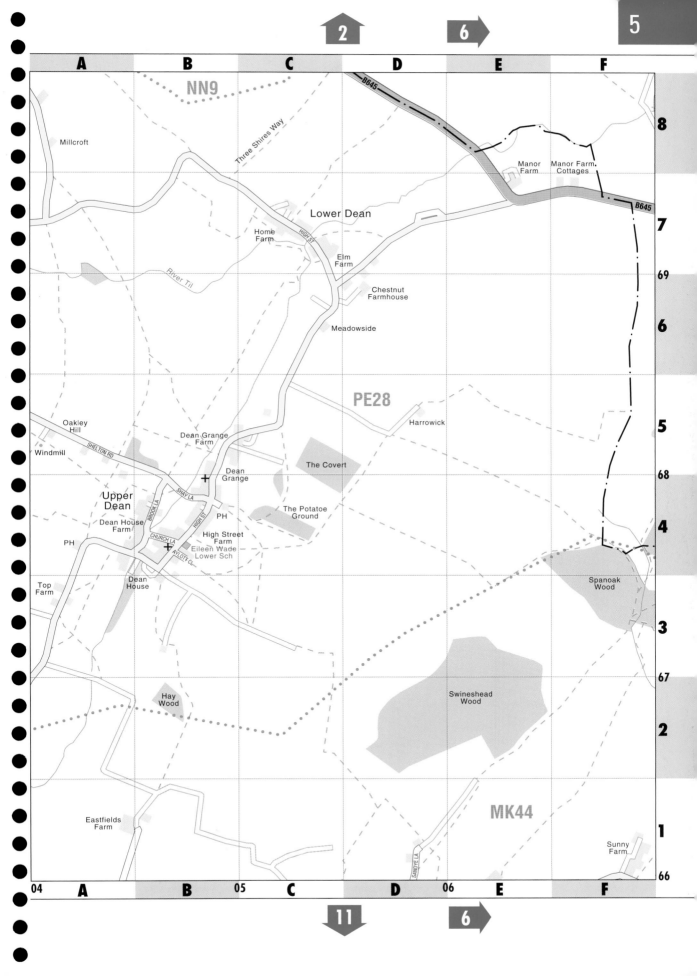

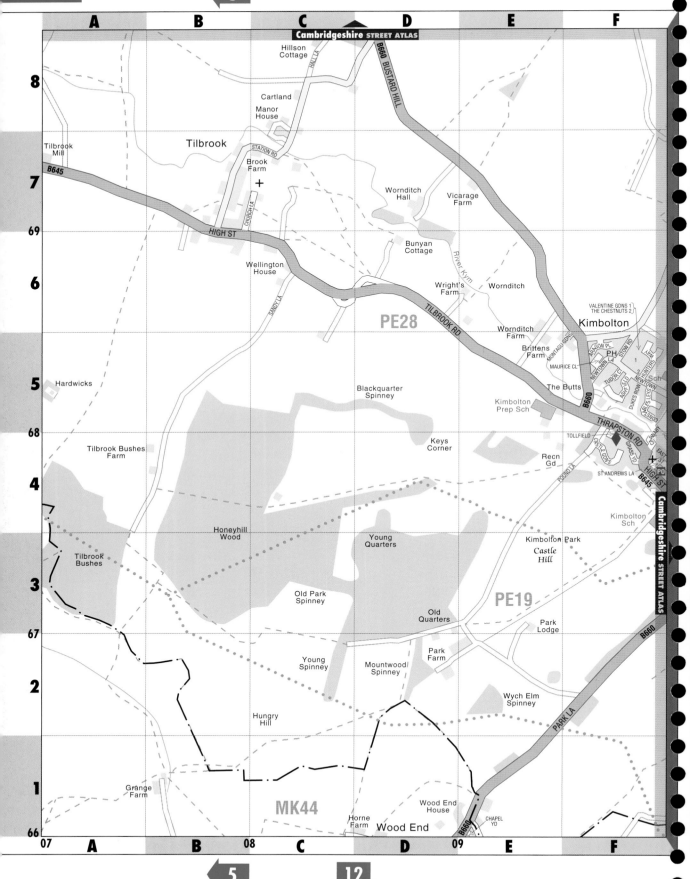

Cambridgeshire STREET ATLAS

A   B   C   D   E   F

8

Hillson
Cottage

Cartland

Manor
House

Tilbrook

B660 BUSTARD HILL

STATION RD

Brook
Farm
+

B645

7

HIGH ST

CHURCH LA

Wornditch
Hall

Vicarage
Farm

69

Bunyan
Cottage

River Kym

Wellington
House

SANDY LA

Wright's
Farm

Wornditch

6

PE28

TILBROOK RD

Wornditch
Farm

Brittens
Farm

VALENTINE GDNS 1
THE CHESTNUTS 2

Kimbolton

ARAGON PL
PH
MONTAGU GDNS
NEWTOWN
MAURICE CL
TUDOR CL
ASH CL
DUKES ROW
STOW RD
HUNTERS
Sch
NEWTOWN
EAST
BELL'S LEYS
CONS

Hardwicks

5

Blackquarter
Spinney

The Butts

B660

Kimbolton
Prep Sch

THRAPSTON RD

HIGH ST

PO

B645

68

Tilbrook Bushes
Farm

Keys
Corner

Recn
Gd

POUND LA

TOLLFIELD

CASTLE GDNS

GRASS TD

ST ANDREWS LA

Kimbolton
Sch

4

Honeyhill
Wood

Young
Quarters

Kimbolton Park
Castle
Hill

Tilbrook
Bushes

3

Old Park
Spinney

Old
Quarters

PE19

Park
Lodge

67

Young
Spinney

Mountwood
Spinney

Park
Farm

B660

2

Wych Elm
Spinney

PARK LA

Hungry
Hill

1

Grange
Farm

MK44

Horne
Farm

Wood End
House

Wood End

B660

CHAPEL
YD

66

07   A   08   B   C   08   D   09   E   F

Cambridgeshire STREET ATLAS

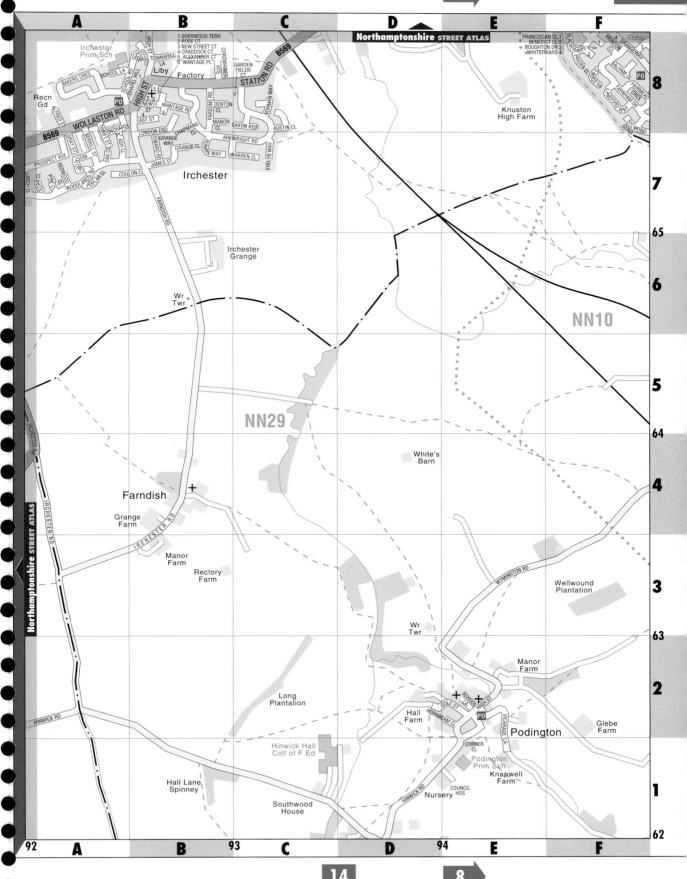

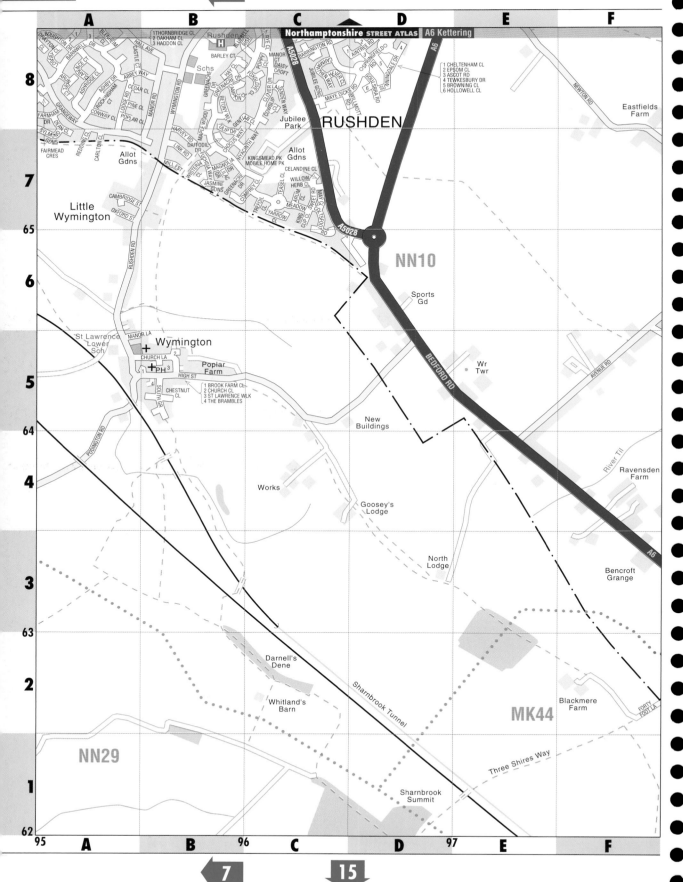

A   B   C   D   E   F

8

7

65

6

5

64

4

3

63

2

1

62

95   A   B   96   C   D   97   E   F

Rushden
H

RUSHDEN

NN10

Little
Wymington

Allot
Gdns

St Lawrence
Lower
Sch

Wymington

Poplar
Farm

PH

Chestnut
Cl

1 BROOK FARM CL
2 CHURCH CL
3 ST LAWRENCE WLK
4 THE BRAMBLES

1 CHELTENHAM CL
2 EPSOM CL
3 ASCOT RD
4 TEWKESBURY DR
5 BROWNING CL
6 HOLLOWELL CL

1 THORNBRIDGE CL
2 OAKHAM CL
3 HADDON CL

Jubilee
Park

Allot
Gdns

Sports
Gd

BEDFORD RD

Wr
Twr

AVENUE RD

Eastfields
Farm

River Til

Ravensden
Farm

New
Buildings

Works

Goosey's
Lodge

North
Lodge

Bencroft
Grange

A6

Darnell's
Dene

Whitland's
Barn

Sharnbrook Tunnel

Blackmere
Farm

MK44

FORTY FOOT LA

NN29

Three Shires Way

Sharnbrook
Summit

A5028

Schs

MANOR LA
CHURCH LA
HIGH ST
SOUTH GR

RUSHDEN RD

PODINGTON RD

CAMBRIDGE ST
OXFORD ST

MILL EST

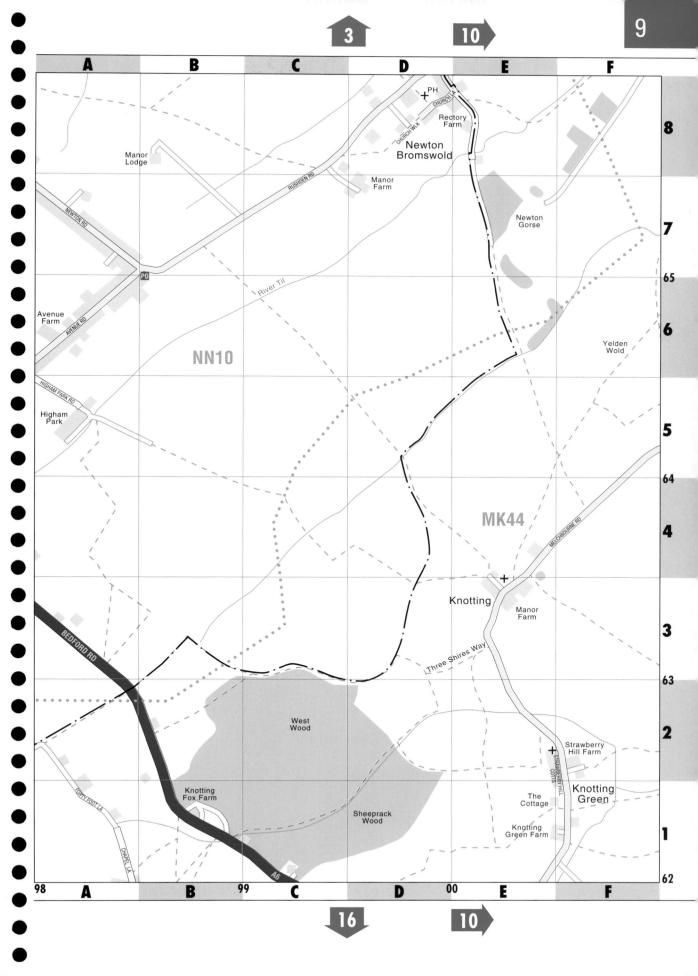

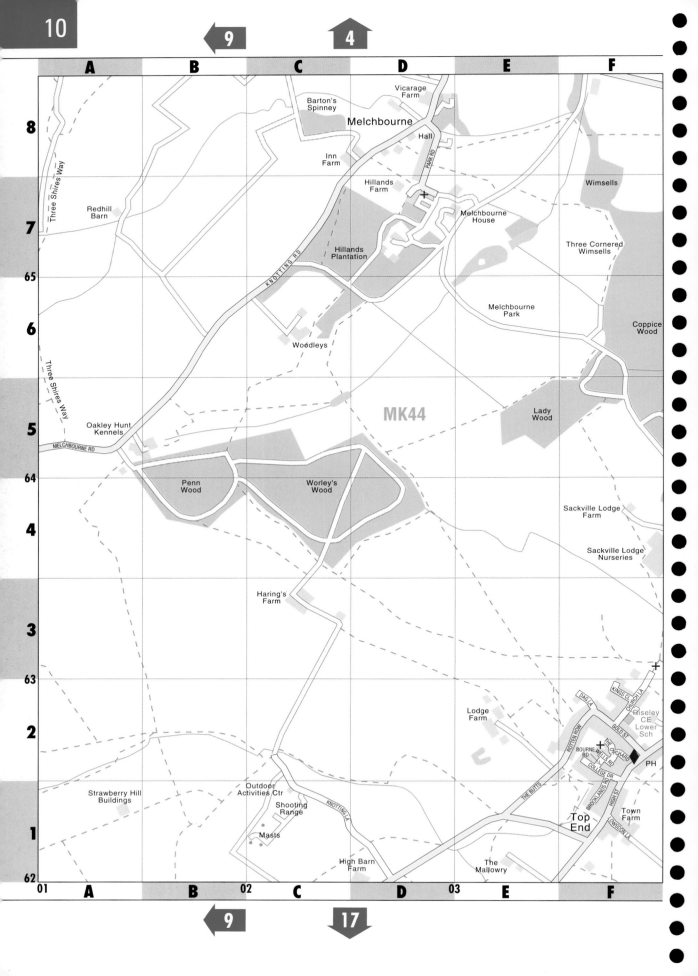

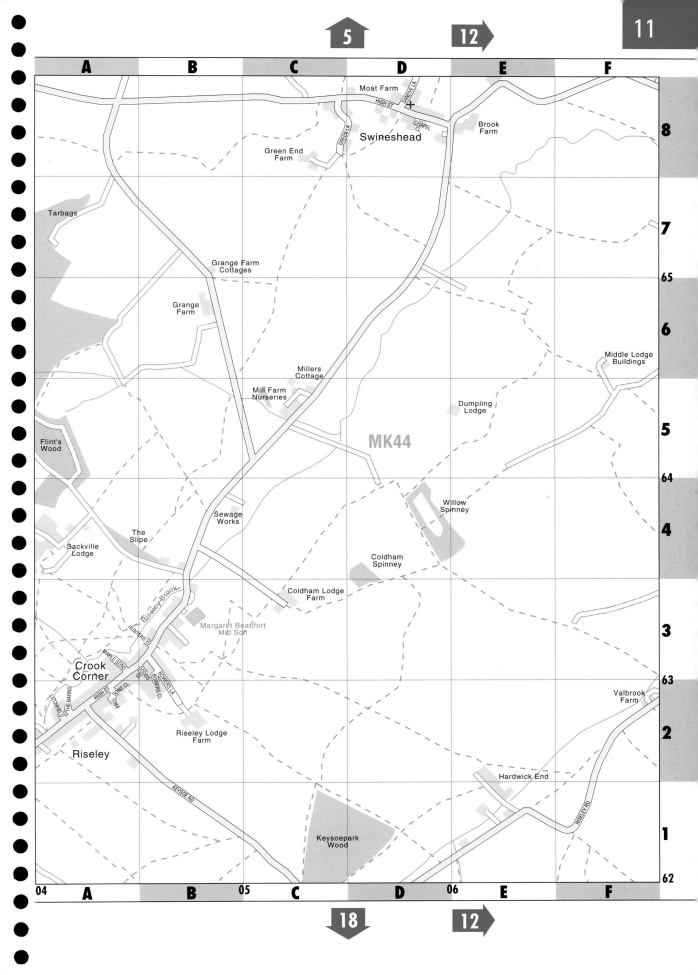

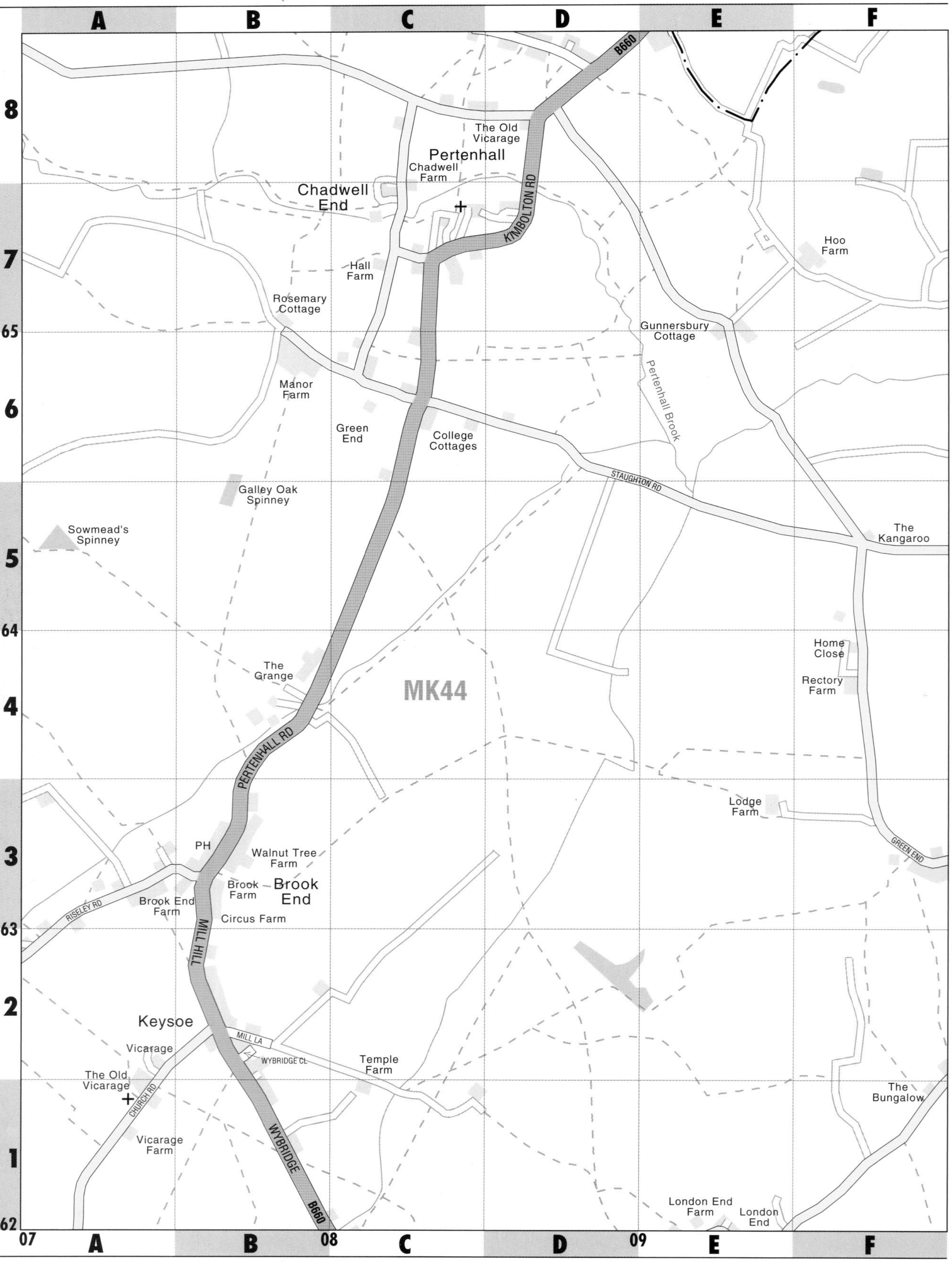

A B C D E F

8
7
65
6
5
64
4
3
63
2
1
62

The Old Vicarage
Pertenhall
Chadwell Farm
Chadwell End
Hall Farm
Rosemary Cottage
Manor Farm
Green End
College Cottages
Galley Oak Spinney
Sowmead's Spinney
The Grange
MK44
PH
Walnut Tree Farm
Brook Farm
Brook End
Brook End Farm
Circus Farm
RISELEY RD
MILL HILL
Keysoe
Vicarage
MILL LA
WYBRIDGE CL
The Old Vicarage
CHURCH RD
Vicarage Farm
WYBRIDGE
B660
Temple Farm
London End Farm
London End
The Bungalow
GREEN END
Lodge Farm
Rectory Farm
Home Close
The Kangaroo
STAUGHTON RD
Pertenhall Brook
Gunnersbury Cottage
Hoo Farm
KIMBOLTON RD
B660
PERTENHALL RD

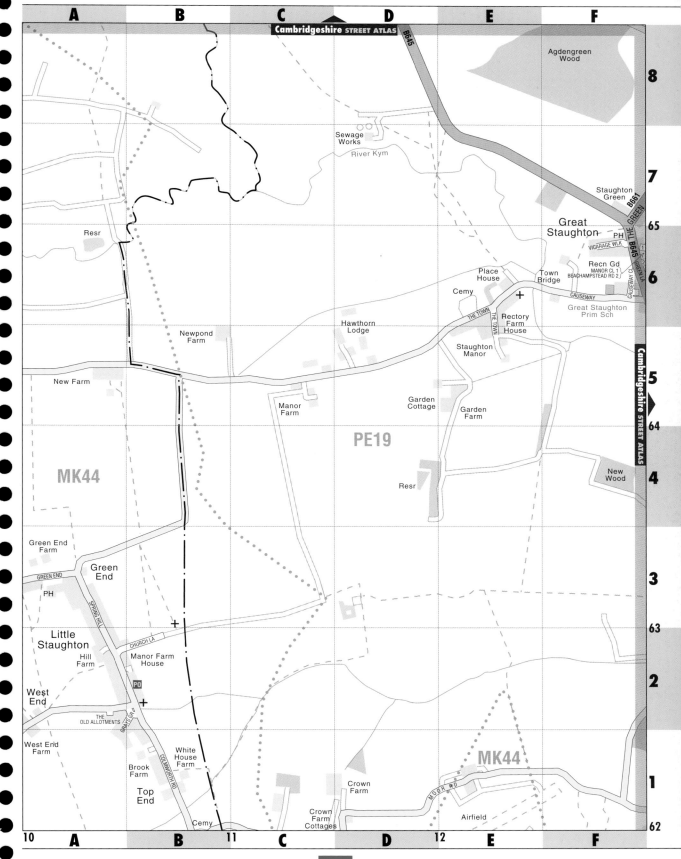

Agdengreen Wood

Sewage Works

River Kym

Staughton Green

Resr

Great Staughton

PH

VICARAGE WLK

Place House

Town Bridge

Recn Gd
MANOR CL 1
BEACHAMPSTEAD RD 2

CAUSEWAY

Cemy

Great Staughton Prim Sch

Newpond Farm

Hawthorn Lodge

THE TOWN

Rectory Farm House

Staughton Manor

New Farm

Manor Farm

Garden Cottage

Garden Farm

PE19

MK44

Resr

New Wood

Green End Farm

Green End

GREEN END

PH

SPRING HILL

Little Staughton

Hill Farm

CHURCH LA

Manor Farm House

PO

West End

THE OLD ALLOTMENTS

GRAYS GR

West End Farm

COLMWORTH RD

White House Farm

Brook Farm

Top End

MK44

Crown Farm

MOOR RD

Crown Farm Cottages

Airfield

Cemy

8

7

65

6

5

64

4

3

63

2

1

62

7

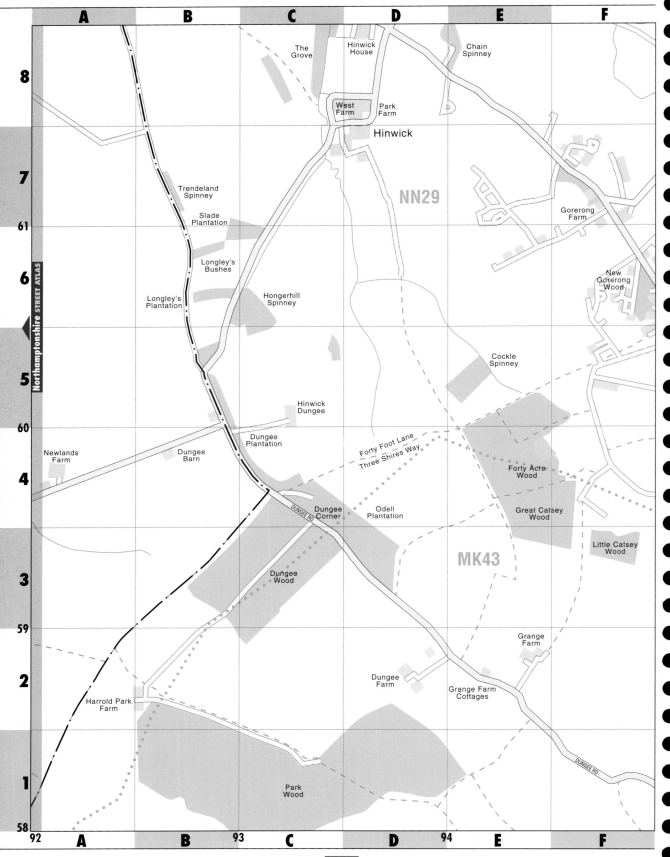

24

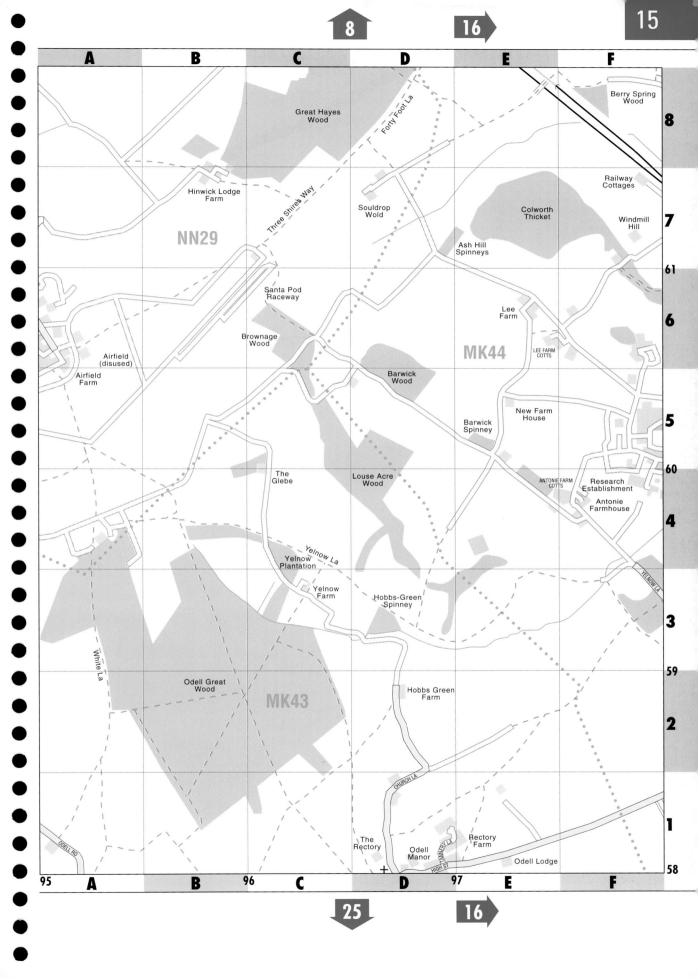

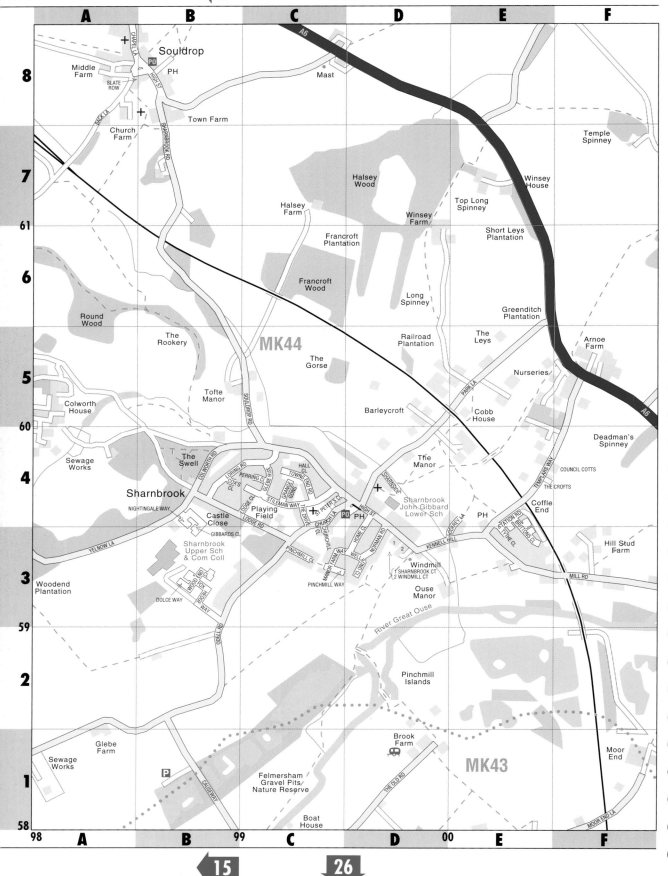

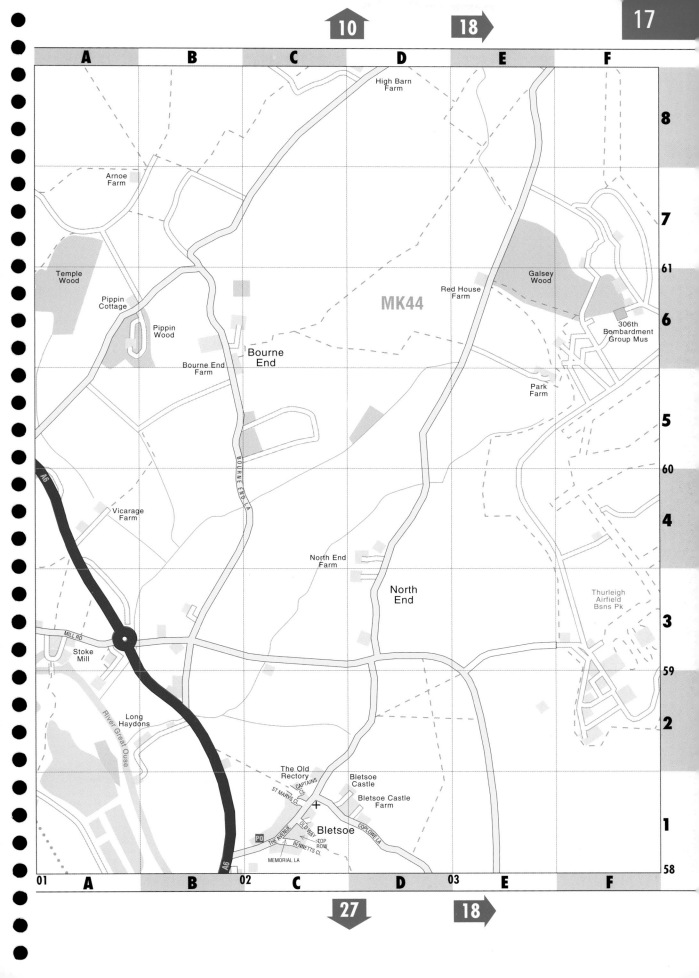

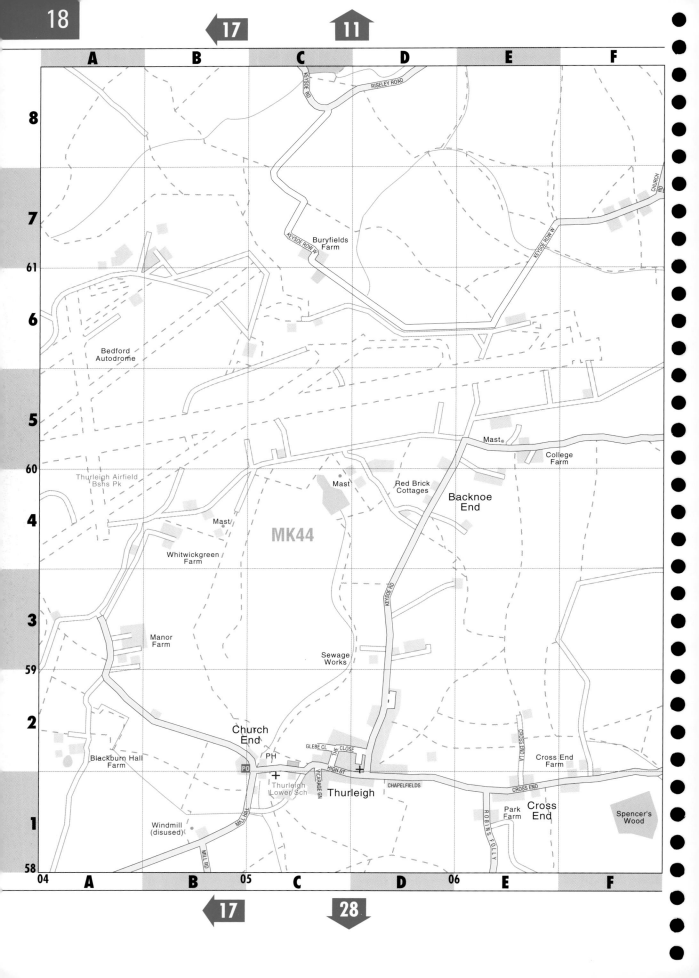

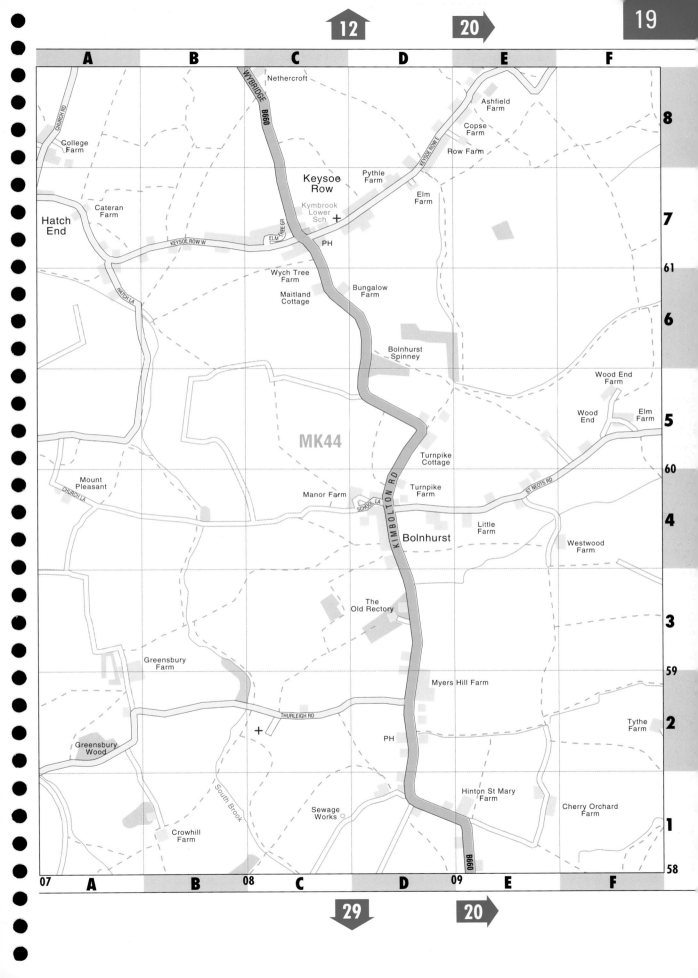

19 13

A B C D E F

8

Top End
Top End Farm
MOOR RD
PE19
Little Staughton Airfield
Works
Staughton Moor

The Wickey Farm

7
HIGH ST
Works
PE19

61
Berrywood Farm
Duloe Brook
Sewage Works

6
Bushmead Priory

Garden Wood
The Camps
Bushmead Big Wood

Steeple Wood
Wood Corner

5
ST NEOTS RD
BUSHMEAD CROSS
Home Farm

60

Honeydon Brook
Bushmead

4
LITTLE STAUGHTON RD
MK44
Upper Honeydon Farm

3
City Farm
CITY LA
SHELFORD LA
The City

59
QUEENS RD
THE TUDORS
PO
Church End

2
Colmworth
SCHOOL LA
HONEYDON RD
Kennels Farm

CHURCH RD
CHURCH LA
Manor Farm
Jewsfield
Lower Goodwick Farm

1
CHAPEL LA
COLLEY CL
Mast
Colley Hill
Coxfield

Chapel End
Chapel Farm

58
10 A B 11 C D 12 E F

19 30

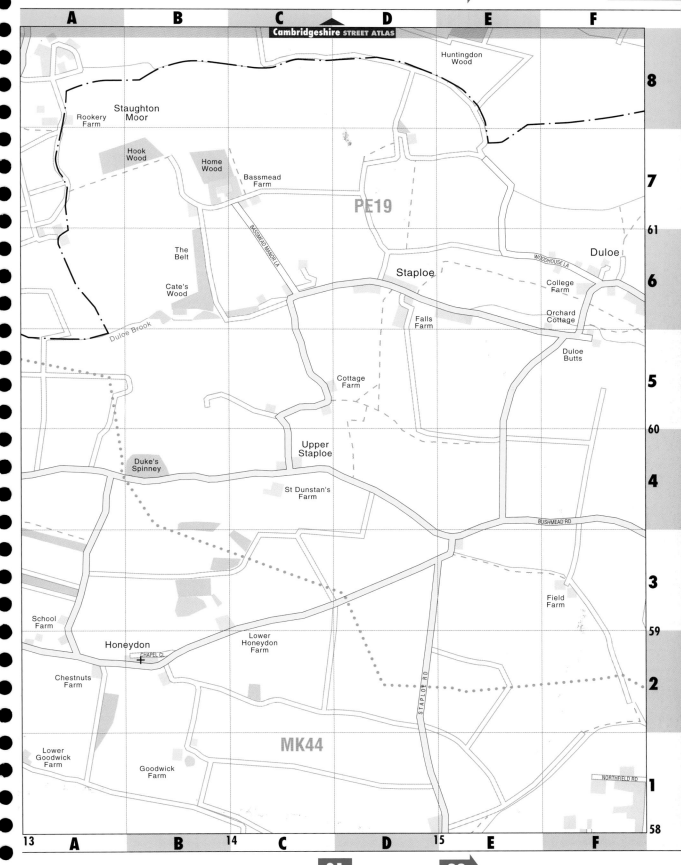

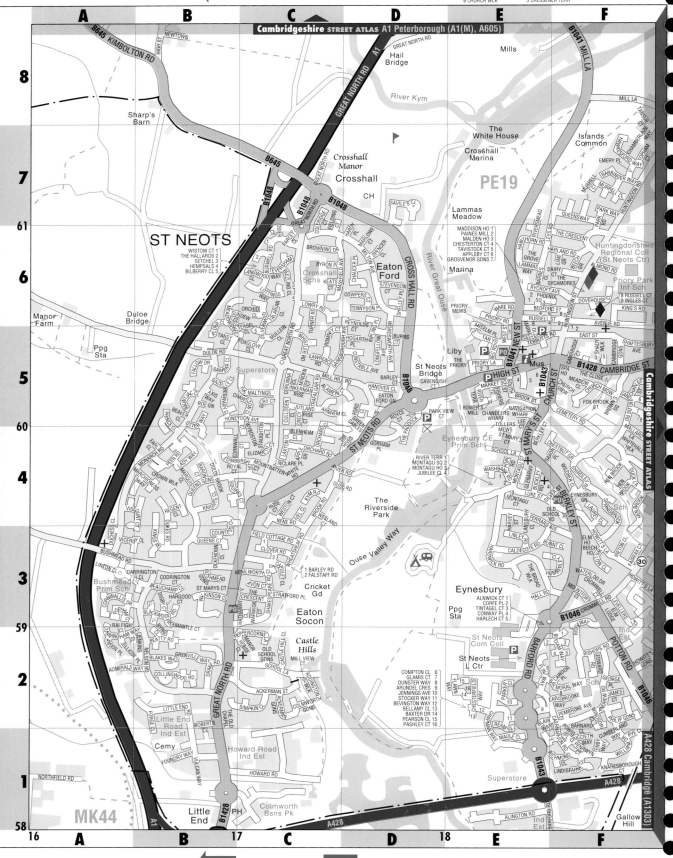

Cambridgeshire STREET ATLAS A1 Peterborough (A1(M), A605)

E5
1 WILLOW VIEWS
2 PRIORY MALL
3 CROSS KEYS MALL
4 IBBETTS YD
5 WINDMILL ROW
6 CHURCH WLK

7 MOORES WLK
F5
1 SUFFIELD HO
2 EAST CT
3 PROSPECT ROW
4 MEDALLION CT
5 CRESSENER TERR

6 MUSGRAVE WAY
7 WINTRINGHAM RD
8 MARSHALL RD

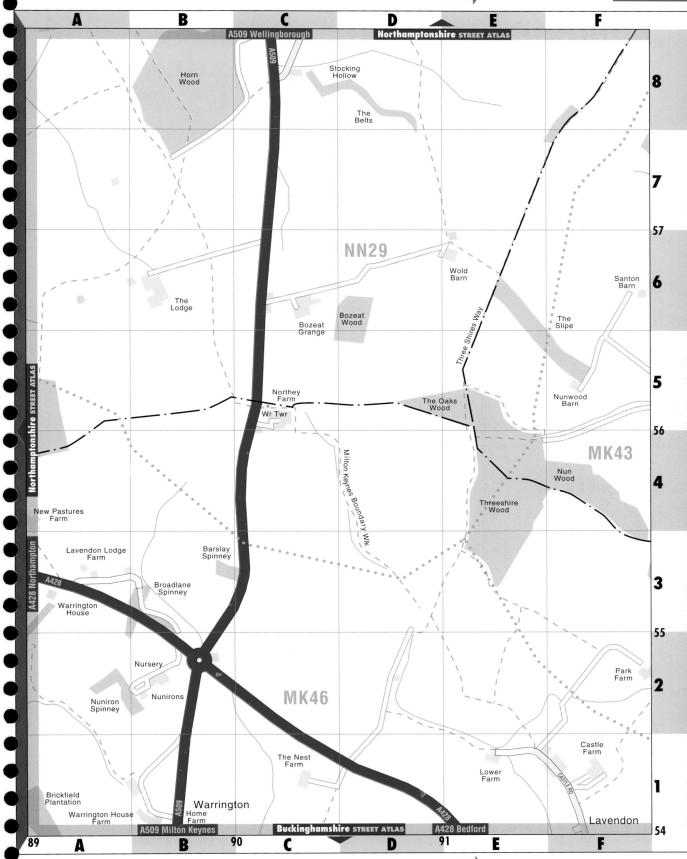

A   B   C   D   E   F

8

7

57

6

56

5

4

55

3

2

1

54

Horn Wood

Stocking Hollow

The Belts

NN29

Wold Barn

The Lodge

Bozeat Grange

Bozeat Wood

Three Shires Way

Santon Barn

The Slipe

Nunwood Barn

Northey Farm

Wr Twr

The Oaks Wood

MK43

Nun Wood

New Pastures Farm

Milton Keynes Boundary Wlk

Threeshire Wood

Lavendon Lodge Farm

Barslay Spinney

Broadlane Spinney

Warrington House

A428 Northampton

A428

Nursery

Nunirons

MK46

Park Farm

Nuniron Spinney

Castle Farm

The Nest Farm

CASTLE RD

Lower Farm

Brickfield Plantation

Warrington House Farm

Warrington Home Farm

A509

Buckinghamshire STREET ATLAS

A428 Bedford

A428

Lavendon

Northamptonshire STREET ATLAS

A B C D E F

8

NN29

Austin's
Spinney

Allot
Gdns

7

Templegrove
Spinney

New
Buildings

WOOD RD

WOOD RD

Allot
Gdns

57

Manor
Farm

ORCHARD LA

BROOK LA

The
Mansion

6

Harrold

MANSION LA

DICKENS CL

HIGH ST

EAGLE WAY

BRAMLEY
CT

NEW RD

Priory
Farm

Harrold
Lower Sch

MOWHILLS

Harrold Priory
Mid Sch

Coldharbour
Hill

5

Middle
Farm

Cracknell Hill
House

Cracknell
Hill

56

MK43

4

River Great Ouse

Millholme
Island

Marsh
Farm

3

Lavendon
Wood

Harrold Lodge
Farm

Milton Keynes Boundary Wlk

Church
Farm

55

Spring Close
Farm

2

MK46

Tollgate
House

TURKEY RD

Carltonhall
Wood

Valley View
Farm

Carlton Hall
Farm

Snelson
Cottages

Snelson

1

HARROLD RD

Snelson
Cobs

CARLTON RD

54

92

A

B

93

C

D

94

E

F

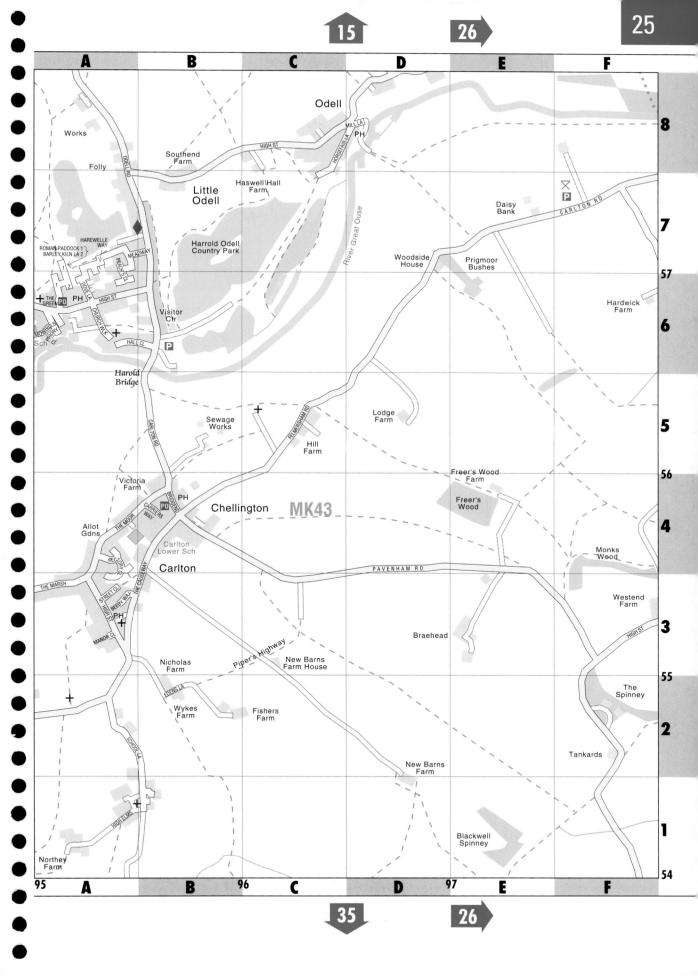

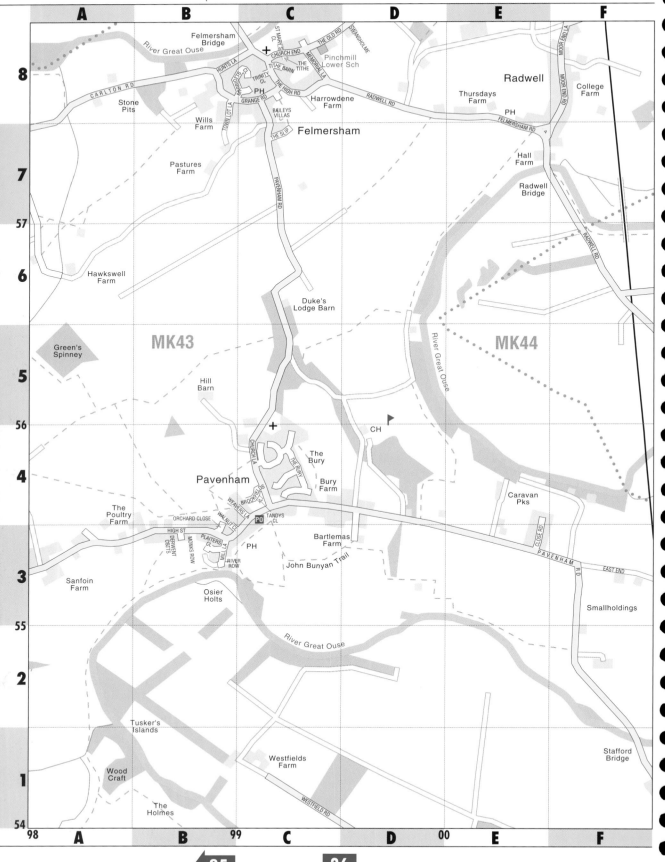

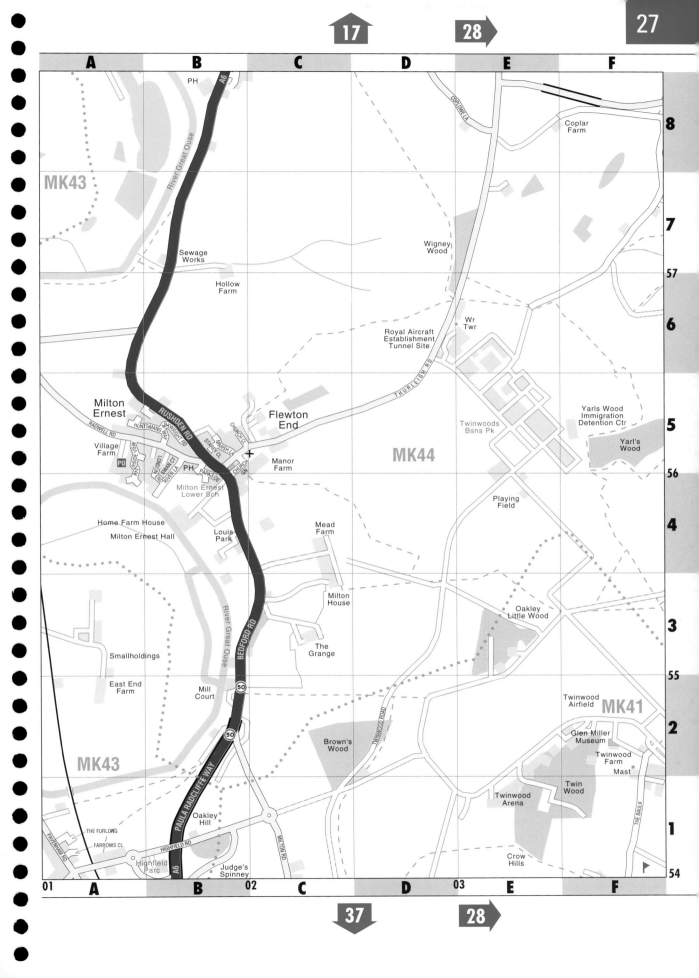

A B C D E F

8

Old Milton Rd

Romp
Hall

Scald End
Farm

Scald
End

Robins Folly

Robins Folly
Farm

Park End
Farm

7

Mill Rd

Waterfall
Farm

Short
Wood

57

Rutter's
Farm

Tilwick
Wood

6

Red Gate
Farm

MK44

Brook
Farm

5

56

4

Traylesfield
Farm

Little
Wood

Great
Wood

Manor
Farm

Wood
End

Brook
Farm

3

Outfields
Farm

Ravensden
House

55

Graze Hill

Gray's Hill
Farm

Thurleigh Rd

Ravensden Brook

Sunderland Hill

B660

2

Highfield
Farm

Graze Hill
House

Willow
Farm

Sunderland
Cl

Butler St

PO

Fairfield
Farm

PH

New Cl

Oldways Rd

MK41

Highfield
House

Bedford Rd

B660

1

54

04 A B 05 C D 06 E F

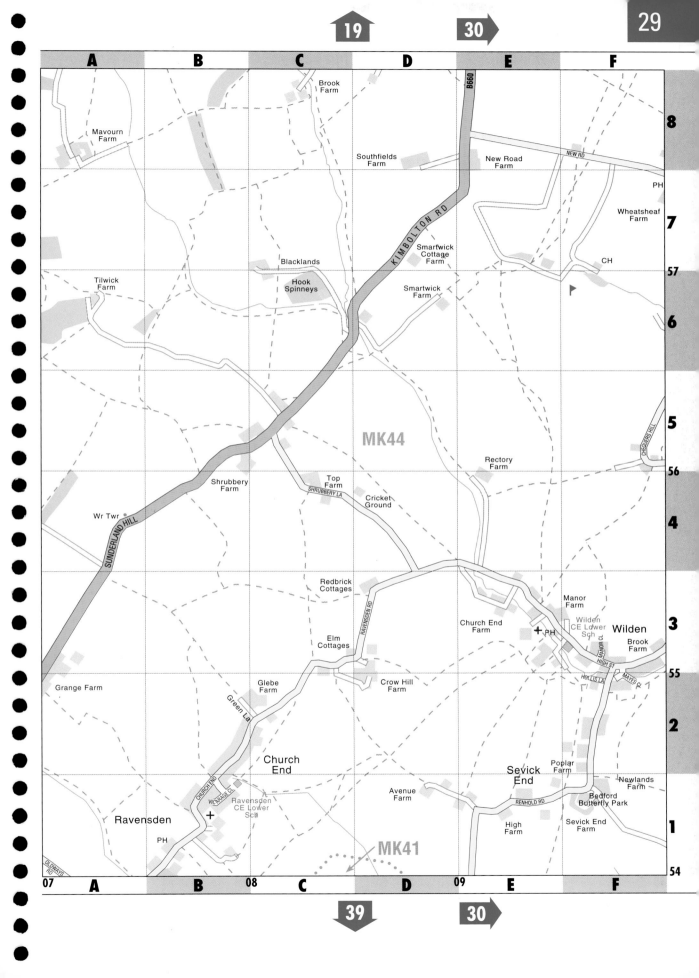

A   B   C   D   E   F

8

CHURCH RD

NEW RD

Mill End

Mill Rd

Rootham's
Green

7

57

Top
Farm

WILDEN RD

Channel's
End
Farm

Begwary Brook

6

Hillview
Farm

CHANNELS END RD

Finsbury Park
Farm

Channel's
End
Farm

Colesden
Wood

5

Channel's End
Farm

Channel's
End

Colesden
Grange
Farm

Dacca
Farm

Duck's
Cross

56

Bryher
Farm

COLESDEN RD

MK44

Colesden

4

CHEQUERS HILL

Bell
Farm

Ley
Farm

East End
Farm

Sewage
Works

3

HIGH ST

EAST END LA

East End

55

Hill
Farm

Lady Wood

2

BARFORD RD

Hill Farm

Palaceyard
Wood

WOODEND LA

1

54

10   A   B   11   C   D   12   E   F

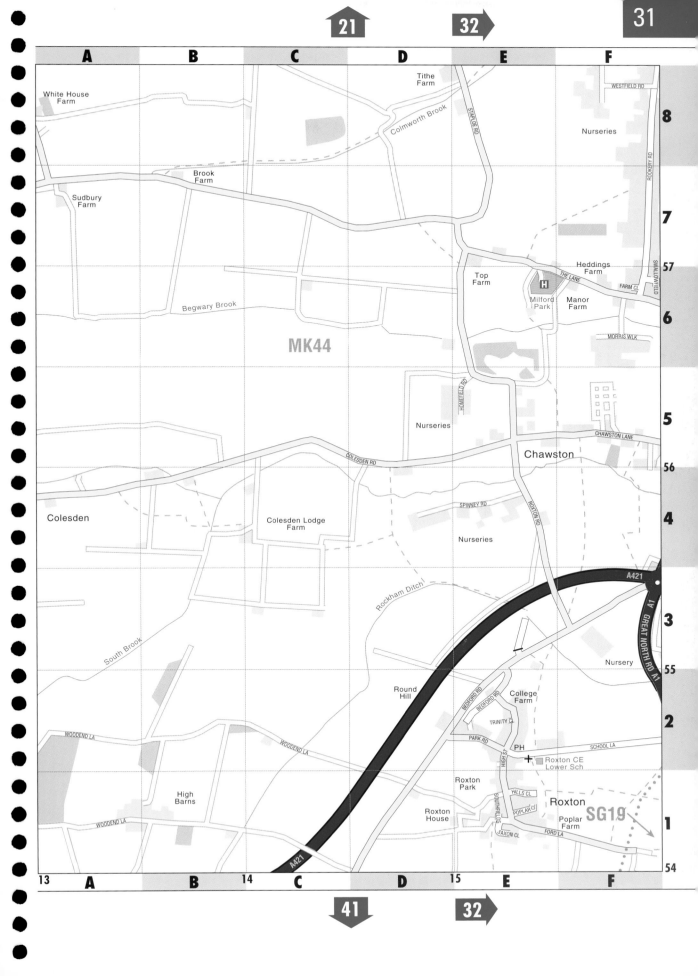

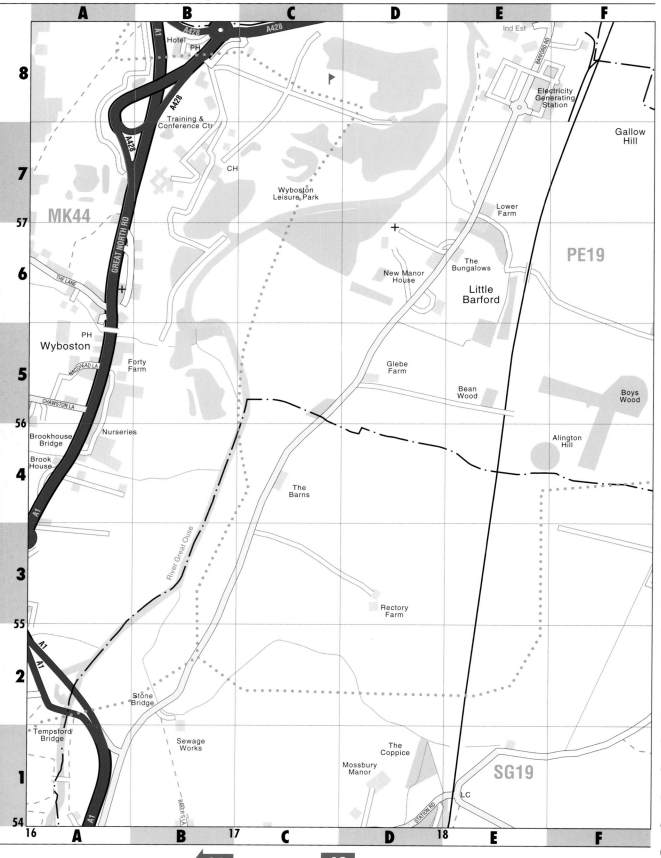

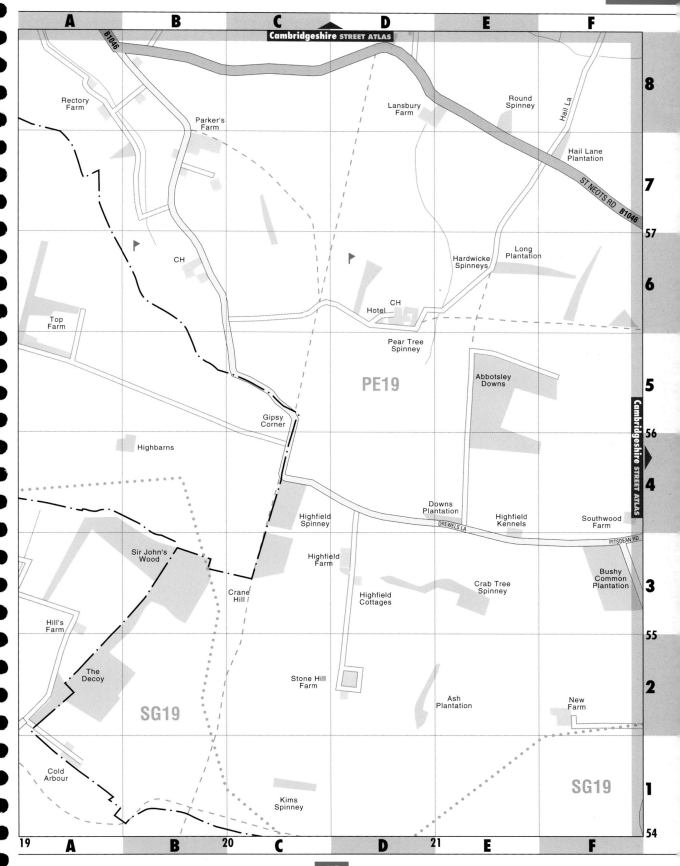

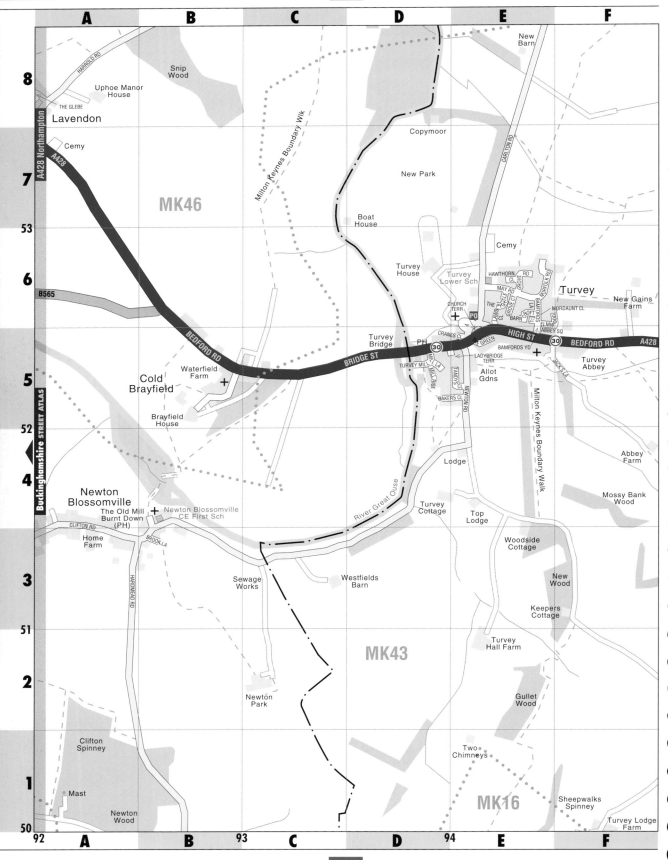

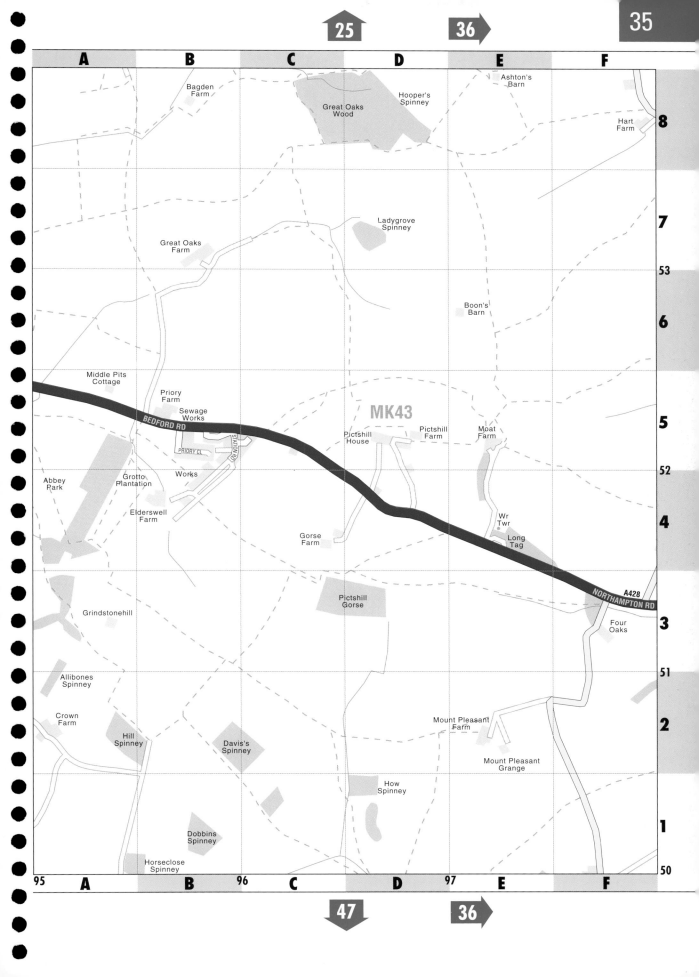

A B C D E F

8
7
53
6
5
52
4
3
51
2
1
50

Bagden Farm

Great Oaks Wood

Hooper's Spinney

Ashton's Barn

Hart Farm

Ladygrove Spinney

Great Oaks Farm

Boon's Barn

Middle Pits Cottage

Priory Farm

Sewage Works

BEDFORD RD

MK43

Pictshill House

Pictshill Farm

Moat Farm

PRIORY CL

STATION RD

Abbey Park

Grotto Plantation

Works

Elderswell Farm

Gorse Farm

Wr Twr

Long Tag

NORTHAMPTON RD

A428

Grindstonehill

Pictshill Gorse

Four Oaks

Allibones Spinney

Crown Farm

Mount Pleasant Farm

Hill Spinney

Davis's Spinney

Mount Pleasant Grange

How Spinney

Dobbins Spinney

Horseclose Spinney

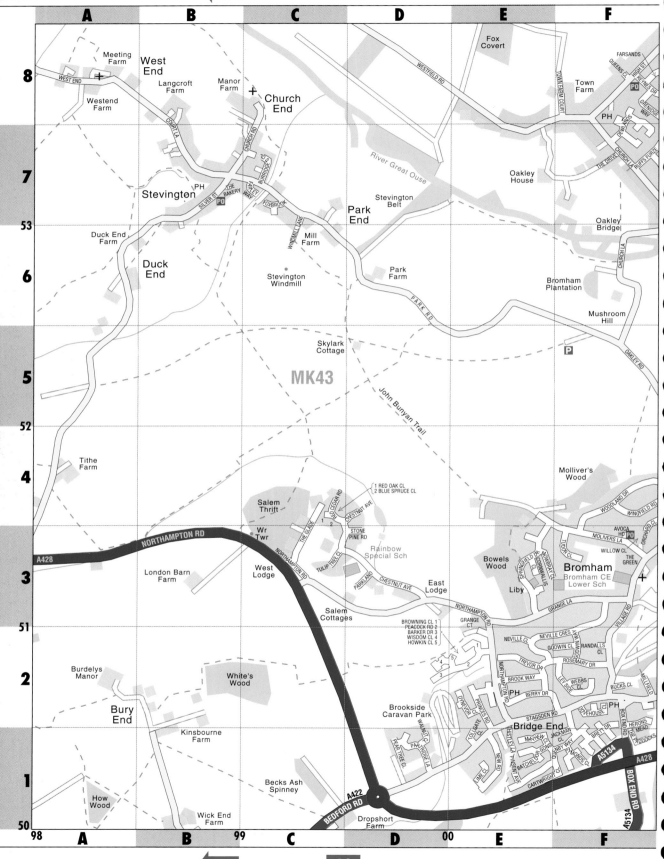

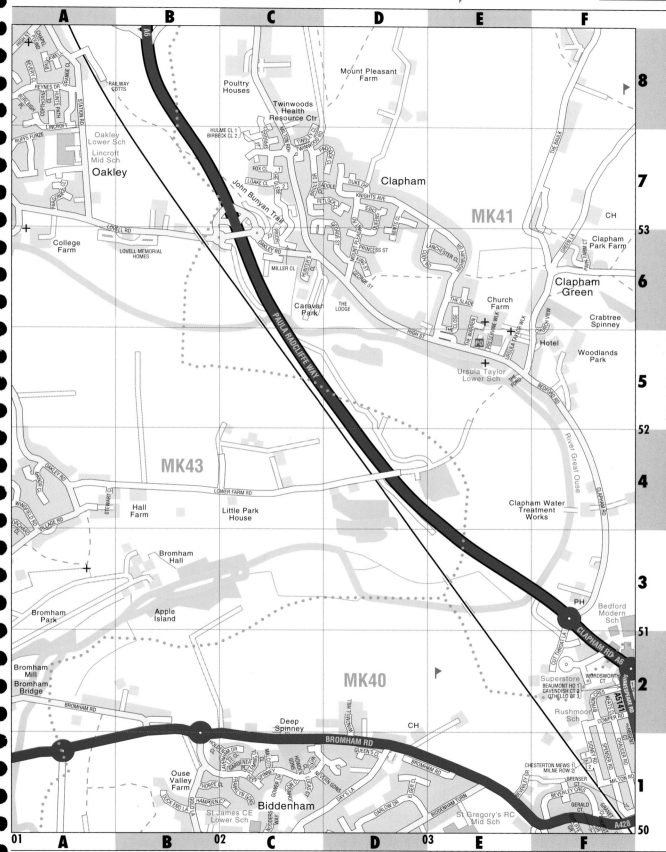

Grid columns: A B C D E F
Grid rows: 8 7 53 6 52 5 52 4 51 3 51 2 1 50

MK44

MK41

MK40

College Farm

GREEN LA

Clapham Park Wood

Clapham Park

Little Park Farm

John Bunyan Trail

Laboratory

Ind Est

Mast

Murdock Rd

Mast

The Manton Ctr

Mast

Bedford Modern Sch

Edith Cavell Lower Sch

Livingstone Lower Sch

A6 CLAPHAM RD

A5141

SHAKESPEARE RD

A428

BROMHAM RD

HM Prison

Robinson Pool

Cemy Crem

Bedford Park

Pilgrims Pre-Prep Sch

Pilgrim Ctr

Brickhill

Brickhill Lower Sch

Beauchamp Mid Sch

Scott Lower Sch

St Thomas More RC Upper Sch

Cleat Hill

CLEAT HILL

BEDFORD RD B660

GRACE HILL

Mowsbury Hill

Putnoe Wood

Mowsbury Park

Putnoe

Liby

KIMBOLTON RD

B660

Newnham Mid Sch

Goldington Mid Sch

Univ of Bedfordshire

A428

GOLDINGTON RD

A5140

NEWNHAM AVE

The Place Theatre

Bedford (North Wing)

Bedford RFC

Castle Lower Sch

Bedford Sch

St Andrew's Sch

AELFRIC CT 1
MERSEY WAY 2
WESTBURY CT 3
LEIGHTON CT 4
HIGHFIELD 5
EVESHAM CT 6
UPTON CT 7
FRAMPTON CT 8

BREAMISH WLK 1
PETTERIL WLK 2
THE GELT 3
SWALE PATH 4

1 IRVINE CT
2 MEDWAY CT
3 WELLAND CT

1 SUNNINGDALE WLK
2 TURNBERRY WLK
3 LOWTHER RD
4 PERSHORE CL

1 LIBRARY WLK
2 LITTLE HEADLANDS
3 GREYSTOKE WLK

1 LINDEN CT
2 CULVER HO
3 WARWICK HO
4 STRATFORD CT

1 BRANGWYN GDNS
2 ROMNEY WLK

NEWBURY HO 1
ST MICHAEL'S CTS 2
KIMBOLTON CT 3
RODEAN CT 4

SIDMOUTH CL 1
SHALDON CT 2

CREDITON CL 1
INSTOW

1 AYLESBURY CT
2 WENDOVER CT
3 RISBOROUGH CT

Index (bottom):

A1
1 REGENT CT
2 MILTON RD
3 STOKE ALBANY MEWS
4 PADBURY HO
5 BEECH CT
6 CYMBELINE CT
7 LANSDOWNE TERR
8 SALISBURY HO
9 BEAUCHAMP CT

B1
1 PRIORY CT
2 NORTH PAR
3 ROISE CT
4 PRIORY TERR
5 GWYN ST
6 BALSALL ST E
7 PEEL ST
8 BOSWELL PL
9 PRINCES ST

10 ALBERT ST
11 COBDEN SQ
12 QUEEN'S CT
13 BOSWELL CT
14 CHANDOS CT
15 ARLINGTON CT

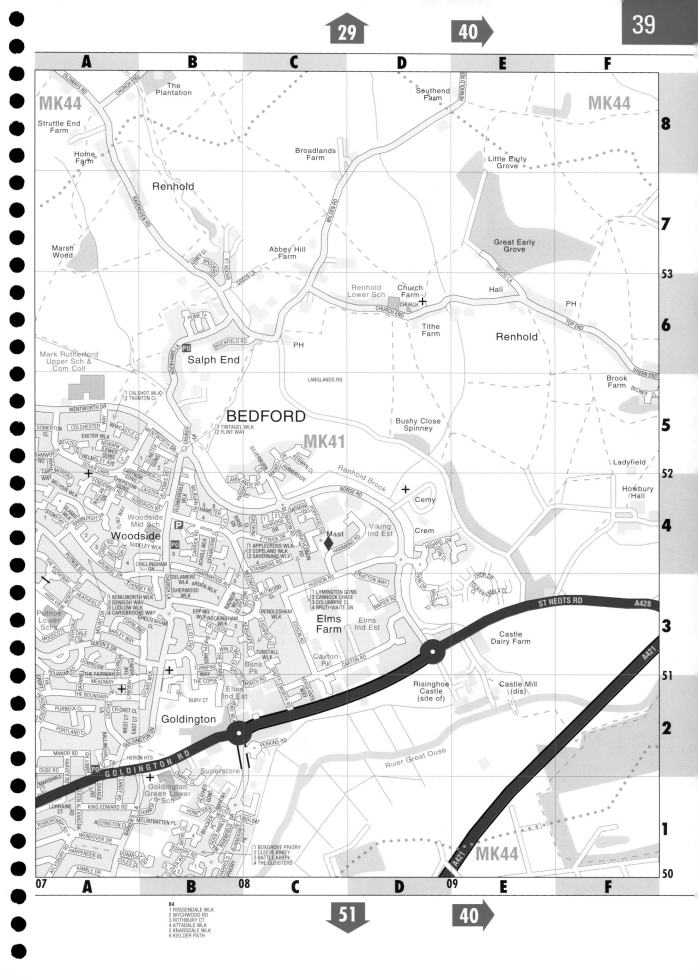

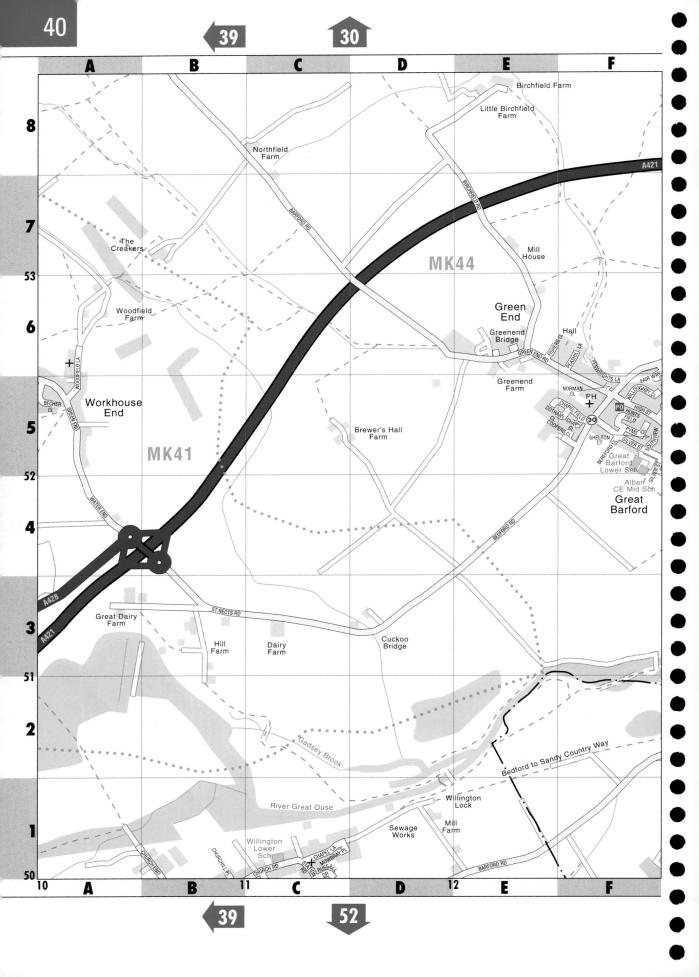

A   B   C   D   E   F

8

7

53

6

5

52

4

3

51

2

1

50

Birchfield Farm
Little Birchfield Farm
Northfield Farm
A421
The Creakers
Mill House
MK44
Green End
Greenend Bridge
Hall
Woodfield Farm
Greenend Farm
Workhouse End
NORMAN CL
PH
PO
30
CHAPEL FIELD
DOTHAMS
CHART
COOPERS CL
BECHER CL
GREEN END
WOODFIELD LA
MK41
Brewer's Hall Farm
SHELTON CT
Great Barford Lower Sch
Alban CE Mid Sch
Great Barford
WATER END
Bedford Rd
A428
A421
St Neots Rd
Great Dairy Farm
Hill Farm
Dairy Farm
Cuckoo Bridge
Gadsey Brook
Bedford to Sandy Country Way
River Great Ouse
Willington Lock
Willington Lower Sch
Church End
Churchill Pl
Church Rd
Chapel La
Mowbray Pl
Russell Dr
Station Rd
Sewage Works
Mill Farm
Barford Rd

FISHERS CL
GREEN END RD
PEASHILL LA
WHEELWRIGHTS LA
WILLOUGHBY CL
FAIR WAY
HIGH ST
HUNTS FIELD
PYMS CL
SILVER ST
SOUTHVIEW
BEDFORD RD

10   A   B   11   C   D   12   E   F

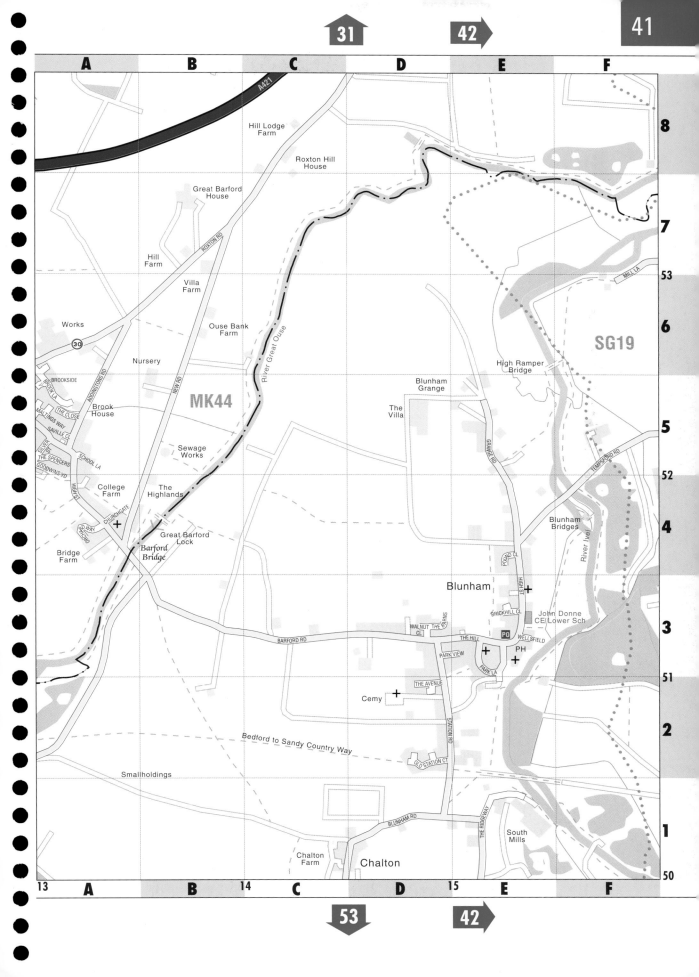

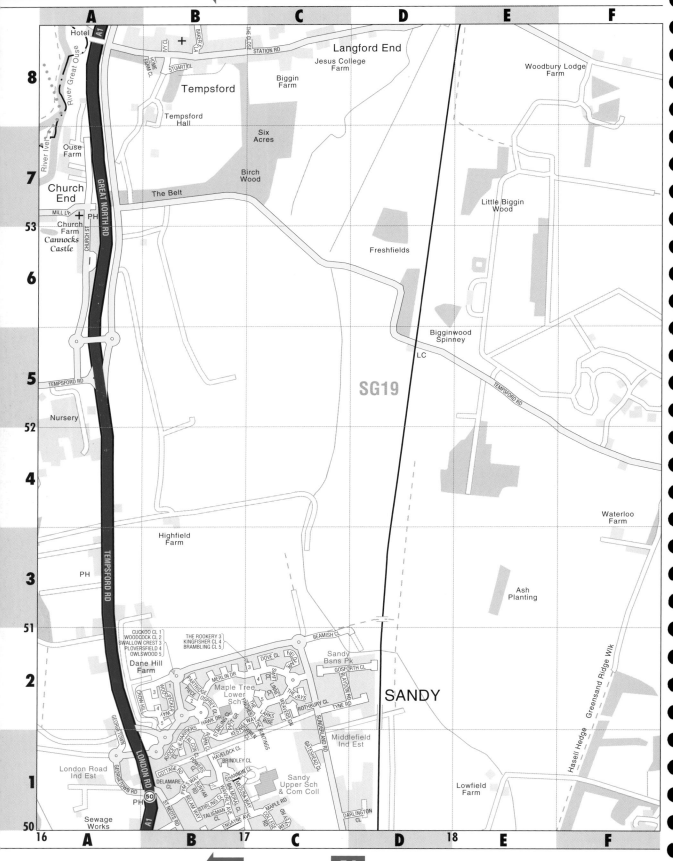

41
32

A   B   C   D   E   F

8

Hotel
A1
BAKER'S LA
THE CLOSE
STATION RD
Langford End
Jesus College Farm
Woodbury Lodge Farm
HOME FARM CL
STUART CL
12 AV
Biggin Farm
Tempsford
Tempsford Hall
Six Acres
Birch Wood
Little Biggin Wood
GREAT NORTH RD
River Great Ouse
Ouse Farm
River Ivel

7

Church End
The Belt
Freshfields

53
MILL LA
PH
Church Farm
Cannocks Castle
CHURCH ST

6
Bigginwood Spinney
LC

5
TEMPSFORD RD
SG19
TEMPSFORD RD

52
Nursery

4
Waterloo Farm

Highfield Farm

3
PH
TEMPSFORD RD
Ash Planting

51
BEAMISH CL
CUCKOO CL 1
WOODCOCK CL 2
SWALLOW CREST 3
PLOVERSFIELD 4
OWLSWOOD 5
THE ROOKERY 3
KINGFISHER CL 4
BRAMBLING CL 5
DOVE CL
Sandy Bsns Pk
Greensand Ridge Wlk

2
Dane Hill Farm
MERLIN DR
PARTRIDGE
FIELD
SWIFT LANE
THE FINCHES
GOSFORTH CL
BLAYTON RD
SANDY
PRESTLAND
OSPREY CL
Maple Tree Lower Sch
WEAVERS RD
ROTHBURY CL
TYNE RD
WOODPECKER
CROWN HILL
HAWK DR
STARLING WAY
KESTREL WAY
THE LARKS RISE
THE BUNTINGS
Haseell Hedge

1
London Road Ind Est
GEORGETOWN RD
LONDON RD
COTTAGE CL
DELAMARE CL
PLOVERS WAY
ROSE
THE HARRIERS
PINTAIL CL
HOME CL
PAINTERS WAY
HAVELOCK CL
BRINDLEY CL
SHANNON CL
SUNDERLAND RD
GATESHEAD RD
Middlefield Ind Est
Sandy Upper Sch & Com Coll
DARLINGTON CL
Lowfield Farm

50
Sewage Works
A1
PH
50
GEORGETOWN RD
ST NEOTS RD
BELAM WAY
STIRLING RD
TALISMAN AVE
WAFERLY WAY
MEDUSA WAY
ENGAYNE AVE
MAPLE RD
COLLEGE RD
DR A434
A434 WEST

16   A   B   17   C   D   18   E   F

41
54

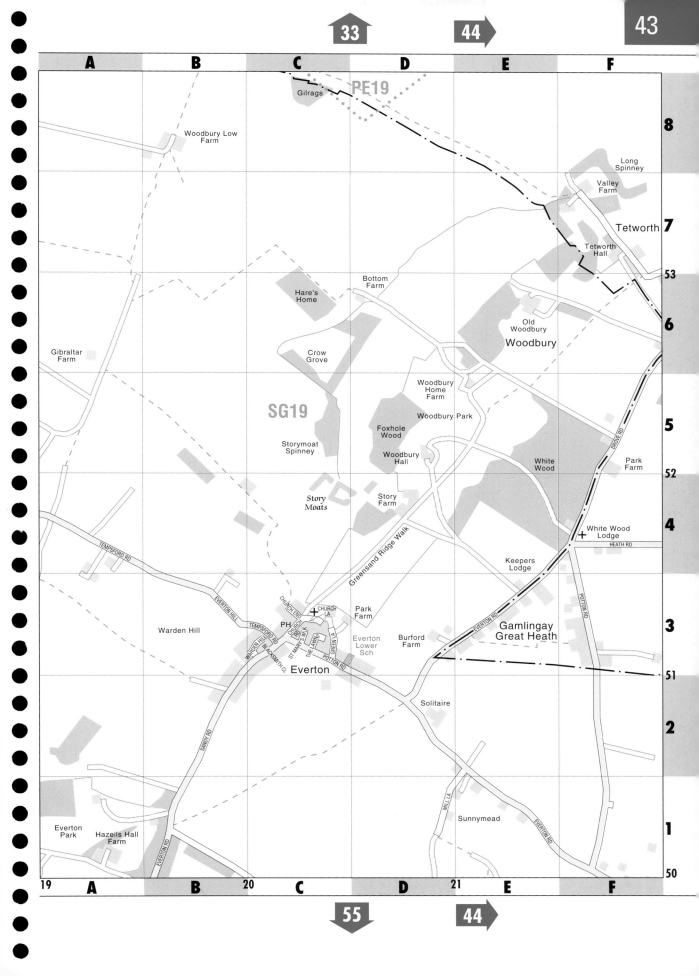

43

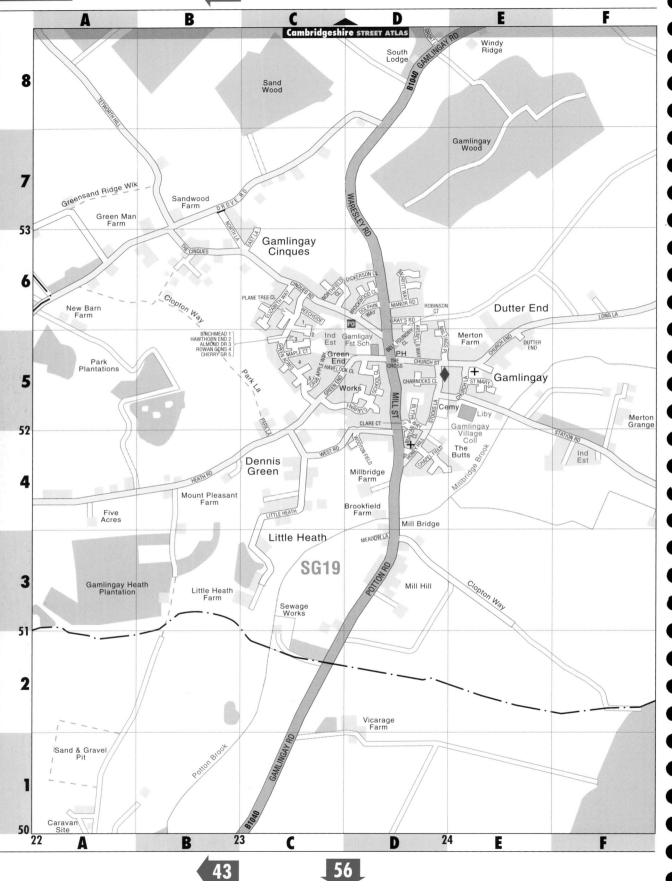

CAMBRIDGESHIRE STREET ATLAS

8

Sand Wood

South Lodge

Windy Ridge

Gamlingay Wood

TETWORTH HILL

7

Greensand Ridge Wlk

Sandwood Farm

DROVE RD

WARESLEY RD

B1040 GAMLINGAY RD

CROXT...

53

Green Man Farm

NORTH LA

CASTLE LA

THE CINQUES

Gamlingay Cinques

6

New Barn Farm

Clopton Way

PLANE TREE CL

CINQUES RD

NORTHFIELD CL

DICKERSON CL

BROOKWOOD CL

DOLPHIN WAY

WUFFITT WAY RD

MANOR CT

ROBINSON CT

Dutter End

LONG LA

ELIZABETH WAY

BEECHSIDE

GRAY'S RD

AVENELLS WAY

MALTINGS PL

CHURCH END

DUTTER END

1

BIRCHMEAD 1
HAWTHORN END 2
ALMOND DR 3
ROWAN GDNS 4
CHERRY GR 5

3

2

Ind Est

Gamlingay Fst Sch

BELL FOUNDRY CL

IPH

Merton Farm

Park Plantations

GREEN ACRES

MAPLE CT

4

Green End

CHURCH ST

St MARY'S

Gamlingay

5

Park La

GREEN END

APPLE WAY

HAVELOCK CL

Works

FAIRFIELD

THE CROSS

CHARNOCKS CL

Cemy

Liby

Merton Grange

PIERCE LA

STOCKS LA

BLYTHE WAY

CHURCH LA

52

CLARE CT

WEST RD

WOOTTON FIELD

MILL ST

Gamlingay Village Coll

STATION RD

Ind Est

Dennis Green

HEATH RD

CHAPEL FIELD

The Butts

Millbridge Brook

4

Mount Pleasant Farm

LITTLE HEATH

Millbridge Farm

MEADOW LA

Five Acres

Brookfield Farm

Mill Bridge

Little Heath

SG19

3

Gamlingay Heath Plantation

Little Heath Farm

Sewage Works

POTTON RD

Mill Hill

Clopton Way

51

2

Sand & Gravel Pit

Potton Brook

GAMLINGAY RD

Vicarage Farm

1

B1040

50

Caravan Site

43   56

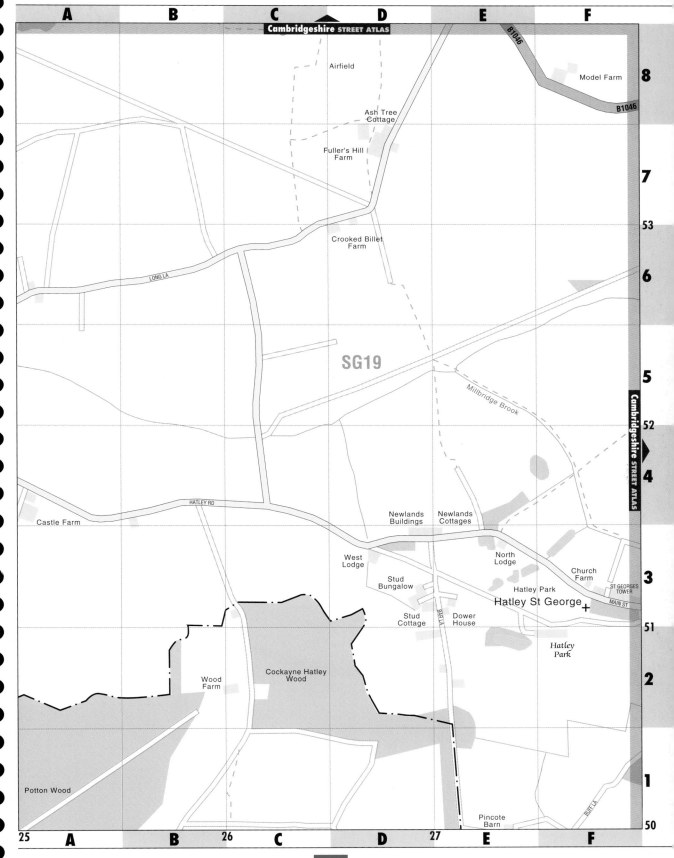

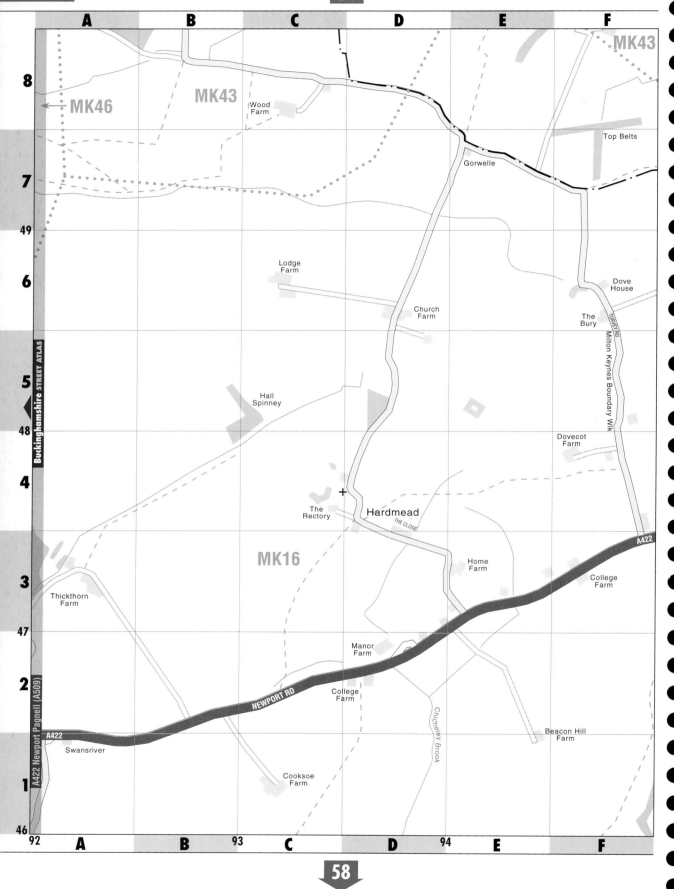

MK43

MK46

MK43

Wood
Farm

Top Belts

Gorwelle

Lodge
Farm

Dove
House

Church
Farm

The
Bury

Hall
Spinney

Dovecot
Farm

The Rectory

Hardmead

THE CLOSE

MK16

Home
Farm

College
Farm

Thickthorn
Farm

A422

Manor
Farm

NEWPORT RD

College
Farm

Beacon Hill
Farm

A422

Swansriver

Chicheley Brook

Cooksoe
Farm

TURVEY RD

Milton Keynes Boundary Wlk

Buckinghamshire STREET ATLAS

A422 Newport Pagnell (A509)

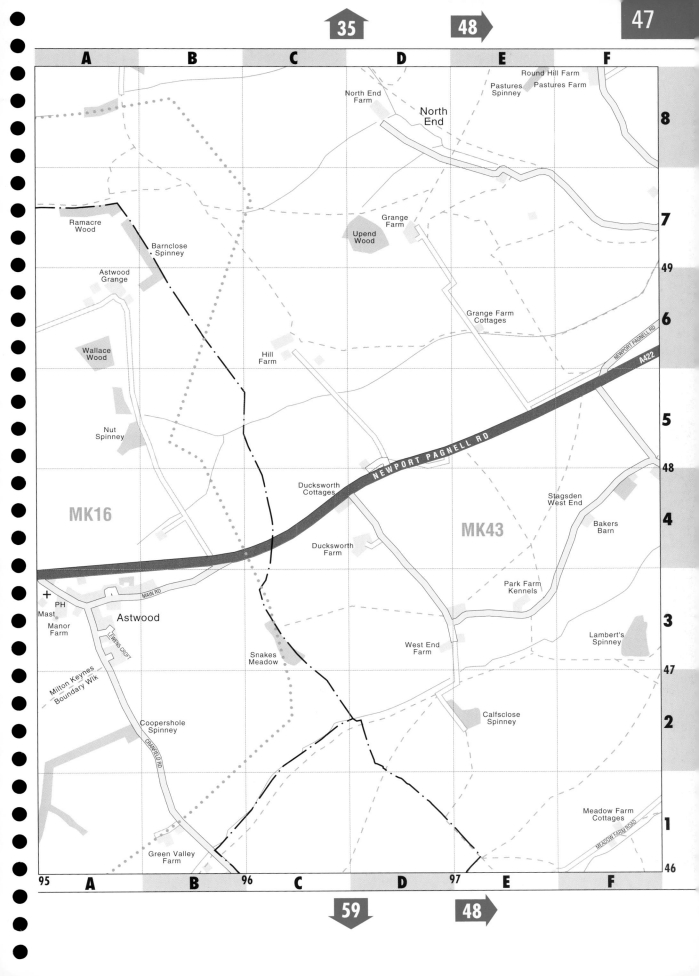

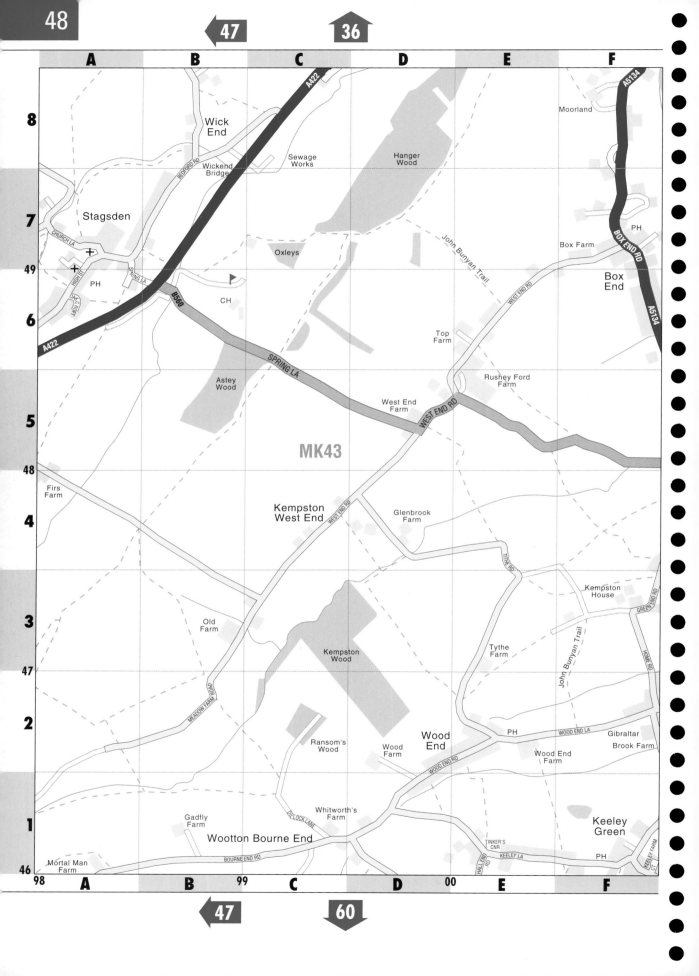

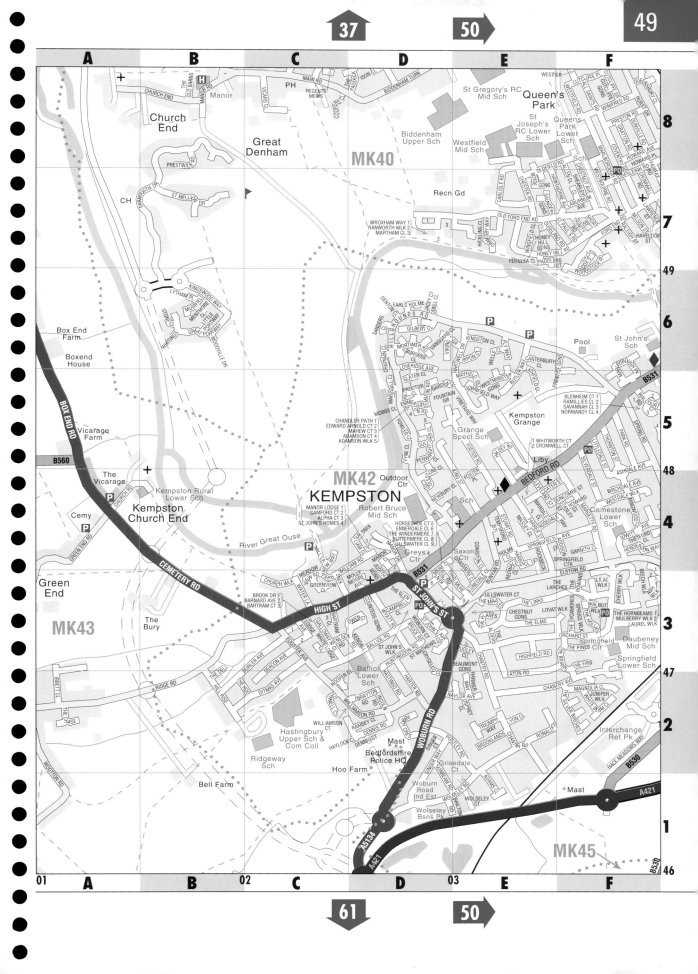

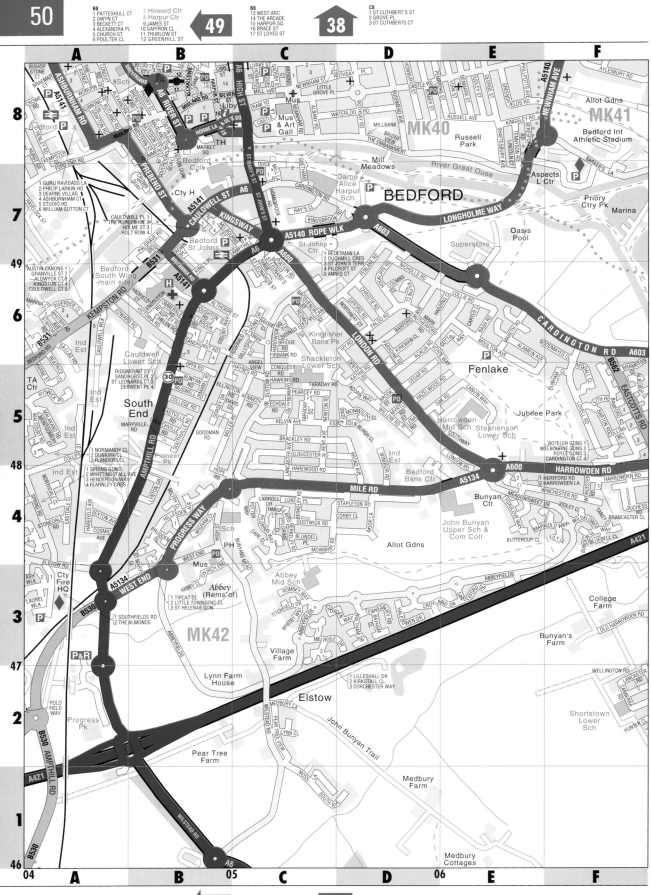

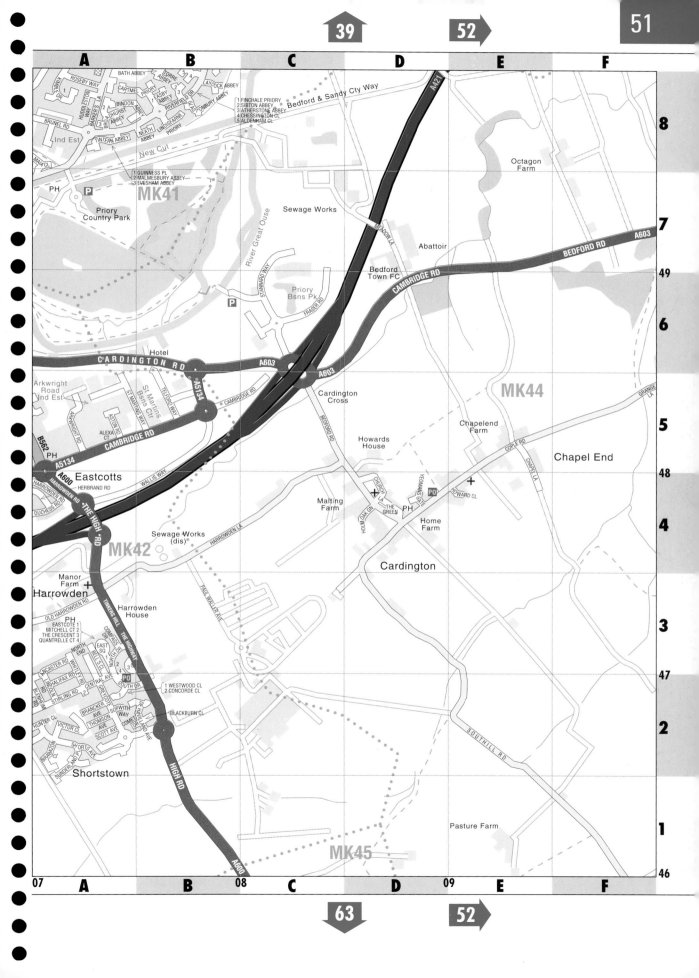

51
40

A B C D E F

8

Works

Dovecote

Willington

CHURCH END

Manor
Farm

+

CHURCH RD

Dog
Farm

Nursery

PH

BARFORD RD

GOSTWICK PL

STATION RD

BALLS LA

GRANGE WAY

PO

Nursery

SANDY RD

Willowhill
Farm

Willowhill
Cottages

A603

BEDFORD RD

A603

7

Gravel Pit
Spinney

Nurseries

49

ALL SAINTS RD

Home
Farm

WOOD LA

Hill
Farm

Conduit
Grove

6

RYE CRES

WILLINGTON RD

Cople

Grange
Farm

Cople
Lower Sch

BURRS CLOSE

+

PH

GRANGE LA

5

WOODLANDS CL

48

MK44

Middle
Farm

4

Water
End

WATER END

Hoo
Farm

NORTHILL RD

3

47

Mox Hill

SG18

2

Wood End
Farm

Moxhill
Farm

Oak
Farm

1

Sweetbrier
Cottage

46

10 A 11 B C 12 D E F

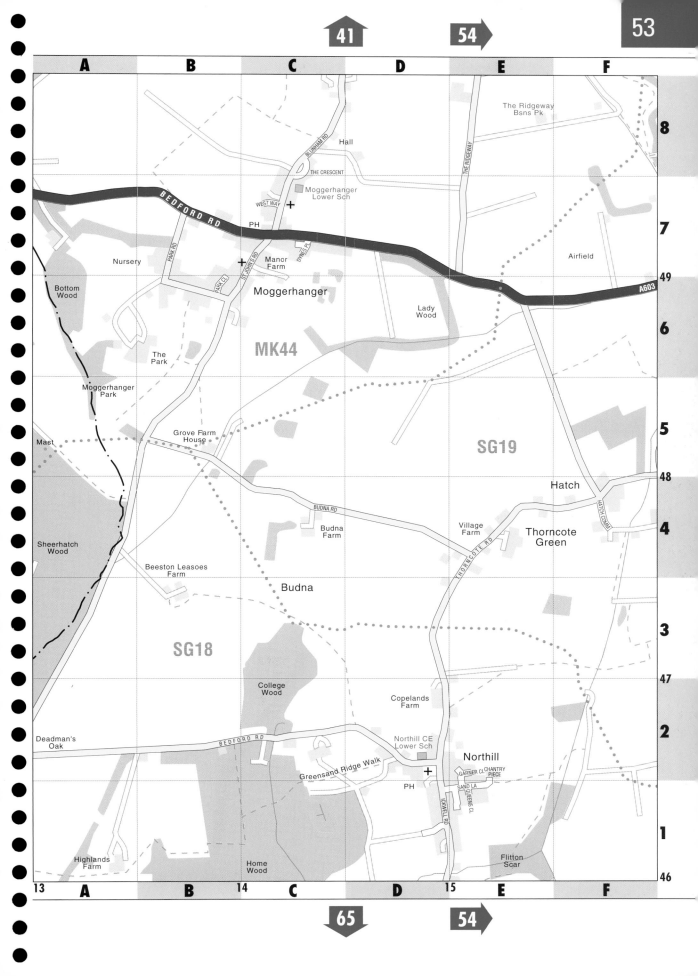

A   B   C   D   E   F

8

The Ridgeway
Bsns Pk

BLUNHAM RD
Hall

THE CRESCENT

Moggerhanger
Lower Sch

7

WEST WAY

BEDFORD RD

PH

THE RIDGEWAY

Airfield

49

Nursery

PARK RD

ST JOHN'S RD

DYNES PL

Manor
Farm

A603

PARK CL

Moggerhanger

Bottom
Wood

Lady
Wood

6

MK44

The
Park

Moggerhanger
Park

SG19

5

Grove Farm
House

Mast

Hatch

48

BUDNA RD

Village
Farm

HATCH COMM

4

Sheerhatch
Wood

Budna
Farm

THORNCOTE RD

Thorncote
Green

Beeston Leasoes
Farm

Budna

SG18

3

College
Wood

47

Copelands
Farm

Deadman's
Oak

BEDFORD RD

2

Northill CE
Lower Sch

Northill

GARNER CL   CHANTRY
PIECE

Greensand Ridge Walk

PH

SAND LA

QUEENS CL

ICKWELL RD

1

Highlands
Farm

Home
Wood

Flitton
Scar

46

13   A   B   14   C   D   15   E   F

53
42

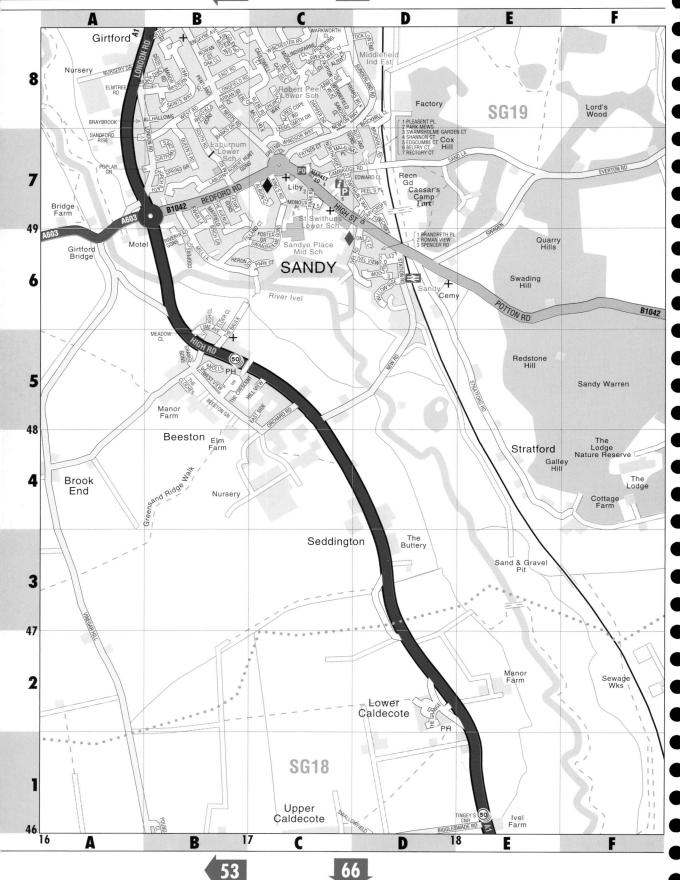

66

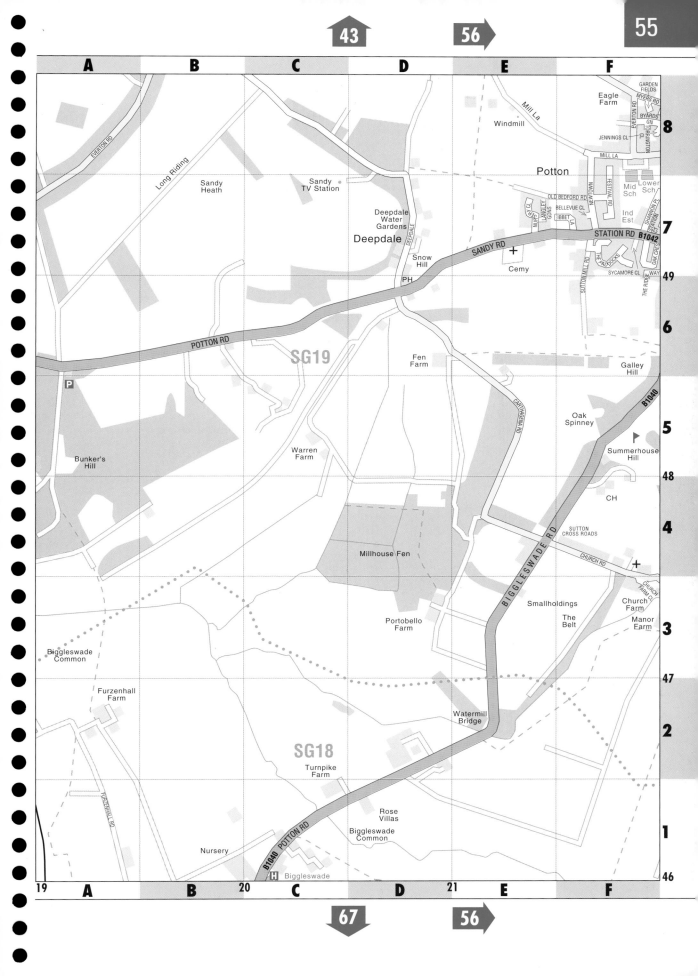

55 44

A **B** **C** **D** **E** **F**

8

ASTWOOD CL
ST PETERS CT
MYERS RD
JACOBS CL
BYARDS GN
COMMON RD
WINGFIELD DR
WEST END LA
DOWNSIDE GDNS
EVERTON RD
BURGOYNE CT
BAKER AVE
CHIPMAN CL
HORSLOW ST
SHEFFIELD CT
CARTERS LA
WILLOW RD
CATHERINES CL
CAVE'S CL
CHAPELS LA
SUN ST
BULL ST
ROYSTON ST
BLACKBIRD ST
BURDETT'S CT
HOPE LA
ORCHARD CL
MEETING LA
MARKET SQ
PO
Liby
BRAYBROOKS DR
BROOK END
BROOKFIELDS
ROYSTON
SHEEPWALK CL
THE HEDGEWALK
KING ST
JUDITH GDNS
WOODLAND AVE
THE MANOR
MANSWAY
AULDGATE CL

GAMLINGAY RD
B1040
B1042
B1040
B1040
BIGGLESWADE RD

Potton

Potton Wood

Clopton Way

Tithe Farm

Poultry Farm

HATLEY RD

Wr Twr

Smallholdings

SUTTON RD

Crossroad Farm

CROFT STEWART

7

49

BURY HILL
B1042

THE BAULK

WRESTLINGWORTH RD

6

Sewage Works

Peg Nut Hill

Smallholdings

B1042

5

Standalone Farm

SG19

48

▶

4

John O'Gaunts Hill

Sutton CE Lower Sch
Ford
Village Farm
HIGH ST
SUTTON RD

Crow Grove

47

PH

Sutton

Manor Farm

3

2

Havannah Farm

Lodge

1

SG18

Dunton Fen

46

22   **A**   **B**   23   **C**   **D**   24   **E**   **F**

55 68

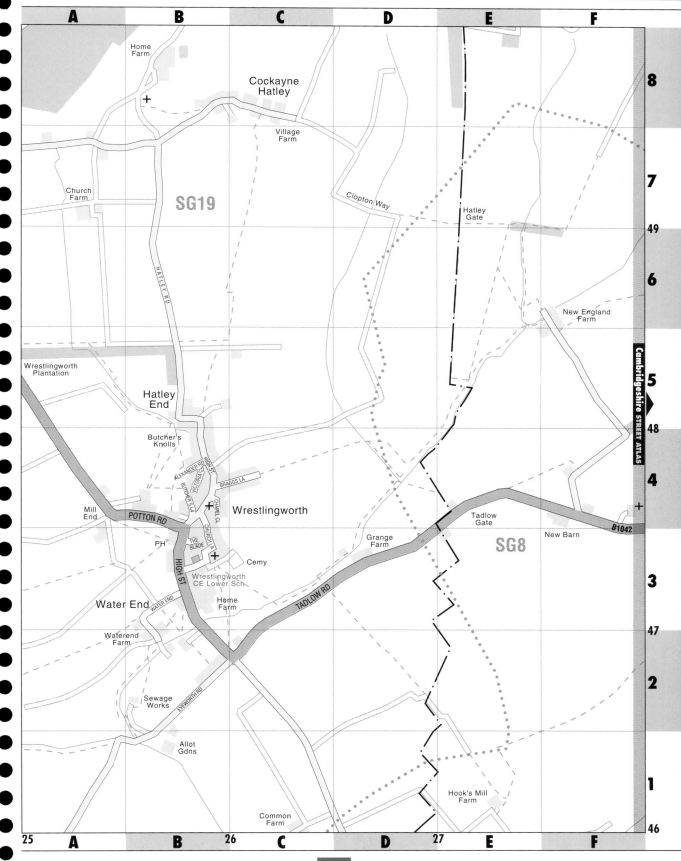

Little Crawley House
Little Crawley
Gumbrills Farm
Old Moat Farm
North Crawley
Crawley Grange
Dollars Grove Farm
Dollars Grove
East End Farm
Quaker's House
East End
ORCHARD WAY
BRYANS CL
HACKETT PL
KILN CRES
NURSERY GDN
VIOLETS CL
CHICHELEY RD
POUND LA
Chicheley Brook
BROOK END
North Crawley CE Fst Sch
PH
HIGH ST
CHEQUERS LA
CHURCH WLK
Church Farm
Broadmead House
Rookery Farm
FOLLY LA
MK16
Lodge Farm
Ringtail Farm
SHIRE LA
Ring Croft Farm
Rings Wharley Farm
Murtland's Farm
Hurstend Farm
Hurst End
Wharley Farm
Shire La
Milton Keynes Boundary Wlk
Sewage Works
FEDDEN HO
ROYCE RD
WEST RD
THE DRIVE
PRINCE PHILIP AVE
EAST RD
MITCHELL RD
THE CRESCENT
DUNCAN RD
REYNOLDS CL
HAWLEY PAGE CL
TO JOSEPH STRINGFELLOW
THE GREEN
COLLEGE RD
Cranfield Conference Ctr
MERCHANT LA
Wharley End
PO
LANCHESTER RD
Moulsoe Old Wood
Chapelclose Spinney
The Cottage
Wharley End Farm
UNIVERSITY WAY
CENTRAL AVE
Cranfield Univ
Liby
MK43
Cranfield Airfield

Buckinghamshire STREET ATLAS

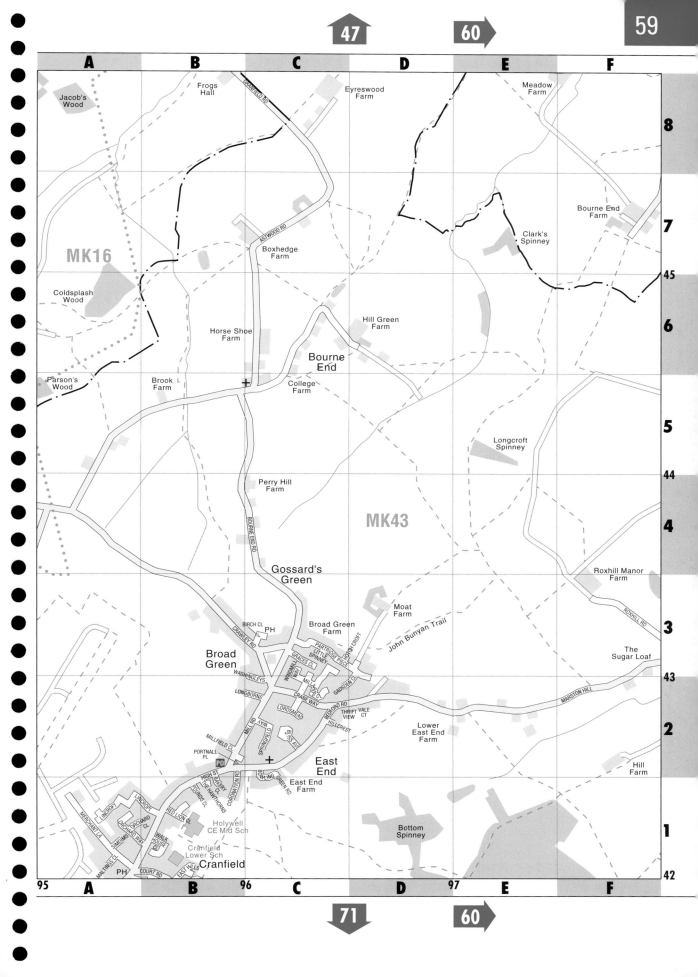

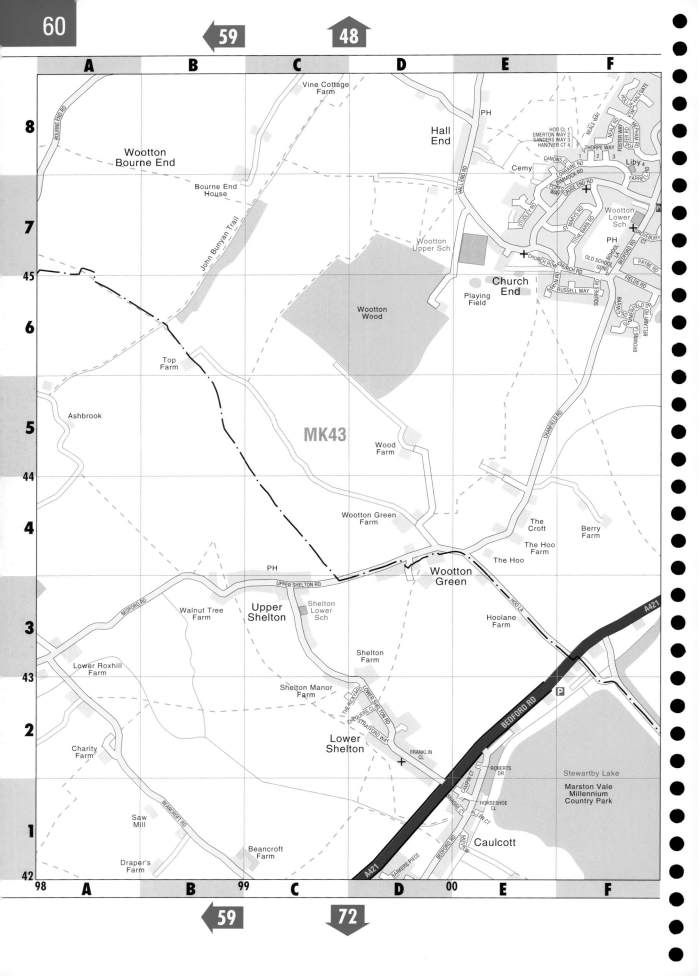

59
48

A   **B**   **C**   **D**   **E**   **F**

8

Wootton
Bourne End

Vine Cottage
Farm

Hall
End

PH

HOO CL 1
EMERTON WAY 2
SANDERS WAY 3
HANOVER CT 4

NEALE WAY
FOSTER WAY
NEALE RD

THORPE WAY

Liby

FARRE

Bourne End
House

Cemy

CANONS CL
DRAME RD
DIMMOCK RD

Wootton
Lower
Sch

GROVEBURY
CT

7

45

John Bunyan Trail

Wootton Upper Sch

Playing
Field

Church
End

Wootton
Wood

MK43

Top
Farm

Ashbrook

STUDLEY RD
ST MARYS RD
CHURCH ROW
PORT WAY
CAUSE END RD

CHURCH RD

OLD SCHOOL LA
BEDFORD RD

PH

OLD SCHOOL
GDNS

PAYNE RD

FIELDS RD

JEAN RD
RUSSELL WAY
SQUIRES RD

BARKES RD

IMMERFIELD RD

BROWNES LA

BELLAMY RD

6

Wood
Farm

CRANFIELD RD

5

44

4

Wootton Green
Farm

The Croft

The Hoo
Farm

Berry
Farm

The Hoo

Wootton
Green

PH

UPPER SHELTON RD

Upper
Shelton

Shelton
Lower
Sch

Hoolane
Farm

HOO LA

A421

Walnut Tree
Farm

3

43

BEDFORD RD

Lower Roxhill
Farm

Shelton
Farm

Shelton Manor
Farm

THE RICKYARD

LOWER SHELTON RD

CHEQUERS CL

STRATFORD WA

2

Charity
Farm

Lower
Shelton

FRANKLIN
CL

ROBERTS
DR

CAMPIN CT

P

BEDFORD RD

Stewartby Lake

Marston Vale
Millennium
Country Park

SNAGGE CL

ALLEN CT

HORSESHOE
CL

1

Saw
Mill

BEANCROFT RD

Caulcott

BEDFORD RD

MEADOW

Draper's
Farm

Beancroft
Farm

A421

BANKERS PIECE

42

98   **A**   **B**   99   **C**   **D**   00   **E**   **F**

59
72

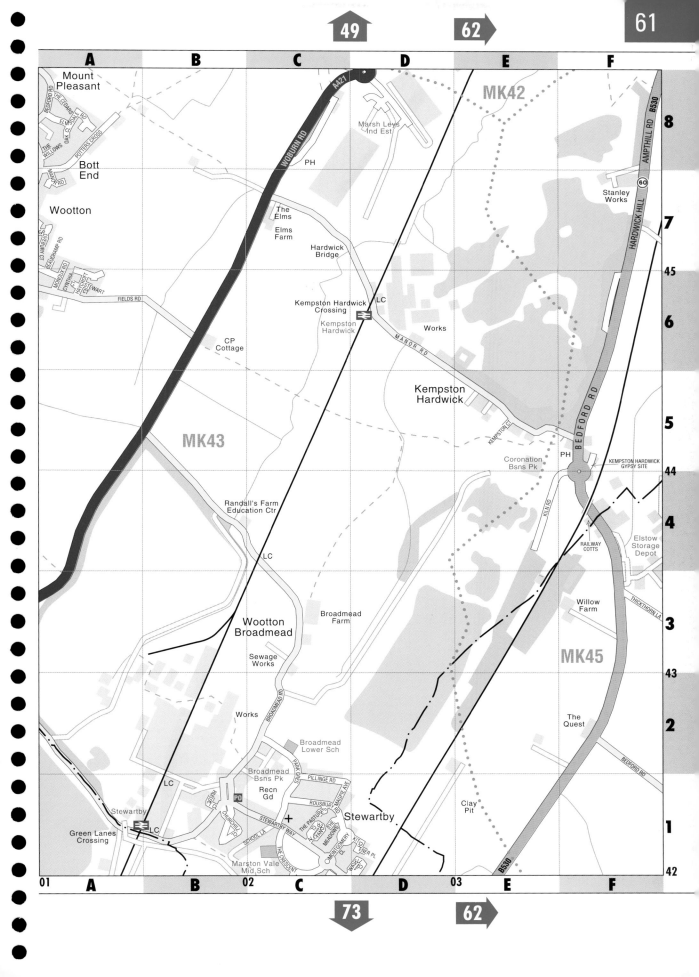

Mount Pleasant
Bott End
Wootton

MK42

Stanley Works
60

Hardwick Hill
AMPTHILL RD
B530

8

WOBURN RD
A421
PH

The Elms
Elms Farm

Hardwick Bridge

7

45

Kempston Hardwick Crossing
LC
Kempston Hardwick
Works

MANOR RD

6

CP Cottage

BEAUCHAMP RD
MONFOLK RD
CYNTHIA
HACROFT
STEWART
CT
BEDFORD RD
OAK CL
FIELDS RD

Kempston Hardwick

5

MK43

Kempston Hardwick Gypsy Site
Kempston Ct
Coronation Bsns Pk
PH

KEMPSTON HARDWICK GYPSY SITE

BEDFORD RD

44

Randall's Farm Education Ctr

LC

Elstow Storage Depot

4

RAILWAY COTTS

KILN RD

Wootton Broadmead

Broadmead Farm

Willow Farm

THICKTHORN LA

MK45

3

Sewage Works

The Quest

Works

BROADMEAD RD

43

Broadmead Lower Sch

BEDFORD RD

2

Broadmead Bsns Pk
Recn Gd
PO
PARK CRES
PILLINGE RD

Clay Pit

1

LC
ASPEN CL
CHURCHILL CL
SCHOOL LA
STEWARTBY WAY
THE CRESCENT
ROUSBURY RD
MAPLE AVE
THE PASTURES
K PRINCES
THE MEADOWS
COMMON
MONTGOMERY
CL
KILN CL
EMER PL
WASEY RD

Stewartby

B530

Green Lanes Crossing
Stewartby
LC
Marston Vale Mid Sch

42

61
50

A B C D E F

8

7

45

6

5

44

4

3

43

2

1

42

B530

A6

WILSTEAD RD

BEDFORD RD

WATSON RD

KENNETH WAY

North End Farm

Wilstead Ind Est

DANE LA

Horton Turn Farm

MK42

MK45

John Bunyan Trail

Works

DUCK END LA

Duck End

Duck End Farm

Vicarage Farm

BEDFORD RD

Manor Farm

CHAPEL LA

THE SQUARE

BLACK HAT CL

DINES CL
BIRD CL
TOWN CL

CASTLE CL

COTTON END RD

WILSON CT

P.H.

PO

CHURCH RD

HOME CL

ARDS CL

HAMPTON CL

BRAMBLES

ARMSTRONG CL

Wilstead Lower Sch

WHITWORTH WAY

PHIPPS CL 1
MORGANS CL 2

1

VICARAGE LA

WILTON RD

Church Farm

CHURCH FARM AVE

OAK

LUTTON RISE

LUTTON RD

HOWARD CL

Wilstead

1 ORCHARD DR
2 CLUB RD

MAPLE CL

SILVER BIRCH AVE

HAWTHORNE DR

LONGMEADOW DR

CHERRY TREE DR

BERKELEY CL

WOODLAND DR

1 HONEYSUCKLE AVE
2 OAK AVE
3 LILAC AVE
4 ASH GR
5 BEECH AVE
6 CEDAR AVE
7 POPLAR AVE
8 WOODLAND PK
9 WOODVIEW

60

60

LABURNHAM AVE 1
WILLOW RD 2
PARK RD 3

Elstow Storage Depot

Great Thickthorn Farm

THICKTHORN LA

Little Thickthorn Farm

BEDFORD RD

DUCK END CL

MILL LA

Duck End

Windmill (dis)

Chapel End

Chapel End Farm

WILSTEAD HILL

A6

04 A B 05 C D 06 E F

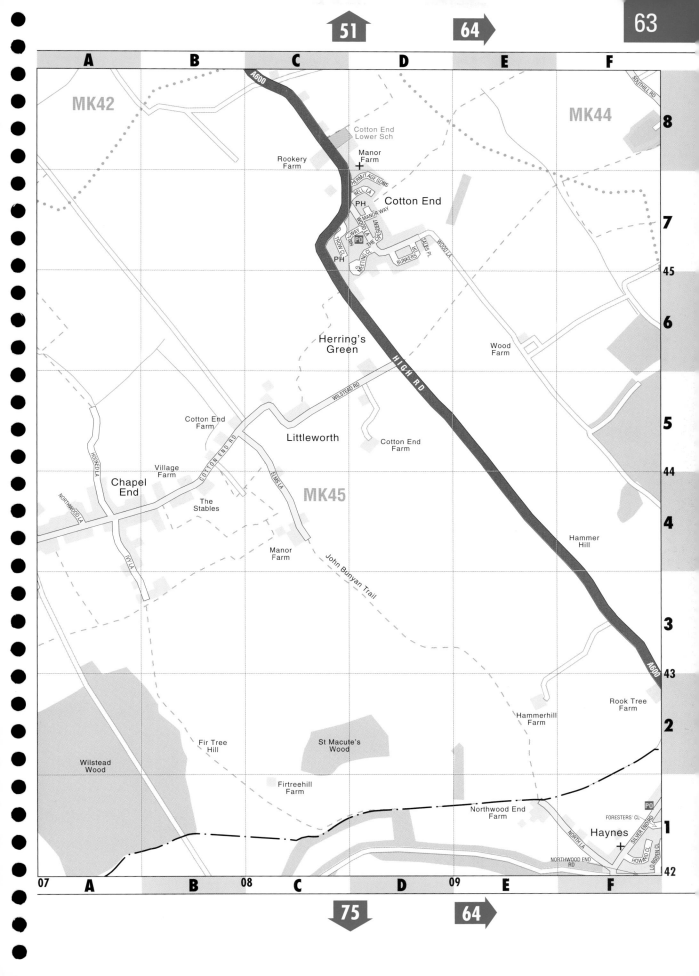

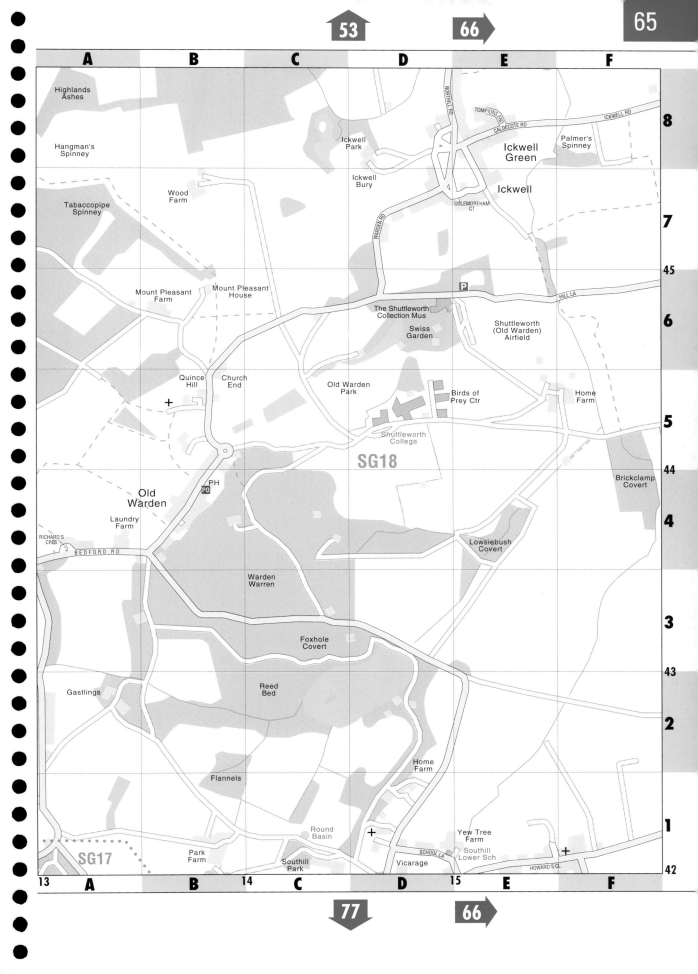

A   B   C   D   E   F

8
7
45
6
5
44
4
3
43
2
1
42

Highlands Ashes

Hangman's Spinney

Ickwell Park

NORTHILL RD
TOMPIONS END
CALDECOTE RD
ICKWELL RD

Ickwell Green

Palmer's Spinney

Tabaccopipe Spinney

Wood Farm

Ickwell Bury

Ickwell

WARDEN RD

COLEMOREHAM CT

Mount Pleasant House

Mount Pleasant Farm

P

HILL LA

The Shuttleworth Collection Mus

Swiss Garden

Shuttleworth (Old Warden) Airfield

Quince Hill

Church End

Old Warden Park

Birds of Prey Ctr

Home Farm

+

Shuttleworth College

SG18

PH
PO

Old Warden

Brickclamp Covert

Laundry Farm

RICHARD'S CRES

BEDFORD RD

Lowsiebush Covert

Warden Warren

Foxhole Covert

Gastlings

Reed Bed

Home Farm

Flannels

Round Basin

+

Yew Tree Farm

SCHOOL LA

Southill Lower Sch

+

SG17

Park Farm

Southill Park

Vicarage

HOWARD'S CL

13   A   B   14   C   D   15   E   F

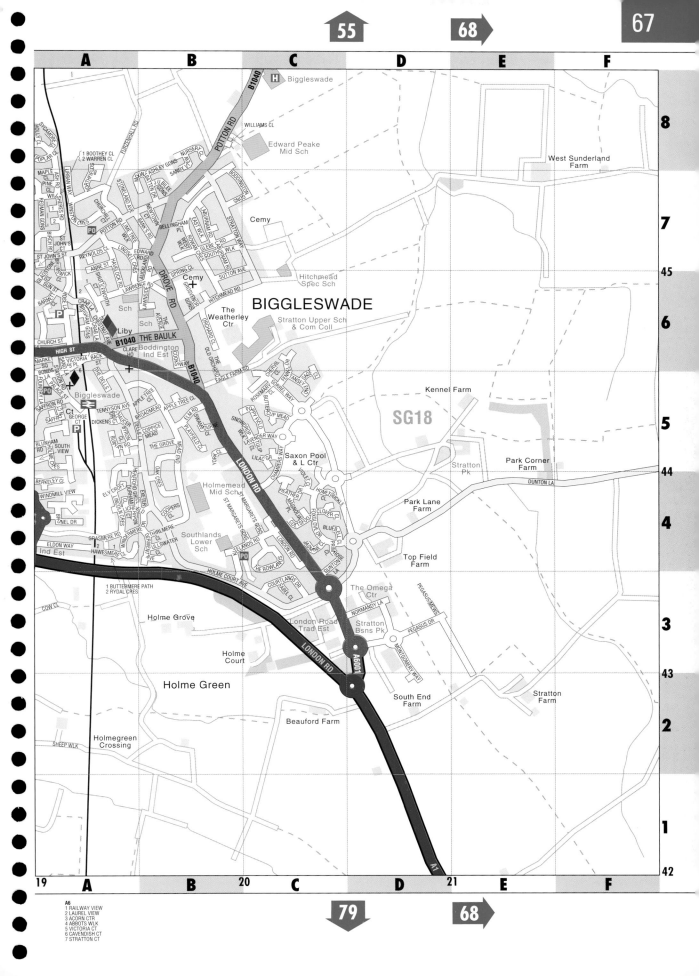

A B C D E F

8

7

45

6

5

44

4

3

43

2

1

42

22 A B 23 C D 24 E F

Dunton Fen

Sunderland Hall Farm

SUTTON RD

SG19

Eyeworth

HIGH ST

SUTTON RD

Church Farm

Water Works

CAMBRIDGE RD

Newton

Newton Grove Farm

Sewage Works

Middlesex Farm

GREENFIELD WAY

OLD BAKERY YD

KINGS POND CL

HORSESH CL

BOTT LA

Dunton Lower Sch

PO

PH

CHURCH ST

MAGDALENE

LEET CL

Dunton

HALLSIDE

HIGH ST

CHAPEL ST

FOX CL

LIMETREE CL

SPRINGFIELD

Church Farm

SG18

BIGGLESWADE RD

Millow Hall Farm

Millow Lodge Farm

Millow

Millow Hill Farm

River Cam or Rhee

Millowbury Farm

Plantation Farm

SG7

Green La

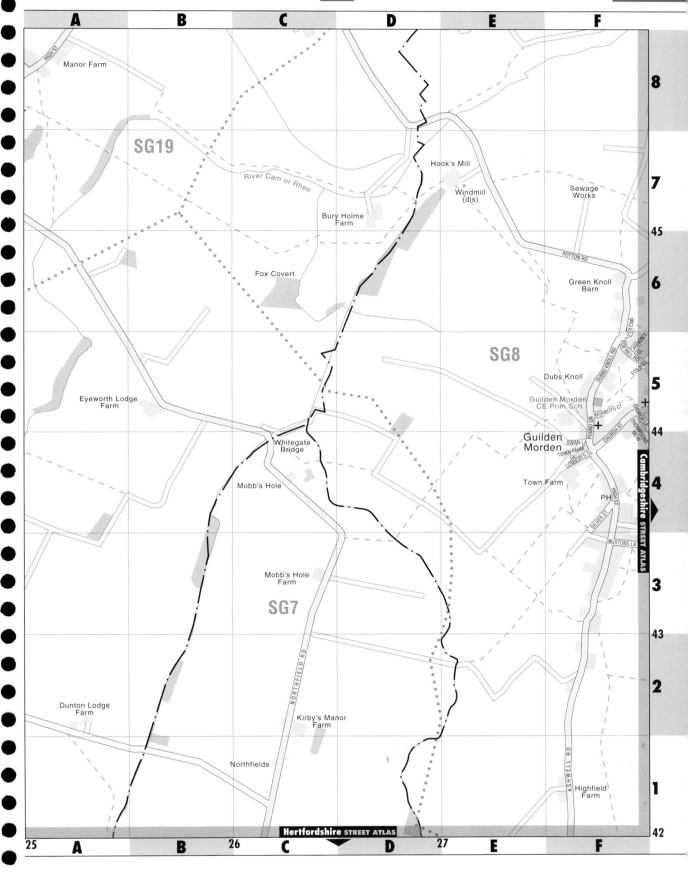

A B C D E F

8

7

45

6

5

44

4

43

3

2

43

1

42

SG19

River Cam or Rhee

Manor Farm

Bury Holme Farm

Fox Covert

Eyeworth Lodge Farm

Whitegate Bridge

Mobb's Hole

SG7

Mobb's Hole Farm

Dunton Lodge Farm

Kirby's Manor Farm

NORTHFIELD RD

Northfields

Hook's Mill

Windmill (dis)

SG8

Sewage Works

POTTON RD

Green Knoll Barn

Dubs Knoll

Guilden Morden CE Prim Sch

Guilden Morden

Town Farm

DUBS KNOLL RD

FOX HILL RD

FOX HILL

CANNON'S CL

CHR

POUND GN

WORBOYS CT

CHURCH ST

CHURCH LA

THOMPSON'S ROW

SWAN LA

TOWN FARM CL

CONNOR'S CL

HIGH ST

SILVER ST

BUXTONS LA

PH

ASHWELL RD

Highfield Farm

25 A B 26 C D 27 E F

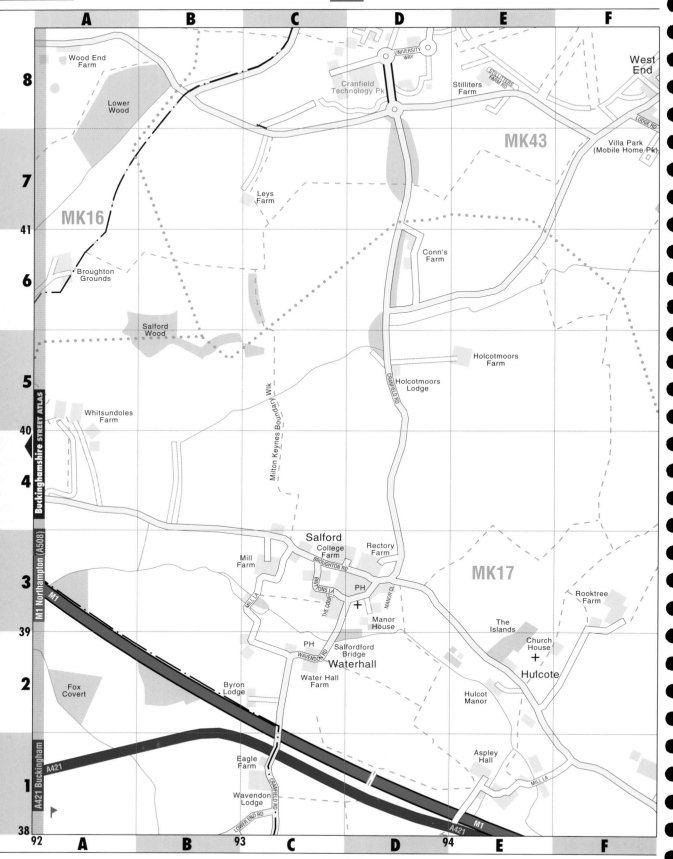

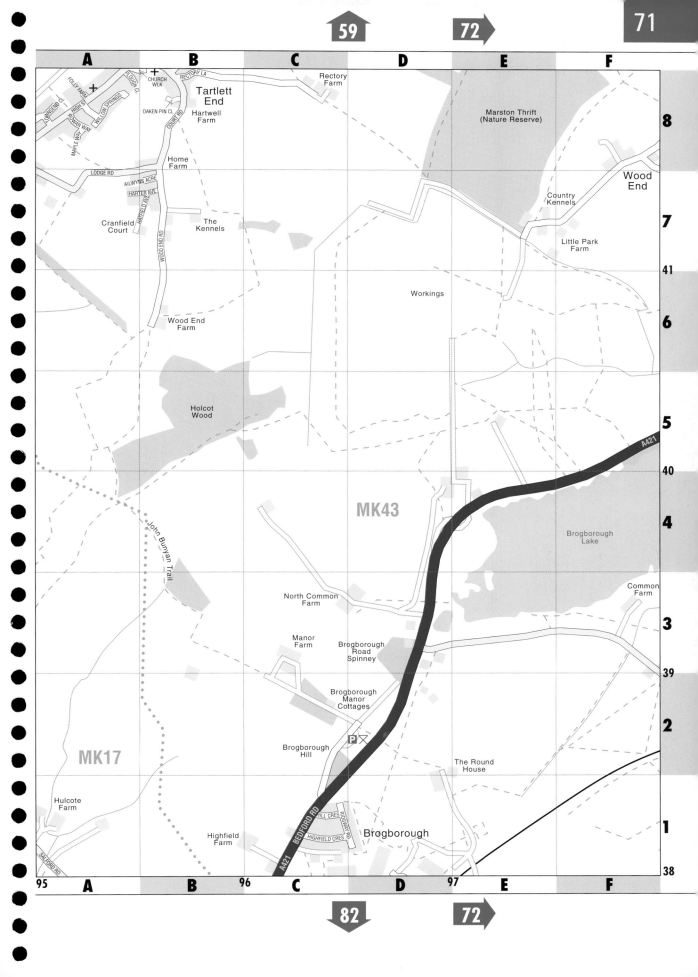

59
72

A   B   C   D   E   F

Rectory La

Rectory
Farm

Tartlett
End

Marston Thrift
(Nature Reserve)

CHURCH
WLK

PLOUGH CL

FOLLY FARM

HIGH ST

TOWNSEND CL

MAPLE WAY

ROWAN WAY

WILLOW SPRINGS

OAKEN PIN CL

COURT RD

Hartwell
Farm

Wood
End

8

LODGE RD

Home
Farm

Country
Kennels

AILWYNS ACRE

HARTER AVE

HATFIELD AVE

WOOD END RD

Cranfield
Court

The
Kennels

Little Park
Farm

7

41

Workings

Wood End
Farm

6

Holcot
Wood

5

A421

40

John Bunyan Trail

MK43

Brogborough
Lake

4

North Common
Farm

Common
Farm

3

Manor
Farm

Brogborough
Road
Spinney

39

Brogborough
Manor
Cottages

2

MK17

P

Brogborough
Hill

The Round
House

BEDFORD RD

HILL CRES

RIDGWAY RD

Hulcote
Farm

Highfield
Farm

HIGHFIELD CRES

Brogborough

1

SALFORD RD

A421

38

95   A   96   B   C   D   97   E   F

82
72

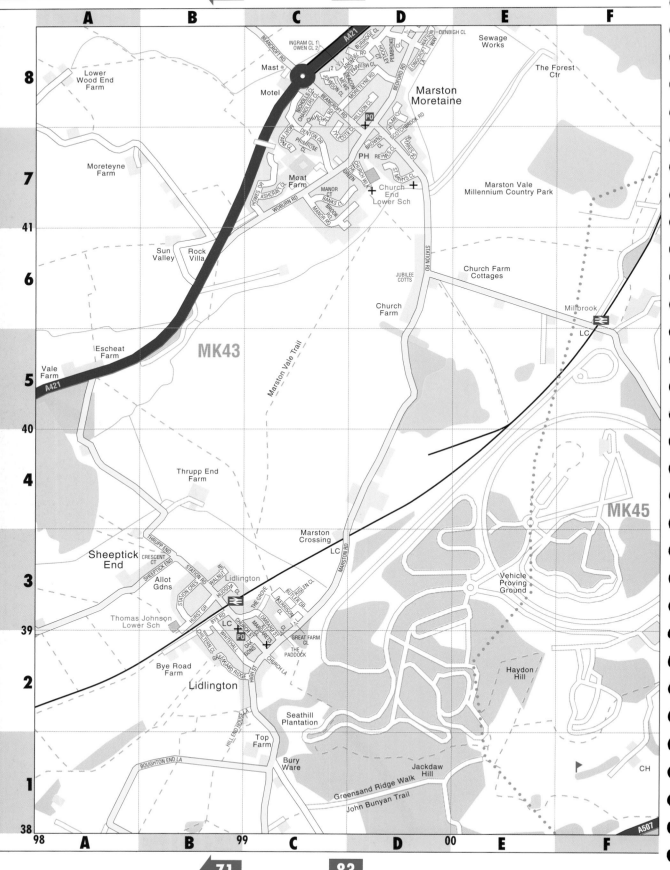

A   B   C   D   E   F

8   Lower Wood End Farm

Marston Moretaine

Sewage Works

The Forest Ctr

Mast
Motel

Moreteyne Farm

7   Moat Farm

Church End Lower Sch

PH

Marston Vale Millennium Country Park

41

Sun Valley   Rock Villa

Jubilee Cotts

Church Farm Cottages

6   Escheat Farm

Church Farm

Millbrook
LC

MK43

Vale Farm
A421

Marston Vale Trail

5   A421

40

Thrupp End Farm

MK45

4

Marston Crossing
LC

Sheeptick End

Allot Gdns

Lidlington

Vehicle Proving Ground

3   Crescent Ct

Thomas Johnson Lower Sch

The Grove

39   LC   PO

Great Farm Cl
THE PADDOCK

Bye Road Farm

2   Lidlington

Haydon Hill

Seathill Plantation

Top Farm

1   Bury Ware

Jackdaw Hill

CH

Greensand Ridge Walk
John Bunyan Trail

38   98   A   B   99   C   D   00   E   F   A507

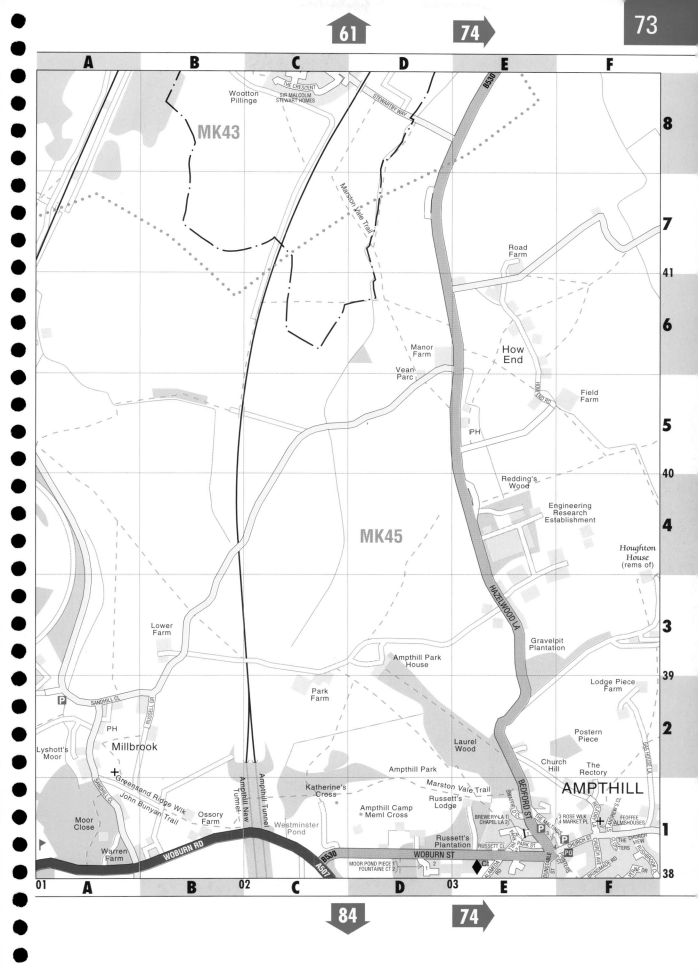

Duck End

MILL LA
BUNYAN CL
FRANCOTT CL
ADELAIDE CL
UXBRIDGE WAY
BEDFORD RD
BROADWAY
DAYSFIELD
HOME CL
CHERRY CL
VICAR DR
ALBERT'S CL
THE ORCHARD
HIGH ST
PO
PH
SYBIL'S WAY

Hill Farm

CHAPEL END RD

A6

West Park Farm

Keyse's Spinney

Houghton Conquest Lower Sch

GRANGE CL
THE GROVE
CHURCH CL
GLEBE WAY
PEMBROKE RD
RECTORY LA
KINGSWOOD CL
PH

Houghton Conquest

Brookside Farm

WILSTEAD HILL

Lark Hill

Bury Leys Farm

Wilstead Hill Farm

The Old Rectory

LONDON LA

Pike Farm

Hawhills Farm

West End Cottage

60

Bury Farm

Barnacles

West End Farm

King's Wood (Nature Reserve)

MK45

Haynes West End

60

A6

Houghton Park

Brickhill Pastures

North Limbersey Farm

Montague Wood

Houghton Park Farm

LIMBERSEY LA

South Limbersey Farm

Limbersey Nurseries

Greensand Ridge Wlk

Maulden Wood

Bolebec Farm

Greensand Ridge Wlk

Kings Farm

Oaklands House

WINGFIELD AVE
KINGS RD
THE BRACHE
1 MOOR LA
2 BRIGHTMANS DR

Maulden

Maulden Grange

ALLESBURY RD
THE PATHWAY
SNOW HILL
SANDY RD
BECK CL
S CL
TAYLORS END
PH
FLITWICK RD
AMPTHILL RD
RECN Gd
THE MAGPIES
BROWNSELL
COBBITTS
ANDREWS RD
GEORGE ST
CHURCH RD

Maulden Grange

Green End

Grid labels: A B C D E F (top and bottom); 8 7 41 6 5 40 4 3 39 2 1 38 (side)

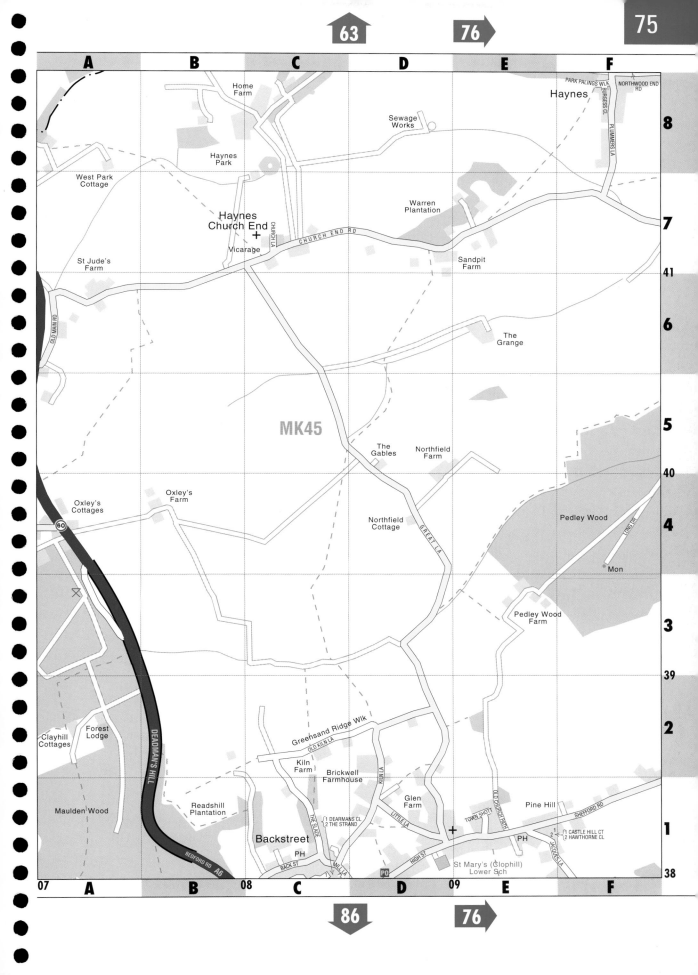

A B C D E F

Haynes

PARK PALINGS WLK
NORTHWOOD END RD
BURGESS CL
PLUMMERS LA

Home Farm

Sewage Works

8

Haynes Park

Warren Plantation

West Park Cottage

Haynes Church End

7

Vicarage

CHURCH LA

CHURCH END RD

41

St Jude's Farm

Sandpit Farm

OLD MAIN RD

The Grange

6

MK45

5

The Gables

Northfield Farm

40

Oxley's Cottages

Oxley's Farm

Pedley Wood

LONGS DR

4

Northfield Cottage

GREAT LA

Mon

60

Pedley Wood Farm

3

39

Clayhill Cottages

Forest Lodge

Greensand Ridge Wlk

2

DEADMAN'S HILL

Kiln Farm

OLD KILN LA

Brickwell Farmhouse

KILN LA

Glen Farm

OLD CHURCH PATH

Pine Hill

SHEFFORD RD

Maulden Wood

Readshill Plantation

THE SLADE

1 DEARMANS CL
2 THE STRAND

LITTLE LA

TOWN SHOTT

PH

1 CASTLE HILL CT
2 HAWTHORNE CL

1

Backstreet

PH

BACK ST

MILL LA

HIGH ST

PO

St Mary's (Clophill) Lower Sch

BEDFORD RD A6

JACKDAWS LA

38

07 A B 08 C D 09 E F

75
64

A   B   C   D   E   F

8
Hill Farm
PH
MEADOW PIECE
Pear Tree Farm
Deadman's Cross
A600
HIGH RD
PH
Old Rowney Farm
Keeper's Warren
Greensand Ridge Walk

NORTHWOOD END RD
Standalone Farm
STANDALONE WARREN

7
Appley Corner

41
Wood Farm
MK45
Greensand Ridge Wlk
John Bunyan Trail
New Rowney Farm

6
Obelisk
LONG DR
Rowney Warren Wood
A600

Chicksands Wood
SANDY LA
P
Rowney Forest Walk

5

40
Secondlodge Farm
Firstlodge Farm

Penseroso Grove
Druids Grove
Chicksands
NIMROD DR
MOUNTBA
TEEN WAY
TRENCHARD LA

4
The Hill
DANGER AREA
Temple Grove
TRENCHARD AVE
NELSON RD
REPTON RD
CHURCHILL DR
WELLINGTON DR
TEMPLER WAY

Obelisk
ROSATA LA
CHICKSANDS AVE
Sewage Works

3
SG17
LONG WLK
BECKMANOK PL
MERCURY PL
Chicksands Priory
KENDAL DR

LITTENHAM PL
Sports Island
LEYDENE PL
MEDMENHAM AVE

39
OSBORNE AVE
ORCHARD CT
WYTON CT
MARESFIELD AVE
WASHINGTON AVE

2
Upper Alders
JT KENNEDY DR
BLOWER PL
JACKSON PL
FRET PL
TRUMAN PL
CHICKSANDS AVE
A507

River Flit
HOOVER PL
AMPTHILL RD

SHEFFORD RD
Speedsdairy Farm
Top Farm
Beadlow
Kiln Farm
PRIORY RD

1
Nursery
Top Farm
RECTORY RD
THE GLEBE

38
A507
Hotel
Campton Lower Sch
ELM CT
GRANGE GDNS

10   A   B   11   C   D   12   E   F

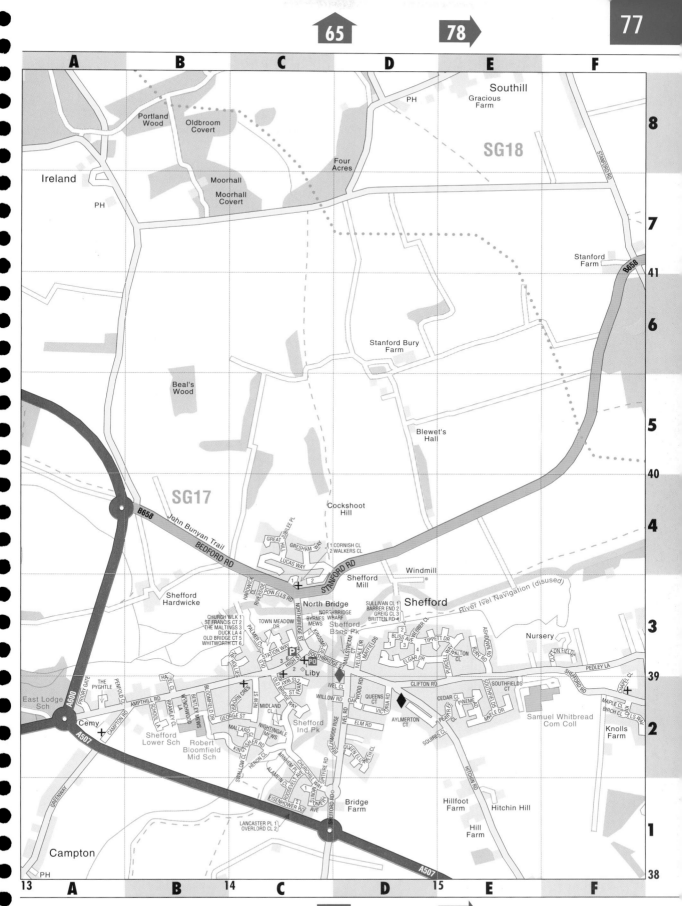

77 66

A B C D E F

8

7

B658

41

SG18

Stanford

6

Allot Gdns

THE CRESCENT
GLEPIN CL
OLD SCHOOL LA

B658

Hill Farm

River Ivel Navigation (dis)

Poplars

Village Farm

MILL RD

A6001
CHURCH ST

VICARAGE CL
HOWARD CL
QUEEN'S WAY
DENNY CRES
EAST RD
ST ANDREW'S WAY

TITHE FARM CL
MILL LANE
MILL LA
OLD MILL CL
CHURCH CRES
CHURCH FARM
Langford Lower Sch

KING GEORGE CL

Langford Mill

POUND CL
PH

THE BUTTS

Garfield Farm

CROWN LA

PROSPECT RD
WINDSOR WAY
THE AVENUE
MANOR CL
ASHBY CT
JUBILEE LA
STATION RD

WEST VIEW
THE LEYS

Langford

PO
CHAPEL CT

HIGH ST

BENTLEY CL

VICTORIA CL

Flexmore End

Water End

RIVERMEAD CT
VIC CL
WILMAN CT

FLEXMORE WAY

RIVERSIDE GDNS

WHITEMAN CL

CAMBRIDGE RD

Boot End

5

Sewage Wks

PH

LAKES CL

CAMBRIDGE GDNS
HLAND RISE
CAMBRIDGE WAY
CAMEY
RIDGE CL

40

SG17

4

Clifton Bury Farm

LANGFORD RD

River Ivel

COMMON RD

3

Clifton Manor

LYS MEAD
SEARS CL
BATH RD
BILBERRY RD

Clifton Farm

Stockbridge Farm

Seedlings Well

SG16

RECTORY LA
CHURCH ST
CLIFTON HOUSE CL
WHISTON CRES
STOCKBRIDGE RD

Clifton

All Saints Lower Sch

Stock Bridge

NEWTOWN CL
THE HAWTHORNS
BURGESS WAY

GARDENERS LA

Poppy Hill Farm

39

PEDLEY LA
MARC
GRANGE ST
LIME TREE RD
LINK WAY

PH
OLD SCHOOL CT
ELM FARM CL
MILL CLOSE WAY
BRICKEL PL

NEWS CRES

1 YEW TREE WLK
2 ROOKERY WLK
3 BROAD WLK

NORTHFIELD

CHURCH RD

JORDAN CL

SPRING RD
SHEFFORD RD
FAIRFAX CL
BURROW
HABBERICK LA
PO

ASHINGTON CT
JUBILEE CL
FAIRGROUND WAY

Old Vicarage Gdns
DEGRAY MANOR
OLD BARN CL
LIME WLK

SPARKSFIELD
PARK LANE CRES
GROVE CL
PARK LA

Henlow Park

2

BUNYAN CL
ALEXANDER CL

Nurseries

HITCHIN LA
BROAD ST

PH

HIGH ST

Henlow Mid Sch

Raynsford Lower Sch

Henlow

The Grange

1

Clifton Park

NEW RD

MANOR RD
CLIFTON RD
WESTFIELD RD

CHILTERN
CHAPEL RD
CROSSWAYS CL

TOWN FARM CT
PO
ELIZABETH CT

BROOK CL
ADDINGTON

CHESTNUT FARM

A6001

DOVE HOUSE DR
OAK DR
ELM CL
COACH RD

THE MALTINGS

OAK DR
MEADOW WLK

38

16   17   18

A B C D E F

77 89

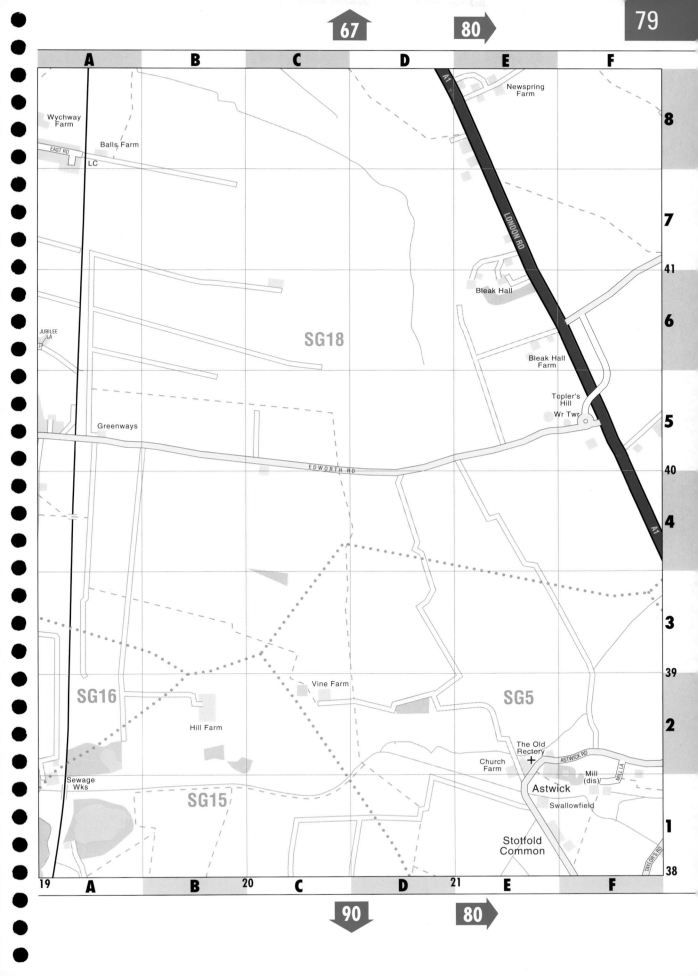

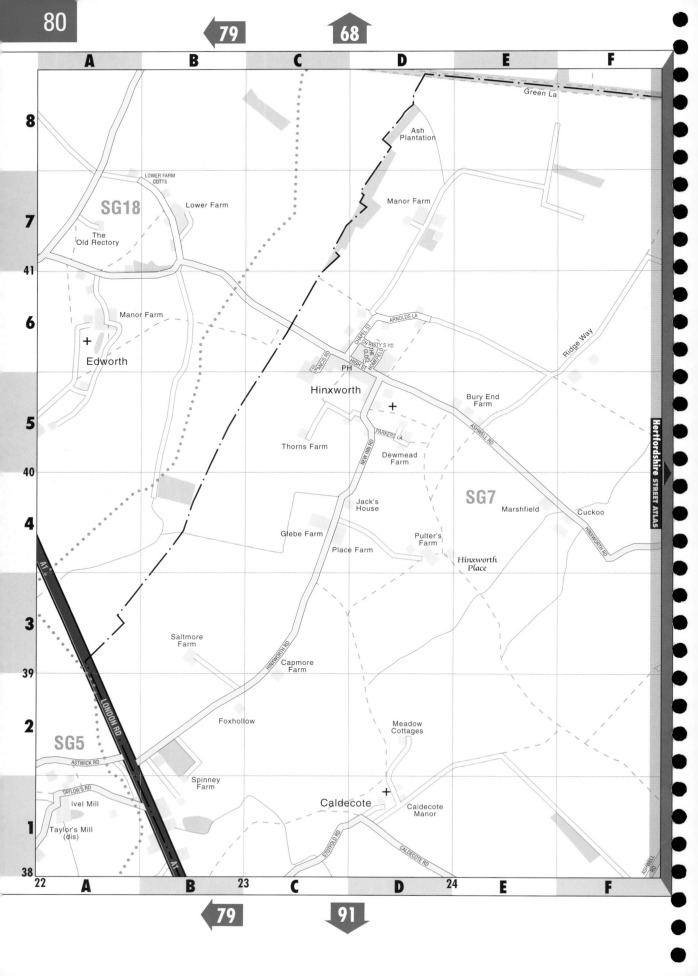

79
68

A B C D E F

8

Green La

Ash
Plantation

LOWER FARM
COTTS

Lower Farm

7

SG18

Manor Farm

The
Old Rectory

41

Arnolds La

Ridge Way

6

Manor Farm

CHAPEL ST
RISTY'S YD
THE CLOSE
HUNNETS LA

+

Edworth

PANG'S RD
HIGH ST
PH

Bury End
Farm

5

Hinxworth

+

ASHWELL RD

Thorns Farm

PARKERS LA

Dewmead
Farm

40

Jack's
House

SG7

Marshfield

Cuckoo

4

Glebe Farm

HINXWORTH RD

Place Farm

Pulter's
Farm

Hinxworth
Place

HINXWORTH RD

A1

3

Saltmore
Farm

Capmore
Farm

39

LONDON RD

HINXWORTH RD

Foxhollow

2

Meadow
Cottages

SG5

ASTWICK RD

Spinney
Farm

TAYLOR'S RD

Ivel Mill

Caldecote

+

Caldecote
Manor

1

Taylor's Mill
(dis)

STOTFOLD RD

CALDECOTE RD

ASHWELL RD

38

22 A B 23 C D 24 E F

Hertfordshire STREET ATLAS

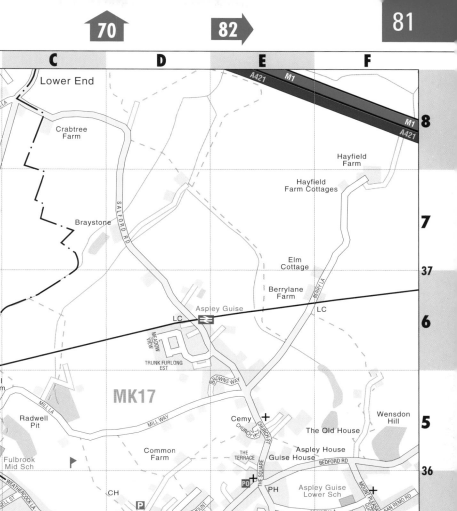

A   B   C   D   E   F

8

Lower End

CH
LOWER END RD
The Lodge
WAVENDON HOUSE DR
CROW LA
Crabtree Farm
WAVENDON HO

Park Farm

A421 M1

M1
A421

Hayfield Farm

Hayfield Farm Cottages

7

Milton Keynes Bdy Wlk
CRANFIELD RD
Wks
Braystone
SALFORD RD

Elm Cottage

37

Nursery

BELLWAY
PARKWAY
Deethe Farm
HILLWAY
RIDGWAY
TAVISTOCK CL
VANDYKE CL
CHANTRY CL
DEETHE CL
TURNPIKE CT

Aspley Guise
LC
Berrylane Farm
BERRY LA
LC

6

A5130 Milton Keynes (A509)

NEWPORT RD

A5130

Woburn Sands

LC
30

HUTTON WAY
Mill Farm
MILL LA
MEADOW VIEW
TRUNK FURLONG EST

MK17

DOWNS WAY

Cemy
CHURCH
CHURCH ST
The Old House
Wensdon Hill

5

SWALLOWFIELD
Lower Sch
SADLEIRS GN
BURROWS CL
Radwell Pit

Common Farm
MILL WAY

THE TERRACE
Aspley House
Guise House
BEDFORD RD

36

Woburn Sands

STATION RD
THE GROVE
CRAMB RD
WEST RD
SPRING GR
Fulbrook Mid Sch
WEATHERDOCK LA
THE CLOSE

CH

PO
THE SQUARE
PH
Aspley Guise Lower Sch
SPINNEY LA
MOUNT PLEASANT
GUISE CT
SAN REMO RD

4

BLACKTHORN GR
PINFOLD
MAPLE GR
ELM GR
THEYDON AVE
THE LEYS
WOOD ST
ASPLANDS CL
CHAPEL ST
RUSSELL ST
PO
VICARAGE ST
CONGRA PK
ST VINCENTS
Aspley Guise

BOW BRICKHILL RD
TILBROOK CL
THE LEYS
HARDWICK GR
SHELDON CL
HIGH ST
Liby
PH
DOWNHAM RD
ASPLEY HILL
DEETH CL
WOODLAND WAY
HARDWICK RD
HARDWICK MDWS
HEATH CL
ASPLEY CT
DUKE ST
MENTONE
WEST HILL
WOOD LA
GREEN LA
WOBURN LA
Allot Gdns

Edgewick Farm
BISHOPS WLK
CHARLEWOOD HO
WOODSIDE
PEERS DR
GYPSY LA

3

Wavendon Wood
Milton Keynes Bdy Wlk
CHURCH RD
WERTHER RD
MARROW PATH
SANDY LA
HOLLY WLK

35

Aspley Heath
SILVERBIRC
DANESBOROUGH DR
HEATH LA
Old Wavendon Heath
Aspley Wood
ASPLEY LA

2

Danesborough
HEATH LA
Fernwood Sch
WOBURN RD
Mermaid's Pond
Birchmoor Lodge

DANESWOOD
THE KNOLL

Shepherd's Cottage
Birchmoor Farm

1

New Wavendon Heath
Fuller's Earth Lodge
A5130

34

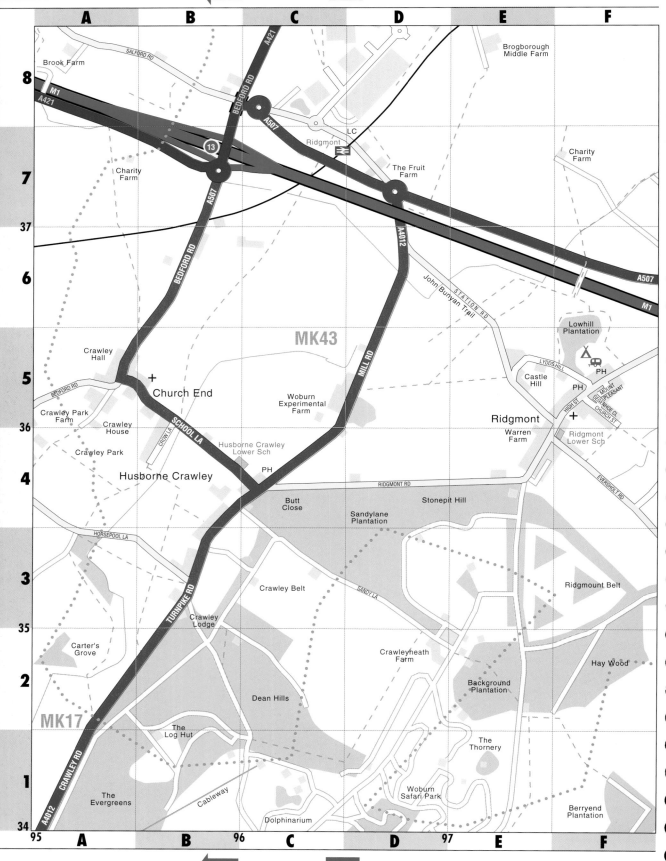

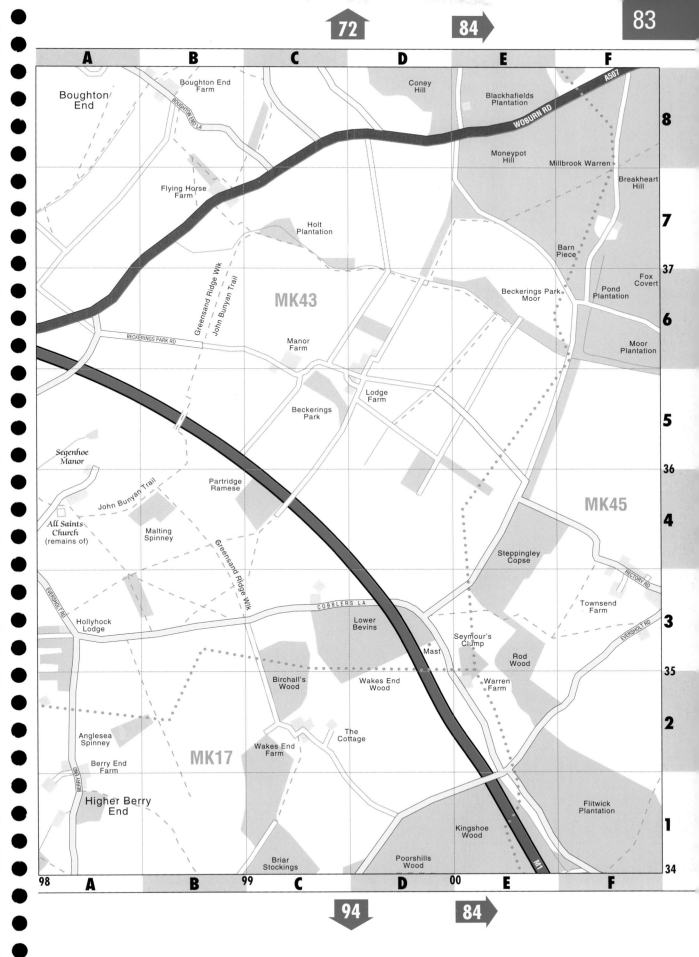

Boughton End Farm

Boughton End

BOUGHTON END LA

Coney Hill

Blackhafields Plantation

WOBURN RD

A507

Flying Horse Farm

Moneypot Hill

Millbrook Warren

Breakheart Hill

Holt Plantation

Greensand Ridge Wlk

John Bunyan Trail

Barn Piece

Fox Covert

8

7

37

Beckerings Park Moor

Pond Plantation

MK43

6

BECKERINGS PARK RD

Manor Farm

Moor Plantation

Lodge Farm

Beckerings Park

5

Segenhoe Manor

36

Partridge Ramese

MK45

4

John Bunyan Trail

Greensand Ridge Wlk

All Saints Church (remains of)

Malting Spinney

Steppingley Copse

RECTORY RD

Townsend Farm

EVERSHOLT RD

EVERSHOLT RD

Hollyhock Lodge

COBBLERS LA

Lower Bevins

Seymour's Clump

Rod Wood

3

Mast

Warren Farm

35

Birchall's Wood

Wakes End Wood

Anglesea Spinney

2

BERRY END

MK17

Wakes End Farm

The Cottage

Berry End Farm

Higher Berry End

Flitwick Plantation

1

Kingshoe Wood

Briar Stockings

Poorshills Wood

M1

34

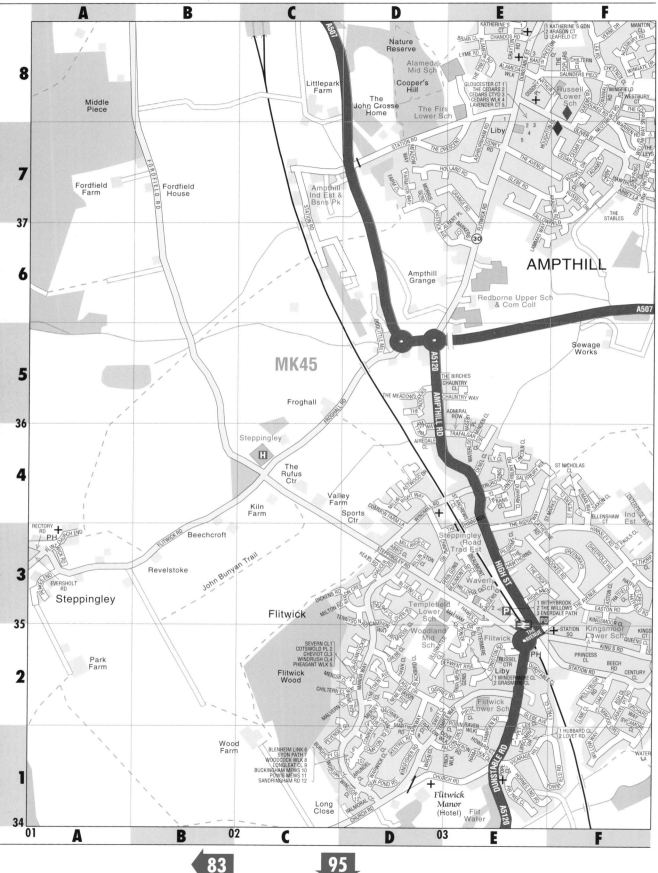

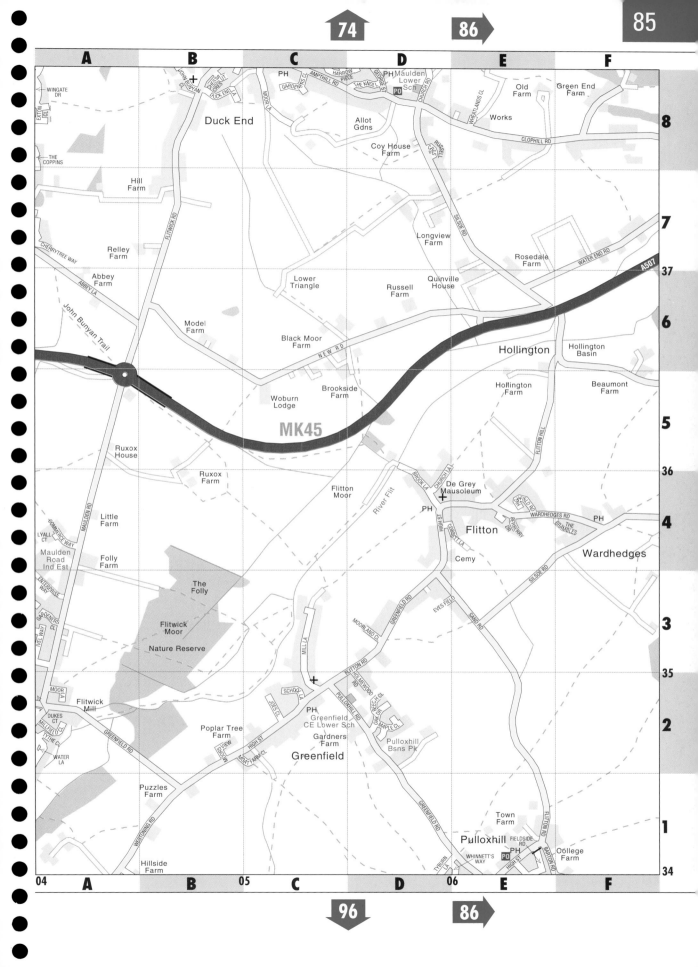

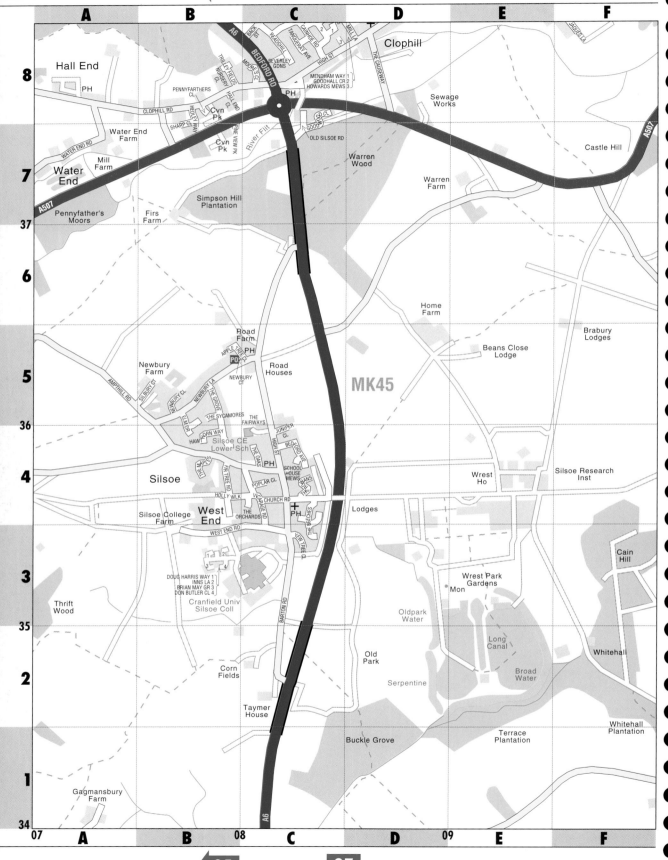

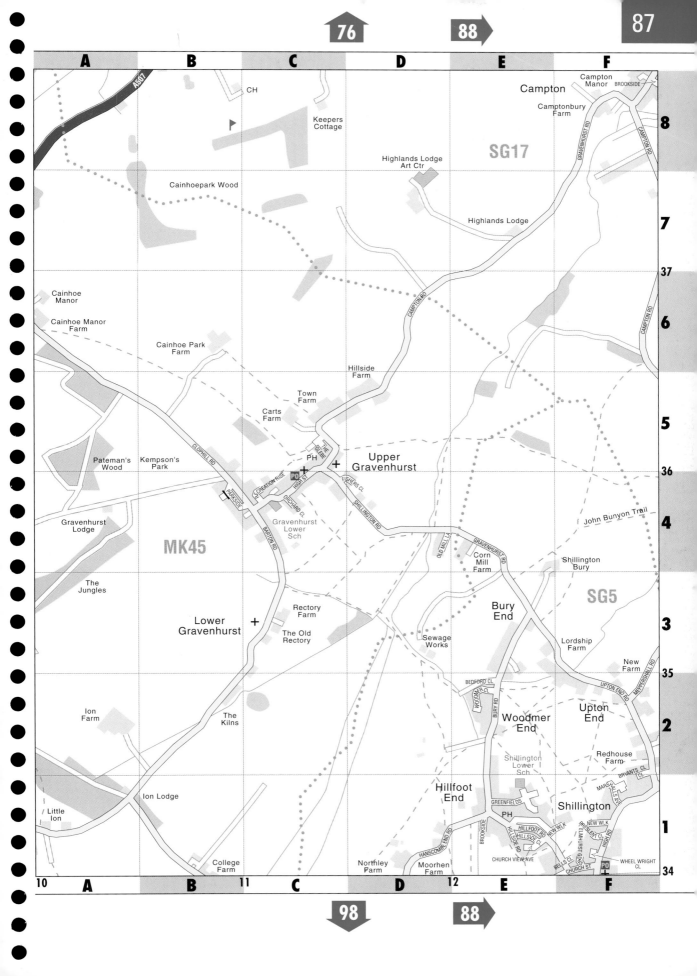

A B C D E F

8 SG17

Campton
Campton Manor
BROOKSIDE
Camptonbury Farm

CH
Keepers Cottage

Highlands Lodge Art Ctr

Cainhoepark Wood

7

37

Highlands Lodge

6
Cainhoe Manor
Cainhoe Manor Farm

Campton Rd

Cainhoe Park Farm

Hillside Farm

5
Town Farm
Carts Farm

Pateman's Wood
Kempson's Park
PH
THE GLEBE
Upper Gravenhurst

36
PO
HIGH ST
ASHERS CL

Gravenhurst Lodge
PARKSIDE
S. CREATION RISE
ORCHARD CL
Gravenhurst Lower Sch
SHILLINGTON RD
John Bunyon Trail

4
BARTON RD
OLD MILL LA
GRAVENHURST RD
Shillington Bury

MK45
Corn Mill Farm

Bury End
SG5

The Jungles
Rectory Farm

3
Lower Gravenhurst
The Old Rectory
Sewage Works
Lordship Farm
New Farm

MEPPERSHALL RD

35
BEDFORD CL
UPTON END RD

Ion Farm
The Kilns
WOODMER CL
BURY RD
Woodmer End
Upton End

2
Redhouse Farm

Shillington Lower Sch
MARSHALLS AVE
BRYANTS CL

Ion Lodge
Hillfoot End
GREENFIELDS
PH
Shillington

Little Ion
HILLFOOT END RD
BROOKSIDE
HILLFOOT RD
HILLSIDE RD
HILLSIDE CL
NEW WLK
NEW WLK
CRESCENT CL
ELMHURST RD
HIGH ST
1

College Farm
HANSCOMBE END RD
CHURCH VIEW AVE
BELLS CL
CHURCH ST
PO
WHEEL WRIGHT CL

Northley Farm
Moorhen Farm

34

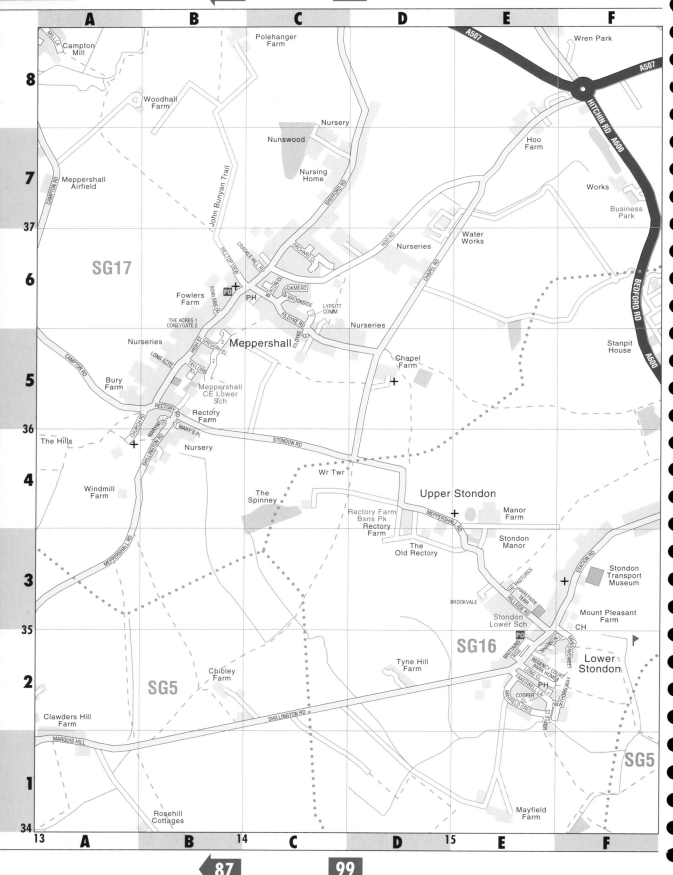

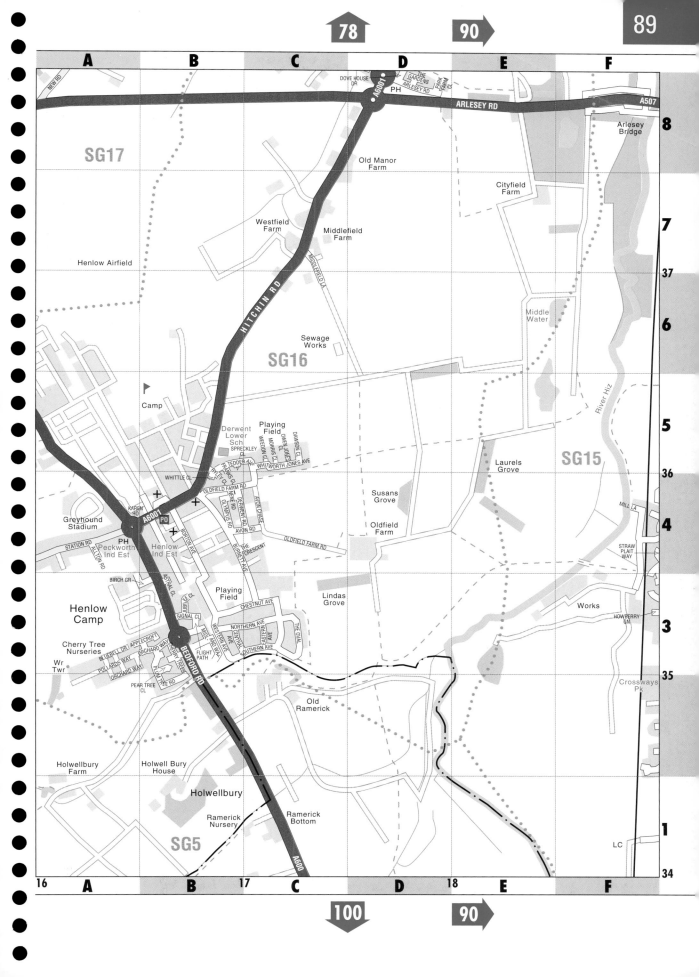

78
90

SG17

NEW RD

DOVE HOUSE DR
THE GARDENS
ARLESEY RD
PARK FARM CL
PH
A6001

ARLESEY RD
A507

Arlesey Bridge

8

Old Manor Farm

Cityfield Farm

Westfield Farm

Middlefield Farm

7

Henlow Airfield

HITCHIN RD

MIDDLEFIELD LA

37

Middle Water

6

Sewage Works

SG16

River Hiz

5

Camp

Playing Field

Derwent Lower Sch
SPRECKLEY CL
DAWSON CL
OWEN JONES CL
MORRIS CL
WEEDON CL
WHITWORTH JONES AVE

Laurels Grove

SG15

36

WHITTLE CL

TEDDER AVE
FRANKS CL
RYLEY CL
OLDFIELD FARM RD
NENE RD
DERWENT RD
OLYMPUS RD

Susans Grove

KAREN HO
A6001 PO

BORTON AVE

AVON CHASE

AVON RD

OLDFIELD FARM RD

Oldfield Farm

4

Greyhound Stadium

STATION RD
ALLTON RD
PH
Peckworth Ind Est
Henlow Ind Est

THE BURNETT AVE
THE CRESCENT

35

BIRCH GR

ASTRAL CL

Playing Field

CHESTNUT AVE

Lindas Grove

Works

HOWBERRY GN

3

MILL LA

STRAW PLAIT WAY

Henlow Camp

LEE CL
EXHIBIT CL
SIGNAL CL

WESTERN AVE
THE DUAL
AND DUAL
NORTHERN AVE
CENTRAL AVE
SOUTHERN AVE
SOUTH EASTERN AVE

THE OVAL

Cherry Tree Nurseries
BLUEBELL DR
APPLECROFT
POLLARDS WAY
ORCHARD WAY
ORCHARD WAY
CHERRY TREES
FLIGHT PATH

Wr Twr

BEDFORD RD

PEAR TREE CL
PLUM TREE RD

Old Ramerick

Crossways Pk

35

Holwellbury Farm

Holwell Bury House

Holwellbury

A600

SG5

Ramerick Nursery

Ramerick Bottom

LC

1

34

16
A
B
17
C
D
18
E
F

100
90

89
79

A B C D E F

8

7

37

6

5

36

4

3

35

2

1

34

19 A B 20 C D 21 E F

89
101

Arlesey
ARLESEY RD A507
OLD OAK CL
VICARAGE CL
THE LIMES
SCH END
1 ARLESEY HO
2 GROVE CT
PH
THE POPLARS
CHASE CL
THE HERMITAGE
THE CHASE
STOTFOLD RD
SCH CL
1
2
CARTERS WLK
ST PETER'S AVE
CHURCH LA
GLOS CL OP WAY
PO
CHANCELLORS
HINWICK
SAFFRON CL
GLEBE AVE
HOUSE LA
Church End
THE RALN
CARTERS WAY
CARTERS
BURY MEAD
GR STH 35 HO
Chase Farm
LEWIS LA
PH
ROSE COTTS
LYMANS RD
COX'S WAY
EVEREST
HIGH ST
GOTHIC WAY
HILLARY RISE
LYNTON AVE
CLUNY WAY
Liby
Gothic Mede Lower Sch
THE GRANARY
CRICKETER'S RD
PH
PRIMLY WAY
ST JOHN'S
Ind Est
WESLEY CL
SCH
CHAPEL
WLK
SG15
DAVIS ROW
Arlesey
PRIMROSE LA
CROWN LODGE
1 PRIMROSE CL
2 CHERRY TREE CL
3 LANTHONY CT
STATION RD
HOSPITAL RD
PO
Church Farm
ALBERT RD
WEST DR
Green Farm
LAMB MDW
HONEYBERRY GN
GEORGINA CT
NIGHTINGALE TERR
LONDON ROW
Portland Ind Est
Hitchin Road Ind & Bsns Ctr
HITCHIN RD
JUBILEE CRES
RAMERICK GDNS
Cemy
Blue Lagoon
Green Lagoon
Sewage Works
HEATHCLIFF AVE
SHAFTESBURY DR
MIDDLEMARCH
KINGSLEY AVE
PALMERSTON WAY
NICKLEBY WAY
DICKENS BVD
CHARLOTTE AVE
BRONTE AVE
FARADAY GDNS
RUSSELL WLK
SALSBURY CL
ELIOT WAY
HITCHIN RD
Pix Brook
STOTFOLD RD
Lower Wilbury Farm
SG6
FLEMING DR
Sewage Works
LETCHWORTH
Stonehill JMI Sch
THE PARADE 1
MIDDLEFIELDS CT 2
MIDDLEFIELDS 3
GAUNTS WAY
CROSSLEYS
BURLEY
KIMBERLEY
STONELEY
AVOCET
NORTHERN WAY
WESTERN CL
WESTERN WAY
SAX HO
BITTERN WAY
FIELDFARE
CURLEW WAY
DUNLIN
FIRECREST
ASHDOWN
SOUTHERN WAY
SOUTHFIELDS
CASLON WAY
NORMANS CL
SAXON CL
HEATHERMERE
ORDELMERE
PARTRIDGE
FIELDFARE
LANGLEIGH
REYNOLDS
PO
NORTHFIELDS
Sch
Waterloo Farm
STOTFOLD RD
Etonbury Mid Sch
PH
ARLESEY RD
THE VINES
Stotfold
Works
Works
Allot Gdns
FERN END RD
ASTWICK RD
TAYLOR'S RD
PINE CL
SAXON AVE
NEL
CASTLE REGATT
COMMON RD
PRINCE S ST
NETHERFIELD
TRINITY RD
REGENT ST
JACLINE
MOWBRAY CRES
OLIVER'S LA
ROOK TREE LA
HONEY CL
SILVERBIRCH AVE
POPLAR DR
PH
Stotfold Green
THE GREEN
BLACKSMITH CL
KINGSWAY
KINGSWAY GDNS
VAUGHAN RD
WHITE CROFTS
MARSCHOFIELD
FRANCIS CL
THE GARTHS
WATERS END
MEADOW WAY
ST OLIVES
HUNTERS CL
WYCKLAND CL
HITCHIN RD
ROE CL
PIX RD
HIGHBUSH RD
HYDE AVE
HOWARD CL
Recn Gd
SPENCER HO
Old Brewery Sch
THE MEWS
ST OLIVES
Liby
STOTFOLD HO
MILLWORTH
BARDELL
COPPICE
HAZEL GR
Brook End
BROOK ST
HALLWORTH HO
MELBOURN CL
CHAPEL PL
THE HAVEN
ALEXANDER RD
THE CRIEFS
THE GRANGE
HIGH ST
ST MARY'S AVE
MULBERRY CL
QUEEN ANNE'S CL
SG5
THE AVENUE
CHURCH RD

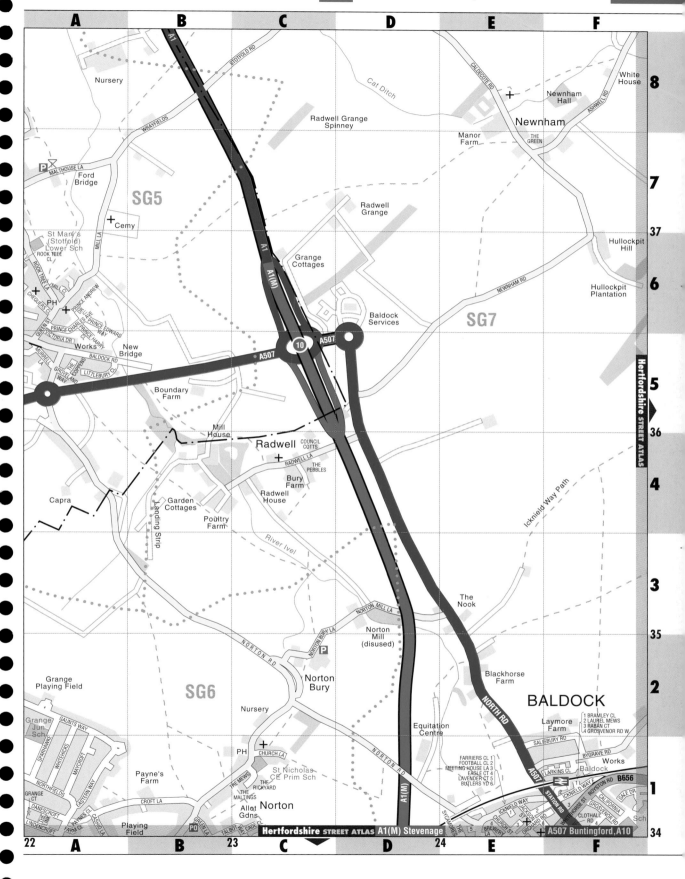

A · B · C · D · E · F

8
7
37
6
5
36
4
3
35
2
1
34

Nursery

STOTFOLD RD

Cat Ditch

CALDECOTE RD

White House

Newnham Hall

8

A1

WRAYFIELDS

Radwell Grange Spinney

Manor Farm

THE GREEN

Newnham

ASHWELL RD

SG5

MALTHOUSE LA
Ford Bridge
P

Radwell Grange

Hullockpit Hill

7

MILL LA

Cemy

St Mary's (Stotfold) Lower Sch
ROOK TREE CL

A1

Radwell Grange

NEWNHAM RD

Hullockpit Plantation

37

ROOK TREE LA
MILL CL
PH
PRINCE ANDREW
PRINCE EDWARD WAY
PRINCE CHARLES AVE
PRINCE HARRY

A1(M)

Grange Cottages

6

QUEEN VICTORIA DR
Works
BALDOCK RD
New Bridge

Baldock Services

SG7

CHECKERS CL
MURBELL LA
THE COPPENS
LITTLEBURY CL
GROVELAND WAY

A507
10
A507

5

Boundary Farm

Hertfordshire STREET ATLAS

Mill House

36

Capra

Landing Strip

Garden Cottages

Radwell

COUNCIL COTTS
RADWELL LA
THE PEBBLES

Icknield Way Path

4

Bury Farm
Radwell House

Poultry Farm

River Ivel

3

The Nook

35

NORTON MILL LA

Norton Mill (disused)

SG6

NORTON ROAD

Grange Playing Field

Norton Bury
NORTON BURY LA
P

Blackhorse Farm

BALDOCK

2

Grange Jun Sch
GAUNTS WAY
SPARHAWKE
WHITEHICKS
MAYCROFT
NORTHFIELDS
EASTERN WAY

Nursery

NORTON RD

Equitation Centre

NORTH RD

Laymore Farm

1 BRAMLEY CL
2 LAUREL MEWS
3 RABAN CT
4 GROSVENOR RD W

SALISBURY RD
BYGRAVE RD
Works
Baldock

PH
CHURCH LA

St Nicholas CE Prim Sch

LARKINS CL

FARRIERS CL 1
FOOTBALL CL 2
MEETING HOUSE LA 3
EAGLE CT 4
LAVENDER CT 5
BUTLERS YD 6

B656

1

GRANGE CT
DANESCROFT
LINDENCROFT
PAYNES CL
FARM CL
CASTLE CL

Payne's Farm

THE MEWS
THE MALTINGS

CROFT LA

THE RICKYARD

Allot Gdns
Norton

TALBOT LA
CADE CL
GREEN LA

A1(M)

A507

STATION RD
ST JAMES
ICKNIELD WAY

ICKNIELD WAY E
WHITE HORSE ST
ROYSTON RD
CALIFORNIA
ISALE DR
Sch

Playing Field

PO

THE CAUSEWAY
CHURCH ST
THE BREWERY
ORCHARD RD

CLOTHALL RD
GROSVENOR RD

A507 Buntingford, A10

34

22 · A · B · 23 · C · D · 24 · E · F

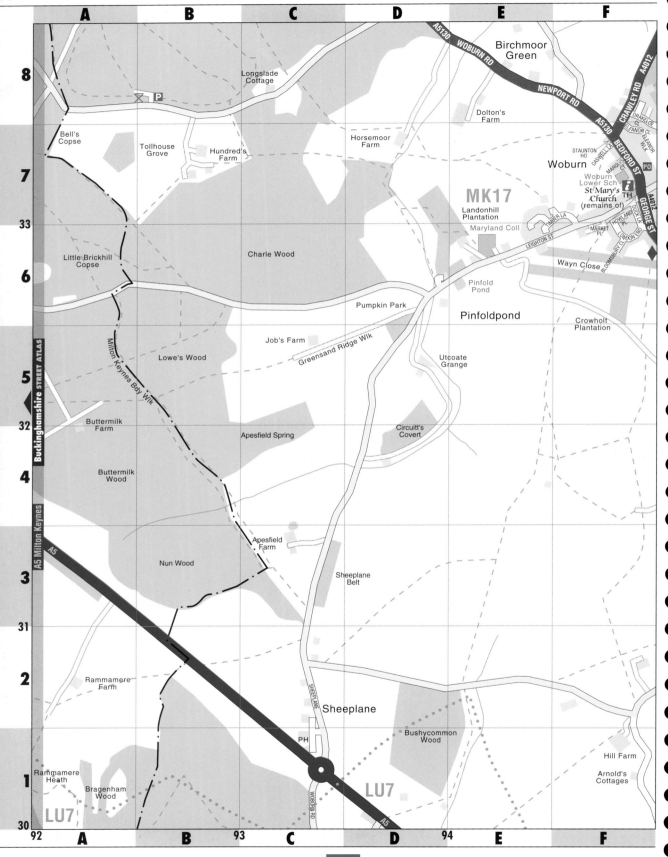

Birchmoor Green

Longslade Cottage

Bell's Copse

Tollhouse Grove

Hundred's Farm

Horsemoor Farm

Dolton's Farm

NEWPORT RD

A5130 WOBURN RD

CRAWLEY RD

A4012

Woburn

MK17

Landonhill Plantation

Maryland Coll

STAUNTON HO

Woburn Lower Sch

St Mary's Church (remains of)

LEIGHTON ST

CASWELL CL

MARQUIS CT

BEDFORD ST

GEORGE ST

A4012

PO

TH

MARKET PL

HOWLAND CL

DUCK LA

LONDON END

DRAKELOE CL

ELEANOR CL

ELEANOR WLK

BLOOMSBURY CL

TIMBER LA

Little Brickhill Copse

Charle Wood

Pinfold Pond

Wayn Close

Crowholt Plantation

Pumpkin Park

Pinfoldpond

Milton Keynes Bdy Wlk

Lowe's Wood

Job's Farm

Greensand Ridge Wlk

Utcoate Grange

Buckinghamshire STREET ATLAS

Buttermilk Farm

Apesfield Spring

Circuitt's Covert

Buttermilk Wood

A5 Milton Keynes

A5

Apesfield Farm

Nun Wood

Sheeplane Belt

Rammamere Farm

SHEEPLANE

Sheeplane

Bushycommon Wood

Hill Farm

Rammamere Heath

Bragenham Wood

PH

WOBURN RD

LU7

Arnold's Cottages

LU7

LU7

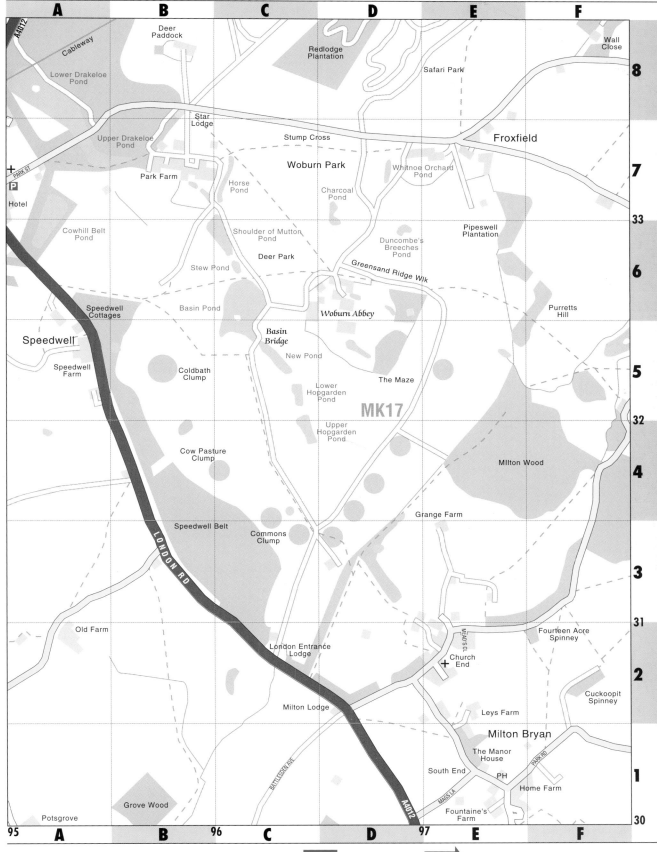

93
83

A | B | C | D | E | F

8

Lower Berry End
Berrystead
New England
Briar Stockings
Meadow Plantation
Town Mead
Alder Spinney
MK45
Priestley Plantation

New Water End

Water End

7

Water End Farm
Eversholt
Town Farm
Home Farm
Trout Farm

Greensand Ridge Wlk

33

Tyrells End
Witts End
Rads End Farm
Lower Rads End
TINGRITH RD
Hill's Plantation

6

Linden Lodge
Higher Rads End

Brook End
PH
Church End

Eversholt Lower Sch

Linden Lake

CHURCH CL
CHURCH RD
HIGH ST

5

Mill Farm
MK17
Tingrith

32

Potter's End

Castle Farm

LONG LA

4

Palmer's Shrubs
Washer's Wood
Wood House

3

Daintry Wood
Oakhill Spinney
Coxley Bushes

31

Longland Spinney

2

Herne Green Farm
LU5
Lodge Farm

Happyland Farm

1

Greatfield Spinney
PARK RD
Manor Wood

Herne Willow Farm

30

98 | A | 99 | B | C | D | 00 | E | F

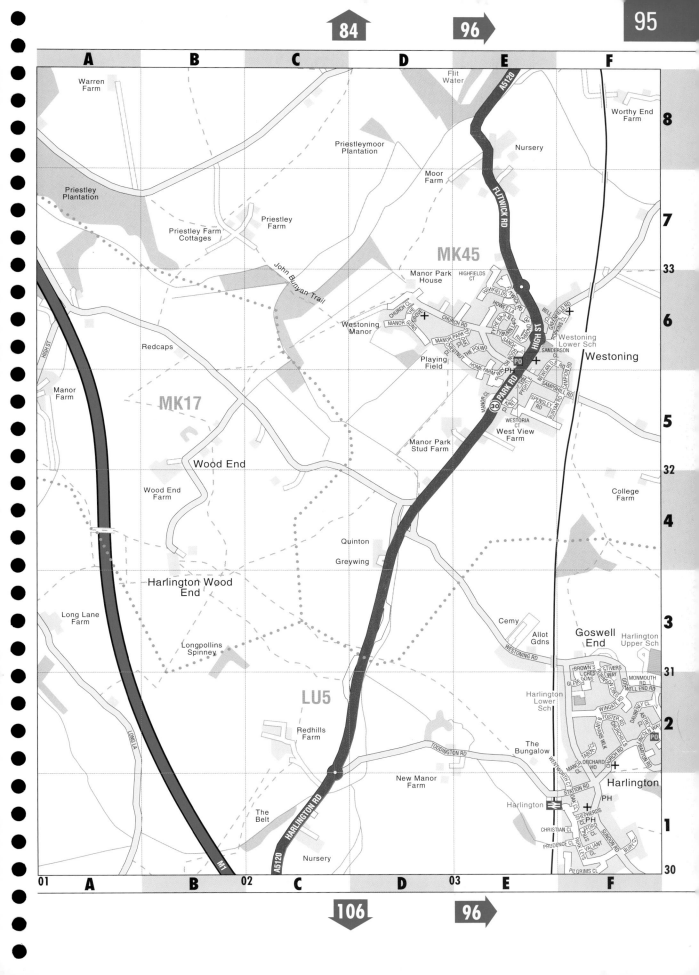

95
85

A B C D E F

8
7
33
6
5
32
4
3
31
2
1
30

HORNES END RD

Old Farm Cottage

Clayhill Farm

The White House

Higham Bury

Hill Farm

John Bunyan Trail

Portobello Farm

Portobello Wood

SAMPSHILL RD

Samshill Farm

Upper Sampshill Farm

MK45

Meadhook

MARGRETT LANE

Meadhook Wood

John Bunyan Trail

TYBURN LA
WHINNETT'S WAY
ST JAMES CL
CHURCH RD
HIGH ST
FIELDSIDE RD
Pulloxhill Lower Sch
BARTON RD
PH
1 ORCHARD RD
2 GREENFIELD RD
STANLEY CL
Pulloxhill
Water Twr
BLACKHILL LA

Harlington Upper Sch
Horse-Hill Farm
Horsehill Spinney
GOSWELL END RD
LINCOLN WAY
BRIAN RD
BARTON RD
Goswell End
LU5
Upper East End Farm
Willow Farm

LOVETT GN
HARLINGTON RD
Mill Farm
Harlington Mill Nurseries
Lower East End Farm
Wa010ff

Grange Farm

Sharpenhoe Grove

Bury Farm

BARTON RD

Sharpenhoe
PH

Priory Farm
Roberts Farm

SHARPENHOE RD

Sharpenhoe Clappers
Mon

Suncote Lodge

04 A B 05 C D 06 E F

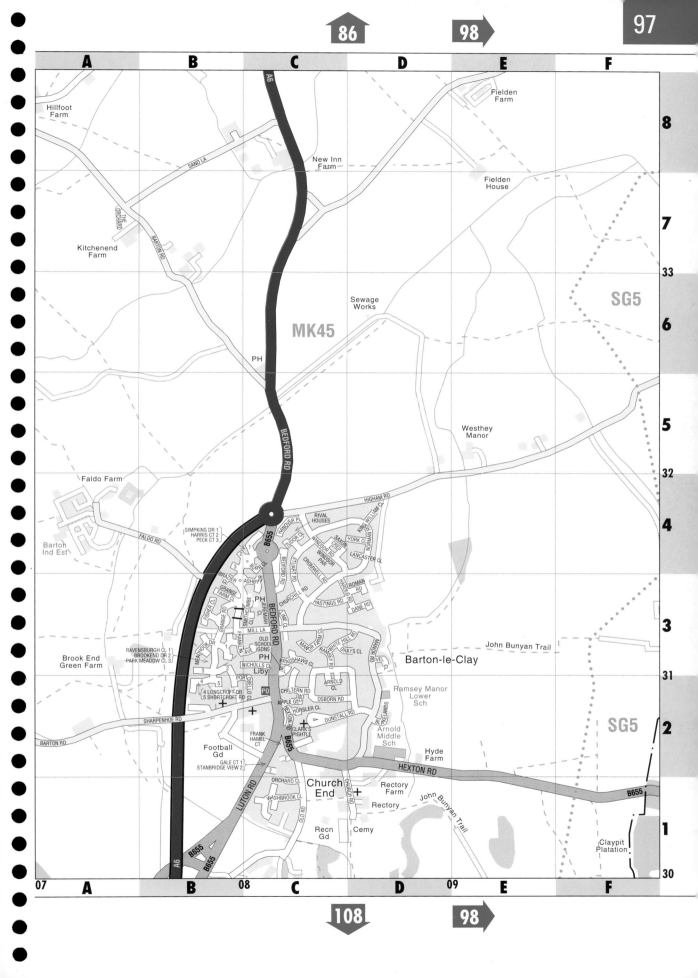

86
98
108
98

A B C D E F

8 7 33 6 5 32 4 3 31 2 1 30

07 08 09

Hillfoot Farm

SAND LA

New Inn Farm

Fielden Farm

Fielden House

THE ORCHARD

BARTON RD

Kitchenend Farm

A6

Sewage Works

MK45

SG5

PH

BEDFORD RD

Westhey Manor

Faldo Farm

FALDO RD

Barton Ind Est

HIGHAM RD

SIMPKINS DR 1
HARRIS CT 2
PECK CT 3

B655

HANOVER PL

RIVAL HOUSES

KING WILLIAM CL

TUDOR CL

WINDSOR RD

SAXON CRES

YORK CL

DURHAM

LANCASTER CL

WINDSOR PAR

BRAZIER

ASHBY

BEDFORD RD

STUART RD

CHURCHILL RD

CROMWELL RD

HARROLD RD

ROMAN

GRANGE FARM CL

JEREMIAH CL

PH

BENDOMS

MILL LA

LYNE CL

HASTINGS RD

DANE RD

FISHER CL

GRANGE RD

FRANKLIN

MEADHOOK DR

OLD SCHOOL GDNS

MANOR RD

WHITE HILL RD

RAMSEY RD

GRAYS CL

John Bunyan Trail

RAVENSBURGH CL 1
BROOKEND DR 2
PARK MEADOW CL 3

Barton-le-Clay

Brook End Green Farm

PH

Liby

NICHOLLS CL

BRADSHAWS CL

RIVEL CL

MANOR RD

4 LONGCROFT DR
5 SHORTCROFT RD

1

3

4 5

POOLE CL

ARNOLD CL

OSBORN RD

Ramsey Manor Lower Sch

PO

CHILTERN RD

APPLE GR

DUNSTALL RD

RELANDS

31

SHARPENHOE RD

HEXTON CL

HORSLER CL

CLARK'S PIGHTLE

Arnold Middle Sch

Hyde Farm

BARTON RD

FRANK HAMEL CT

B655

HEXTON RD

B655

GALE CT 1
STANBRIDGE VIEW 2

2

LUTON RD

ORCHARD RD

WASHBROOK CL

Football Gd

OLD RD

CHURCH RD

Church End

Rectory Farm

Rectory

John Bunyan Trail

B655

A6

B655

Recn Gd

Cemy

Claypit Platation

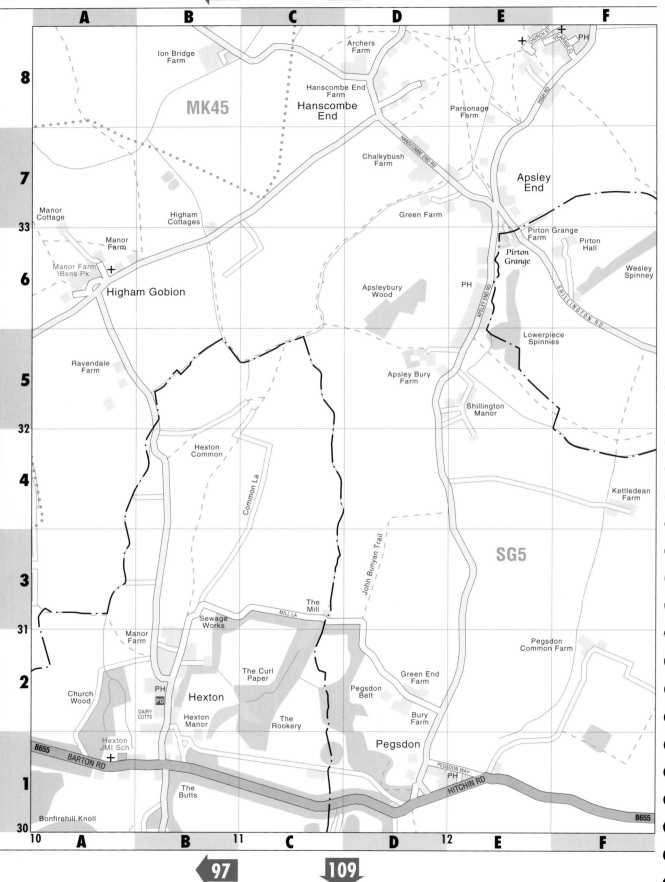

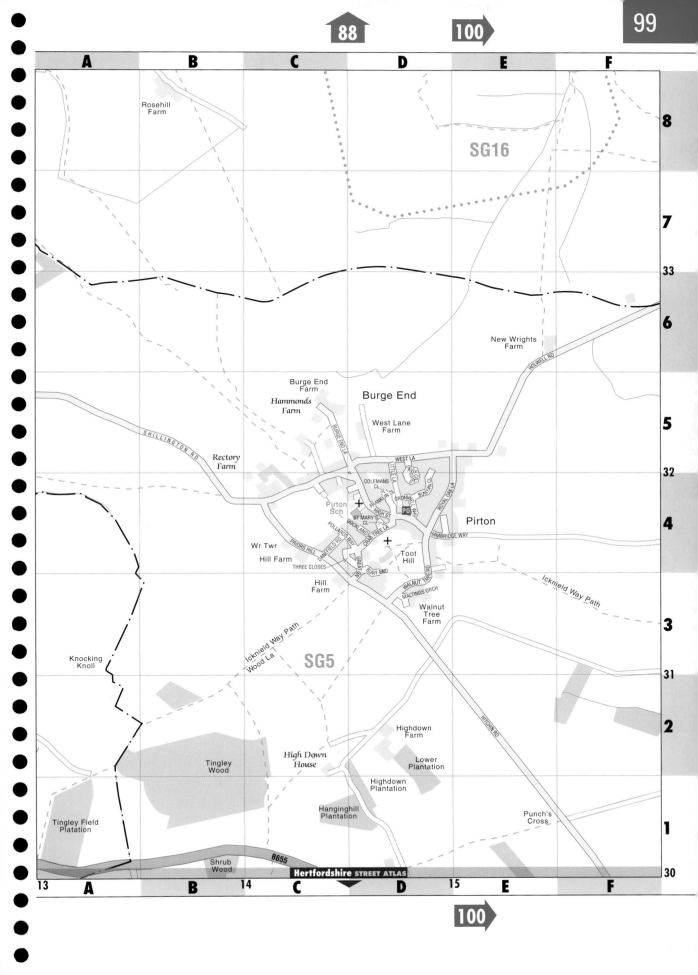

SG15

8

North Farm

Holwell

Sewage Works

GURNEY'S LA

RAND'S CL

Riddy Park Farm

New Ramerwick Farm

Meadow Farm

HOLWELL RD

7

RAND'S COTTS

RAND'S MDW

The Old Rectory

Ashcroft Farm

Ickleford Common

Pestol Farm

33

Lordship Farm

PIRTON RD

WATERLOO LA

Elmdene Farm

River Hiz

6

Holme Farm

Lower Green Farm

Snailswell

SNAILSWELL LA

THE POPLARS

ARLESEY RD

Cadwell Farm

BEDFORD RD

Pinchgut Hall

ABBIS ORCH

Lower Green

LONGMEADOW DR

CLAYMORE DR

5

SG5

Pound Farm

PH

32

Ickleford Prim Sch

WITTER AVE

RIVER CT

RAYMOND COTTS

Ickleford

Cadwell Crossing

4

Hambridge Way

WYATT CL

GALLEYWOOD

CEDAR AVE

WALNUT WAY

GREENFIELD AVE

PO

LODGE CL

TRINDER RD

CHAMBERS LA

NOONFIELD CL

FREEWATERS CL

GREENFIELD LA

PH

3

Icknield Way Path

RYDER AVE

RYDER WAY

ST KATHARINES CL

TURNPIKE LA

MANOR CL

LODGE CT

DUNCOTS CL

LAUREL WAY

Ickleford Bury

31

Mill Way

WESTMILL LA

ICKLEFORD GATE

Flour Mill

Allot Gdns

SG4

Westmill Farm

River Oughton

Burford Ray Bridge

BESSEMER CL

WILLOW TREE WAY

Our Lady RC Prim Sch

Allot Gdns

Sewage Works

BILTON RD

CANHILL LA

2

Icknield Way

WESTMILL LA

Allot Gdns

BURFORD WAY

PORTMILL CL

TIMES CL

Strathmore Inf Sch

SHEPHERDS MEAD

THE MEAD

Westmill

SWINBURNE AVE

PIXIE WAY

SEDGWICK RD

JOHN BARKER PL

TRUEMANS RD

BEECH DALE

RIVER MEAD

MULBERRY CL

MILESTONE RD

MICHAEL MUIR HO

KING GEORGES CL

The Priory Sch

King George V Playing Field

OLD HALE WAY

LAMMAS MEAD

THE MEAD

BRAMPTON PARK RD

WILTON RD

WHITEHURST AVE

STRATHMORE AVE

HEATHFIELD RD

BURY MEAD RD

1

Oughtonhead Common

BINGEN RD

CHURINGA

DUNDALE

MOSS WAY

KINGS HEDGES

WELLINGHAM AVE

WESTMILL LAWNS

BEDFORD RD

BOWYER'S CL

THE CRESCENT

MATTOCKE RD

NORTH PL

CASTLE CT

A600

DEACONS WAY

KING GEORGES

BEARTON RD

TA Ctr

BALMORAL RD

ST MARK'S CL

BEARTON CT

JAMES FOSTER HO

BRAMPTON CL

WILTON RD

PERIWINKLE LA

ICKLEFORD LA

GROVE RD

STORMONT RD

STRATHMORE CT

GLOVERS CT

KIWI CT

ALEXANDRA RD

30

FREEMANS CL

LYTTELTON RD

REDMILL CL

PO

A600 Hitchin

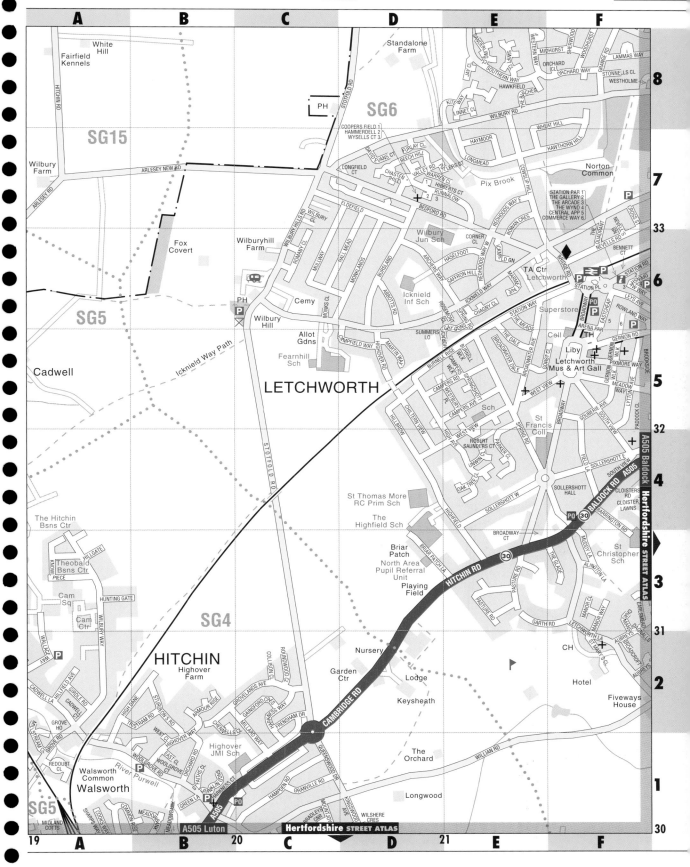

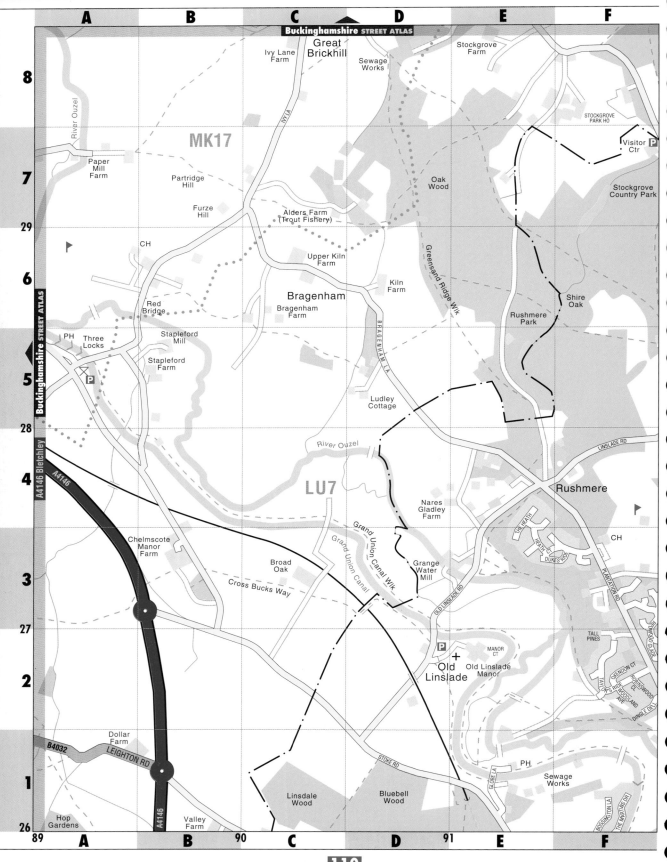

Great Brickhill

MK17

Ivy Lane Farm

Sewage Works

Stockgrove Farm

STOCKGROVE PARK HO

Visitor Ctr P

River Ouzel

Paper Mill Farm

Partridge Hill

Oak Wood

Stockgrove Country Park

Furze Hill

Alders Farm (Trout Fishery)

CH

Upper Kiln Farm

Bragenham

Kiln Farm

Greensand Ridge Wlk

Shire Oak

Rushmere Park

Red Bridge

Bragenham Farm

BRAGENHAM LA

PH Three Locks

Stapleford Mill

Stapleford Farm

P

Ludley Cottage

River Ouzel

LU7

Linslade Rd

Rushmere

Nares Gladley Farm

THE HEATH

HEATH RD

DUKES RIDE

CH

A4146 Bletchley

A4146

Chelmscote Manor Farm

Broad Oak

Cross Bucks Way

Grand Union Canal Wlk

Grand Union Canal

Grange Water Mill

OLD LINSLADE RD

PLANTATION RD

TALL PINES

BRINDWOOD GLADE

27

P

MANOR CT

Old Linslade

Old Linslade Manor

OXENDON CT

TAYLOR'S RIDE

WOODLAND AVE

HORSESWOOD

DINGLE DELL

Dollar Farm

B4032

LEIGHTON RD

A4146

STOKE RD

PH

GLOBE LA

Sewage Works

Hop Gardens

Valley Farm

Linsdale Wood

Bluebell Wood

BOSSINGTON LA

THE MARTINS DRI

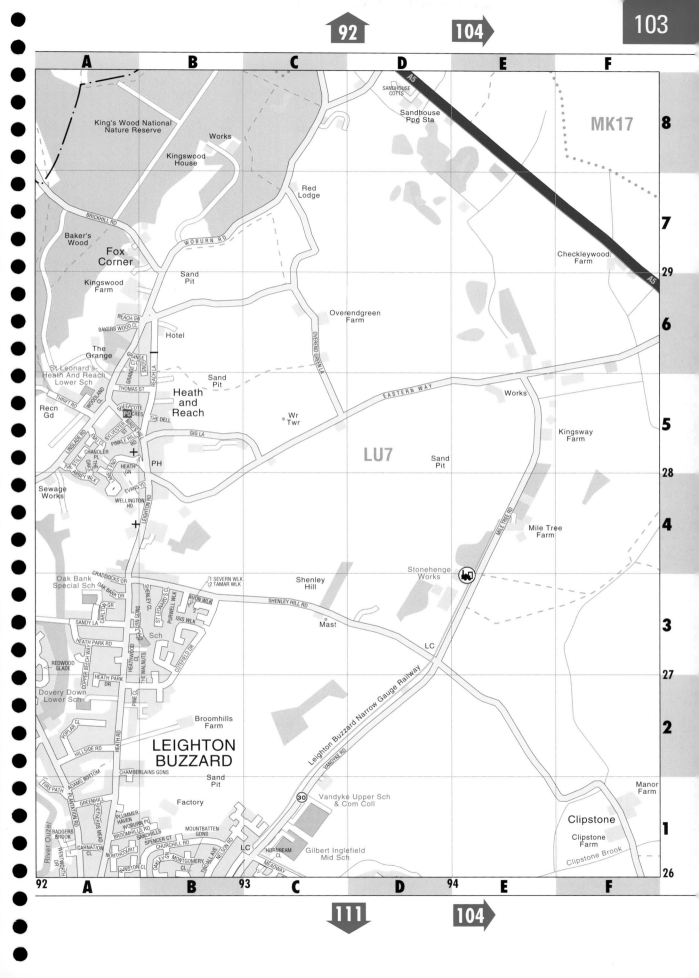

A B C D E F

8

SANDHOUSE COTTS

Sandhouse Ppg Sta

A5

Sandhouse

King's Wood National
Nature Reserve

Works

Kingswood
House

Red
Lodge

BRICKHILL RD

7

WOBURN RD

Checkleywood
Farm

Baker's
Wood

Fox
Corner

Sand
Pit

29

A5

Kingswood
Farm

OVEREND GREEN LA

Overendgreen
Farm

6

REACH GN

BAKERS WOOD CL

Hotel

Sand
Pit

The
Grange

GRANGE GDNS

REACH LA

GRANGE CL

St Leonard's
Heath And Reach
Lower Sch

THOMAS ST

Sand
Pit

EASTERN WAY

Works

Kingsway
Farm

5

THRIFT RD

WOODLAND CL

Heath
and
Reach

THE DELL

SHEEPCOTE
CRES

BIRDS HILL

Recn
Gd

LINSLADE RD

FLAT CL

THE
OAKS

PINKLE HILL
RD

GIG LA

Wr
Twr

LU7

Sand
Pit

28

TK STILE

ABBEY WLK

CHANDLER
PL

LANE'S END

HEATH
GN

PH

Sewage
Works

EVANS YD

WELLINGTON
HO

LEIGHTON RD

Mile Tree
Farm

MILE TREE RD

4

CRADDOCKS DR

Oak Bank
Special Sch

OAK BANK DR

SHENLEY CL

1 SEVERN WLK
2 TAMAR WLK

AVON WLK

Shenley
Hill

Stonehenge
Works

Oak Bank
Special Sch

CARLTON
GR

SANDY LA

PURWELL WLK

ST LEONARD'S CL

ISIS WLK

SHENLEY HILL RD

3

HEATH PARK RD

CHILTERN GDNS

Sch

COTERFIELD DR

Mast

LC

REDWOOD
GLADE

COPPER BEECH WAY

HEATHWOOD
CL

The Walnuts

27

Dovery Down
Lower Sch

HEATH PARK
DR

PINE CL

Leighton Buzzard Narrow Gauge Railway

2

POPLAR CL

HEATH RD

Broomhills
Farm

ADAMS BOTTOM

CHAMBERLAINS GDNS

LEIGHTON
BUZZARD

Sand
Pit

VANDYKE RD

HILLSIDE RD

FIRS PATH

PLANTATION RD

GREENHILL

SHEPHERDS MEAD

Factory

30

Vandyke Upper Sch
& Com Coll

Manor
Farm

BADGERS
BROOK

River Ouzel

WEYMOUTH

CARNATION
CL

PLUMMER
HAVEN

WOBURN PL

BROOMHILLS RD

SANDHILLS

SPENCER CT

CHURCHILL RD

MOUNTBATTEN
GDNS

LC

HORNBEAM
CL

Gilbert Inglefield
Mid Sch

Clipstone

Clipstone
Farm

1

NORTHCOURT

SUNSTON CL

OAKLEY RD

MONTGOMERY
CL

TINDALL AVE

NELSON RD

MEADWAY

Clipstone Brook

26

A B C D E F

103
93

A B C D E F

8

Manor Farm
The Old Rectory
+ Potsgrove

New Planting

LONDON RD
A4012

Town Farm

Home Wood

Hungerhill Wood

BATTLESDEN AVE

Battlesden House

7

Ford Spinney

MK17

+

29

Battlesden Park

Centre Farm

Mast

6

A5

EASTERN WAY

HOCKLIFFE RD

5

Fourne Hill Farm

Battlesden Lodge

Hill Farm

28

The Coops

4

LU7

Watergate Lodge

WOBURN RD

3

Ground Farm

Hockliffe Grange

The Lodge

Hockliffe Lower Sch

Hockliffe Grounds

CHURCH LA

Rectory

OLD SCHOOL CT

27

MANOR AVE

Hockliffe

+ Church End

AUGUSTUS RD

WHITE HORSE CL

THE BLACKBIRDS

NINER RD

BRACKLEY RD

2

Grange Farm

GOOSE GN

Clipstone Brook

A4012

PH

HOCKLEY CT

PO

BLACK'S CL

Old Stock Farm

Hockliffe Bsns Pk

Hockliffe House

1

Hawthorns

LEIGHTON RD

LITTLE LA

Bull Farm

A5

26

95 A B 96 C D 97 E F

103
112

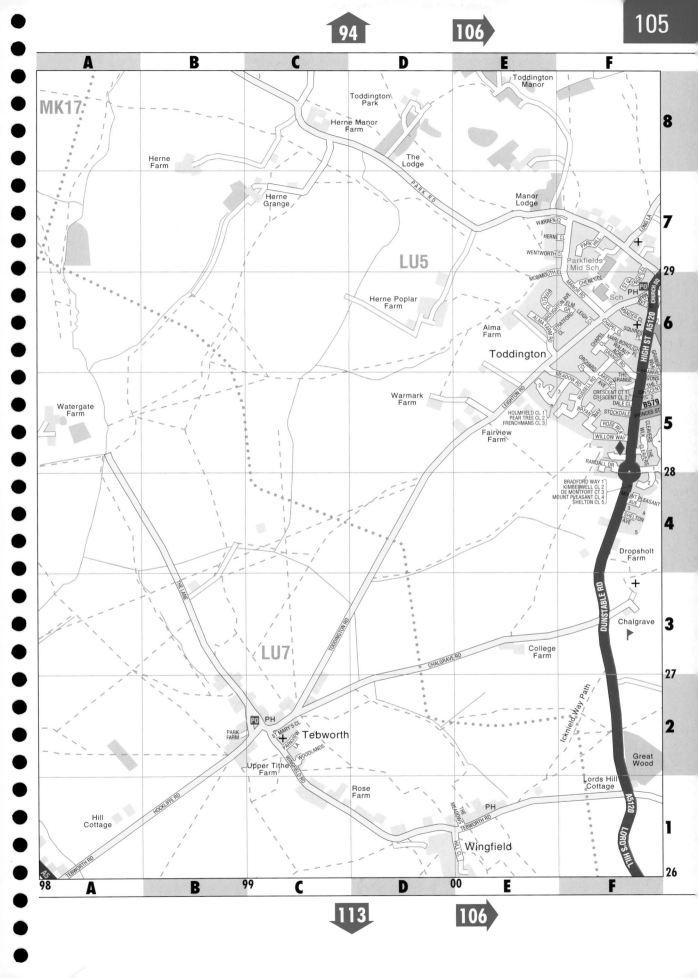

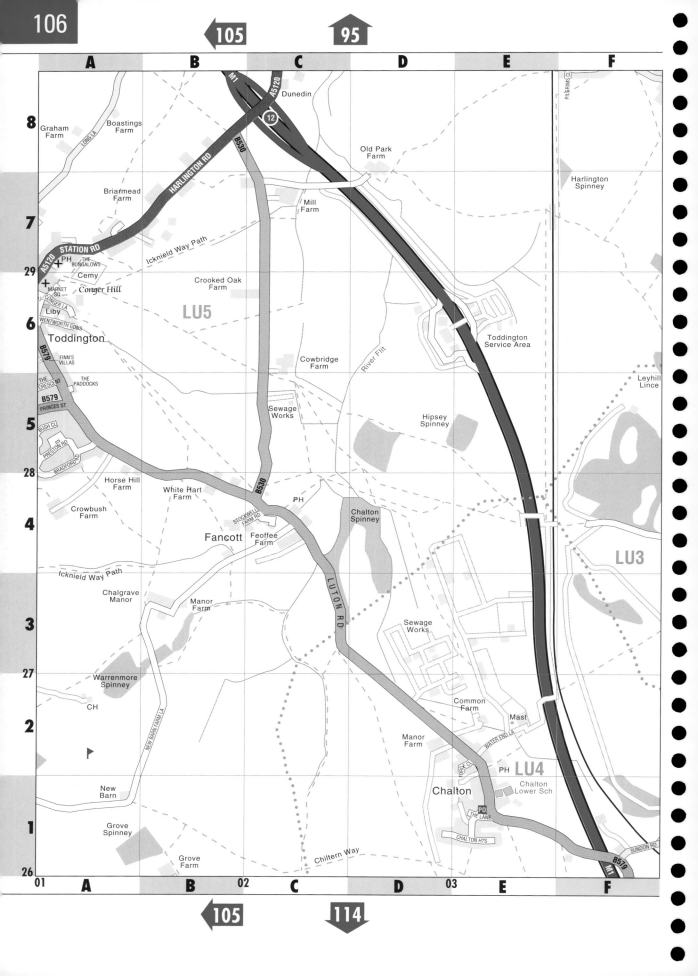

A B C D E F

8

Graham Farm
Boastings Farm
LONG LA
Dunedin
M1
A5120
12
Old Park Farm
Harlington Spinney

7

Briarmead Farm
HARLINGTON RD
B530
Mill Farm

STATION RD
A5120
PH
THE BUNGALOWS
Cemy
Icknield Way Path

29

MARKET SQ
Conger Hill
Crooked Oak Farm

CONGER LA
Liby
WENTWORTH GDNS
LU5

6

Toddington
B579
FINN'S VILLAS
Cowbridge Farm
River Flit
Toddington Service Area
Leyhill Lince

THE CRESCENT
THE PADDOCKS
B579
PRINCES ST
Sewage Works
Hipsey Spinney

5

BUSH CL
PRESTON RD
BRADFORD

28

Horse Hill Farm
White Hart Farm
B530
PH

Crowbush Farm
STOCKWELL FARM RD
Chalton Spinney

4

Fancott
Feoffee Farm
LU3

Icknield Way Path
Chalgrave Manor
Manor Farm
LUTON RD

3

Sewage Works

27

Warrenmore Spinney
CH
NEW BARN FARM LA
Common Farm
Mast

2

Manor Farm
WATER END LA
PH
LU4

New Barn
FORGE CL
Chalton
Chalton Lower Sch

1

Grove Spinney
PO
THE LANE
CHALTON HTS
SUNDON RD
B579
M1

26

Grove Farm
Chiltern Way

01 A B 02 C D 03 E F

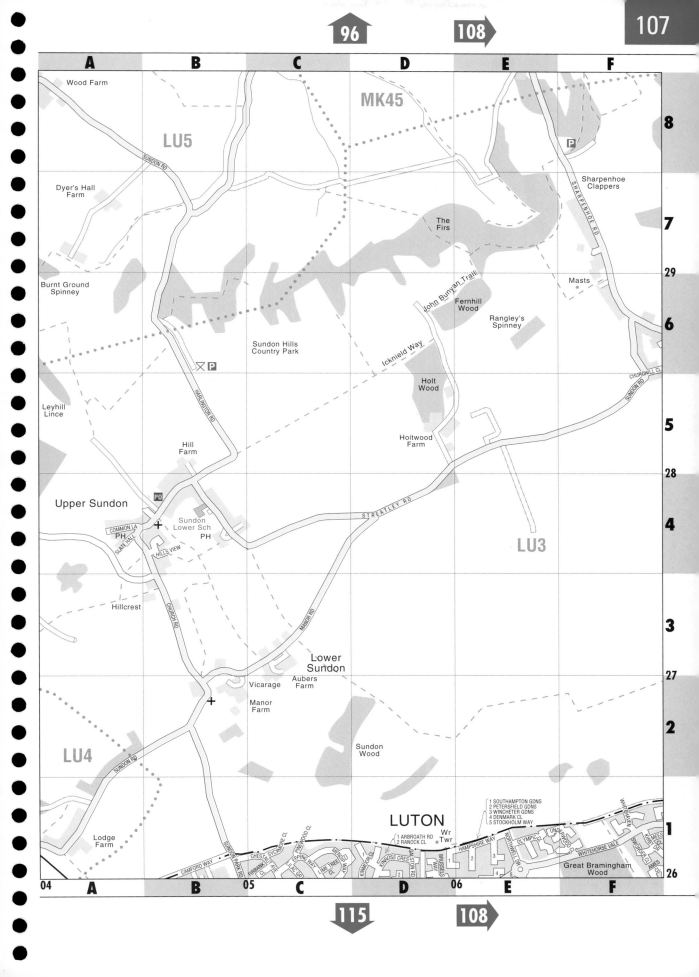

A   B   C   D   E   F

Wood Farm

LU5

SUNDON RD

MK45

8

Dyer's Hall
Farm

Sharpenhoe
Clappers

7

The Firs

29

Burnt Ground
Spinney

John Bunyan Trail

Fernhill
Wood

Rangley's
Spinney

Masts

6

Icknield Way

SHARPENHOE RD

Sundon Hills
Country Park

Holt
Wood

CHURCHILL CL

SUNDON RD

Leyhill
Lince

HARLINGTON RD

Holtwood
Farm

5

Hill
Farm

28

Upper Sundon

PO

STREATLEY RD

LU3

4

COMMON LA
PH
SLATE HALL

Sundon Lower Sch
PH

HILLS VIEW

Hillcrest

CHURCH RD

MANOR RD

3

Lower
Sundon

27

Vicarage

Aubers
Farm

Manor
Farm

2

LU4

SUNDON RD

Sundon
Wood

1 SOUTHAMPTON GDNS
2 PETERSFIELD GDNS
3 WINCHETER GDNS
4 DENMARK CL
5 STOCKHOLM WAY

LUTON

Wr
Twr

1 ARBROATH RD
2 RANOCK CL

1

Lodge
Farm

CAMFORD WAY

SUNDON PARK RD

SYCAMORE CL
PINEWOOD CL
FIRBANK
CHESTNUT AVE
LILAC GR
ESPING WAY
LIME TREE WAY
MEAD CL

KINPISS CRES
KINROSS CL

GRASTON RD
BRUSSELS WAY

HAMPSHIRE WAY
NORTHWELL DR

OLYMPIC
LINGSWOOD CL
WHITEHAVEN

WHITEHORSE VALE
SWORDS CL
KIRBY
AMES
MEES

Great Bramingham
Wood

26

04   A   B   05   C   D   06   E   F

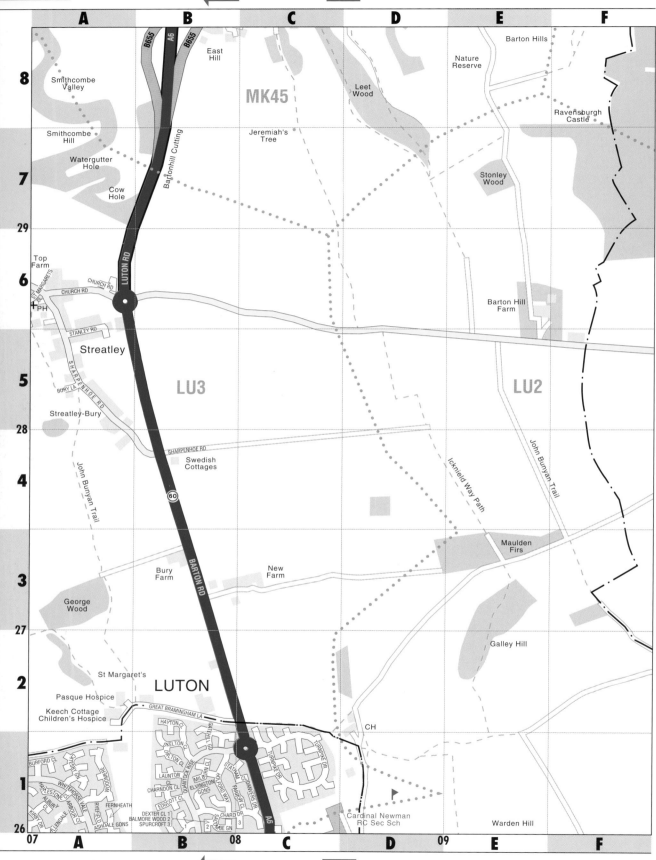

A   **B**   **C**   **D**   **E**   **F**

8

Church Hole

Claypit Plantation

Butts Hill

Lion Hill

Moor Hill

Clark's Hill

Deacon Hill

Cank Hill

Burwell Platation

Gravel Hill

The Meg

Devil's Ditch

7

Claypit Hole

Fairy Hole

Hoo Bit

Icknield Way Path

SG5

Wicks Spring

Pegdons Spring

29

6

Telegraph Hill

Nature Reserve

Muzzleford Wood

Mortgrove Farm

John Bunyan Trail

Staple Knoll

Brogsdell Plantation

Brogsdell

Lilley Hoo

Wasgrove Wood

Newfield Wood

5

28

Walk Spring

Burnwell Spinneys

Lilley Manor Farm

Kingshill Plantation

Wasgrove Plantation

4

LU2

HEXTON RD

Kingshill La

Mazebeard Spring

Ward's Spring

Pond Farm

Ward's Farm

Stockinghill Plantation

3

Ward's Wood

John Bunyan Trail

Wardswood La

Lilley

RECTORY LA

GREEN ACRES

RUELEY DELL RD

THE BAULK

EAST ST

Lilley Hoo Farm

27

LILLEYHOO LA

A505 Hitchin

2

Lilleypark Plantation

PH

WEST ST

Church Farm

Hollybush Hill

A505

George's Plantation

Lilley Park

LILLEY BOTTOM

Ralphs Farm

HOLLYBUSH HILL

SG5

1

Mushroom Elders

Lilleypark Wood

Allot Gdns

A505

26

10   **A**   **B**   **11**   **C**   **D**   **12**   **E**   **F**

Hertfordshire STREET ATLAS

102

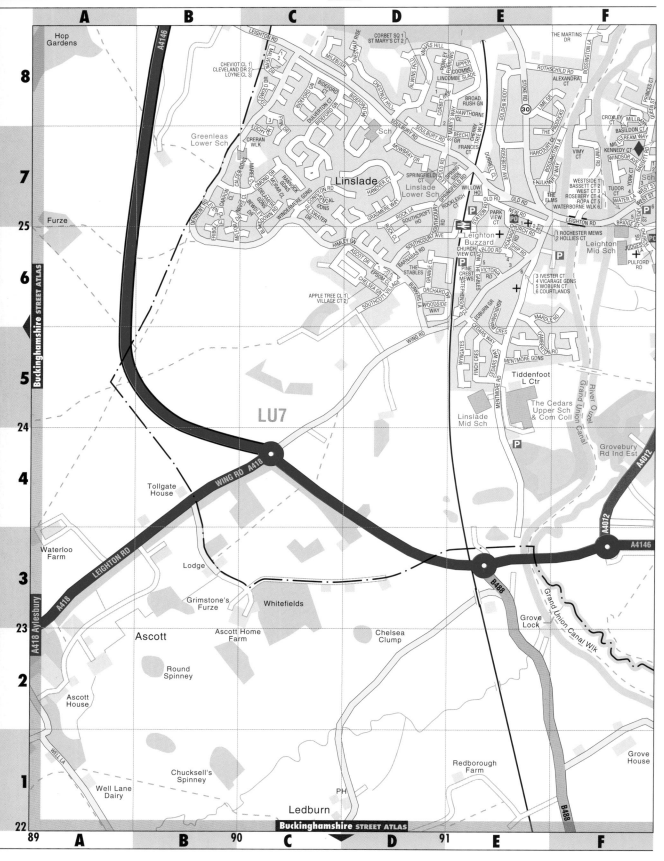

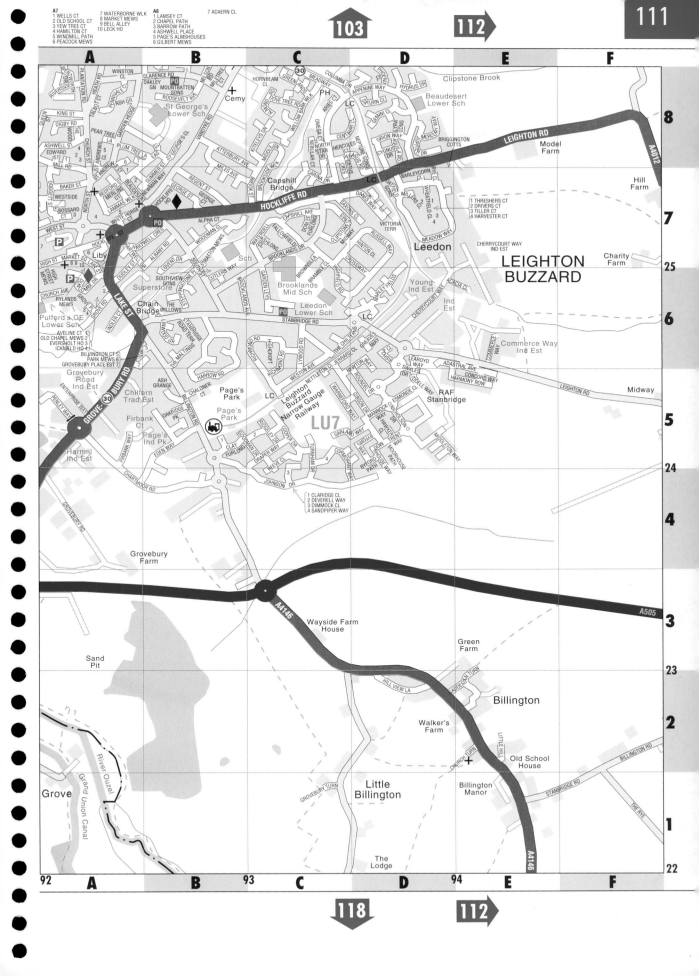

A B C D E F

8

A4012 LEIGHTON RD

Hill Farm

7

Hill Farm

Eggington

Manor Farm

Eggington House

Claridge's Farm

CHURCH WLK

HIGH ST

PH

25

ORCHARD EST

Ppg Sta

LEIGHTON RD

6

MILL RD

Old Windmill

The Old Vicarage

Hill Farm

HIGH BANKS

Stanbridge Lower Sch

BURY RISE

BLACK HL

5

Stanbridge

TILSWORTH RD

PO

ORCHARD WAY

HOWS WAY

GREEN END

PH

PH

DUNSTABLE RD

STANBRIDGE RD

Tilsworth

LU7

LORDS CL

BEACON VIEW

Tilsworth Manor

Mast

24

LEIGHTON RD

PH

ST JOHNS CL

4

Corner Farm

PEDDARS LA

Bluegate Farm

Stanbridge Wood

Tullian Park

BILLINGTON RD

STATION RD

Blackgrove Wood

Greenacre Farm

A505

3

STANBRIDGE CROSSING

50

50

Deans Farm

Stanbridgeford

STANBRIDGE RD

50

50

A505

23

Mead Open Farm & Rare Breeds

BILLINGTON RD

2

Works

Sewage Works

STANBRIDGE RD

Allot Gdns

KNOLLS VIEW

Works

1

LU6

Lower End

CASTLE HILL RD

Castle Hill

22

THE RYE

EATON BRAY RD

Manor Farm

95 A B 96 C D 97 E F

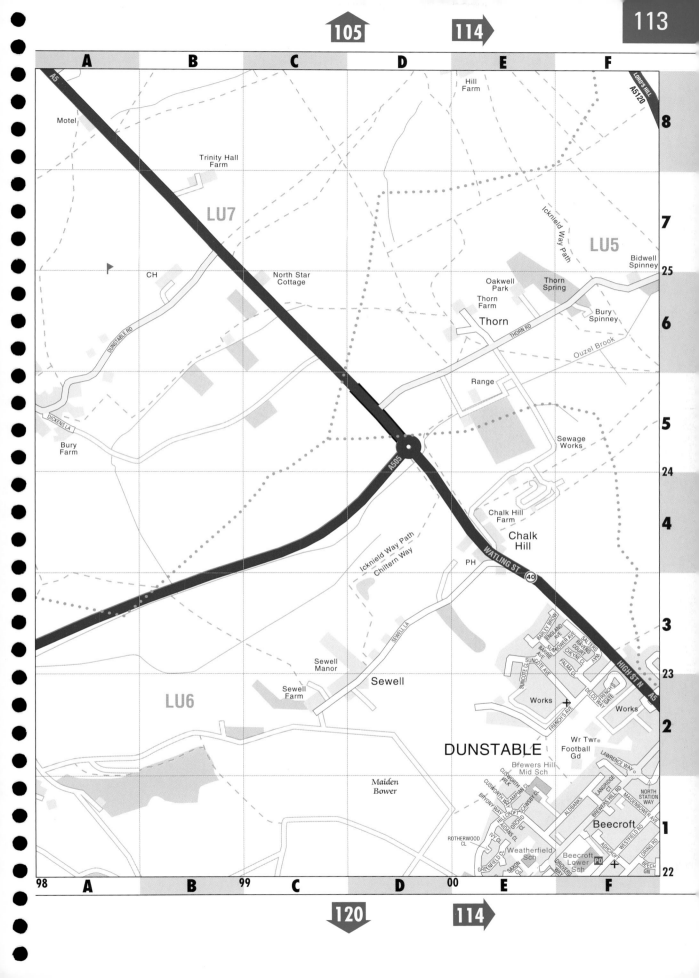

105
114

A5

A

B

C

D

E

F

A5120

LORD'S HILL

Motel

Hill Farm

8

Trinity Hall Farm

LU7

Icknield Way Path

7

LU5

Bidwell Spinney

CH

North Star Cottage

25

Oakwell Park

Thorn Spring

Thorn Farm

DUNSTABLE RD

Thorn

Bury Spinney

6

THORN RD

Ouzel Brook

Range

DICKENS LA

Bury Farm

Sewage Works

5

A505

24

Chalk Hill Farm

4

Chalk Hill

Icknield Way Path

Chiltern Way

WATLING ST

PH

40

3

SEWELL LA

BARLEY BROW

ENGLAND AVE

SALTERS

RAVENS COURT

CHEYNE CL

HIGH ST N

A5

Sewell Manor

SUNCOTE CL

BARRIE

RD

SUNCOTE AVE

PALMA CL

FRENCH'S

GATE

FRENCH'S

DELCO WAY

23

Sewell Farm

Sewell

Works

Works

2

LU6

FRENCH'S AVE

Wr Twr Football Gd

LAWRENCE WAY

DUNSTABLE

Brewers Hill Mid Sch

CUSWORTH WALK

CAMPIAN CL

LANGRIDGE

BREWERS HILL RD

MAIDENBOWER AVE

NORTH STATION WAY

Maiden Bower

CUSWORTH RD

HILLCROFT

ORCHID

OLDSWINFORD CL

ALDANS CL

ALDBANKS

ASHGROFT

WESTFIELD RD

LORING RD

Beecroft

1

BRYONY WAY

IVY CL

ROTHERWOOD CL

Weatherfield Sch

GREENFIELD CL

SAXON

CL

DROVERS WAY

Beecroft Lower Sch

PO

BEECH GN

22

98

A

B

99

C

D

00

E

F

120
114

A   B   C   D   E   F

LU5

HOUGHTON REGIS

Grove Farm

Calcutt Lodge

The Orchard

Chiltern Way

Bidwell Farm

Bidwell

VICTORIA COTTS

Dunstablians Rugby Football Club

Tithe Farm

Tithe Farm Lower Sch

Recn Gd

Thornhill Lower Sch

Osborne House

Chalton Cross Lodge

Chalton Cross Farm

LU4

Kings Houghton Mid Sch

Hillcrest Sch (Regis Education Ctr)

Houghton Park

1 THERFIELD WLK
2 ABBEY WLK
3 ASH WELL WLK
4 ROSE WLK
5 NEPTUNE CL
6 NEPTUNE SQ
7 LEASIDE

SHORT PATH 1
BORDERS WAY 2
THE CLOISTERS 3
GRASMERE WLK 4
GABLE WAY 5
WILLOW WAY 6
ST DAVID'S WAY 7

Hawthorn Park Lower Sch

Parkside

The Hyde

Thorn View Rd

CHURCH END 1
HARRINGTON HTS 2

Houghton Regis Lower Sch

Liby PO

The Green

Houghton Hall

Townsend Ind Est

FREEMANS CL 1
TOWNSEND TERR 2

Northfields Tech Coll

Woodside Park Ind Est

Nimbus Pk

Works
1 The Townsend Ctr
2 Circle Bsns Ctr
3 Arianne Bsns Ctr
4 Ivinghoe Bsns Ctr

Centrus Ind Est

Apex Bsns Ctr

1 HIGH ST N
2 WATLING CT
3 HOUGHTON PAR

LU6

Woodside Ind Est

Mill Vale Mid Sch

Hadrian Lower Sch

DUNSTABLE DVROCOBRIVIS

Works

Dunstable Coll

White Lion Ret Pk (dis)

Ashton CE Mid Sch

Superstore Liby

TA Ctr

Dukeminster Trad Est

Superstore

Sceptre Sch

Lewsey Farm

Liby PO

St Dominics Sq

Chantry Prim Sch

Halyard High Sch

1 GAINSBOROUGH DR
2 WINDSOR PL

1 WHEATFIELD CT
2 PLOUGH CT

KENSINGTON CL

LU4

Longmeadow

BEDFORD RD
HOUGHTON RD
HIGH ST
HIGH ST N
A5120
A5
LUTON RD
A505

1 THE PARADE
2 CROSS ST N
3 JUBILEE CT
4 STEWART CLARK CT
5 WATERLOW CHAPEL
6 LYNWOOD LODGE
7 BROOK CL

1 WATLING CT
2 ROMAN CT

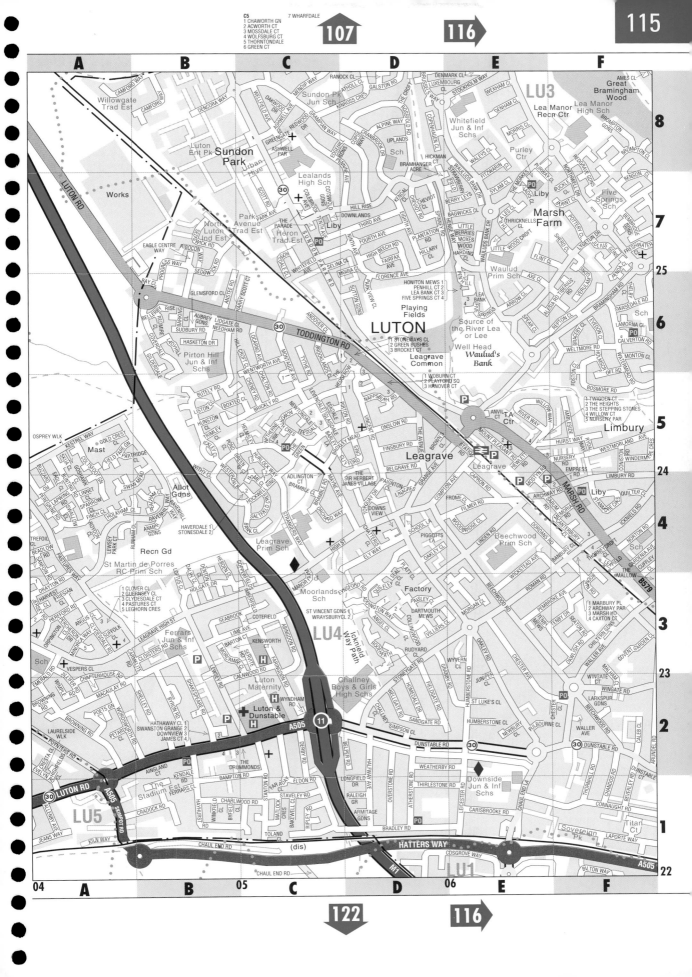

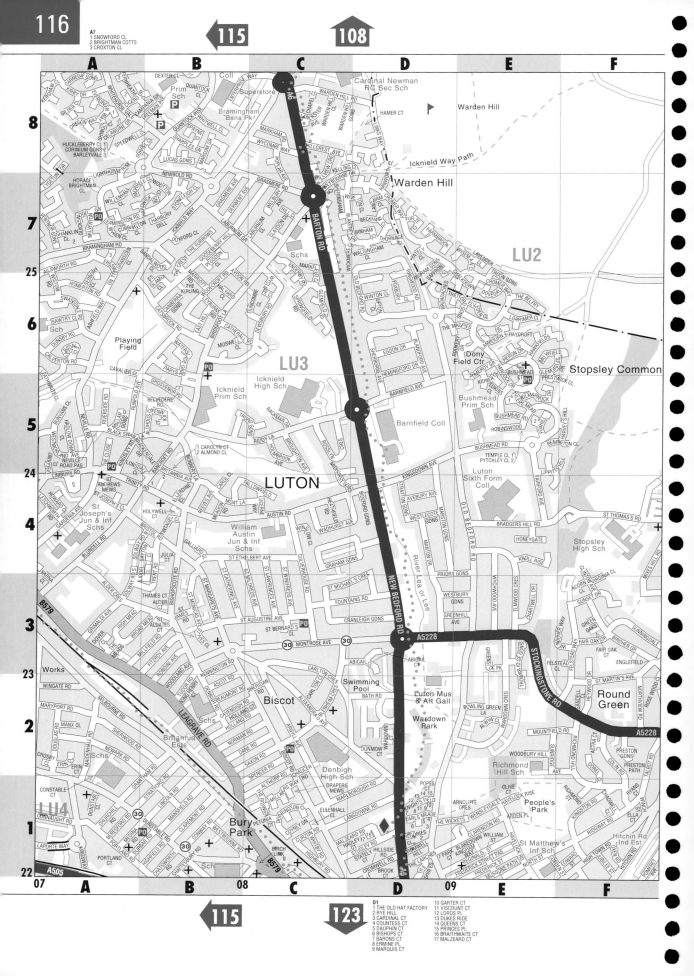

D1
1 THE OLD HAT FACTORY
2 RYE HILL
3 CARDINAL CT
4 COUNTESS CT
5 DAUPHIN CT
6 BISHOPS CT
7 BARONS CT
8 ERMINE PL
9 MARQUIS CT
10 GARTER CT
11 VISCOUNT CT
12 LORDS PL
13 DUKES RIDE
14 QUEENS CT
15 PRINCES PL
16 BRAITHWAITE CT
17 MALZEARD CT

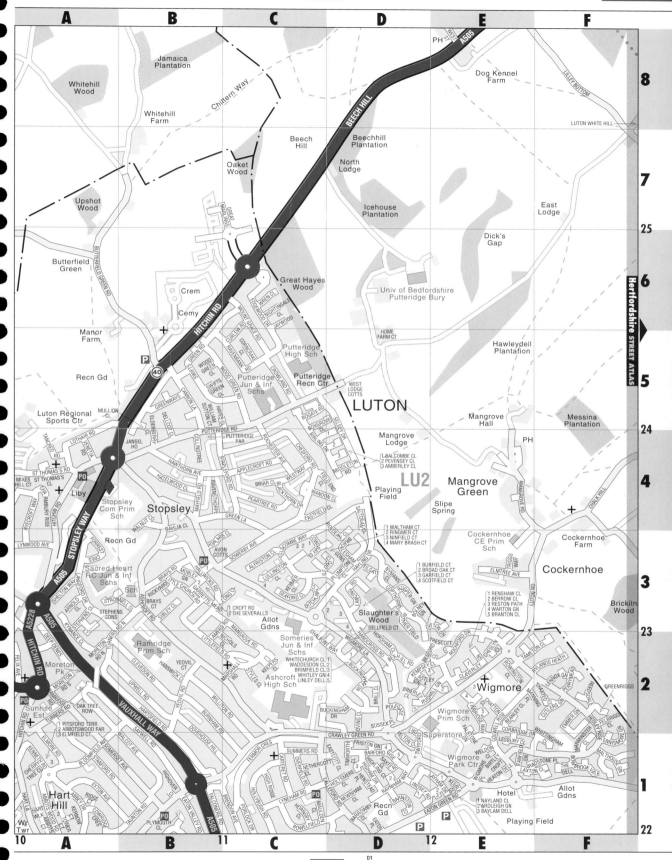

D1
1 CHELSWORTH CL
2 MUTFORD CROFT
3 MELFORD CL
4 PINFORD DELL
5 ALDERTON CL

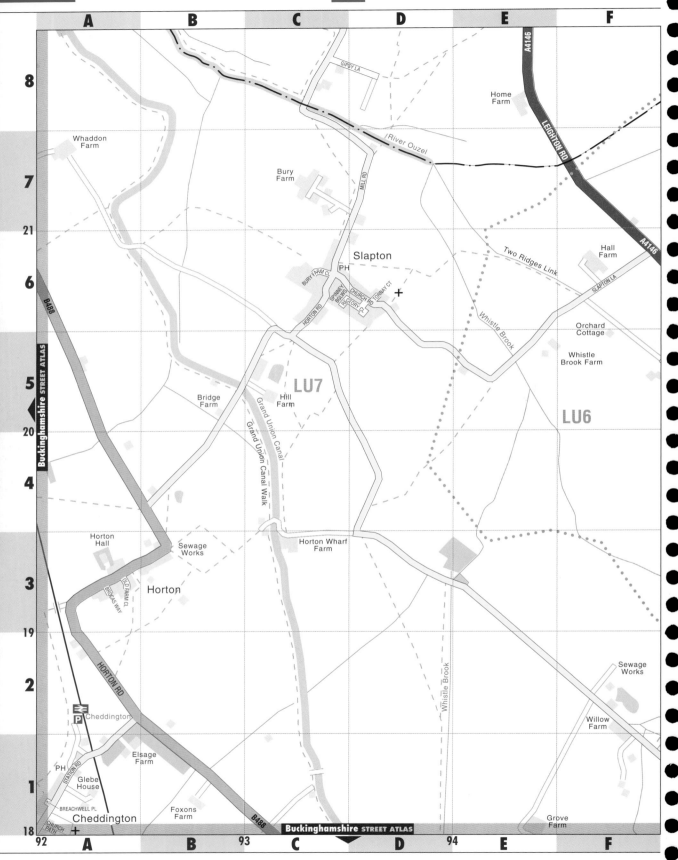

A B C D E F

8

Whaddon
Farm

GIPSY LA

Home
Farm

LEIGHTON RD

A4146

River Ouzel

7

Bury
Farm

MILL RD

21

Slapton

Two Ridges Link

Hall
Farm

A4146

SLAPTON LA

6

B488

BURY FARM CL

PH

SPINNEY BRLWK

CHURCH RD

HORTON RD

RECTORY CL

TORNAY CT

Whistle Brook

Orchard
Cottage

Whistle
Brook Farm

5

Buckinghamshire STREET ATLAS

Bridge
Farm

Hill
Farm

LU7

LU6

20

Grand Union Canal

Grand Union Canal Walk

4

Horton
Hall

Sewage
Works

Horton Wharf
Farm

3

OLD FARM CL

BROCAS WAY

Horton

19

HORTON RD

Whistle Brook

Sewage
Works

2

Cheddington

Willow
Farm

1

PH

STATION RD

Glebe
House

Elsage
Farm

Grove
Farm

18

BREACHWELL PL

CHURCH PATH

Cheddington

Foxons
Farm

B488

Buckinghamshire STREET ATLAS

92 A B 93 C D 94 E F

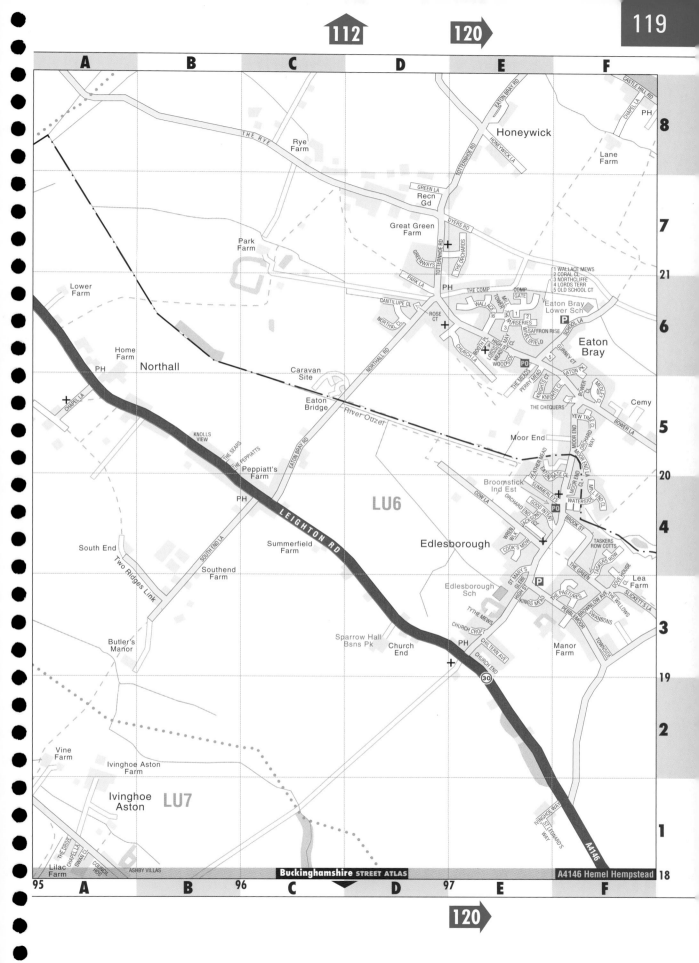

112
120
120

Honeywick

CASTLE HILL RD
CHAPELLA
PH
Lane Farm

THE RYE
Rye Farm

EATON BRAY RD
TOTTERNHOE RD
HONEYWICK LA

GREEN LA
Recn Gd
DYERS RD

Great Green Farm

Park Farm

GREENWAYS
TOTTERNHOE RD
THE ORCHARDS

PARK LA
PH
THE COMP
GATE
COMP

1 WALLACE MEWS
2 CORAL CL
3 NORTHCLIFFE
4 LORDS TERR
5 OLD SCHOOL CT

Lower Farm

CANTILUPE CL
NORTHALL
ROSE CT

NORTHALL RD

WALLACE DR
MILL
TOWER
HIGH WAY CL
LORDS MEAD
WOODSIDE
SAFFRON RISE
WINDSFIELD

Eaton Bray Lower Sch
SCHOOL LA
Eaton Bray
GURNEY CT
EATON PK
BOWER RD
MEDLEY
Cemy

Home Farm
PH
Northall

CHURCH LA
THE MEADS
PERRY MEAD
PO
KNIGHTS CL
KNITS CL
THE CHEQUERS
YEW TREE CL
MOOR END
BOWER LA
MOOR END LA

Caravan Site

Eaton Bridge

River Ouzel

Moor End
FEATHER MEAD
EATON GATE CL
MOOR END
MITRE CL
WATERSIDE
PO
ORCHARD CL

KNOLLS VIEW
THE SEARS
THE PEPPIATTS
Peppiatt's Farm

SUMMERLEYS
Broomstick Ind Est
COW LA
ORCHARD END
GOOD INTENT
JACKSONS CL
BROOK ST

PH

LEIGHTON RD

LU6

Summerfield Farm

WREN
CL
Edlesborough

TASKERS ROW COTTS
THE GREEN
TASKERS ROW
DOVE HOUSE
Lea Farm
SLICKETT'S LA

South End

SOUTH END LA

Southend Farm

COOK'S MDW

ST MARY'S
GLEBE
Edlesborough Sch
HIGH ST
KINGS MEAD
P
THE PASTURES
PEBBLEMOOR
BROWNLOW AVE
SWANSONS
THE WILLOWS
TOWNSEND

Butler's Manor

Two Ridges Link

Sparrow Hall Bsns Pk

Church End

TYTHE MEWS
CHURCH CROFT
CHILTERN AVE
PH
Manor Farm

CHURCH END
30

Vine Farm

Ivinghoe Aston Farm

LU7
Ivinghoe Aston

Lilac Farm
THE DRIVE
CHAPEL LA
SWAN CL
COUNCIL HOS
ASHBY VILLAS

IVINGHOE WAY
ST LEONARD'S
WAY
A4146

A4146 Hemel Hempstead

119
113

A B C D E F

8

Middle End

Brookfield Pk CVN Pk

Poplar Farm

Castle Hill Rd

Park Ave

Totternhoe Knolls Nature Reserve

SAXON CL 1 REDFIELD CL 2

WEATHERBY

NORMAN WAY

GREEN LA

BURHILL CL

CROOKFIELD CL

DROVERS CL

AYNSCOMBE CL

SPRG RD

PASCOMB RD

BEECROFT WAY

HAMBLING PL

WORTHINGTON RD

FRANKLIN RD

30

Lancot Lower Sch

LANCOT PL

LANCOT DR

SPINNEY CRES

7

Totternhoe

Church End Farm

CHURCH GN

Recn Gd

Allot Gdns

Church End

Dunstable Rd

HARVEY RD

MAYNARD RD

GARDNER'S CL

BEACON AVE

COMBE DR

BADGERS GATE

Totternhoe Rd

LANCOT AVE

OAKWELL CL

MELTON CT

BEECHWOOD CT

B489

WESTDOWN GDNS

MEADWAY

B4541

WHIPSNADE RD

SPIXWORTH

21

Totternhoe Lower Sch

PH

FURLONG LA

BRIGHTWELL AVE

THE AVENUE

TRING RD

Five Knolls

Pillow Mounds

The Vicarage

THE RIDE

ELLESMERE CL

California

Pascomb Pit

6

CHURCH RD

WELL HEAD RD

LU6

60

CH

5

Ware Hill Cottage

DUNSTABLE RD

Doolittle Mill (disused)

BOTTOM DR

SPRINGFIELD RD

MANTON RD

ICKNIELD WAY

Well Head

London Gliding Club

20

BOWER LA

Visitor Ctr

P

4

Rosebury Farm

Wellhead Farm

ROBERTSON CNR

P

Bellows Mill

HARLING RD

Norfolk House Farm

Harling House

Shepherds Farm

ICKNIELD WAY FARM COTTS

Dunstable Downs Ctry Pk

3

SLICKETT'S LA

Patrick's Cottage

PH

Icknield Way Farm

Icknield Way Path

19

Edlesborough Mills (disused)

Edlesborough Hill

B4506

Mast

2

TRING RD

B4540

Sallowspring Wood

Chute Farm

SALLOWSPRINGS

Valance-end Farm

DAGNALL RD

P

1

ICKNIELD WAY

B4506

B4540

Tree Cathedral

Whipsnade

18

B489

Willow Farm

P

98 A B 99 C D 00 E F

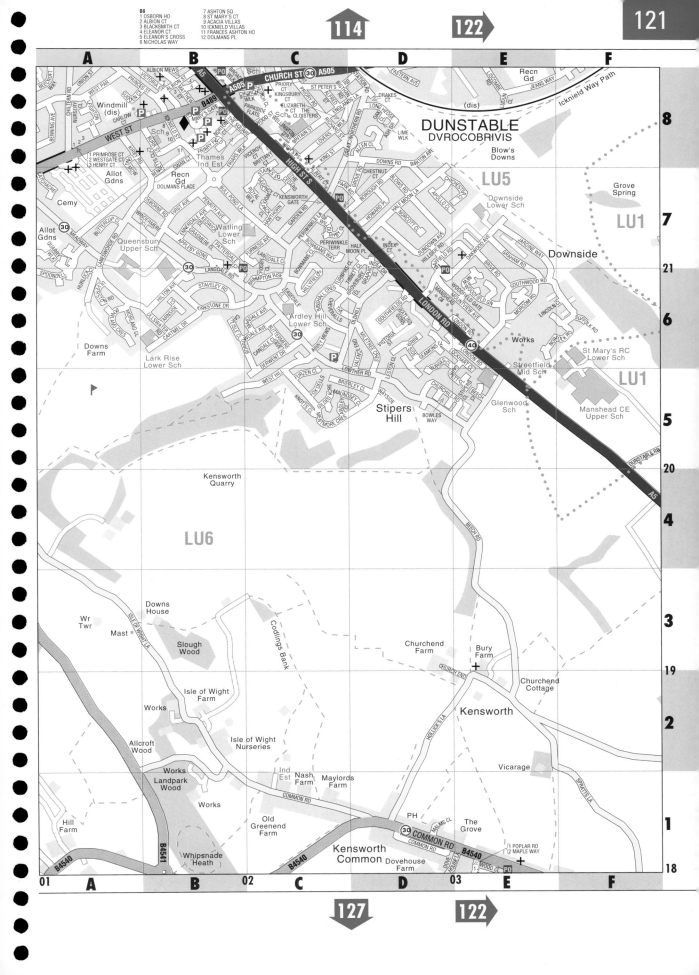

121
115

A **B** **C** **D** **E** **F**

LU5

LU4

LU4

Skimpot Wood

Stanner's Wood

Mast

Cultivation Terraces

Foxdell Jun Sch

COSGROVE WAY

Ind Est

BILTON WAY

BILTON WAY

COULSON CT

FINWAY

DALLOW RD

HAREFIELD CT

CASTINGWOLD GDNS

WARREN RD

KENT RD

HAREFIELD RD

SUMMERFIELD RD

RUNLEY RD

Chaul End Farm

Chaul End

Zouches Farm

Twentynine Wood

CH

Round Wood

Bush Wood

Badgerdell Wood

BLUEBELL WOOD CL

Mast

Thirty Wood

LU5

Dame Ellen's Wood

Castlecroft Wood

Brickkiln Farm

LU1

Blossom Spring

Little John's Wood

Folly Wood

Manor Farm

Cvn Pk

RUSHALL WELLS CL

COLLINGS CL

CADMAN CL

MANOR CT

LUTON RD

MEADOW CROFT

Turnpike Farm

Bury Farm

Cradle Spinney

FOLLY LA

MEADOW WAY

HEATHFIELD CL

HYDE RD

Willowfield Lower Sch

Lodge Farm

PO

PH

ORCHARD CL

DELFIELD GDNS

Heathfield Lower Sch

FIVE OAKS

Gatehouse

DUNSTABLE RD

MOSSMAN DR

HOLLY FARM CL

THE DELL

THE CRESCENT

Five Oaks Mid Sch

Buncer's Wood

Garden Centre

HAWTHORN CRES

SUTTON GDNS

CULWORTH CL

ELM AVE

ADSTONE RD

FAIRGREEN RD

LEDWELL RD

Jockey Farm

CROS LANDS

WILLOW GR

EDGECOTE CL

ENSLOW CL

Caddington

THE GLEN

LU6

MILLFIELD WAY

MARDLE RD

LITTLEGREEN LA

WOOD LANDS

MANOR RD

Tipplehill Farm

PH Motel

Piper's Farm

Heron Farm

MANCROFT RD

Kensworth House

MILLFIELD LA

MILLFIELD MEWS

Cotswold Bsns Pk

Millfield Farm

Aley Green

Corner Farm

Lynch Farm

Nurseries

Kensworth Lynch

Hill Farm

PIPERS LA

Cemy

AL3

04 **A** **B** 05 **C** **D** 06 **E** **F**

8 7 21 6 5 20 4 3 19 2 1 18

M1

A5

121
128

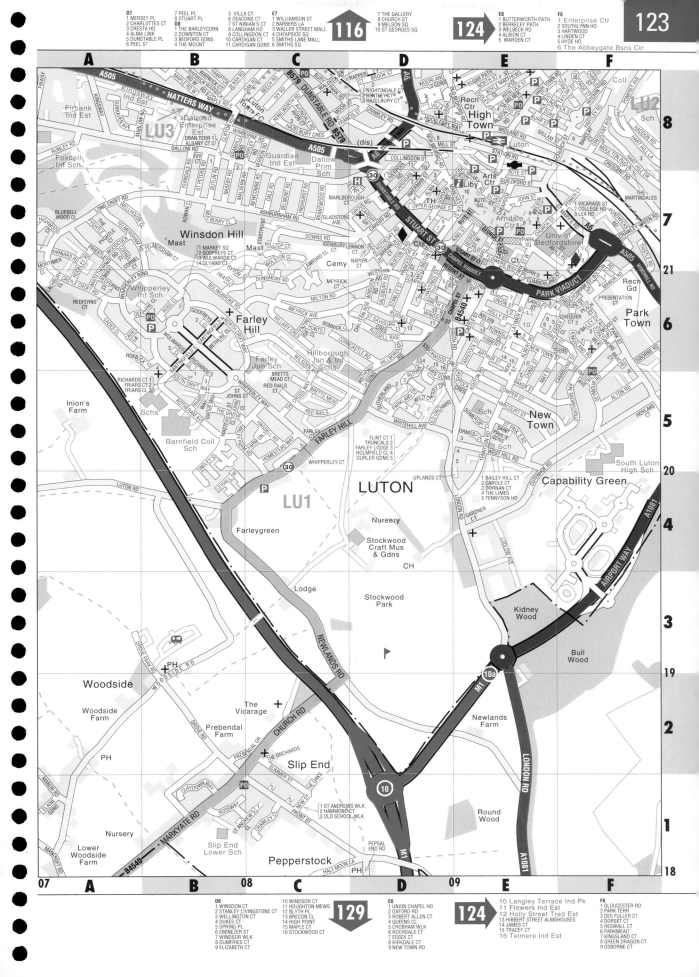

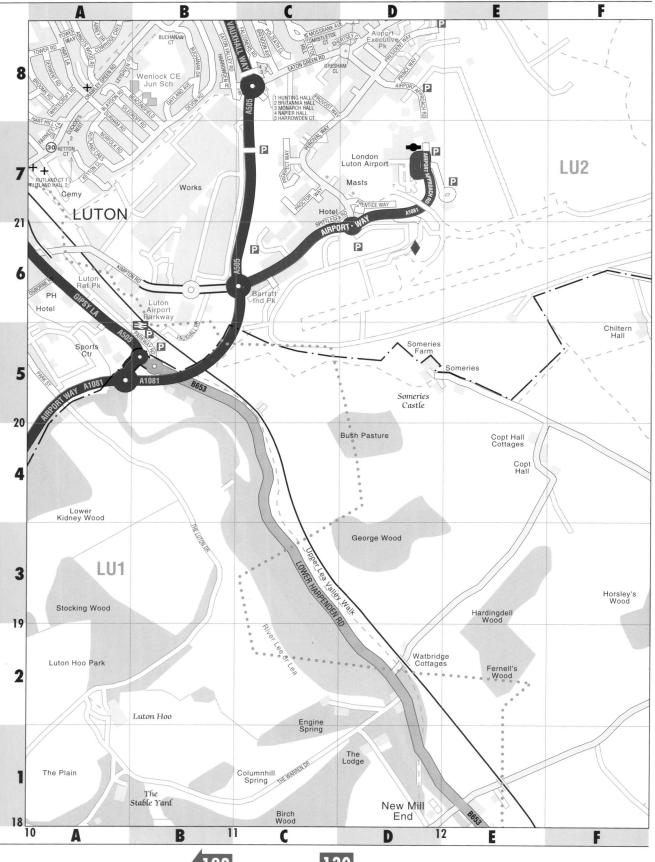

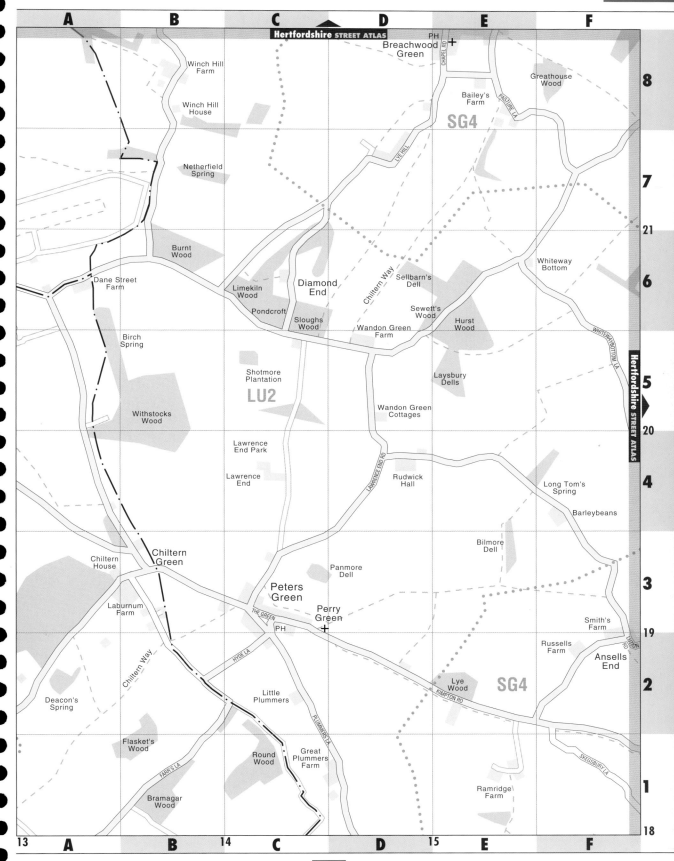

Hertfordshire STREET ATLAS

Breachwood Green

PH

Winch Hill Farm

Winch Hill House

SG4

Bailey's Farm

Greathouse Wood

8

Netherfield Spring

CHAPEL RD

PASTURE LA

7

21

Burnt Wood

Dane Street Farm

Limekiln Wood

Diamond End

LYE HILL

Chiltern Way

Sellbarn's Dell

Whiteway Bottom

6

Pondcroft

Sloughs Wood

Wandon Green Farm

Sewett's Wood

Hurst Wood

WHITEWAYBOTTOM LA

Birch Spring

Shotmore Plantation

LU2

Laysbury Dells

Hertfordshire STREET ATLAS

5

Withstocks Wood

Wandon Green Cottages

20

Lawrence End Park

LAWRENCE END RD

Rudwick Hall

Long Tom's Spring

4

Lawrence End

Barleybeans

Bilmore Dell

Chiltern House

Chiltern Green

Panmore Dell

Smith's Farm

3

Laburnum Farm

Peters Green

THE GREEN

Perry Green

PH

Russells Farm

19

PH

Ansells End

LUTON RD

Deacon's Spring

Chiltern Way

HYDE LA

Little Plummers

Lye Wood

SG4

2

KIMPTON RD

PLUMMERS LA

Flasket's Wood

Round Wood

Great Plummers Farm

Ramridge Farm

SKEGSBURY LA

1

FARR'S LA

Bramagar Wood

18

120

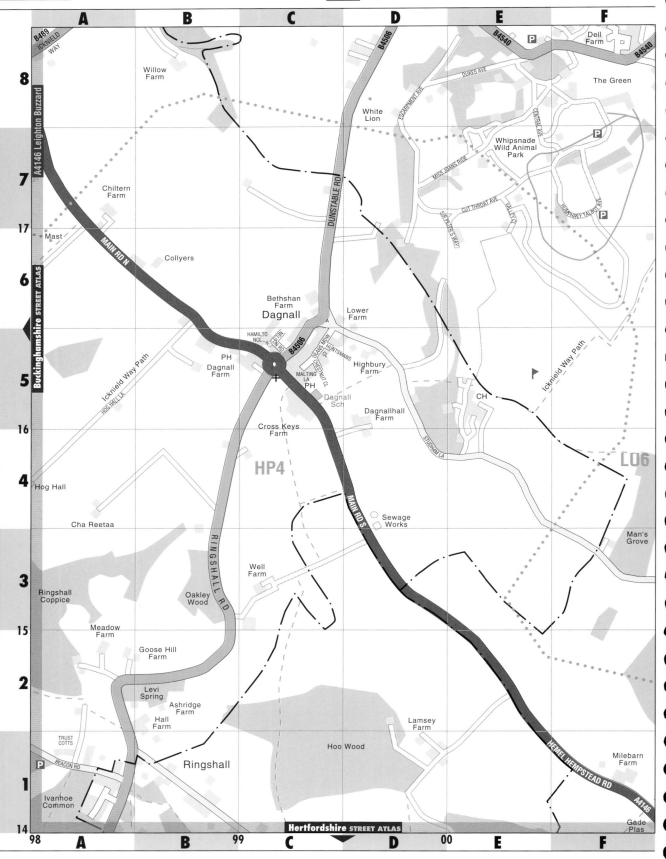

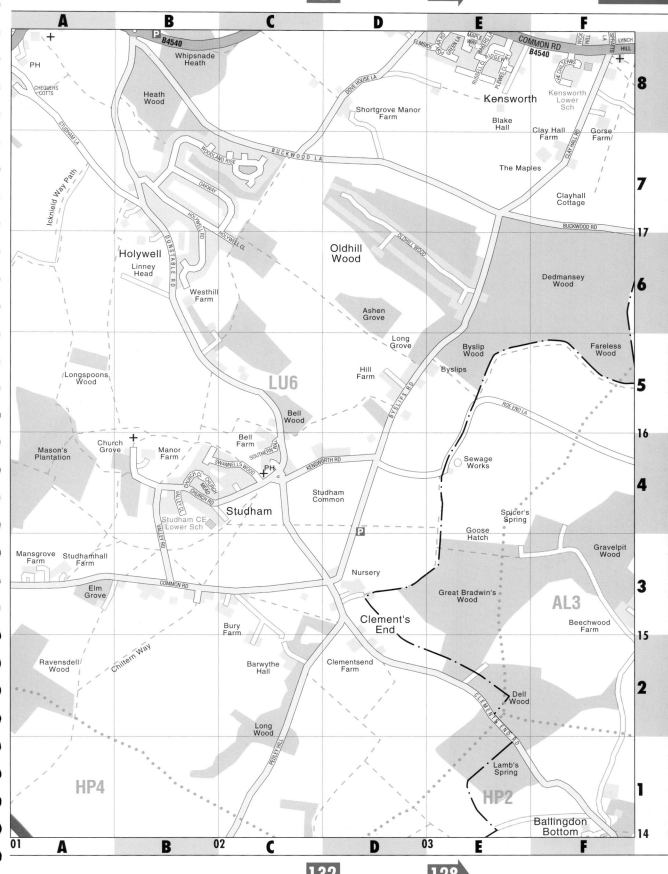

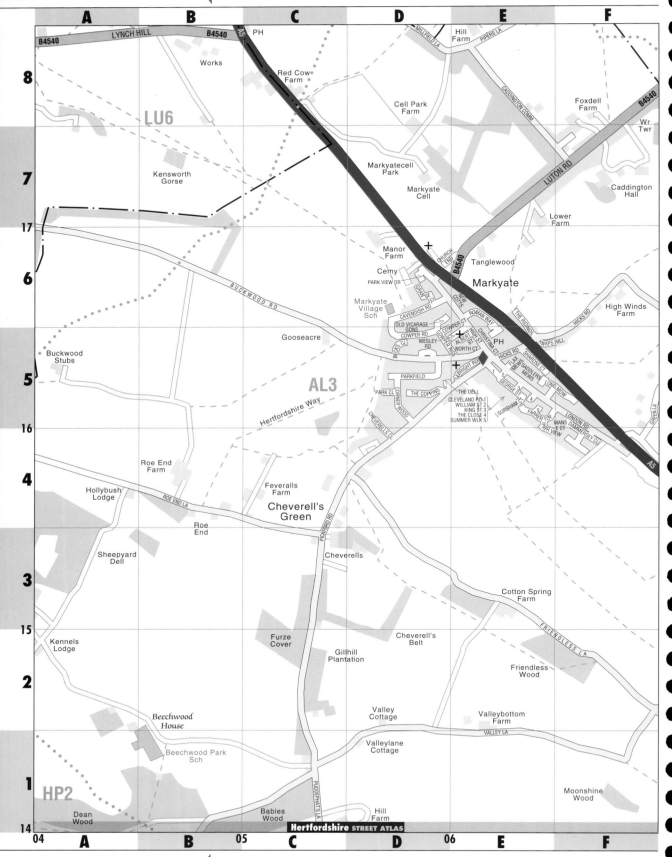

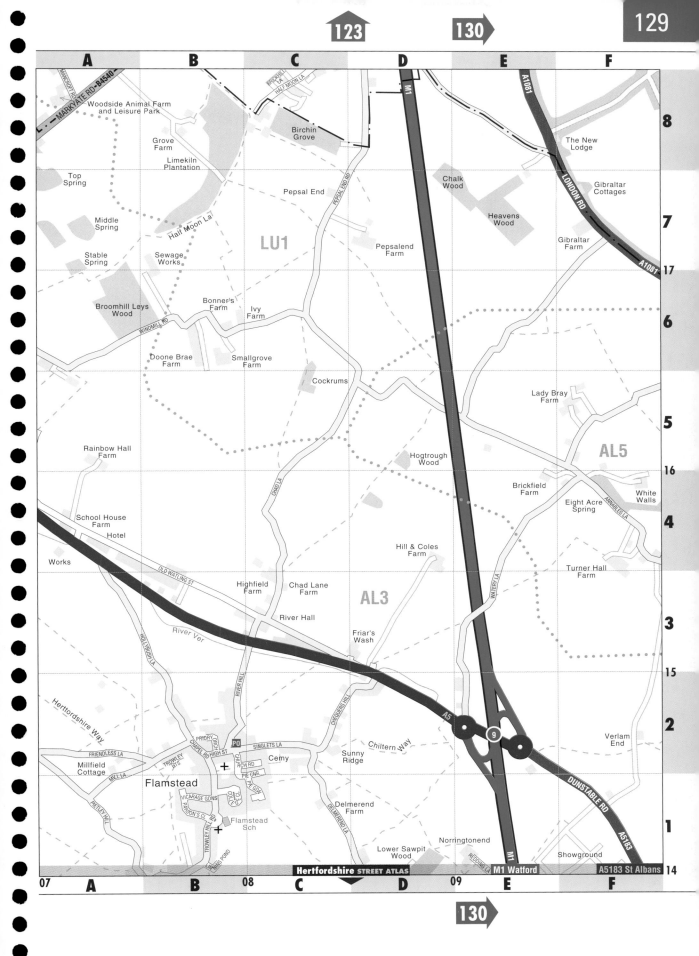

A B C D E F

Woodside Animal Farm
and Leisure Park
Grove
Farm
Limekiln
Plantation
Top
Spring
Pepsal End
Birchin
Grove
Chalk
Wood
The New
Lodge
Gibraltar
Cottages
8

Middle
Spring
Half Moon La
LU1
Heavens
Wood
Gibraltar
Farm
7

Stable
Spring
Sewage
Works
Pepsalend
Farm
London Rd
A1081
17

Broomhill Leys
Wood
Bonner's
Farm
Ivy
Farm
6

WINDMILL RD
Doone Brae
Farm
Smallgrove
Farm
Cockrums
Lady Bray
Farm
AL5
5

Rainbow Hall
Farm
Hogtrough
Wood
Brickfield
Farm
White
Walls
16

CHAD LA
Eight Acre
Spring
ANNABLES LA
4

School House
Farm
Hotel
Works
OLD WATLING ST
Hill & Coles
Farm
Turner Hall
Farm
Highfield
Farm
Chad Lane
Farm
AL3
River Hall
River Ver
Friar's
Wash
WATERY LA
3

HOLLYBUSH LA
RIVER HILL
CHEQUERS HILL
15
A5
9
Verlam
End
2

Herttordshire Way
PRIORY
ORCH
CHAPEL RD HIGH ST
PO
SINGLETS LA
Cemy
Chiltern Way
Sunny
Ridge
FRIENDLESS LA
TROWLEY HTS
Millfield
Cottage
MILL LA
Flamstead
VICARAGE GDNS
CHURCH RD
PIE CNR
PARSON'S CL
DUNSTABLE RD
A5183
1

PIETLEY HILL
TROWLEY HILL RD
Flamstead
Sch
DELMEREND LA
Delmerend
Farm
Lower Sawpit
Wood
Norringtonend
REDDING LA
M1
Showground
14

LU1

Luton Hoo
Home Farm

Saw Mill

The Gables

Birch
Wood

Hillside

Tumble
Grove

Graves
Wood

B653

Sewage
Works

River Lea or Lee

Upper Lea Valley Walk

VIADUCT COTTS

SOUTHERN RISE

LOWER HARPENDEN RD

East
Hyde

TAMBRO CL

LEA
BRIDGE
CNR

FARRS LA

PH

B653

LU2

A1081

LONDON RD

LIMETREE AVE

FARM RD

Lady Bute's
Lodge

Circus
Wood

West
Hyde

Thrales
End

Thrales End
Rd

COOTERS END LA

Cooters Hill
Farm

Kennel La

Beech
Ridge

Kinsbourne
Green

PH

PH

PO

THE COMMON

LUTON RD

Thrales End
Farm

KINSBOURNE CRES

Kinsbourne

Klondyke

RIDGEWAY

Cooters End
Farm

Long
Spring

Chamber Almes

Spring Rd

Annables La

Pollard's
Farm

DERWENT RD

TINTERN CL

GREATFIELD

CROSSPATHS

SHEP HERDS WAY

VALE CL

TUFFNELLS WAY

AM LA

PENSHURST CL

FARM RD

MOLESCROFT

RIDGE AVE

WELLS CL

LUTON RD

AMBROSE LA

Dove House
Farm

AL5

KENNESBOURNE
CT

CARDENER'S CT

RICKWOOD GDNS

HOMEDELL
HO

1 ROUNDWOOD CT
2 ST NICHOLAS CT
3 KINSBOURNE CT
4 BRAMBLE CL

Annables
Farm

Mast

KINSBOURNE GREEN LA

Faulkners End
Farm

Wood End
JM Sch

YEOMANS AVE

ASHLEY GDNS

BRACKENDALE GR

HASLINGDEN CL

WOOD END RD

WOOD END HILL

RIDGEWOOD DR

WOODLANDS DR

HIGH RIDGE

MAYFIELD CL

HOW FIELD

APTS

Harpenden RISE

BLOOMFIELD RD

HILLSIDE RD

BEECH

LAMBOURN
GDNS

REED
PL

BOND
CT

BRIDGE CT

HOLLYBUSH LA

OVERTREES

A1081

Delgarth

Roundwood La

HARPENDEN

Roundwood
Park Sch

Roundwood
Prim Sch

Chiltern Way

Nicky Line

Chiltern Way

AL3

Northfield
Spring

LUTON LA

Harpenden
Stables

OTTERTON CL

PARK RISE CL

APTS

FALOWE CL

PARK RISE

THE SPINNEY

ROUNDWOOD

ROUNDWOOD GDNS

MEDOWS

Park RISE

HARPENDEN RISE

Park Mount

PARK HILL

MEADOW CL

MORTON END LA

MORTON AVE

DOUGLAS RD

MORTON
DR

ST ANDREW'S
AVE

CLAYGATE AVE

POMWICK CL

ALBERS END LA

BROADFIELDS

BARNS DENE

HARTWELL GDNS

TOWNSEND CL

TOWNSEND LA

PARK AVE N

MAPLE RD

LONGCROFT AVE

St Hilda's
Sch

TANGLEWOOD

MORETON

CHEPSTOW

TIMBERS CT

THE
COPPICE

SALISBURY AVE

ROSEBERY AVE

AMENBURY LA

PARK AVE S

KIRKWICK AVE

ORCHARD AVE

ROTHAMSTED AVE

BADINGHAM DR

F2
1 THE BOURNE
2 THE BOURNE APTS

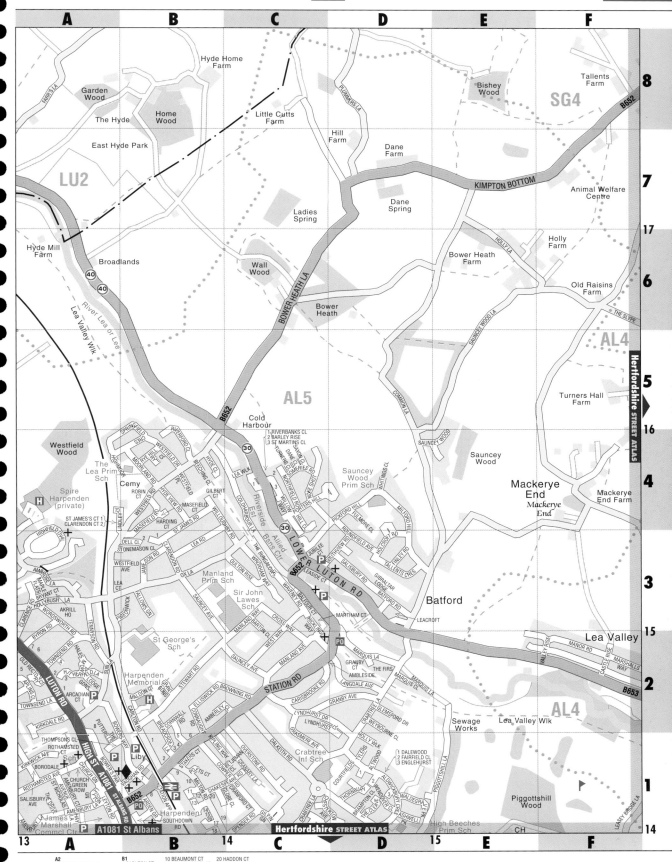

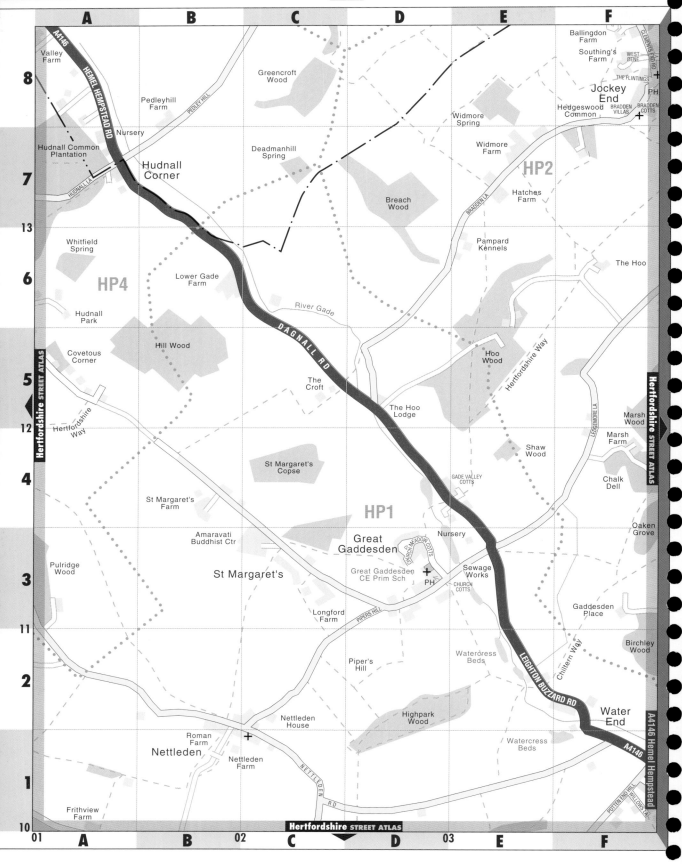

127

Index

Place name May be abbreviated on the map

Location number Present when a number indicates the place's position in a crowded area of mapping

Locality, town or village Shown when more than one place has the same name

Postcode district District for the indexed place

Page and grid square Page number and grid reference for the standard mapping

Church Rd 6 Beckenham BR2..........**53** C6

Cities, towns and villages are listed in CAPITAL LETTERS

Public and commercial buildings are highlighted in magenta   **Places of interest** are highlighted in blue with a star★

Abbreviations used in the index

Acad	Academy	Comm	Common	Gd	Ground	L	Leisure	Prom	Promenade
App	Approach	Cott	Cottage	Gdn	Garden	La	Lane	Rd	Road
Arc	Arcade	Cres	Crescent	Gn	Green	Liby	Library	Recn	Recreation
Ave	Avenue	Cswy	Causeway	Gr	Grove	Mdw	Meadow	Ret	Retail
Bglw	Bungalow	Ct	Court	H	Hall	Meml	Memorial	Sh	Shopping
Bldg	Building	Ctr	Centre	Ho	House	Mkt	Market	Sq	Square
Bsns, Bus	Business	Ctry	Country	Hospl	Hospital	Mus	Museum	St	Street
Bvd	Boulevard	Cty	County	HQ	Headquarters	Orch	Orchard	Sta	Station
Cath	Cathedral	Dr	Drive	Hts	Heights	Pal	Palace	Terr	Terrace
Cir	Circus	Dro	Drove	Ind	Industrial	Par	Parade	TH	Town Hall
Cl	Close	Ed	Education	Inst	Institute	Pas	Passage	Univ	University
Cnr	Corner	Emb	Embankment	Int	International	Pk	Park	Wk, Wlk	Walk
Coll	College	Est	Estate	Intc	Interchange	Pl	Place	Wr	Water
Com	Community	Ex	Exhibition	Junc	Junction	Prec	Precinct	Yd	Yard

Index of towns, villages, streets, hospitals, industrial estates, railway stations, schools, shopping centres, universities and places of interest

306–Ara

306th Bombardment Group Mus★ MK44 .... **17** F6

A

Abbey Cl
Ampthill MK45 .... **84** F7
Elstow MK42 .... **50** B3
Renhold MK41 .... **39** B7
Abbey Dr LU2 .... **117** A1
Abbeyfields MK42 ..... **50** C3
Abbeygate Bsns Ctr The 6
LU2 .... **123** F8
Abbey Gr SG19 .... **54** C8
Abbey La MK45 .... **85** A6
Abbey Mews LU6 .... **121** C6
Abbey Mid Sch MK42... **50** C3
Abbey Rd MK41 .... **39** A2
Abbey Sq MK43 .... **34** E5
Abbey Way NN10....... **8** A8
Abbey Wlk
Heath and Reach LU7 .. **103** A4
Houghton Regis LU5 .... **114** E6
Abbis Cl MK45 .... **84** D3
Abbis Orch SG5 .... **100** E5
Abbot Cres MK42 ...... **49** D2
Abbots Ct LU2 .... **117** A1
Abbots Wlk 4 SG18.... **67** A6
Abbotswood Par LU2... **117** A1
Abbots Wood Rd LU2.. **124** A8
Abbotts Rd SG6......... **101** D6
Abercorn Rd LU4 ...... **114** F3
Abigail Cl LU3 .... **116** D3
Abigail Ct LU3 .... **116** D3
Abingdon Rd LU4 ...... **115** C3
Abrahams Cl MK40..... **38** E1
Acacia Cl LU7........... **111** E6
Acacia Rd MK42 .... **50** D6
Acacia Villas 9 LU6... **121** B8
Ackerman Gdns PE19 .. **22** C2
Ackerman St PE19 ..... **22** C2
Acorn Cl LU2 .... **116** F3
Acorn Ctr 3 SG18...... **67** A6
Acorn Ho SG18 .... **66** F7
Acorn Way MK42 .... **50** D5
Acres The SG17......... **88** B5
Acworth Cres LU4...... **115** C5
Acworth Ct 2 LU4 ..... **115** C5
Adaern Cl 7 LU7 .... **111** A8
Adams Bottom LU7..... **103** A1
Adams Cl
Ampthill MK45 .... **84** F7

Adams Cl continued
Kempston MK42 .... **49** E1
Adamson Ct MK42 ..... **49** D5
Adamson Wlk MK42..... **49** D5
Adastral Ave LU7 ...... **111** E6
Addington Cl
Bedford MK41 .... **39** A1
Henlow SG16............. **78** D1
Addingtons Rd MK44... **41** A5
Addington Way LU4.... **115** D3
Addington Wlk PE19 ... **22** C2
Addison Cl MK42........ **49** F4
Addison Rd LU4 .... **115** A7
Adelaide Cl MK45 ...... **74** B8
Adelaide Sq MK40...... **38** B1
Adelaide St LU1........ **123** D7
Adlington Ct LU4 ...... **115** C4
Admiral Row MK45..... **84** E4
Admirals Way PE19 ... **22** A2
Adstone Rd LU1........ **122** F3
Aelfric Ct MK41.......... **38** C5
Aidans Cl LU6 .... **113** E1
Ailesbury Rd MK45..... **84** F8
Ailsworth Rd LU3 ...... **116** A7
Ailwyns Acre MK43 .... **71** B7
Ainsland Ct LU4........ **115** B2
Aintree Rd NN10....... **8** D8
Airedale Ct MK45 ...... **84** D4
Aire Wlk MK41.......... **38** C7
Airport Approach Rd
LU2 .... **124** D8
Airport Executive Pk
LU2 .... **124** D8
Airport Way LU1, LU2 .. **124** A5
Akrill Ho AL5 .... **131** A3
Alameda Mid Sch MK45.. **84** E8
Alameda Rd MK45 ...... **84** E8
Alameda Wlk MK45 ..... **84** E8
Alamein Ave MK42 ..... **50** E6
Alamein Cl SG17........ **77** C1
Alamein Ct PE19 .... **22** C5
Alban CE Mid Sch MK44.. **40** F5
Albany Ct LU1 .... **123** B8
Albany Rd
Bedford MK40 .... **50** C8
Leighton Buzzard LU7 .. **111** B7
Albermarle Cl LU4 ..... **114** F3
Albert Cl LU6 .... **121** C7
Albert Pl
Ampthill MK45 .... **84** D6
Houghton Conquest MK45.. **74** B8
Albert Rd
Arlesey SG15............. **90** A4
Luton LU1 .... **123** E6

Albert St
10 Bedford MK40 .... **38** B1
Markyate AL3 .... **128** E5
Albion Ct
2 Dunstable LU6 ...... **121** B8
4 Luton LU2 .... **123** E8
Sandy SG19 .... **54** C7
Albion Mews LU6 ...... **121** B8
Albion Rd LU2 .... **123** E8
Albion St LU6........... **121** B8
Albone Way SG18...... **66** F4
Albone Way Ind Est SG18.. **66** F4
Alburgh Cl MK42........ **50** F5
Albury Cl LU3 .... **108** A1
Aldbanks LU6........... **113** F1
Aldenham Cl
Bedford MK41 .... **51** B8
Luton LU4 .... **114** F3
Aldens Mead MK41..... **38** F4
Alder Cl LU3 .... **116** A3
Alder Cres LU3 .... **116** A3
Alder Ct LU3 .... **116** B3
Alders End La AL5 ..... **130** F2
Alders The MK42........ **49** E3
Alderton Cl 5 LU2 ..... **117** D1
Aldgate Cl SG19 .... **56** B7
Aldhous Cl LU3 .... **116** B5
Aldwickbury Cres AL5.. **131** D1
Aldwyck Ct MK42....... **50** A6
Alesia Rd LU3........... **115** F6
Alexa Ct MK42.......... **51** A5
Alexander Cl
Clifton SG17............. **78** A2
Stewartby MK43......... **61** C1
Alexander Ct NN29......**7** B8
Alexander Rd
Stotfold SG5.............. **90** F6
Wrestlingworth SG19 ... **57** B4
Alexandra Ave LU3..... **116** C2
Alexandra Ct LU7 ...... **110** F8
Alexandra Pl 4 MK40.. **50** B8
Alexandra Rd
Bedford MK40 .... **50** A8
Hitchin SG5.............. **100** F1
ALEY GREEN **122** E1
Alfred Cope Rd SG19.. **54** C8
Alfred St
Dunstable LU5.......... **121** C8
Irchester NN29........... **7** A8
Alfriston Cl LU2 .... **117** C3
Alington La SG6 .... **101** F3
Alington Rd PE19 ...... **22** E1
Allenby Ave LU5 .... **115** A1

Allen Cl
Bedford MK40 .... **49** F8
Dunstable LU5.......... **121** D8
Allen Ct MK43 .... **60** E1
Allendale LU3 .... **108** A1
Allhallows
Bedford MK40 .... **50** B8
Sandy SG19 .... **54** B8
Allied Bsns Ctr AL5 ... **131** C3
All Saints CE Lower Sch
SG17 .... **78** B2
All Saints Rd
Bedford MK40 .... **49** F8
Cople MK44 .... **52** A7
Houghton Regis LU5 ... **114** B5
All Saints Way SG19... **54** B8
Allton Rd SG16......... **89** A4
Alma Farm Rd LU5 .... **105** E6
Alma Link 4 LU1 ...... **123** D7
Alma St LU1 .... **123** D7
Almer's Cl MK45 .... **74** B8
Almond Cl LU3........... **116** B4
Almond Dr SG19 .... **44** C5
Almond Rd
Leighton Buzzard LU7... **111** C8
St Neots PE19 .... **22** F6
Almonds The MK42 .... **50** A3
Alnwick Cl SG19 .... **54** C8
Alnwick Ct PE19 .... **22** F2
Alpha Ct
Kempston MK42 .... **49** D3
Leighton Buzzard LU7 .. **111** B7
Alpine Way LU3......... **115** D8
Alsop Cl LU5............ **114** B5
Althorp Cl MK45 .... **84** F3
Althorpe St MK42 ...... **50** B6
Althorp Rd LU3 .... **116** C1
Alton Rd LU1 .... **123** F5
Altwood AL5............. **131** D1
Alwen Wlk MK41........ **38** C5
Alwins Field LU7 .... **110** D8
Alwyn Cl LU2 .... **116** E2
Amaravati Buddhist Ctr
HP1......................... **132** C3
Amberley Cl
Harpenden AL5 .... **131** B2
Luton LU2 .... **117** D4
Amberley Gdns MK40 .. **38** D2
Ambleside
Harpenden AL5 .... **131** D2
Luton LU3 .... **115** F5
Ambrose La AL5 .... **130** F4
Amenbury Ct AL5....... **131** A1

Amenbury La AL5 ...... **131** A1
Ames Cl LU3............. **107** F1
Amhurst Rd LU4 .... **114** F3
AMPTHILL **84** E6
Ampthill Ind Est & Bsns Pk
MK45 .... **84** C7
Ampthill Rd
Bedford MK42 .... **50** B5
Chicksands SG17 .... **76** E2
Silsoe MK45.............. **86** B5
Steppingley MK45 ...... **84** D5
Ampthill St MK42 ...... **50** C7
Andover Cl LU4 .... **115** C6
Andrew Rd PE19 .... **22** F2
Andrews Cl MK45 ...... **74** C1
Angel Cl LU4 .... **115** D3
Angels La LU5 .... **114** B5
Angel View MK42 ...... **50** C5
Angus Cl LU4 .... **115** A3
Anmer Gdns LU4 ...... **115** B4
Annables La AL5 .... **130** A4
Annes Ct MK42 .... **50** C7
Anne St SG18........... **67** A7
ANSELLS END **125** F2
Anson Pl PE19 .... **22** A2
Anstee Rd LU4 .... **115** B6
Anthony Gdns LU1 .... **123** D6
Antonie Farm Cotts MK44. **15** F4
Anvil Cl LU3 .... **115** E5
Anvil Ho 8 AL5......... **131** A1
Apex Bsns Ctr LU5 .... **114** C2
Aplins Cl AL5 .... **131** A2
Apollo Cl LU5........... **121** D7
Appenine Way LU7 .... **111** D8
Appleby Ct PE19 ...... **22** E6
Appleby Gdns LU6 .... **121** B7
Applecroft SG16........ **89** B3
Applecroft Rd LU2 .... **117** C4
Applecross Wlk MK41.. **39** B3
Appledore Rd MK40.... **38** D1
Apple Glebe MK45 .... **97** C2
Apple Gr PE19 .... **22** C4
Apple Tree Cl
Biggleswade SG18...... **67** B5
Leighton Buzzard LU7 .. **110** D6
Silsoe MK45.............. **86** B5
Applewood Cl AL5 ..... **130** E3
Apsley End Rd SG5.... **98** E6
Aquila Rd LU7 .... **111** D8
Aragon Ct MK45 .... **84** E8

Aragon PI PE28 . . . . 6 F5
Aragon Rd MK45 . . . . 84 F7
Arbour CI LU3 . . . . 108 A1
Arbroath Rd LU3 . . . . . . 107 D1
Arcade The
  14 Bedford MK40 . . . . . 50 B8
  Letchworth SG6 . . . . . . 101 F6
Arcadian Ct AL5 . . . . . . 131 A2
Archers Way SG6 . . . . . . 101 B6
Archway Par LU3 . . . . . . 115 E4
Archway Rd LU3 . . . . . . 115 E4
Arden Gr AL5 . . . . 131 B1
Arden PI LU2 . . . . 116 E1
Arden Wlk MK41 . . . . 39 B3
Ardleigh Gn LU2 . . . . . . 117 E1
Ardley CI LU6 . . . . 121 C5
Ardley Hill Lower Sch
  LU6 . . . . 121 C6
Arena Par SG6 . . . . 101 F6
Arenson Way LU5 . . . . . 114 C2
Argyll Ave LU3 . . . . 116 C2
Argyll St MK40 . . . . 38 B2
Arianne Bsns Ctr LU5 . . 114 B3
Aries Ct LU7 . . . . 111 C4
Arkwright Rd
  Bedford MK42 . . . . 51 A5
  Irchester NN29 . . . . 7 C7
  Milton Ernest MK44 . . . . 27 B5
Arkwright Road Ind Est
  MK42 . . . . 51 A5
ARLESEY 90 A4
Arlesey Ho SG15 . . . . 90 A8
Arlesey New Rd SG6,
  SG15 . . . . 101 B7
Arlesey Rd
  Church End SG16 . . . . . 89 E8
  Henlow SG16 . . . . 89 D8
  Ickleford SG5 . . . . 100 F5
Arlesey Sta SG15 . . . . . . 90 A4
Arlington Ct 15 MK40 . . . . 38 B1
Armitage Gdns LU4 . . . . 115 D1
Armour Rise SG4 . . . . . . 101 B2
Armstrong CI MK45 . . . . . 62 F3
Armstrong Dr MK42 . . . . . 50 C6
Arnald Way LU5 . . . . . . 114 A4
Arncliffe Cres LU2 . . . . . 116 E1
Arndale Ctr LU1 . . . . 123 E4
Arnhem PI PE19 . . . . 22 C5
Arnhem PI SG17 . . . . 77 C2
Arnold CI
  Barton-le-C MK45 . . . . . 97 C2
  Luton LU2 . . . . 117 A3
Arnold Middle Sch MK45 . 97 C2
Arnolds La SG7 . . . . 80 D6
Arran CI SG19 . . . . 54 B8
Arran Ct LU1 . . . . 123 D7
Arrow CI LU3 . . . . 115 E6
Arrow Leys MK41 . . . . . . 38 F4
Arthur St
  Ampthill MK45 . . . . 84 E8
  Luton, New Town LU1 . . 123 E6
Arum CI NN10 . . . . 8 C7
Arun CI MK41 . . . . 38 D5
Arundel CI MK45 . . . . 84 D1
Arundel Cres PE19 . . . . . 22 E2
Arundel Ct NN10 . . . . 8 A8
Arundel Dr MK41 . . . . . . 39 A4
Arundel Rd
  Luton LU1 . . . . 115 F2
  Marston Moretaine MK43 . 72 C8
Ascot Dr LU7 . . . . 110 D6
Ascot Rd
  Luton LU3 . . . . 116 B2
  Rushden NN10 . . . . 8 D8
ASCOTT 110 B2
Ascott House★ LU7 . . . . 110 A2
Asgard Dr MK41 . . . . 39 D4
Ashburnham Cres LU7 . . 110 E6
Ashburnham Ct MK40 . . . 50 A8
Ashburnham Rd
  Ampthill MK45 . . . . 84 E7
  Bedford MK40 . . . . 50 A8
  Luton LU3 . . . . 123 C7
Ashby Ct SG18 . . . . 78 F4
Ashby Dr
  Barton-le-C MK45 . . . . . 97 C3
  Rushden NN10 . . . . 8 A8
  Upper Caldecote SG18 . . 66 B8
Ashby Villas LU6 . . . . . . 119 A1
Ash CI
  Beeston SG19 . . . . 54 B6
  Flitwick MK45 . . . . 84 F2
  Irchester NN29 . . . . 7 A7
Ashcraft CI MK43 . . . . . . 72 C7
Ashcroft LU6 . . . . 113 F1
Ashcroft High Sch LU2 . . 117 C2
Ashcroft Rd LU2 . . . . . . 117 B3
Ashdale Ave MK42 . . . . . 49 F5
Ashdale Gdns LU3 . . . . . 108 A1
Ashdown SG6 . . . . 90 F1
Ashdown Rd SG17 . . . . . . 77 E3
Ashfield PE28 . . . . 6 F5
Ashfield Way LU3 . . . . . 116 A6
Ash Gr
  Biggleswade SG18 . . . . . 66 F8
  Dunstable LU5 . . . . . . 121 D8
  Leighton Buzzard LU7 . . 111 A8
  Wilstead MK45 . . . . 62 F2
Ash Grange LU7 . . . . . . 111 A8
Ashington Ct SG17 . . . . . 78 B2
Ashley Gdns
  Biggleswade SG18 . . . . . 67 B7
  Harpenden AL5 . . . . . . 130 A5
Ashlong CI LU7 . . . . 111 C4
Ashmead Rd MK41 . . . . . 38 C7

Ash Rd
  Biggleswade SG18 . . . . . 67 A7
  Luton LU4 . . . . 123 B8
Ashridge CI NN10 . . . . . . 8 A8
Ashridge Dr MK41 . . . . . . 39 C4
Ashton CE Mid Sch LU6 . 114 B1
Ashton Rd
  Dunstable LU6 . . . . . . 114 B1
  Luton LU1 . . . . 123 B5
Ashton Sq 7 LU6 . . . . . . 121 B8
Ash Tree Rd LU5 . . . . . . 114 B6
Ashwell Ave LU3 . . . . . . 115 C8
Ashwell Ct LU3 . . . . 115 C8
Ashwell Pk AL5 . . . . 131 D1
Ashwell Place 4 LU7 . . . 111 A8
Ashwell Rd
  Guilden Morden SG8 . . . 69 F1
  Hinxworth SG7 . . . . 80 E5
  Newnham SG7 . . . . 91 F8
Ashwell St LU7 . . . . 111 A8
Ash Well Wlk LU5 . . . . . 114 C6
Ash Wlk MK41 . . . . 49 F3
Aspects L Ctr MK41 . . . . . 50 F7
Aspen Ave MK41 . . . . 38 E4
Asplands CI MK17 . . . . . . 81 B4
Aspley CI LU4 . . . . 114 E3
Aspley Ct
  Bedford MK40 . . . . 38 A1
  Woburn Sands MK17 . . . . 81 C3
ASPLEY END 98 E7
ASPLEY GUISE 81 F4
Aspley Guise Lower Sch
  MK17 . . . . 81 F4
Aspley Guise Sta MK17 . . . 81 D6
ASPLEY HEATH 80 B2
Aspley Hill MK17 . . . . 81 C4
Aspley La MK17 . . . . 81 E2
Aspley Rd MK42 . . . . 50 B8
Astley Gn LU2 . . . . 117 D2
Aston Rd MK42 . . . . 51 A5
Astra Ct LU2 . . . . 116 F2
Astral CI SG16 . . . . 89 B3
Astrey CI LU5 . . . . 95 F2
ASTWICK 79 E1
Astwick Rd SG5 . . . . 79 F2
ASTWOOD 47 A3
Astwood CI SG19 . . . . . . 56 A8
Astwood Dr MK45 . . . . . . 84 D4
Astwood Rd MK43 . . . . . . 59 C7
Atherstone Abbey MK41 . . 51 B8
Atherstone Rd LU4 . . . . . 115 D1
Atholl CI LU3 . . . . 115 D8
Atholl Wlk MK41 . . . . 39 B4
Attadale Wlk 4 MK41 . . . . 39 B4
Atterbury Ave LU7 . . . . . 111 B8
Aubrey Gdns LU4 . . . . . . 115 B6
Aubreys SG6 . . . . 101 F2
Auckland Rd SG18 . . . . . . 67 B7
Augustus Rd LU7 . . . . . . 104 E2
Austin Canons MK42 . . . . 50 A6
Austin CI NN29 . . . . 7 C8
Austin Rd LU3 . . . . 116 C4
Avebury Ave LU2 . . . . . . 116 D4
Aveline CI LU7 . . . . 111 A6
Avenells Way SG19 . . . . . 44 D5
Avenue Rd
  Rushden NN10 . . . . 8 F5
  St Neots PE19 . . . . 22 F6
Avenue St Nicholas AL5 . 131 D5
Avenue The
  Ampthill MK45 . . . . 84 E7
  Bedford MK40 . . . . 50 A8
  Biggleswade SG18 . . . . . 67 B6
  Bletsoe MK44 . . . . 17 C1
  Blunham MK44 . . . . 41 D2
  Dunstable LU6 . . . . . . 120 F7
  Flitwick MK45 . . . . 84 F3
  Langford SG18 . . . . 78 F4
  Luton LU4 . . . . 115 D5
  Sandy SG19 . . . . 54 B7
  Stotfold SG5 . . . . 90 F6
Aviary Wlk MK41 . . . . 38 C5
Avoca Ho MK43 . . . . 36 F3
Avocet SG6 . . . . 90 E1
Avocet CI
  Biggleswade SG18 . . . . . 66 F4
  Sandy SG19 . . . . 42 B1
Avon Chase SG16 . . . . . . 89 C4
Avon Cotts LU2 . . . . 117 B3
Avon Ct
  17 Harpenden AL5 . . . . 131 B1
  Luton LU1 . . . . 123 C8
  St Neots PE19 . . . . 22 C3
Avondale Rd LU1 . . . . . . 123 C8
Avon Dr MK41 . . . . 38 C5
Avon Rd SG16 . . . . 89 B4
Avon Rise MK45 . . . . 84 D2
Avon Wlk LU7 . . . . 103 B3
Axe CI LU3 . . . . 115 E6
Axis Way PE19 . . . . 22 B5
Aydon Rd LU3 . . . . 116 B6
Aylesbury Ct MK41 . . . . . 38 F1
Aylesbury Rd MK41 . . . . . 50 F8
Aylmerton Ct SG17 . . . . . 77 D2
Aylott CI PE28 . . . . 5 D1
Aynscombe CI LU6 . . . . . 120 F8

B

Back La MK44 . . . . 16 A8
BACKNOE END 18 E4
Back St
  Biggleswade SG18 . . . . . 67 A6
  Clophill MK45 . . . . 75 C1
  Luton LU2 . . . . 123 E8

BACKSTREET 75 C1
Badgers Brook LU7 . . . . 103 A1
Badgers CI MK45 . . . . 84 E3
Badgers Gate LU6 . . . . . 120 E8
Badingham Dr AL5 . . . . . 130 E1
Bagwicks CI LU3 . . . . . . 115 E7
Bailey Hill Ct LU1 . . . . . 123 E5
Bailey St LU1 . . . . 123 F6
Baileys Villas MK43 . . . . . 26 C8
Baker Ave SG19 . . . . 56 A7
Bakers CI MK43 . . . . 34 C5
Bakers Cres NN29 . . . . . . 7 A8
Baker's La SG19 . . . . 42 B8
Baker St
  Ampthill MK45 . . . . 84 E8
  Leighton Buzzard LU7 . . 111 A7
  Luton LU1 . . . . 123 E5
Bakers Wood CI LU7 . . . 103 A6
Bakery CI MK43 . . . . 59 B1
Bakery The MK43 . . . . . . 36 B7
Bakewell CI LU4 . . . . 115 C1
Balcombe CI LU2 . . . . . . 117 D4
BALDOCK 91 F2
Baldock CI LU4 . . . . 114 F3
Baldock Rd
  Letchworth SG6 . . . . . . 101 F4
  Stotfold SG5 . . . . 91 A5
Baldock Sta SG7 . . . . 91 F1
Baldur CI MK41 . . . . 39 D3
Balfour Ct AL5 . . . . 131 A1
Balham CI NN10 . . . . 7 F8
BALLINGDON BOTTOM . . 127 F1
Ballinghall CI MK41 . . . . . 39 A2
Balliol Lower Sch MK42 . . 49 D3
Balliol Rd MK42 . . . . 49 D3
Balls La MK45 . . . . 52 B8
Balmoral Ave MK40 . . . . . 38 D2
Balmoral CI
  Flitwick MK45 . . . . 84 D1
  Sandy SG19 . . . . 42 B1
Balmoral Rd SG5 . . . . . . 100 E1
Balmoral Way PE19 . . . . . 22 F2
Balmore Wood LU3 . . . . 108 B1
Balsall St E 6 MK40 . . . . . 38 B1
Balsall St W MK40 . . . . . . 38 B1
Bamburgh Dr MK41 . . . . . 39 A4
Bamford Rd MK42 . . . . . . 50 F5
Bamfords La MK43 . . . . . . 34 C5
Bamfords Yd MK43 . . . . . . 34 E5
Bampton Rd LU4 . . . . . . 115 B2
Banbury CI LU4 . . . . 115 F4
Bancroft Ave SG18 . . . . . 66 B2
Bancroft Rd LU3 . . . . . . 116 B5
Bank CI LU4 . . . . 115 C5
Banks CI MK43 . . . . 72 C7
Banks Dr SG19 . . . . 54 B7
Bankside CI LU5 . . . . . . 114 A5
Bank's Rd SG18 . . . . 67 B7
Barber End SG17 . . . . 77 D3
Barbers La 2 LU1 . . . . . 123 E7
Barclay Ct LU2 . . . . 123 F8
Barford Ave MK42 . . . . . . 50 D6
Barford Rd
  Blunham MK44 . . . . 41 C3
  St Neots PE19 . . . . 22 E2
  Willington MK44 . . . . . . 40 C7
Barford Rise LU2 . . . . . . 117 D1
Barker Dr MK43 . . . . 36 D2
Barkers CI MK45 . . . . 84 E6
Barker's La MK41 . . . . . . 51 A8
Barkers Piece MK43 . . . . . 60 D1
Barking CI LU4 . . . . 115 B6
Bar La SG19 . . . . 45 E3
Barley Brow LU6 . . . . . . 113 E3
Barleycorn CI LU7 . . . . . 111 D7
Barleycorn The 1 LU3 . . 123 D8
Barley Ct
  Rushden NN10 . . . . 8 C8
  St Neots PE19 . . . . 22 D5
Barleyfield Way LU5 . . . . 114 A4
Barley Kiln La MK43 . . . . . 25 A6
Barley La LU5 . . . . 115 C5
Barley Rd PE19 . . . . 22 C3
Barley Rise AL5 . . . . 131 C4
Barleyvale LU3 . . . . 116 A8
Barley Way MK41 . . . . 39 A3
Barnabas Rd LU7 . . . . . . 110 D6
Barnard Ave MK42 . . . . . . 49 C3
Barnard Ct PE19 . . . . 22 F1
Barnard Rd LU1 . . . . 123 D4
Barncroft MK43 . . . . 34 E6
Barndell CI SG5 . . . . 90 F6
Barnfield Ave LU2 . . . . . 116 D5
Barnfield Coll
  Luton LU2 . . . . 116 D5
  Luton LU2 . . . . 123 F8
  Luton LU3 . . . . 116 B8
Barnfield Coll South
  LU1 . . . . 123 B5
Barnhill MK41 . . . . 39 A2
Barns Dene AL5 . . . . 130 E4
Barnstaple Rd MK40 . . . . . 38 E2
Barns The
  Blunham MK44 . . . . 41 D3
  Riseley MK44 . . . . 11 A4
Barnston Ct LU2 . . . . . . 117 D1
Barnwell Dr NN10 . . . . . . 8 A8
Baron Ct PE19 . . . . 22 B4
Barons Ct 7 LU2 . . . . . . 116 D1
Barrie Ave LU3 . . . . 113 E3
Barringer Way PE19 . . . . . 22 F7
Barrington Rd
  Letchworth SG6 . . . . . . 101 F4

Barrington Rd continued
  Rushden NN10 . . . . 8 C8
Barrowby CI LU2 . . . . . . 117 D1
Barrow Path 3 LU7 . . . . 111 A8
Barton Ave LU5 . . . . 121 D8
Barton CI AL5 . . . . 131 C3
Barton Ct LU4 . . . . 115 B3
Barton Ind Est MK45 . . . . 97 F4
BARTON-LE-CLAY 97 D3
Barton Rd
  Barton-le-C MK45 . . . . . 97 B7
  Bedford MK42 . . . . 50 F5
  Gravenhurst MK45 . . . . . 87 C4
  Harlington LU5 . . . . 96 A2
  Hexton SG5 . . . . 98 A1
  Luton LU3 . . . . 116 C7
  Sharpenhoe MK45 . . . . . 96 F2
  Silsoe MK45 . . . . 86 C3
Bartram CI MK42 . . . . 49 C3
Bartram Rd MK42 . . . . . . 49 C3
Basildon Ct LU7 . . . . 110 F7
Bassett Ct LU7 . . . . 110 F7
Bassett Rd LU7 . . . . 110 F7
Bassie Rd MK42 . . . . 50 C6
Bassmead Manor La PE19 21 C6
Batcheldor Gdns MK43 . . . 36 E1
BATFORD 131 D3
Batford Rd AL5 . . . . 131 D3
Bath Abbey MK41 . . . . . . 51 B8
Bath PI SG17 . . . . 78 B3
Bath Rd LU3 . . . . 116 D2
Battison St MK40 . . . . 50 B8
Battle Abbey MK41 . . . . . 39 B1
Battlesden Ave MK17 . . . 104 C8
Baulk The
  Beeston SG19 . . . . 54 B6
  Biggleswade SG18 . . . . . 67 B6
  Clapham MK41 . . . . 37 F7
  Lilley SG5 . . . . 109 D2
  Potton SG19 . . . . 56 C5
Baxter Dr PE19 . . . . 22 E2
Bay CI LU4 . . . . 115 B6
Bayham CI MK42 . . . . 50 D3
Baylam Dell LU2 . . . . . . 117 E1
Baylie Rd PE19 . . . . 22 B2
Beachampstead Rd PE19 . 13 F6
Beacon Ave LU6 . . . . . . 120 E7
Beacon Rd HP4 . . . . 126 C1
Beaconsfield LU2 . . . . . . 124 B8
Beaconsfield St MK41 . . . . 38 B2
Beacon View LU7 . . . . . . 112 D5
BEADLOW 76 B1
Beadlow Rd LU4 . . . . 114 F4
Beale St LU6 . . . . 114 A1
Beamish CI SG19 . . . . 42 C2
Beancroft Rd MK43 . . . . . 60 B1
Beanley Ct LU2 . . . . 117 E2
Bearton Ct SG5 . . . . 100 E1
Bearton Gn SG5 . . . . 100 D1
Bearton Rd SG5 . . . . 100 E1
Beatrice St MK42 . . . . 50 A5
Beatty Rd PE19 . . . . 22 B2
Beauchamp CI PE19 . . . . . 22 B3
Beauchamp Ct 9 MK40 . . . 38 A1
Beauchamp Mid Sch
  MK41 . . . . 38 C5
Beauchamp Rd MK43 . . . . 61 A7
Beaudesert LU7 . . . . 111 A7
Beaudesert Lower Sch
  LU7 . . . . 111 D8
Beaufort Way AL5 . . . . . . 38 C5
Beaulieu Way MK41 . . . . . 38 E5
Beaumanor PI SG17 . . . . . 76 E3
Beaumont Ct
  Flitwick MK45 . . . . 84 E3
  10 Harpenden AL5 . . . . 131 B1
Beaumont Gdns MK42 . . . 49 E3
Beaumont Ho MK40 . . . . . 37 F2
Beaumont Rd
  Flitwick MK45 . . . . 84 E3
  Luton LU3 . . . . 116 B2
Beaver CI PE19 . . . . 22 B5
Becher CI MK41 . . . . 39 F5
Beckerings Park Rd MK43 83 A6
Beckett Ct 3 MK40 . . . . . 50 B8
Becketts CI MK45 . . . . . . 74 B1
Beckett St MK40 . . . . 50 B8
Beckham CI LU2 . . . . 116 D7
Becks CI AL3 . . . . 128 D5
Bec Rd PE19 . . . . 22 E5
Bedesman La MK42 . . . . . 50 A7
BEDFORD 50 D7
Bedford Autodrome
  MK44 . . . . 18 A6
Bedford Ave MK45 . . . . . . 86 C4
Bedford Bsns Ctr MK42 . . 50 D4
Bedford Butterfly Pk★
  MK44 . . . . 29 F1
Bedford CI SG5 . . . . 87 E2
Bedford Coll MK42 . . . . . 50 B7
Bedford CI LU5 . . . . 114 B5
Bedford CI 3 LU2 . . . . . 123 D8
Bedford High Sch MK40 . . 38 B1
Bedford Hospl (North Wing)
  MK40 . . . . 38 A3
Bedford Hospl (South Wing-
  main site) MK42 . . . . . . 50 F8
Bedford Int Athletic Stadium
  MK41 . . . . 50 F8
Bedford Modern Sch
  MK41 . . . . 38 A3
Bedford Mus★ MK40 . . . . 50 C8
Bedford Rd
  Aspley Guise MK17 . . . . 81 F5
  Barton-le-C MK45 . . . . . 97 C3
  Brogborough MK43 . . . . 82 C8
  Cardington MK44 . . . . . 51 C5
  Clapham MK41 . . . . 37 F5
  Clophill MK45 . . . . 86 C8

Bedford Rd continued
  Cold Brayfield MK46 . . . . 34 B5
  Cranfield MK43 . . . . 59 C2
  Cranfield MK43 . . . . 60 A3
  Great Barford SG18 . . . . 40 E4
  Haynes SG18 . . . . 64 E5
  Hitchin SG5 . . . . 100 D3
  Hitchin, Westmill SG5 . . 100 D1
  Houghton Conquest MK45 62 A1
  Houghton Regis LU5 . . . 114 A6
  Kempston Hardwick MK45 61 D7
  Kempston MK42 . . . . . . 49 E4
  Letchworth SG6 . . . . . . 101 D7
  Lower Stondon SG16 . . . 89 B3
  Marston Moretaine MK43 . 72 D8
  Milton Ernest MK44 . . . . 27 B3
  Moggerhanger MK44 . . . . 53 B7
  Northill SG18 . . . . 53 B2
  Ravensden MK44 . . . . . . 28 E1
  Roxton MK44 . . . . 31 E2
  Rushden NN10 . . . . 8 D5
  Sandy SG19 . . . . 54 B7
  Shefford SG17 . . . . 77 B4
  Stagsden MK43 . . . . 36 C1
  Turvey MK43 . . . . 35 B5
  Wick End MK43 . . . . 48 B8
  Willington MK44 . . . . . . 52 B7
  Wilstead, Duck End MK45 . 62 D7
  Wilstead MK45 . . . . 62 D5
  Wootton MK43 . . . . 61 A8
Bedford RFC MK40 . . . . . 38 D1
Bedford Road Lower Sch
  MK42 . . . . 49 E4
Bedford St Johns Halt
  MK42 . . . . 50 B7
Bedford Sch MK40 . . . . . 38 C1
Bedford Sq LU5 . . . . 114 B5
Bedford St
  Ampthill MK45 . . . . 73 E1
  Leighton Buzzard LU7 . . 111 A7
  St Neots PE19 . . . . 22 E6
  Woburn MK17 . . . . 92 E1
Bedford Sta MK40 . . . . . . 50 A8
Beeby Way MK43 . . . . . . 25 A3
Beech Ave
  Biggleswade SG18 . . . . . 66 F8
  Wilstead MK45 . . . . 62 F2
Beech CI
  Dunstable LU6 . . . . . . 121 E5
  Greenfield MK45 . . . . . . 85 D2
Beech Cres NN29 . . . . . . 7 A7
Beech Ct
  5 Bedford MK40 . . . . . . 38 A1
  Harpenden AL5 . . . . . . 130 F3
Beechdale Rd MK42 . . . . . 50 C5
Beeches The MK45 . . . . . 86 C4
Beech Gn LU6 . . . . 114 A1
Beech Gr
  Leighton Buzzard LU7 . . 110 E7
  St Neots PE19 . . . . 22 F6
Beech Hill
  Letchworth SG6 . . . . . . 101 D8
  Luton LU2 . . . . 117 D8
Beech Hill Com Prim Sch
  LU4 . . . . 116 B1
Beech Ho PE19 . . . . 22 F3
Beeching CI AL5 . . . . . . 131 B4
Beech Rd
  Dunstable LU6 . . . . . . 121 E4
  Flitwick MK45 . . . . 84 F2
  Luton LU1 . . . . 123 C8
Beech Ridge AL5 . . . . . . 130 B5
Beechside SG19 . . . . 44 C6
Beech Tree Way LU5 . . . 114 B5
Beechwood CI SG5 . . . . . 100 D2
Beechwood CI LU6 . . . . . 120 F7
Beechwood Park Sch
  AL3 . . . . 128 B1
Beechwood Prim Sch
  LU4 . . . . 115 E3
Beechwood Rd LU4 . . . . . 115 E3
Beechwood Rise SG17 . . . 77 D2
BEECROFT 113 F1
Beecroft Lower Sch LU6 . 113 F1
Beecroft Way LU6 . . . . . 121 A8
BEESTON 54 B4
Beeston Gn SG19 . . . . . . 54 B5
Beezling CI PE19 . . . . 22 C6
Begwarie PI PE19 . . . . . . 22 B5
Belam Way SG19 . . . . . . 42 B1
Belfry CI MK42 . . . . 50 B4
Belfry Ct SG19 . . . . 54 C7
Belfry The LU2 . . . . 116 E6
Belgrave Rd LU4 . . . . . . 115 D5
Bell Alley 9 LU7 . . . . . . 111 A7
Bellamy CI PE19 . . . . 22 E2
Bellamy Rd MK43 . . . . . . 60 F6
Bell CI MK45 . . . . 95 E6
Bellerby Rise LU4 . . . . . 115 B6
Bellevue CI SG19 . . . . . . 55 F7
Bell Foundry CI SG19 . . . 44 D5
Bellingham PI SG18 . . . . . 67 B7
Bell La MK45 . . . . 63 D7
Bells CI SG5 . . . . 87 F1
Bell's Ct MK42 . . . . 51 A3
Bellway MK17 . . . . 81 A6
Belmont Rd LU1 . . . . 123 C7
Belper Rd LU4 . . . . 115 D2
Belsize Rd LU4 . . . . 114 F3
Belvedere Rd LU3 . . . . . 116 B5
Belvoir Wlk MK41 . . . . . . 39 A4
Bembridge Gdns LU3 . . . 115 F7
Benedict CI NN10 . . . . . . 7 F8
Benington Ct LU2 . . . . . . 116 F5
Bennett Ct SG6 . . . . 101 F6
Bennetts CI
  Bletsoe MK44 . . . . 17 C1

Bennetts Cl continued
Dunstable LU6 . . . . 121 B7
Benning Ave LU6 . . . . 121 A8
Benson Cl LU3 . . . . 115 F7
Bentley Cl SG18 . . . . 78 F6
Bentley Ct LU1 . . . . 123 C8
Bentley Mews SG17 . . . . . . 77 B2
Bents Cl MK41 . . . . 37 D7
Berberry Dr MK45 . . . . 85 E4
Bereford Cl MK44 . . . . 40 F5
Beresford Rd
Bedford MK40 . . . . 50 E8
Luton LU4 . . . . 116 A1
Berkeley Cl SG18 . . . . 67 A4
Berkeley Ct 6 AL5 . . . . . . 131 C4
Berkeley Path 2 LU2 . . . . 123 E8
Berkeley Rd MK42 . . . . 50 C4
Berkley Ct PE19 . . . . 22 E4
Berkley St PE19 . . . . 22 F4
Bernard Cl LU5 . . . . 114 C1
Berrill St NN29 . . . . 7 A7
Berrow Cl LU2 . . . . 117 E2
Berry Dr MK43 . . . . 36 E2
Berry End MK17 . . . . 83 A1
Berry La MK17 . . . . 81 F6
Berry Leys LU3 . . . . 115 E7
Berwick Way SG19 . . . . . . 54 C8
Besford Cl LU2 . . . . 117 E2
Bessemer Cl SG5 . . . . 100 E2
Bethune Cl LU1 . . . . 123 B6
Betjeman Cl AL5 . . . . 131 C1
Betony Wlk NN10 . . . . .8 B8
Beverley Cres MK40 . . . . . 37 F1
Beverley Gdns MK45 . . . . . 86 C8
Beverley Gn MK40 . . . . . . 37 E1
Beverley Rd LU4 . . . . 115 F1
Bevery MK43 . . . . 37 A8
Bevington Way PE19 . . . . . 22 E2
Bewcastle Cl MK41 . . . . . . 39 A5
Bewdley Dr LU7 . . . . 110 C7
Bexhill Rd LU2 . . . . 117 D2
Bibshall Cres LU6 . . . . . . 121 C6
BIDDENHAM 37 C1
Biddenham Turn MK40 . . . 37 E1
Biddenham Upper Sch
MK40 . . . . 49 D8
Bideford Ct LU7 . . . . 110 C7
Bideford Gdns LU3 . . . . . 116 D4
Bideford Gn LU7 . . . . 110 C8
BIDWELL 114 A6
Bidwell Hill LU5 . . . . 114 B5
Bidwell Path LU5 . . . . . . 114 B4
BIGGLESWADE 67 C8
Biggleswade Hospl SG18 . 67 C8
Biggleswade Rd
Dunton SG18 . . . . 68 B5
Sutton SG19 . . . . 55 E4
Upper Caldecote SG18 . . . 66 C8
Biggleswade Sta SG18 . . . 67 A5
Bigthan Rd LU3 . . . . 121 C8
Bilberry Cl PE19 . . . . 22 C5
Bilberry Rd SG17 . . . . 78 B3
BILLINGTON 111 E2
Billington Cl MK45 . . . . . . 84 D3
Billington Ct LU7 . . . . . . 111 B6
Billington Rd
Billington LU7 . . . . 112 A2
Stanbridge LU7 . . . . . . 112 B4
Bilsdon Cl NN10 . . . . .7 F8
Bilton Rd SG4 . . . . 100 F2
Bilton Way LU1 . . . . 115 F1
Binder Cl LU4 . . . . 114 E4
Bindon Abbey MK41 . . . . . 51 A8
Bingen Rd SG5 . . . . 100 C1
Binham Cl LU2 . . . . 116 D2
Birbeck Cl MK41 . . . . 37 C7
Birch Cl
Broom SG18 . . . . 66 C2
Clifton SG17 . . . . 77 F2
Cranfield MK43 . . . . 59 C3
Birchdale Ave MK42 . . . . . 49 F4
Birchen Gr LU2 . . . . 116 F3
Birches The
Flitwick MK45 . . . . 84 D5
Letchworth SG6 . . . . . . 101 E8
Birchfield Rd MK44 . . . . . 40 E7
Birch Gr
Lower Stondon SG16 . . . 89 B3
Sandy SG19 . . . . 54 B6
Birch Link LU4 . . . . 116 C1
Birchmead 44 C6
BIRCHMOOR GREEN 92 E8
Birch Rd SG18 . . . . 67 A7
Birch's Cl LU7 . . . . 104 C3
Birch Side LU6 . . . . 121 D6
Bird Ct MK45 . . . . 62 E4
Birdsfoot La LU3 . . . . 116 B6
Bird's Hill LU7 . . . . 103 A5
Birds of Prey Ctr SG18 . . . 65 D5
Birkdale Rd MK41 . . . . 38 E5
Birling Dr LU2 . . . . 117 C4
Birse Gn MK41 . . . . 39 B4
Birtley Croft LU2 . . . . 117 E1
BISCOT 116 C2
Biscot Rd LU3 . . . . 116 C2
Bishop Cl LU7 . . . . 111 D6
Bishopscote Rd LU3 . . . . 116 B3
Bishops Ct 6 LU3 . . . . . . 116 D1
Bishops Rd
Bedford MK41 . . . . 39 B1
St Neots PE19 . . . . 22 E4
Bishopstone Ct MK40 . . . . 50 A8
Bishops Wlk MK17 . . . . . . 81 B3
Bittern Cl MK45 . . . . 84 D2
Bittern Way SG6 . . . . 90 E1
Blackbird Cl MK45 . . . . . . 84 D2
Blackbird St SG19 . . . . . . 56 A7

Blackbirds The LU7 . . . . . 104 E2
Blackburn Cl MK42 . . . . . . 51 B2
Blackburn Rd LU5 . . . . . . 114 B3
Blackfriars NN10 . . . . .7 B8
Black Hat LU5 . . . . 62 E4
Blackhill LU7 . . . . 112 F5
Blackhill La MK45 . . . . 96 E8
Blacksmith Cl
Everton SG19 . . . . 43 C3
Stotfold SG5 . . . . 90 F7
Blacksmith Ct 3 LU6 . . . 121 B8
Black Swan La LU3 . . . . . . 116 A5
Blackthorn Dr LU2 . . . . . . 117 C4
Blackthorn Rd MK41 . . . . . 81 A4
Black Thorn Rd LU5 . . . . . 114 C6
Blackwood Rd PE19 . . . . . 22 B2
Blair Way PE19 . . . . 22 E2
Blakedown Cl LU2 . . . . . . 116 E1
Blakedown Rd LU7 . . . . . . 110 C7
Blakelands MK45 . . . . 97 D2
Blakeney Dr LU2 . . . . 116 C7
Blakes Way PE19 . . . . 22 B2
Blandford Ave LU2 . . . . . . 116 D6
Blaydon Rd
Luton LU2 . . . . 124 A8
Sandy SG19 . . . . 42 C2
Blenheim Cl
Rushden NN10 . . . . 8 A8
St Neots PE19 . . . . 22 C4
Blenheim Cres LU3 . . . . . 116 C2
Blenheim Link MK45 . . . . . 84 D1
Blenheim Rd MK42 . . . . . . 51 A2
BLETSOE 17 C1
Bliss Ave
Cranfield MK43 . . . . 59 C2
Shefford SG17 . . . . 77 D3
Bloomfield Ave LU2 . . . . . 117 A1
Bloomfield Dr SG17 . . . . . 77 B2
Bloomfield Rd AL5 . . . . . 130 F3
Bloomsbury Cl MK17 . . . . 92 F6
Bloomsbury Gdns LU5 . . . 114 D5
Blows Rd LU5 . . . . 121 D7
Bluebell Cl
Bedford MK42 . . . . 50 F4
Biggleswade SG18 . . . . . 67 C4
Flitwick MK45 . . . . 84 D3
Bluebell Dr SG16 . . . . 89 A3
Bluebell Rise NN10 . . . . . . .8 B8
Bluebell Wood Cl LU1 . . . 123 A7
Blue Spruce Cl MK43 . . . . 36 C4
Blundell Pl MK42 . . . . 50 C4
Blundell Rd LU3 . . . . 116 A4
BLUNHAM 41 E3
Blunham Rd
Biggleswade SG18 . . . . . 66 F5
Moggerhanger MK44 . . . . 53 C8
Blythe Way SG19 . . . . 44 D5
Blyth Pl 12 MK42 . . . . 51 A1
Boddington Gdns SG18 . . . 67 C7
Boddington Ind Est SG18 . 67 B6
Bodiam Way PE19 . . . . 22 F2
Bodmin Rd LU4 . . . . 115 F3
Bolingbroke Rd LU1 . . . . . 123 B6
Bolney Gn LU2 . . . . 117 D3
BOLNHURST 19 D4
Bolton Rd LU1 . . . . 123 E7
Bond Cl AL5 . . . . 130 F3
Bonds La SG18 . . . . 67 A5
Bonnick Cl LU1 . . . . 123 C6
Boothey Cl SG18 . . . . 67 A7
Booth Pl LU6 . . . . 119 E6
Boot La SG18 . . . . 68 D5
Borden La SG18 . . . . 64 C5
Borders Way LU5 . . . . 114 C6
Borodale AL5 . . . . 131 A1
Borough Rd LU5 . . . . 121 D7
Borrowdale Ave LU6 . . . . . 121 C6
Borton Ave SG16 . . . . 89 B4
Boscombe Rd LU5 . . . . . . 114 C2
Bosmore Rd LU3 . . . . 115 F5
Bossard Ct LU7 . . . . 111 A7
Bossington La
Leighton Buzzard, Linslade
LU7 . . . . 110 F7
Leighton Buzzard LU7 . . 110 F8
Boswell Ct 13 MK40 . . . . . 38 B1
Boswell Dr SG5 . . . . 100 E4
Boswell Pl 8 MK40 . . . . . . 38 B1
Boteler Gdns MK42 . . . . . . 50 F5
Bothy The SG18 . . . . 66 C2
BOTT END 61 A7
Bottom Dr LU6 . . . . 120 D5
Boughton Dr NN10 . . . . 8 A8
BOUGHTON END 83 A8
Boughton End La MK43 . . . 72 B1
Boundary The MK41 . . . . . 39 A2
Bourne Apts The 2 AL5 . . 130 F2
BOURNE END
MK43 . . . . 59 C6
MK44 . . . . 17 C6
Bourne End La MK44 . . . . 17 B4
Bourne End Rd
Cranfield MK43 . . . . 59 C4
Kempston MK43 . . . . 48 B1
Bourne Rd MK44 . . . . 10 F2
Bourneside MK41 . . . . 38 D6
Bourne The 1 AL5 . . . . . 130 F2
Bow Brickhill Rd MK17 . . . 81 A4
Bowbrook Vale LU2 . . . . . 117 D3
Bower Cl LU6 . . . . 119 F5
Bower Heath La AL5 . . . . 131 C6
Bower La LU6 . . . . 119 F5
Bowers Cl MK44 . . . . 11 B3
Bowers La MK44 . . . . 11 B3
Bower's Mill PE19 . . . . 22 E5
Bower's Par AL5 . . . . 131 A1
Bower St MK40 . . . . 50 D8
Bowers Way AL5 . . . . 131 A1

Bowhill MK41 . . . . 38 F3
Bowland Cres LU6 . . . . . . 121 A6
Bowles Way LU6 . . . . 121 D5
Bowling Green La LU2 . . . 116 E2
Bowling Green Rd MK43 . . 59 C1
Bowmans Cl LU6 . . . . 121 C7
Bowmans Way LU6 . . . . . . 121 C7
Bowyer's Cl SG5 . . . . 100 D1
BOX END 48 F6
Box End Rd MK43 . . . . 48 F7
Boxgrove Cl LU2 . . . . 117 C5
Boxgrove Priory MK41 . . . . 39 B1
Boxted Cl LU5 . . . . 115 C5
Boyde Gdns MK40 . . . . . . 49 E7
Boyle Ct LU2 . . . . 123 E8
Brabazon Cl MK42 . . . . . . 51 A2
Braceby Cl LU3 . . . . 115 F6
Brace St 16 MK40 . . . . 50 B8
Brache The MK45 . . . . 74 C1
Brackendale Gr
Harpenden AL5 . . . . 130 D3
Luton LU3 . . . . 116 B5
Bracken Pl MK41 . . . . 39 B1
Bracklesham Gdns LU2 . . 117 B3
Brackley Rd MK42 . . . . 50 C5
Bracknell Cl LU4 . . . . 114 F3
Bradden Cotts HP2 . . . . . 132 F8
Bradden La HP1, HP2 . . . 132 E7
Bradden Villas HP2 . . . . . 132 F8
Bradford Rd LU5 . . . . 106 A5
Bradgate Rd MK40 . . . . . . 38 D1
Bradgers Hill Rd LU2 . . . . 116 E4
Bradley Rd LU4 . . . . 115 F7
Bradleys Cnr SG4 . . . . . . 101 C1
Bradshaws Cl MK45 . . . . . 97 C3
Braemar Ct MK40 . . . . 50 A8
Braeside MK41 . . . . 38 F4
BRAGENHAM 102 C6
Bragenham La LU7 . . . . . 102 D5
Braggs La SG19 . . . . 57 C4
Braintree Cl LU4 . . . . 114 F3
Braithwaite Ct 16 LU3 . . . 116 D1
Bramble Cl
Harpenden AL5 . . . . 130 F3
Leighton Buzzard LU7 . . 111 C7
Luton LU4 . . . . 115 C4
Bramble Rd LU4 . . . . 115 C4
Brambles MK45 . . . . 62 F4
Brambles The MK45 . . . . . 85 F4
Brambling Cl MK45 . . . . . . 42 C2
Bramhanger Acre LU3 . . . 115 D7
Bramingham Bsns Pk
LU3 . . . . 116 B8
Bramingham Prim Sch
LU3 . . . . 116 B8
Bramingham Rd LU3 . . . . 115 F6
Bramley Cl
Baldock SG7 . . . . 91 F1
Shefford SG17 . . . . 77 B2
Bramley Ct MK43 . . . . 24 F6
Brampton Cl
Bedford MK42 . . . . 50 F5
Harpenden AL5 . . . . 131 C1
Brampton Park Rd SG5 . . 100 E1
Brampton Rise LU6 . . . . . 121 C6
Brancaster Cl MK42 . . . . . 50 F4
Brancker Ave MK42 . . . . . . 51 A2
Brandreth Ave LU4 . . . . . 114 E1
Brandreth Pl SG19 . . . . . . 54 D6
Brangwyn Gdns MK41 . . . . 38 B3
Branton Cl LU2 . . . . 117 C2
Brantwood Rd LU1 . . . . . . 123 C7
Braybrook SG19 . . . . 54 A8
Braybrooks Dr SG19 . . . . . 56 A7
Brayes Manor SG5 . . . . . . 90 F6
Brays Ct LU2 . . . . 117 B3
Brays Rd LU2 . . . . 117 B3
Brazier Cl MK45 . . . . 97 B3
Breachwell Pl LU7 . . . . . . 118 A1
BREACHWOOD GREEN . . 125 D8
Breadcroft La AL5 . . . . . . 131 B1
Breamish Wlk MK41 . . . . . 38 C7
Brecon Cl LU1 . . . . 123 D6
Brecon Way MK41 . . . . . . 38 E5
Brendon Ave
Bedford MK41 . . . . 38 E3
Luton LU2 . . . . 117 C1
Brentwood Cl LU5 . . . . . . 114 D6
Brereton Rd MK40 . . . . . . 50 B8
Brett Dr MK43 . . . . 36 F1
Bretts Mead LU1 . . . . 123 C5
Bretts Mead Ct LU1 . . . . . 123 C5
Brewers Hill Mid Sch
LU6 . . . . 113 E1
Brewers Hill Rd LU6 . . . . 113 F1
Brewery La
Ampthill MK45 . . . . 73 C1
Baldock SG7 . . . . 91 E1
Brian May Gr MK43 . . . . . . 86 B3
Brian Rd LU5 . . . . 96 A2
Briar Bank Cvn Pk MK45 . . 62 F2
Briar Cl
Ampthill MK45 . . . . 84 E8
Luton LU2 . . . . 117 C4
Briar Patch La SG6 . . . . . 101 D3
Briars The MK42 . . . . 49 F3
Brickfield Rd MK41 . . . . . . 39 B6
BRICKHILL 38 C4
Brickhill Cl
Blunham MK44 . . . . 41 E3
Sandy SG19 . . . . 54 D8
Brickhill Dr MK41 . . . . 38 C4
Brickhill La LU1 . . . . 129 C8
Brickhill Lower Sch MK41 . 38 D5
Brickhill Rd
Heath and Reach LU7 . . 103 A7

Brickhill Rd continued
Sandy SG19 . . . . 54 D7
Brickle Pl SG17 . . . . 78 B2
Brickly Rd LU4 . . . . 115 C5
Bridge Ct AL5 . . . . 130 F3
BRIDGE END 36 E2
Bridgeman Dr LU5 . . . . . . 114 D5
Bridgend MK43 . . . . 25 B4
Bridge Rd
Bedford MK42 . . . . 50 C6
Letchworth SG6 . . . . . . 101 F6
Bridge St
Leighton Buzzard LU7 . . 110 F7
Luton LU2 . . . . 123 E8
Turvey MK43 . . . . 34 D5
Bridge View MK40 . . . . 50 D8
Bridle Dr MK41 . . . . 37 C7
Brierley Cl
Dunstable LU6 . . . . 121 D5
Luton LU2 . . . . 117 D2
Briggington Cotts LU7 . . . 111 D8
Brigham Gdns SG18 . . . . . 67 A6
Brightman Cotts 2 LU3 . . 116 A7
Brightmans Dr MK45 . . . . . 74 B1
Brightwell Ave LU6 . . . . . 120 C7
Brill Cl LU2 . . . . 117 D2
Brimfield Cl LU2 . . . . 117 D2
Brindley Cl SG19 . . . . 42 B1
Brinsmade Rd MK45 . . . . . 73 F1
Bristol Rd LU3 . . . . 116 B4
Britannia Ave LU3 . . . . . . 116 B4
Britannia Ests LU3 . . . . . 116 B4
Britannia Hall LU2 . . . . . 124 C8
Britannia Rd MK42 . . . . . . 50 B6
Brittains Rise SG16 . . . . . . 88 E2
Brittany Ct LU1 . . . . 121 C8
Brittaniere Rise SG16 . . . . 88 E2
Britten Cl NN9 . . . . 3 C8
Britten Rd SG17 . . . . 77 D3
Brittons Cl MK44 . . . . 16 E3
Brittons La MK17 . . . . 70 C3
Brive Rd LU5 . . . . 121 E6
Brixham Ct MK40 . . . . 38 E2
Broadacres LU2 . . . . 116 D6
Broad Ave MK42 . . . . 50 D4
Broadcroft SG6 . . . . 101 E5
Broadfields AL5 . . . . 130 F2
BROAD GREEN 59 B3
Broadhurst Abbey MK41 . . 51 A8
Broadmead SG18 . . . . 67 B5
Broad Mead LU3 . . . . 116 A3
Broadmead Bsns Pk
MK43 . . . . 61 C2
Broadmead Lower Sch
MK43 . . . . 61 C2
Broadmead Rd MK43 . . . . 61 C2
Broadmead Sch LU3 . . . . 123 E5
Broad Oak Ct LU2 . . . . . . 117 D3
Broad Rush Gn LU7 . . . . . 110 E8
Broad St SG17 . . . . 78 B2
Broadwater Ave SG6 . . . . 101 E5
Broadwater Dale SG6 . . . . 101 E5
Broadway
Houghton Conquest MK45 . 74 B8
Letchworth SG6 . . . . . . 101 F5
Broadway Ct SG6 . . . . . . 101 E3
Broadway The MK40 . . . . . 38 B1
Broad Wlk
Clifton SG17 . . . . 78 B2
Dunstable LU6 . . . . 121 B8
Broad Wlk The PE19 . . . . . 22 E3
Brocas Way LU7 . . . . 118 A3
Brocket Ct LU4 . . . . 115 D5
Brockwell MK43 . . . . 37 A8
Brockwood Cl SG19 . . . . . 44 D6
BROGBOROUGH 71 C1
BROMHAM 36 F3
Bromham CE Lower Sch
MK43 . . . . 36 F3
Bromham Mill ★ MK43 . . . 37 A2
Bromham Rd
Biddenham MK40 . . . . . . 37 D1
Bromham MK40 . . . . 37 A2
Bromley Gdns LU5 . . . . . 114 D5
Brompton Cl LU3 . . . . 115 F8
Bronte Ave SG5 . . . . 90 C2
Brook Cl
7 Dunstable LU6 . . . . . 114 A1
Henlow SG16 . . . . 78 D1
Upper Caldecote SG18 . . 66 B8
Brook Ct LU3 . . . . 116 D1
Brook Dr MK42 . . . . 49 C3
BROOK END
MK17 . . . . 94 A6
MK44 . . . . 12 B3
SG5 . . . . 90 E5
SG19 . . . . 54 A4
Brook End
North Crawley MK16 . . . 58 A6
Potton SG19 . . . . 56 A7
Brookend Dr MK45 . . . . . . 97 B3
Brookes Rd MK45 . . . . 84 F3
Brook Farm Ct NN10 . . . . . 8 B5
Brookfield Ave LU5 . . . . . 114 C5
Brookfield Pk LU5 . . . . . . 114 C5
Brookfield Pk Cvn Pk
LU6 . . . . 120 A8
Brookfield Rd MK41 . . . . . 38 F7
Brookfields
Pavenham MK43 . . . . . . 26 C4
Potton SG19 . . . . 56 B7
Brook La
Flitton MK45 . . . . 85 D4
Great Barford MK44 . . . . 41 A5
Harrold MK43 . . . . 24 B3
Newton Blossomville MK43 . 34 A3
Renhold MK41 . . . . 39 B6
Upper Dean PE28 . . . . . . 5 B4

Brooklands MK42 . . . . 49 E2
Brooklands Ave LU7 . . . . . 111 B6
Brooklands Cl LU4 . . . . . . 115 C6
Brooklands Dr LU7 . . . . . . 111 C7
Brooklands Mid Sch LU7 . 111 C6
Brooklands Rd MK44 . . . . . 10 F1
Brookmead SG17 . . . . 88 C6
Brook Rd
Marston Moretaine MK43 . 73 D6
St Neots PE19 . . . . 22 C4
Brookside
Campton SG17 . . . . 87 F8
Great Barford MK44 . . . . 41 A5
Letchworth SG6 . . . . . . 101 F5
Meppershall SG17 . . . . . 88 C6
Renhold MK41 . . . . 39 B7
Shillington SG5 . . . . 87 E1
Brookside Wlk LU7 . . . . . 111 C7
Brook St
Bedford MK42 . . . . 50 D5
Edlesborough LU6 . . . . . 119 F4
Hargrave NN9 . . . . 1 E3
Leighton Buzzard LU7 . . 111 C7
Luton LU3 . . . . 123 D8
St Neots PE19 . . . . 22 E5
Stotfold SG5 . . . . 90 E6
Brookvale SG16 . . . . 88 E3
Brook Way MK43 . . . . 36 E2
BROOM 66 C3
Broom Crossroads SG18 . . 66 A1
Broom Hall SG18 . . . . 66 C2
Broomhills Rd LU7 . . . . . 103 A1
Brooms Rd LU2 . . . . 124 A8
Broomstick Ind Est LU6 . 119 E4
Broughton Ave
Luton LU3 . . . . 116 C5
Toddington LU5 . . . . 105 E6
Broughton Rd MK17 . . . . . 70 C3
Browning Cl
Bromham MK43 . . . . 36 E2
Rushden NN10 . . . . 8 D8
Browning Dr PE19 . . . . . . 22 C6
Browning Rd
Harpenden AL5 . . . . 131 C2
Luton LU4 . . . . 115 A2
Brownlow Ave LU6 . . . . . 119 F3
Brownlow Rise LU6 . . . . . 120 A8
Browns Cl MK43 . . . . 72 D7
Brown's Cl LU3 . . . . 115 D5
Browns Cres LU5 . . . . 95 F3
Browns Ct MK40 . . . . 50 C8
Brownshill MK45 . . . . 74 C1
Browns La MK43 . . . . 60 F6
Brownslea LU7 . . . . 111 C7
Brown's Sq PE19 . . . . 22 F5
Browns Way MK17 . . . . . . 81 E5
Broxley Mead LU4 . . . . . . 115 D5
Bruce Rd MK42 . . . . 49 D3
Brunel Cl LU4 . . . . 114 E3
Brunel Dr SG18 . . . . 67 A4
Brunel Rd
Bedford MK41 . . . . 51 A8
Luton LU4 . . . . 114 E3
Brunswick Cl SG18 . . . . . 67 A6
Brunswick St LU2 . . . . . . 123 F8
Brunt's La SG18 . . . . 66 F6
Brussels Way LU3 . . . . . . 115 D8
Bruthwaite Gn MK41 . . . . . 39 C4
Bryans Cres MK16 . . . . . . 58 A6
Bryant Ct AL5 . . . . 131 A3
Bryants Cl SG5 . . . . 87 F2
Bryant Way LU5 . . . . 105 F5
Bryony Cl MK41 . . . . 39 B1
Bryony Way LU6 . . . . 113 C1
Buchanan Ct LU2 . . . . . . 124 B8
Buchanan Dr LU2 . . . . . . 124 B8
Buckfast Ave MK41 . . . . . . 38 F5
Buckingham Dr LU2 . . . . . 117 D2
Buckingham Mews MK45 . 84 D1
Buckle Cl LU3 . . . . 115 F7
Buckley Rd PE19 . . . . 22 E4
Bucks Cl MK43 . . . . 36 F2
Buckwood Ave LU5 . . . . . 114 F1
Buckwood La LU6 . . . . . . 127 C7
Buckwood Rd AL3 . . . . . . 128 C6
BUDNA 53 C3
Budna Rd SG19 . . . . 53 C4
Buff La SG19 . . . . 45 F1
Bull Pond La LU6 . . . . . . 121 B7
Bull St SG19 . . . . 56 A7
Bungalows The
Harpenden AL5 . . . . 131 C3
Toddington LU5 . . . . 106 A7
Bunhill Cl LU6 . . . . 120 F8
Bunkers Dr MK45 . . . . 63 D7
Bunkers La LU7 . . . . 110 D6
Bunting Rd LU4 . . . . 115 A4
Buntings The
Bedford MK41 . . . . 38 D4
Sandy SG19 . . . . 42 C2
Bunyan Cl
Clifton SG17 . . . . 78 A2
Gamlingay SG19 . . . . . . 44 D4
Houghton Conquest MK45 . 74 A8
Pirton SG5 . . . . 99 D4
Bunyan Ctr MK42 . . . . 50 E4
Bunyan Meeting Ho & Mus ★
MK40 . . . . 50 C8
Bunyan Rd
Bedford MK42 . . . . 50 B5
Biggleswade SG18 . . . . . 67 A5
Kempston MK42 . . . . 49 E3
Sandy SG19 . . . . 42 B1
Westoning MK45 . . . . 95 E5
Bunyans Cl LU3 . . . . 116 A5

Bunyans Mead MK42 . . . . . **50** C3
Bunyans Wlk LU5 . . . . **95** F2
Burdett's Ct SG19 . . . . . . **56** A7
Bure Cl MK41 . . . . **38** D6
Burfield Ct LU2 . . . . **117** D3
Burford Cl LU3 . . . . **108** A1
Burford Way SG5 . . . . . . **100** D2
Burford Wlk LU5 . . . . **114** E5
BURGE END **99** C5
Burge End La SG5 . . . . . . **99** C5
Burges Cl LU6 . . . . **121** D6
Burgess Cl
 Haynes MK45 . . . . **75** F8
 Kempston MK42 . . . . . . **49** D6
Burgess Way SG16 . . . . . **78** D3
Burghley Cl MK45 . . . . . . **84** C1
Burgoyne Mid Sch SG19 . . **55** F7
Burgoyne Ct SG19 . . . . . . **56** A8
Burleigh Pl MK43 . . . . **37** A8
Burley SG6 . . . . **90** F2
Burnaby Rd MK40 . . . . **38** C1
Burnell Rise SG6 . . . . **101** D5
Burnell Wlk SG6 . . . . **101** E5
Burnett Ave SG16 . . . . . . **89** B4
Burnham Rd LU2 . . . . **117** B2
Burnt Cl
 Luton LU3 . . . . **115** F7
 St Neots PE19 . . . . **22** F3
Burr Cl MK45 . . . . **97** C4
Burridge Cl MK43 . . . . . . **72** D8
Burridge's Cl MK43 . . . . . **36** C7
Burrows Cl
 Clifton SG17 . . . . **78** A2
 Woburn Sands MK17 . . . . **81** B5
Burrsholt MK44 . . . . **52** A5
Burr's Pl LU1 . . . . **123** E6
Burr St
 Dunstable LU6 . . . . **121** B8
 Luton LU2 . . . . **123** E8
Bursland SG6 . . . . **101** D6
Burwell Rd PE19 . . . . **22** C6
Bury Cl LU5 . . . . **95** F1
Bury Ct MK41 . . . . **39** B2
BURY END
 MK43 . . . . **36** A2
 SG5 . . . . **87** E3
Bury End SG5 . . . . **99** D4
Bury Farm Cl LU7 . . . . . . **118** C6
Bury Hill SG19 . . . . **56** B7
Bury La LU3 . . . . **108** A5
Bury Mead SG5 . . . . **90** A7
Bury Mead Rd SG5 . . . . . **100** F1
BURY PARK **116** B1
Bury Park Rd LU1 . . . . . . **123** C8
Bury Rd
 Shefford SG17 . . . . **77** E3
 Shillington SG5 . . . . **87** E2
Bury Rise LU7 . . . . **112** F5
Bury The MK43 . . . . **26** C4
Bury Wlk MK41 . . . . **39** B2
Bush Cl LU5 . . . . **106** A5
BUSHMEAD **20** D4
Bushmead Ave MK40 . . . . **50** D8
Bushmead Cross MK44 . . . **20** C5
Bushmead Ct LU2 . . . . . . **116** E5
Bushmead PE19 . . . . **22** B3
Bushmead Prim Sch
 Luton LU2 . . . . **116** E5
 St Neots PE19 . . . . **22** A3
Bushmead Priory ✱ MK44 . **20** D6
Bushmead Rd
 Luton LU2 . . . . **116** E5
 St Neots PE19 . . . . **22** A3
Bustard Hill PE28 . . . . **6** D8
Butcher's La SG19 . . . . . . **57** B4
Butely Rd LU4 . . . . **115** B5
Bute Sq LU1 . . . . **123** E7
Bute St LU1 . . . . **123** E7
Butler Dr MK43 . . . . **72** C3
Butler St MK44 . . . . **28** F1
Butlers Yd SG7 . . . . **91** E1
Butler Way MK42 . . . . . . **49** E5
Butlin Rd LU1 . . . . **123** B7
Buttercup Cl
 Bedford MK42 . . . . **50** F4
 Dunstable LU6 . . . . **121** A4
Buttercup Mead SG18 . . . **67** C5
Butterfield Green Rd
 LU2 . . . . **117** A6
Buttermere Ave LU6 . . . . **121** C6
Buttermere Cl
 Flitwick MK45 . . . . **84** E3
 Kempston MK42 . . . . . . **49** D3
Buttermere Path SG18 . . . **67** A4
Butterworth Path [1]
 LU2 . . . . **123** E8
Butts The
 Langford SG18 . . . . **78** F6
 Riseley MK44 . . . . **10** E1
Buxton Cl SG17 . . . . **88** C6
Buxton Rd LU1 . . . . **123** D7
Buxtons La SG8 . . . . **69** F3
Buzzard Rd LU4 . . . . **115** A4
Byards Gn SG19 . . . . **55** F8
Bye Rd MK43 . . . . **72** B3
Byfield Cl
 Luton LU4 . . . . **115** B1
 Toddington LU5 . . . . . . **105** E6
Byford Path LU7 . . . . **111** D5
Byford Way LU7 . . . . **111** D5
Bygrave Rd SG7 . . . . **91** F1
Byng Cl PE19 . . . . **22** B2
Byrnes Mews SG17 . . . . . **77** C3

Byron Cl
 Biggleswade SG18 . . . . . **67** A5
 Upper Caldecote SG18 . . **66** C8
Byron Cres
 Bedford MK40 . . . . **37** F2
 Flitwick MK45 . . . . **84** D3
Byron Pl PE19 . . . . **22** C6
Byron Rd
 Harpenden AL5 . . . . . . **131** A2
 Luton LU1 . . . . **115** B2
Byslips Rd LU6 . . . . **127** D5

C

CADDINGTON **122** D3
Caddington Comm AL3 . . **128** E8
Cade Cl SG6 . . . . **91** C1
Cades Cl LU1 . . . . **123** A6
Cades La LU1 . . . . **123** A6
Cadia Cl LU1 . . . . **122** E4
Cadwell Ct SG4 . . . . **101** A2
Cadwell La SG4 . . . . **101** A2
Caernarvon Rd PE19 . . . . **22** F1
Cainhoe Rd MK45 . . . . . . **86** C8
Caister Rd MK41 . . . . **39** B4
Calcutt Cl LU5 . . . . **114** F2
CALDECOTE **80** D1
Caldecote Lower Sch
 SG18 . . . . **66** B8
Caldecote Rd
 Ickwell SG18 . . . . **65** E8
 Newnham SG7 . . . . **91** E8
 St Neots PE19 . . . . **22** E3
CALDECOTT **3** C6
Caldecott Rd NN9 . . . . **3** B7
Calder Gdns LU7 . . . . . . **110** B7
Calder Rise MK41 . . . . . . **38** D6
Caleb Cl LU4 . . . . **115** F2
Calnwood Rd LU4 . . . . . . **115** C3
Calshot Wlk MK41 . . . . . . **39** A5
Calverton Rd LU3 . . . . . . **116** A6
Camberton Rd LU7 . . . . . **110** E5
Cambrian Way MK41 . . . . **38** E3
Cambridge Cl SG18 . . . . . **78** F4
Cambridge Ct PE19 . . . . . **22** F5
Cambridge Gdns
 Langford SG18 . . . . **78** F5
 St Neots PE19 . . . . **22** F5
Cambridge Rd
 Bedford MK42, MK44 . . . . **51** A5
 Cardington MK44 . . . . . . **51** D6
 Dunton SG18 . . . . **68** D6
 Hitchin SG4 . . . . **101** C2
 Langford SG18 . . . . **78** F5
 Sandy SG19 . . . . **54** C7
Cambridge St
 Luton LU1 . . . . **123** F6
 St Neots PE19 . . . . **22** F5
 Wymington NN10 . . . . . . **8** A7
Cambridge Way SG18 . . . **78** F5
Cam Ctr SG4 . . . . **101** A3
Camestone Lower Sch
 MK42 . . . . **49** F4
Camford Ct MK42 . . . . . . **49** D4
Camford Way LU3 . . . . . . **107** B1
Campania Gr LU3 . . . . . . **116** A4
Campbell Cl MK42 . . . . . . **49** D3
Campbell Rd MK40 . . . . . **38** D1
Camp Dr LU5 . . . . **114** B5
Campers Ave SG6 . . . . . . **101** E5
Campers Rd SG6 . . . . **101** E5
Campers Wlk SG6 . . . . . . **101** E5
Campfield Way SG6 . . . . . **101** D5
Campian Cl LU6 . . . . **113** E1
Campin Cl MK43 . . . . **60** E1
Campion Cl NN10 . . . . **8** B8
Campion Rd MK45 . . . . . . **95** F5
Campion Way MK45 . . . . . **84** D3
CAMPTON **87** F8
Campton Lower Sch SG17 **76** F1
Campton Rd
 Gravenhurst MK45, SG17 . **87** D6
 Meppershall SG17 . . . . . **87** F6
 Shefford SG17 . . . . **77** A2
Cam Sq SG4 . . . . **101** A3
Canberra Gdns LU3 . . . . **116** B6
Canberra Rd MK42 . . . . . **50** F2
Candale Cl LU6 . . . . **121** C6
Canesworde Rd LU6 . . . . **121** A7
Cannock Chase MK41 . . . **39** C4
Cannon La LU2 . . . . **117** B5
Cannon's Cl SG8 . . . . **69** F5
Canons Cl MK43 . . . . **60** F8
Canterbury Cl
 Kempston MK42 . . . . . . **49** E6
 Luton LU3 . . . . **115** F4
Canterbury Rd MK45 . . . . **84** E4
Cantilupe Cl LU6 . . . . . . **119** D6
Canvin Way MK45 . . . . . . **50** D8
CAPABILITY GREEN **123** F4
Capron Cl LU5 . . . . **114** A2
Capron Rd
 Dunstable LU5 . . . . **114** A2
 Luton LU4 . . . . **115** E4
Capshill Ave LU7 . . . . . . **111** C7
Captains Cl MK44 . . . . . . **17** C1
Capulet Cl PE19 . . . . **22** C3
Cardiff Gr LU1 . . . . **123** D7
Cardiff Rd LU1 . . . . **123** D7
Cardigan Ct [10] LU1 . . . . **123** D7
Cardigan Gdns [11] LU1 . . **123** D7
Cardigan St LU1 . . . . **123** D7
Cardinal Ct [3] LU2 . . . . . **116** D1
Cardinal Newman RC Sec
 Sch LU2 . . . . **108** C1

CARDINGTON **51** D4
Cardington Ct MK42 . . . . . **50** F5
Cardington Rd MK42,
 MK44 . . . . **50** F6
Carfax Cl LU4 . . . . **114** E3
Carina Dr LU7 . . . . **111** C7
Carisbrooke Rd
 Harpenden AL5 . . . . . . **131** C2
 Luton LU4 . . . . **115** E1
Carisbrooke Way
 Bedford MK41 . . . . **39** A4
 St Neots PE19 . . . . **22** F2
Carlisle Cl
 Dunstable LU6 . . . . **121** B6
 Sandy SG19 . . . . **54** C8
Carlisle Rd MK40 . . . . . . **49** E7
Carlow Ct LU6 . . . . **121** A8
CARLTON **25** B4
Carlton Bank [2] AL5 . . . . **131** B1
Carlton Cl
 Luton LU3 . . . . **116** C2
 Rushden NN10 . . . . **8** A7
Carlton Cres LU3 . . . . . . **116** C2
Carlton Ct [1] AL5 . . . . . . **131** B1
Carlton Gdns MK41 . . . . . **38** D4
Carlton Gr LU7 . . . . **103** A3
Carlton Lower Sch MK43 . **25** A4
Carlton Rd
 Felmersham MK43 . . . . . **25** F7
 Harpenden AL5 . . . . . . **131** B2
 Harrold MK43 . . . . **25** B5
 Turvey MK43 . . . . **34** E7
Carmarthen Way NN10 . . . **8** C8
Carmelite Rd LU4 . . . . . . **115** A3
Carnaby PE28 . . . . **6** F4
Carnation Cl LU7 . . . . . . **103** A1
Carnegie Gdns LU3 . . . . **116** A8
Carnell Cl MK42 . . . . **49** C2
Carnoustie Dr MK40 . . . . **49** B7
Carol Cl LU3 . . . . **116** B4
Carole Ct LU1 . . . . **123** E5
Carolyn Ct LU3 . . . . **116** B4
Carpenders Cl AL5 . . . . . **130** D4
Carrick Rd MK41 . . . . **39** B4
Carriers Way MK43 . . . . . **25** B4
Carroll Dr MK42 . . . . **50** C4
Carron Ct LU7 . . . . **110** B7
Carron Rd MK41 . . . . **38** C7
Carsdale Cl LU3 . . . . **116** A6
Carter Cl MK42 . . . . **50** E6
Carteret Rd LU2 . . . . **117** C1
Carters Cl SG15 . . . . **90** A7
Carters La SG19 . . . . **56** A7
Carter St SG19 . . . . **54** B8
Carters Way SG15 . . . . . . **90** A7
Carters Wlk SG15 . . . . . . **90** A7
Carterweys LU5 . . . . **114** E2
Cartmel Dr LU6 . . . . **121** B6
Cartmel Priory MK41 . . . . **51** B8
Cartwright Cl MK43 . . . . . **36** F1
Cashio La SG6 . . . . **91** A1
Caslon Way SG6 . . . . **90** F1
Castle Cl
 Totternhoe LU6 . . . . . . **120** A8
 Wilstead MK45 . . . . **62** F4
Castle Croft Rd LU1 . . . . **123** A6
Castle Ct
 Hitchin SG5 . . . . **100** D1
 Rushden NN10 . . . . **8** A8
Castle Gdns PE28 . . . . . . **6** F4
Castle Hill Cl PE19 . . . . . **22** C2
Castle Hill Ct MK45 . . . . . **75** C1
Castle Hill Rd LU6 . . . . . **119** F8
Castle La MK40 . . . . **50** C8
Castle Lower Sch MK40 . **38** D1
Castle Rd
 Bedford MK40 . . . . **50** D8
 Lavendon MK46 . . . . . . **23** F1
Castle Rise AL4 . . . . **131** F2
Castles Cl SG15 . . . . **90** F8
Castle St
 Luton, High Town LU1 . . **123** E7
 Luton, New Town LU1 . . **123** E6
Caswell La MK17 . . . . **92** F7
Catchacre LU1 . . . . **121** A7
Cater St MK42 . . . . **49** E4
Catesby Gn LU3 . . . . **108** A1
Catherall Rd LU3 . . . . . . **116** B6
Catherine Rd MK45 . . . . . **84** E3
Catherines Cl SG19 . . . . . **56** A7
Catsbrook Rd LU3 . . . . . **116** B6
CAULCOTT **60** E1
Cauldwell Ct
 Bedford MK42 . . . . **50** A6
 Sandy SG19 . . . . **54** C8
Cauldwell Lower Sch
 MK42 . . . . **50** B6
Cauldwell Pl MK42 . . . . . **50** B7
Cauldwell St MK42 . . . . . **50** B7
Cauldwell Wlk MK42 . . . . **50** A6
Cause End Rd MK43 . . . . **60** F7
Causeway
 Felmersham MK43 . . . . . **16** B1
 Great Staughton PE19 . . **13** F6
Causeway Cl PE19 . . . . . **13** F6
Causeway The
 Carlton MK43 . . . . **25** B3
 Clophill MK45 . . . . **86** D8
Cavalier Cl LU3 . . . . **116** A5
Cavendish Ct
 Bedford MK40 . . . . **37** F2
 [6] Biggleswade SG18 . . **67** A6
 St Neots PE19 . . . . **22** D5
Cavendish Rd
 Luton LU3 . . . . **116** B2
 Markyate AL3 . . . . **128** D6
Cavendish St MK40 . . . . . **38** B1

Cave's Ct SG19 . . . . **56** A7
Cave's La MK40 . . . . **38** E2
Cawdor Cl MK41 . . . . **39** B4
Cawdor Pl PE19 . . . . **22** F2
Caxton Cl LU3 . . . . **115** F4
Caxton Pk MK41 . . . . **39** C3
Caxton Rd MK41 . . . . **39** D3
Cedar Ave
 Biggleswade SG18 . . . . . **66** F7
 Ickleford SG5 . . . . **100** E4
 Wilstead MK45 . . . . **62** F4
Cedar Cl
 Ampthill MK45 . . . . **84** F7
 Irchester NN29 . . . . **7** A7
 Luton LU4 . . . . **114** E3
 Rushden NN10 . . . . **8** A8
 Shefford SG17 . . . . **77** E2
Cedar Gdns SG19 . . . . . . **54** B7
Cedar Rd MK45 . . . . **50** D5
Cedars Ctyd MK45 . . . . . **84** E7
Cedars The
 Ampthill MK45 . . . . **84** E7
 Dunstable LU6 . . . . **121** C7
 [13] Harpenden AL5 . . . **131** B1
 Wootton MK43 . . . . **61** A8
Cedars Upper Sch & Com
 Coll The LU7 . . . . **110** E5
Cedars Way LU7 . . . . . . **110** E5
Cedars Wlk MK45 . . . . . . **84** E7
Celandine Cl NN10 . . . . . . **8** C7
Celandine Dr LU3 . . . . . . **116** A8
Cemetery Rd
 Houghton Regis LU5 . . . **114** B3
 Kempston MK43 . . . . . . **49** B3
 St Neots PE19 . . . . **22** F5
Centauri Cl LU7 . . . . **111** C8
Central App SG6 . . . . **101** F6
Central Ave
 Henlow SG16 . . . . **89** B3
 Shortstown MK42 . . . . . **51** A2
 Wharley End MK43 . . . . **58** E2
 Whipsnade LU6 . . . . . . **126** E8
Centrus Ind Est LU5 . . . . **114** B2
Century Cl MK45 . . . . **84** F2
Cetus Cres LU7 . . . . **111** C7
Chad La AL3 . . . . **129** C4
Chadwell Cl LU2 . . . . . . **116** F1
CHADWELL END **12** C7
Chadwick Cl LU6 . . . . . . **114** A1
Chagford Cl MK40 . . . . . . **38** E1
Chagny Cl SG6 . . . . **101** E6
Chainbridge La PE28 . . . . . **2** F8
Chalfont Way LU2 . . . . . . **117** D2
Chalgrave Rd LU5, LU7 . . **105** D3
Chalkdown LU2 . . . . **116** E6
CHALK HILL **113** E4
Chalk Hill LU7 . . . . **117** F4
Challney Boys High Sch
 LU4 . . . . **115** D2
Challney Cl LU4 . . . . **115** D2
Challney Girls High Sch
 LU4 . . . . **115** D2
Chaloner Ct LU7 . . . . . . **111** B5
CHALTON
 LU4 . . . . **106** E1
 MK44 . . . . **41** D1
Chalton Hts LU4 . . . . **106** E1
Chalton Lower Sch LU4 . **106** E1
Chalton Rd LU4 . . . . **115** C1
Chamberlaines AL5 . . . . **130** A5
Chamberlains Gdns LU7 . **103** A2
Chamberlain Way PE19 . . **22** F7
Chambers La SG5 . . . . . **100** E4
Chambers Way SG18 . . . . **67** C5
Chancellors SG15 . . . . . . **90** B7
Chandler Path MK42 . . . . **49** D5
Chandler Pl LU3 . . . . **103** A5
Chandlers Cl MK43 . . . . . **72** C8
Chandlers Wharf PE19 . . . **22** E5
Chandos Ct [14] MK40 . . . **38** B1
Chandos Rd
 Ampthill MK45 . . . . **84** E8
 Luton LU4 . . . . **115** F1
Chandos St MK40 . . . . . . **38** B1
CHANNEL'S END **30** C5
Channels End Rd MK44 . . **30** C6
Chantry Ave MK42 . . . . . **49** F2
Chantry Cl MK17 . . . . **81** A6
Chantry Piece SG18 . . . . **53** E2
Chantry Prim Sch LU4 . . **114** F4
Chantry Rd MK42 . . . . . . **49** E3
Chaomans SG6 . . . . **101** F3
Chapel Cl
 Bedford MK41 . . . . **39** B1
 Great Barford MK44 . . . . **40** F5
 Honeydon MK44 . . . . . . **21** B2
 Luton LU2 . . . . **116** C8
 Shefford SG17 . . . . **77** F2
 Swineshead MK44 . . . . . **11** D8
 Toddington LU5 . . . . . . **105** F6
 Wrestlingworth SG19 . . . **57** B4
Chapel Ct SG18 . . . . **78** F6
Chapel Dr SG15 . . . . **90** A4
CHAPEL END
 MK44 . . . . **20** A1
 MK44 . . . . **51** E6
 MK45 . . . . **62** C1
 MK54 . . . . **63** A4
Chapel End Rd MK45 . . . . **74** D8
Chapel Field
 Gamlingay SG19 . . . . . . **44** D4
 Great Barford MK44 . . . . **40** F5
Chapelfields MK44 . . . . . **18** D1
Chapel Fields SG18 . . . . . **66** F6
Chapel Hill NN29 . . . . **7** B8
Chapel La
 Ampthill MK45 . . . . **73** E1
 Cardington MK44 . . . . . . **51** E5

Chapel La continued
 Colmworth MK44 . . . . . . **20** A1
 Ivinghoe Aston LU7 . . . **119** A1
 Northall LU6 . . . . **119** A5
 Souldrop MK44 . . . . **16** A8
 Totternhoe LU6 . . . . . . **119** F8
 Willington MK44 . . . . . . **40** C1
 Wilstead MK45 . . . . **62** F4
Chapel Path
 Houghton Regis LU5 . . . **114** B4
 [2] Leighton Buzzard LU7 **111** A8
Chapel Pl SG5 . . . . **90** F6
Chapel Pound MK43 . . . . **37** A8
Chapel Rd
 Breachwood Green SG4 . **125** E8
 Flamstead AL3 . . . . **129** B2
 Flitwick MK45 . . . . **84** D3
 Meppershall SG17 . . . . . **88** D6
Chapel St
 Dunton SG18 . . . . **68** D5
 Hinxworth SG7 . . . . **80** D6
 Luton, High Town LU1 . . **123** E7
 Luton, New Town LU1 . . **123** E6
 Potton SG19 . . . . **56** A7
 Woburn Sands MK17 . . . . **81** B4
Chapel Viaduct LU1 . . . . **123** E7
Chapel Way SG16 . . . . . . **78** D3
Chapel Yd MK44 . . . . **6** E1
Chapman Cl
 Kempston MK42 . . . . . . **49** D5
 Potton SG19 . . . . **56** A7
Chapmans Cl NN29 . . . . . . **7** B8
Chapman Way PE19 . . . . . **22** E2
Chapterhouse Rd LU4 . . . **115** A3
Chard Dr LU3 . . . . **108** B1
Charlbury Ct MK40 . . . . . **38** D1
Charles St LU2 . . . . **123** F8
Charles' St PE19 . . . . **22** F5
Charlewood Ho MK17 . . . . **81** B3
Charlotte Ave SG5 . . . . . . **90** C2
Charlottes Ct [2] LU1 . . . **123** D7
Charlwood Rd LU4 . . . . . **115** B1
Charmbury Rise LU2 . . . . **117** A4
Charndon Cl LU3 . . . . . . **108** B1
Charnocks Cl SG19 . . . . . **44** D5
Charnwood Ave MK41 . . . **39** B3
Chartmoor Rd LU7 . . . . . **111** A4
Chartwell Dr LU2 . . . . . . **116** E3
Chase Cl SG15 . . . . **90** A8
Chase Hill Rd SG15 . . . . . **90** A7
Chase St LU1 . . . . **123** E6
Chase The MK43 . . . . **49** A2
Chasten Hill SG6 . . . . . . **101** D7
Chatsworth Rd LU4 . . . . **116** B1
Chatteris Cl LU4 . . . . . . **115** D4
Chatton Cl LU2 . . . . **117** E2
Chaucer Dr SG18 . . . . . . **67** A5
Chaucer Pl PE19 . . . . **22** D6
Chaucer Rd
 Bedford MK40 . . . . **37** F1
 Flitwick MK45 . . . . **84** D3
 Luton LU3 . . . . **116** C2
CHAUL END **122** C7
Chaul End La LU4 . . . . . **115** E1
Chaul End Rd
 Caddington LU1, LU4 . . . **122** D6
 Luton LU4 . . . . **115** B1
Chauntry Cl MK45 . . . . . . **84** E5
Chauntry Way MK45 . . . . **84** E5
Chaworth Gn [1] LU4 . . . **115** C5
CHAWSTON **31** E5
Chawston Cl PE19 . . . . . . **22** C5
Chawston La MK44 . . . . . **31** F5
Cheapside LU1 . . . . **123** E7
Cheapside Sq [4] LU1 . . . **123** E7
CHEDDINGTON **118** A1
Cheddington Sta LU7 . . . **118** A2
CHELLINGTON **25** B4
Chelmer Cl MK41 . . . . . . **38** D7
Chelsea Gdns LU5 . . . . . **114** D5
Chelsea Gn LU7 . . . . **110** D6
Chelsworth Cl [1] LU2 . . . **117** D1
Cheltenham Cl
 Bedford MK41 . . . . **39** B3
 Rushden NN10 . . . . **8** C8
CHELVESTON **3** C8
Chelveston Base Cres NN9 **3** D5
Chelveston Rd NN9 . . . . . . **3** A7
Cheney Cl LU5 . . . . **105** F6
Cheney Rd LU4 . . . . **115** C5
Chennells Cl SG4 . . . . . . **101** B2
Chepstow AL5 . . . . **130** F2
Chepstow Gdns MK41 . . . **39** A4
Chequer Ct LU1 . . . . **123** F6
Chequers Cl
 Marston Moretaine MK43 . **60** D2
 Stotfold SG5 . . . . **91** A6
Chequers Cotts LU6 . . . . **127** A8
Chequers Hill
 Flamstead AL3 . . . . **129** C2
 Wilden MK44 . . . . **30** A4
Chequers La MK16 . . . . . **58** B6
Chequer St LU1 . . . . **123** F6
Chequers The LU6 . . . . . **119** F5
Cherry Cl MK45 . . . . **74** B8
Cherrycourt Way LU7 . . . **111** D6
Cherrycourt Way Ind Est
 LU7 . . . . **111** C7
Cherrycroft SG19 . . . . . . **54** D7
Cherry Gr SG19 . . . . **44** C5
Cherry Tree Cl
 Arlesey SG15 . . . . **90** A4
 Luton LU2 . . . . **117** A1
Cherry Trees SG16 . . . . . **89** B3
Cherrytree Way MK45 . . . **85** A7
Cherry Tree Wlk
 Houghton Regis LU5 . . . **114** B6
 Leighton Buzzard LU7 . . **110** E7

Cherry Wlk MK42 . . . . 49 F3
Chertsey Cl LU2. . . . . 124 D8
Cherwell Rd MK41 . . . . 38 C5
Chesford Rd LU2. . . . . 117 C4
Cheslyn Cl LU2 . . . . 117 E2
Chessington Cl MK41. . . . . 51 B8
Chester Ave LU4 . . . . 115 E3
Chester Cl LU4. . . . . 115 F2
Chesterfield Way PE19 . . . 22 E2
Chester Rd MK40 . . . . 49 E7
Chesterton Ave AL5 . . . . . 131 D1
Chesterton Ct PE19 . . . . . . 22 E6
Chesterton Mews MK40 . . 37 F1
Chestnut Ave
Bedford MK40 . . . . 49 F7
Biggleswade SG18. . . . . 67 A6
Bromham MK43. . . . . 36 D3
Henlow SG16. . . . . 89 C3
Luton LU3 . . . . 107 C1
Chestnut Cl
Ampthill MK45. . . . . 84 F8
Dagnall HP4. . . . . 126 C5
Westoning MK45 . . . . 95 D6
Wymington NN10. . . . . 8 B5
Chestnut Cres MK45. . . . . . 85 B8
Chestnut Ct LU6 . . . . 121 C7
Chestnut Farm SG16 . . . . . 78 D1
Chestnut Gdns MK42 . . . . . 49 E3
Chestnut Gr PE19 . . . . 22 F4
Chestnut Hill LU7 . . . . 110 D8
Chestnut Rise LU7 . . . . . . 110 D8
Chestnuts The PE28. . . . . 6 F5
Chethams MK42 . . . . 50 C7
Cheveralls The LU6 . . . . . 121 C6
Cheverells Cl AL3 . . . . 128 D4
CHEVERELL'S GREEN 127 C4
Cheviot Cl
Bedford MK41 . . . . 38 E3
Flitwick MK45 . . . . 84 D2
Leighton Buzzard LU7 . . . . 110 C8
Luton LU3 . . . . 115 D7
Cheviot Rd LU3 . . . . 115 D7
Cheyne Cl LU6 . . . . 113 F3
Cheynes Inf Sch LU3 . . . . 115 D8
Chicheley Rd MK16 . . . . . . 58 A7
Chichester Cl LU5. . . . . . . 121 E7
CHICKSANDS 76 E4
Chicksands Ave SG17 . . . . 76 F2
Chillingham Gn MK41 . . . . 39 B4
Chiltern Ave
Bedford MK41 . . . . 38 E3
Edlesborough LU6 . . . . 119 E3
Chiltern Cl
Ampthill MK45. . . . . 84 F8
Flitwick MK45 . . . . 84 D2
Lidlington MK43. . . . . 72 B2
Chiltern Ct 19 AL5 . . . . . . 131 B1
Chiltern Gdns
Leighton Buzzard LU7 . . . . 103 A3
Luton LU4 . . . . 115 F3
CHILTERN GREEN 124 B3
Chiltern Pk LU5. . . . . 114 D2
Chiltern Pl SG16 . . . . 78 C1
Chiltern Rd
Barton-le-C MK45 . . . . 97 C2
Dunstable LU6. . . . . 114 A1
Chiltern Rise LU1 . . . . 123 D6
Chilterns The
Kensworth LU6 . . . . 127 F8
Leighton Buzzard LU7 . . . . 111 D6
Chiltern Trad Est LU7. . . . 111 A5
Chiltern View SG6 . . . . . . 101 D5
Chinnor Cl MK41. . . . . 39 B1
Chobham St LU1. . . . . 123 F6
Chobham Wlk 5 LU1 . . . 123 E6
Christchurch Ct LU6 . . . . 114 A1
Christian Cl LU5 . . . . 95 F1
Christie Rd MK42 . . . . 50 D6
Christina Ct AL3 . . . . 128 E5
Christy's Yd SG7 . . . . 80 D6
Chudleigh Cl MK40. . . . . . . 38 E2
Church Ave
Ampthill MK45. . . . . 73 F1
Leighton Buzzard LU7 . . . . 111 A6
Church Cl
Bedford MK41 . . . . 39 D6
Dunstable LU5. . . . . 121 C8
Houghton Conquest MK45. . 74 A7
Milton Ernest MK44. . . . . . . 27 B5
Rushden NN10. . . . . 8 B5
Studham LU6 . . . . 127 B4
Westoning MK45 . . . . 95 D6
Church Cotts HP1. . . . . . . 132 D3
Church Cres SG18. . . . . 78 F7
Church Croft LU6 . . . . 119 E3
CHURCH END
LU6 . . . . 120 C7
LU7 . . . . 104 D2
MK17 . . . . 94 B5
MK40 . . . . 49 B8
MK43 . . . . 36 C8
MK43 . . . . 60 E6
MK43 . . . . 82 B5
MK44 . . . . 18 C2
MK44 . . . . 20 B2
MK44 . . . . 29 C2
MK45 . . . . 97 C1
SG15 . . . . 90 B7
SG19 . . . . 42 A7
Church End
Arlesey SG15. . . . . 90 A8
Biddenham MK40. . . . . 49 B8
Edlesborough LU6 . . . . 119 E3
Elstow MK42 . . . . 50 B3
Everton SG19. . . . . 43 C3
Felmersham MK43. . . . . 26 C8
Gamlingay SG19 . . . . 44 E5
Houghton Regis LU5 . . . . . 114 B5
Church End *continued*
Kensworth LU6 . . . . 121 E2
Markyate AL3 . . . . 128 D6
Milton Bryan MK17 . . . . 93 E2
Ravensden MK44. . . . . 29 B1
Renhold MK41 . . . . 39 D6
Steppingley MK45 . . . . 84 A3
Willington MK44 . . . . 52 B8
Church End Farm LU6 . . . 120 B7
Church End Lower Sch MK43 . . . . 72 D7
Church End Rd MK45. . . . . . 75 C7
Church Farm Ave MK45 . . 62 E3
Church Farm Cl
Langford SG18. . . . . 78 F7
Sutton SG19. . . . . 55 F3
Churchfield Rd LU5 . . . . . 114 B5
Churchgate MK44. . . . . 41 A4
Church Gn
Harpenden AL5 . . . . 131 A1
Milton Ernest MK44. . . . . . . 27 B5
Totternhoe LU6 . . . . 120 B7
Church Green Row AL5. . 131 A1
Church Hill MK17 . . . . 81 E5
Churchill Cl
Sharnbrook MK44 . . . . 16 C3
Stewartby MK43 . . . . 61 B1
Streatley LU3. . . . . 107 F6
Churchill Dr SG17. . . . . 76 F4
Churchill Pl MK44. . . . . 40 B1
Churchill Rd
Barton-le-C MK45 . . . . 97 C3
Dunstable LU6. . . . . 121 D5
Leighton Buzzard LU7 . . . . 103 B1
Luton LU4 . . . . 116 A1
Marston Moretaine MK43 . . 72 C8
Churchills LU5. . . . . 95 F2
Churchill Way
Sandy SG19 . . . . 54 C8
Shefford SG17 . . . . 77 C1
Church La
Arlesey SG15. . . . . 90 A7
Bedford MK41 . . . . 39 B3
Bolnhurst MK44. . . . . 19 A4
Cardington MK44. . . . . 51 D4
Colmworth MK44. . . . . 19 D4
Colmworth MK44. . . . . 20 B2
Covington PE28 . . . . 2 C2
Eaton Bray LU6 . . . . 119 E6
Everton SG19. . . . . 43 C3
Flitton MK45 . . . . 85 D4
Gamlingay SG19 . . . . 44 E5
Guilden Morden SG8 . . . . . . 69 F5
Haynes Church End MK45 . . 75 C7
Hockliffe LU7. . . . . 104 D3
Letchworth SG6. . . . . 91 C1
Lidlington MK43. . . . . 72 C2
Little Staughton MK44. . . . . 13 B2
Newton Bromswold NN10 . . . 9 D8
Oakley MK43 . . . . 36 F6
Odell MK43 . . . . 15 D1
Pavenham MK43 . . . . 26 C4
Riseley MK44. . . . . 10 F2
Sharnbrook MK44 . . . . 16 C4
Stagsden MK43 . . . . 48 A7
Tilbrook PE28 . . . . 6 B7
Upper Dean PE28 . . . . 5 B4
Wrestlingworth SG19 . . . . . 57 B3
Wymington NN10. . . . . 8 B5
Yelden MK44 . . . . 4 A3
Church Mdw PE19 . . . . 22 F5
Church Mead LU6. . . . . . . 127 B4
Church Meadow Cotts HP1 . . . . 132 D3
Church Path
Cheddington LU7. . . . . 118 A1
Sandy SG19. . . . . 54 B7
Church Rd
Barton-le-C MK45 . . . . 97 D1
Colmworth MK44. . . . . 20 B1
Everton SG19. . . . . 43 C3
Flamstead AL3. . . . . 129 B2
Flitwick MK45 . . . . 84 D1
Hargrave NN9 . . . . 1 F1
Harlington LU5 . . . . 95 F2
Henlow SG16. . . . . 78 D2
Kempston MK43 . . . . 49 A4
Keysoe MK44. . . . . 12 A1
Leighton Buzzard LU7 . . . . 110 E6
Maulden MK45. . . . . 85 D8
Meppershall SG17. . . . . 88 A5
Pulloxhill MK45 . . . . 96 E8
Silsoe MK45. . . . . 86 C4
Slapton LU7 . . . . 118 D6
Slip End LU1 . . . . 123 C2
Steppingley MK45 . . . . 84 A3
Stevington MK43 . . . . 36 C7
Stotfold SG5 . . . . 90 F6
Streatley LU3. . . . . 108 A6
Studham LU6 . . . . 127 B4
Sutton SG19. . . . . 55 F4
Tingrith MK17 . . . . 94 F5
Totternhoe LU6 . . . . 120 B6
Upper Sundon LU3. . . . . . . 107 B3
Westoning MK45 . . . . 95 E6
Willington MK44 . . . . 52 B8
Wilstead MK45 . . . . 62 E4
Woburn Sands MK17. . . . . . . 81 B3
Wootton MK43. . . . . 60 F7
Church Row MK43 . . . . 60 E7
Church Sq
Leighton Buzzard LU7 . . . . 110 F6
Toddington LU5 . . . . 105 F6
Church St
Ampthill MK45. . . . . 73 F1
Aspley Guise MK17 . . . . 81 E5
Baldock SG7 . . . . 91 E1
5 Bedford MK40 . . . . 50 B8
Church St *continued*
Biggleswade SG18. . . . . 67 A6
Clifton SG17. . . . . 78 B3
Dunstable LU5. . . . . 121 C8
Dunton SG18 . . . . 68 D5
Gamlingay SG19 . . . . 44 D5
Guilden Morden SG8 . . . . . . 69 F5
Hargrave NN9 . . . . 1 E2
Langford SG18. . . . . 78 F7
Langford SG18. . . . . 78 F8
Leighton Buzzard LU7 . . . . 111 A8
Lidlington MK43. . . . . 72 C3
Luton, High Town LU2 . . . . 123 F8
8 Luton LU1 . . . . 123 E7
Luton LU2 . . . . 123 E7
Ridgmont MK43 . . . . 82 F5
Shillington SG5 . . . . 98 E8
St Neots PE19 . . . . 22 F5
Tempsford SG19 . . . . 42 A6
Church Terr MK43 . . . . 34 E5
Church Turn LU7 . . . . 111 E2
Church View
Ampthill MK45. . . . . 73 F1
Clapham MK41. . . . . 37 F5
St Neots PE19 . . . . 22 F5
Church View Ave SG5 . . . . 87 E1
Church View Ct LU7. . . . . . 110 E6
Churchville Rd MK42 . . . . . 50 B5
Church Wlk
Cranfield MK43 . . . . 71 A8
Dunstable LU5. . . . . 121 C8
Eggington LU7 . . . . 112 B7
Harrold MK43 . . . . 25 A6
Kempston MK42 . . . . 49 C3
Marston Moretaine MK43 . . 72 D7
Newton Bromswold NN10 . . . 9 D8
North Crawley MK16 . . . . . . 58 B6
Shefford SG17 . . . . 77 C3
6 St Neots PE19 . . . . 22 E5
Churnet Cl MK41. . . . . 38 D7
Cicero Dr LU3 . . . . 116 A8
Cinques Rd SG19. . . . . 44 C6
Cinques The SG19 . . . . 44 B6
Circle Bsns Ctr LU5 . . . . . 114 B3
City La MK44. . . . . 20 C3
CLAPHAM 37 D7
CLAPHAM GREEN 36 F6
Clapham Rd MK41 . . . . 37 F4
Clare Ct SG19. . . . . 44 D5
Clare Ho SG18 . . . . 67 A6
Claremont Rd LU4 . . . . . . 116 B1
Clarence Ct NN10. . . . . 8 A8
Clarence Rd
Harpenden AL5 . . . . 131 A3
Leighton Buzzard LU7 . . . . 111 B8
Clarendon Ct AL5 . . . . 131 B3
Clarendon Rd
Harpenden AL5 . . . . 131 B3
Luton LU2 . . . . 116 E1
Clarendon St MK41 . . . . . . 38 A2
Clare Rd MK41. . . . . 38 F5
Claridge Cl LU7. . . . . 111 B5
Clarkes Way LU5. . . . . 114 C4
Clark's Pightle MK45. . . . . 97 C2
Claverley Gn LU2 . . . . 117 E2
Claydon Cl LU3 . . . . 116 C7
Claydon Ct MK40. . . . . 38 B1
Claydown Way LU1. . . . . . 123 B1
Clay Furlong LU7 . . . . 111 B5
Claygate Ave AL5 . . . . 130 E2
Clay Hall Rd LU6. . . . . 127 F7
Claymore Dr SG5 . . . . 100 F5
CLEAT HILL. 38 E7
Cleat Hill MK41, MK44. . . . . 38 E7
Cleavers The LU5 . . . . 105 F5
Cleavers Wlk LU5 . . . . 105 F5
Cleave The AL5 . . . . 131 D1
Cleeve Abbey MK41 . . . . . . 39 B1
CLEMENT'S END 127 D3
Clements End Rd LU6, HP2 . . . . 127 E2
Clevedon Rd LU2 . . . . 117 B2
Cleveland Dr LU7 . . . . 110 C8
Cleveland Rd AL3 . . . . 128 E5
Cleveland St MK42 . . . . 49 E4
Clifford Cres LU4 . . . . 115 D5
CLIFTON 78 B3
Clifton Fields SG17. . . . . . . 77 F3
Clifton House Cl SG17. . . . 78 B3
Clifton Pk SG17 . . . . 78 A1
Clifton Rd
Dunstable LU6. . . . . 114 A1
Henlow SG16. . . . . 78 C1
Luton LU1 . . . . 123 B8
Newton Blossomville MK43. 34 A4
Shefford SG17 . . . . 77 D2
Clinton Ave LU2 . . . . 116 F3
CLIPSTONE 103 F1
Clipstone Brook Lower Sch LU7 . . . . 111 B7
Clipstone Cl MK41 . . . . 39 B3
Clipstone Cres LU7. . . . . . 111 C7
Clive Ct LU2 . . . . 116 E1
Cloches The SG19. . . . . 54 B5
Cloister Lawns SG6 . . . . . 101 F4
Cloisters Rd
Letchworth SG6. . . . . 101 F4
Luton LU4 . . . . 115 B3
Cloisters The
Ampthill MK45. . . . . 73 F1
Bedford MK41 . . . . 39 B1
Dunstable LU5. . . . . 121 C8
Houghton Regis LU5 . . . . . 114 C6
CLOPHILL 86 D8
Clophill Rd
Gravenhurst MK45 . . . . 87 B5
Maulden MK45. . . . . 85 E8
Close Rd MK43. . . . . 26 E3
Close The
Biggleswade SG18. . . . . 66 F6
Clapham MK41. . . . . 37 E5
Great Barford MK44 . . . . . . 41 A5
Hardmead MK16 . . . . 46 D4
Harpenden AL5 . . . . 130 D4
Hinxworth SG7. . . . . 80 D6
Luton LU3 . . . . 116 A5
Markyate AL3 . . . . 128 E5
St Neots PE19 . . . . 22 F5
Tempsford SG19 . . . . 42 C8
Thurleigh MK44 . . . . 18 C2
Woburn Sands MK17. . . . . . . 81 B4
Clothall Rd SG7. . . . . 91 F1
Clovelly Way MK40. . . . . . . 38 F1
Clover Ave MK41. . . . . 39 B1
Clover Cl
Biggleswade SG18. . . . . 67 C4
Luton LU4 . . . . 115 A3
Clover Dr NN10 . . . . 8 C8
Clover Rd
Flitwick MK45 . . . . 84 D3
St Neots PE19 . . . . 22 C3
Club Rd MK45. . . . . 62 E3
Cluny Way SG15 . . . . 90 A5
Clyde Cres MK41. . . . . 38 D5
Clydesdale Ct LU4 . . . . . . 115 A3
Clydesdale Rd LU4 . . . . . . 115 A3
Coach Rd SG16 . . . . 78 D1
Cobbett La MK45. . . . . 85 D4
Cobbitts Rd MK45 . . . . 74 C1
Cobblers La MK17. . . . . 83 C3
Cobden Sq 11 MK40 . . . . . 38 B1
Cobden St LU2. . . . . 116 F1
COCKERNHOE. 117 F3
Cockernhoe CE Prim Sch LU2 . . . . 117 E3
COCKHAYNE HATLEY 57 C8
Codrington Ct PE19 . . . . . . 22 B3
Cody Rd MK41 . . . . 37 D6
Colchester Way MK41 . . . . 39 A5
COLD BRAYFIELD. 34 B5
Coldharbour La AL5. . . . . 131 C4
Colebrook Ave LU3 . . . . . . 115 C7
Colemans Cl SG5 . . . . 99 D4
Colemoreham Ct SG18 . . . 65 E7
Coleridge Ct
9 Harpenden AL5 . . . . . . 131 B1
St Neots PE19 . . . . 22 C7
Coles Cl MK41 . . . . 39 A1
COLESDEN 30 E4
Colesden Rd
Chawston MK44. . . . . 31 D5
Wilden MK44 . . . . 30 C4
Colin Rd LU2 . . . . 116 F2
College Cl AL3. . . . . 129 B1
College Dr MK44. . . . . 10 F2
College Ho LU1 . . . . 123 F7
College Rd
Bedford MK42 . . . . 50 B5
Sandy SG19 . . . . 42 C1
Wharley End MK43 . . . . 58 E2
College St Ind Est MK42. . 50 A5
College St MK42 . . . . 50 A5
Colley Cl MK44. . . . . 20 A1
Collie Rd MK42 . . . . 50 E6
Collingdon Ct 9 LU1. . . . . 123 D8
Collingdon St LU1 . . . . . . 123 D8
Collings Wells Cl LU1 . . . 122 E4
Collingtree LU2. . . . . 117 B4
Collingwood Cl LU4 . . . . . 115 D3
Collingwood Rd PE19 . . . . 22 B2
Collins Pl MK42. . . . . 50 F5
Collison Cl SG4 . . . . 101 C2
COLMWORTH 20 B2
Colmworth Bsns Pk PE19. 22 C1
Colmworth Gdns PE19 . . . 22 C2
Colmworth Rd MK44 . . . . . 13 B1
Coltsfoot SG18. . . . . 67 C4
Coltsfoot Gn LU4 . . . . 115 A5
Coltsfoot Rd NN10 . . . . 8 C7
Columba Dr LU7 . . . . 111 C8
Columbine Cl MK41 . . . . . . 39 C4
Colwell Rise LU2. . . . . 117 E2
Colworth Rd MK44 . . . . 16 B4
Comet Dr MK42. . . . . 51 A2
Comfrey Cl NN10 . . . . 8 C7
Commerce Way
Flitwick MK45 . . . . 85 A4
Leighton Buzzard LU7 . . . . 111 E6
Letchworth SG6. . . . . 101 F6
Commerce Way Ind Est LU7 . . . . 111 E6
Commercial Rd MK40 . . . . 50 B8
Common Farm La MK45 . . 84 D4
Common La
Harpenden AL5 . . . . 131 D5
Upper Sundon LU3. . . . . . . 107 A4
Common Rd
Kensworth LU6 . . . . 121 D1
Langford SG18. . . . . 78 E4
Potton SG19. . . . . 56 A8
Stotfold SG5 . . . . 90 F7
Studham LU6 . . . . 127 B3
Common Rise SG4 . . . . . . 101 A1
Common The AL5. . . . . 130 C4
Compass Dr MK42 . . . . 51 A3
Comp Gate LU6 . . . . 119 E6
Comp The LU6. . . . . 119 E6
Compton Ave LU4. . . . . . . 115 D4
Compton Cl
Flitwick MK45 . . . . 84 D1
St Neots PE19 . . . . 22 E2
Concorde Cl MK42 . . . . 51 A2
Concorde St LU2. . . . . 123 F8
Concord Way LU7. . . . . . . 111 E5
Concra Pk MK17 . . . . 81 C4
Conduit Rd MK40 . . . . 50 A8
Coneygate SG17 . . . . 88 B5
Conger La LU5. . . . . 106 A6
Coniston Cl MK42 . . . . 49 E4
Coniston Rd
Flitwick MK45 . . . . 84 E2
Leighton Buzzard LU7 . . . . 110 C7
Luton LU3 . . . . 115 F5
Connaught Rd
Harpenden AL5 . . . . 131 B2
Luton LU4 . . . . 115 F1
Connaught Way MK41. . . . 38 D6
Connor's Cl SG8 . . . . 69 F4
Conquest Rd
Bedford MK42 . . . . 50 C5
Houghton Regis LU5 . . . . . 114 E5
Constable Ave PE19. . . . . . 22 D5
Constable Cl LU5 . . . . 114 D5
Constable Ct LU4 . . . . 116 A1
Constable Hill MK41. . . . . . 38 A2
Constables Leys PE28 . . . . . . 6 F5
Conway Cl
Houghton Regis LU5 . . . . . 114 E5
Rushden NN10. . . . . 8 A8
Conway Cres MK41. . . . . . . 38 C5
Conway Dr MK45. . . . . 84 D1
Conway Pl PE19 . . . . 22 F2
Conway Rd LU4 . . . . 116 B1
Cookfield Cl LU6. . . . . 120 E8
Cook's Mdw LU6. . . . . 119 E4
Cooks Way
Biggleswade SG18. . . . . 67 B6
Hitchin SG4 . . . . 101 A1
Coombe Dr LU6. . . . . 120 E7
Coombs Cl MK42. . . . . 50 D6
Cooper Cl SG16. . . . . 88 E2
Cooper Dr LU7. . . . . 111 C5
Coopers Cl
Biddenham MK40. . . . . 49 C8
Biggleswade SG18. . . . . 67 B4
Great Barford MK44 . . . . . . 40 F5
Sandy SG19. . . . . 54 B6
Coopers Field SG6 . . . . . . 101 D7
Coopers Way LU5. . . . . . . 114 A4
Cooters End La AL5 . . . . . 130 F5
Copeland Wlk MK41. . . . . . 39 B3
Copenhagen Cl LU3 . . . . . 115 D8
COPLE 52 A6
Cople Lower Sch MK44 . . . 52 A6
Cople Rd MK44 . . . . 51 E5
Coplowe La MK44 . . . . 17 D1
Coppens The SG5. . . . . 91 A5
Copper Beeches 11 AL5 . . 131 B1
Copper Beech Way LU7 . 103 A3
Copperfields LU4 . . . . 115 C3
Copperfields Cl LU5. . . . . 114 D4
Coppice Mead
Biggleswade SG18. . . . . 67 B5
Stotfold SG5 . . . . 90 E5
Coppice The AL5. . . . . 130 F2
Coppins The
Ampthill MK45. . . . . 84 F8
Markyate AL3 . . . . 128 D5
Copse The MK41 . . . . 39 B2
Copse Way LU3 . . . . 115 D8
Copthorne LU2 . . . . 117 D3
Copthorne Cl MK43 . . . . . . 37 A8
Coral Cl LU6. . . . . 119 E6
Corbet Ride LU7 . . . . 110 D8
Corbet Sq LU7 . . . . 110 D8
Corbridge Dr LU2 . . . . 117 E1
Corby Cl MK42. . . . . 50 D4
Cordwainer Hts NN29 . . . . . . 7 B8
Corfe Pl PE19. . . . . 22 F2
Corfe Rd MK41. . . . . 39 A4
Corinium Gdns LU3 . . . . . 116 A8
Cormorant Way LU7 . . . . 111 C5
Corncastle Rd LU1 . . . . . . 123 D6
Corncrake Cl LU2 . . . . 117 C5
Cornel Cl LU1. . . . . 123 A7
Cornel Ct LU1 . . . . 123 A7
Cornelia Ct 3 AL5 . . . . . . 131 A2
Corner Cl
Letchworth SG6. . . . . 101 E6
Podington NN29 . . . . 7 E1
Corner Wood AL3. . . . . . . 128 D5
Cornish Cl SG17 . . . . 77 C3
Cornland MK41 . . . . 39 A3
Cornwall Ct PE19 . . . . 22 C4
Cornwallis Cl MK43 . . . . . . 36 E3
Cornwallis Dr PE19 . . . . . . 22 A3
Cornwall Rd
Ampthill MK45. . . . . 84 F8
Bedford MK40 . . . . 38 D2
Harpenden AL5 . . . . 131 B2
Coronation Bsns Pk MK43 61 E5
Coronation Rd MK43 . . . . . 59 B1
Corunna Cl PE19. . . . . 22 C5
Cosgrove Way LU1. . . . . . 115 D1
Cosmic Ave MK42. . . . . 50 A4
Costin St MK40 . . . . 50 B8
Cotefield LU4. . . . . 115 C3
Cotefield Dr LU7. . . . . 103 B3
Cotman Cl MK41. . . . . 38 B3
Cotswold Bsns Pk LU1 . . 122 D2
Cotswold Cl MK41. . . . . 38 F2
Cotswold Dr LU7. . . . . 110 C8
Cotswold Gdns LU3 . . . . . 115 C7
Cotswold Pl MK45. . . . . 84 D2
Cottage Rd SG19. . . . . 42 B1
COTTON END 63 D7
Cotton End Lower Sch MK45 . . . . 63 D8
Cotton End Rd MK45 . . . . . 63 B5
Cottril Way MK42 . . . . 50 E6
Coulon Cl NN29. . . . . 7 A7

Coulson Ct LU1 . . . . **122** F8
Council Cotts
Radwell SG7 . . . . **91** C4
Sharnbrook MK44 . . . . **16** F4
Council Hos
Ivinghoe Aston LU6 . . . . . . **119** A1
Podington NN29 . . . . **7** E1
Countess Cl PE19 . . . . **22** B3
Countess Ct ⁴ LU2 . . . . . . **116** D1
Countess Gdns MK42 . . . . . **49** D3
Court Dr LU5 . . . . **114** B1
Courtfields AL5 . . . . **131** C1
Court La MK43 . . . . **36** B7
Courtlands LU1 . . . . **110** E6
Courtlands Dr SG18 . . . . . . **67** C3
Court Rd MK43 . . . . **71** B8
Court The MK17 . . . . **70** C3
Covent Garden Cl LU4 . . . . **115** F3
Coventry Rd MK40 . . . . **49** F8
Coverdale LU4 . . . . **115** B6
COVINGTON **2** D2
Cow Cl SG18 . . . . **67** A3
Cowdray Cl LU2 . . . . **117** C3
Cow La LU6 . . . . **119** E4
Cowper Cl AL3 . . . . **128** D5
Cowper Rd
Bedford MK40 . . . . **37** F2
Harpenden AL5 . . . . **131** C4
Markyate AL3 . . . . **128** D5
Cowper Rise AL3 . . . . **128** D5
Cowpers Ct PE19 . . . . **22** A4
Cowper St LU1 . . . . **123** E5
Cowridge Cres LU2 . . . . . . **124** A8
Cowslip Cl NN10 . . . . **8** C8
Cowslip Hill SG6 . . . . **101** E7
Cox's Cl
Bedford MK40 . . . . **49** F7
Sharnbrook MK44 . . . . **16** B4
Cox's Way SG5 . . . . **90** A6
Coyney Gn LU3 . . . . **116** C1
Crab Apple Way SG19 . . . . . **44** C5
Crab La SG18 . . . . **67** A6
Crabtree Inf Sch AL5 . . . . . **131** C1
Crabtree La
Harpenden AL5 . . . . **131** C1
Harpenden AL5 . . . . **131** D1
Crab Tree La SG5 . . . . **99** D4
Crabtree Way LU4 . . . . **114** B2
Crackle Hill Rd SG17 . . . . . **88** C6
Craddock Ct NN29 . . . . **7** B8
Craddocks Dr LU7 . . . . **103** A3
Cradock Rd LU4 . . . . **115** B1
Cranborne Cl MK41 . . . . . . **39** B4
Cranbrook MK41 . . . . **81** B5
Cranbrook Dr LU3 . . . . **115** D8
Crancott Cl MK45 . . . . **74** B8
Cranes Cl MK43 . . . . **34** E5
Crane Way MK43 . . . . **59** C2
CRANFIELD **59** B1
Cranfield Lower Sch
MK43 . . . . **59** B1
Cranfield Rd
Astwood MK16 . . . . **47** B2
Salford MK17 . . . . **70** C4
Woburn Sands MK17 . . . . . **81** B7
Wootton MK43 . . . . **60** E5
Cranfield Technology Pk
MK43 . . . . **70** D8
Cranfield Univ MK43 . . . . . **58** E2
Cranfield Univ Silsoe Coll
MK45 . . . . **86** C3
Cranford Cl AL5 . . . . **131** C1
Cranleigh Gdns LU3 . . . . . **116** C3
Crawley Cl LU3 . . . . **123** C1
Crawley Green Inf Sch
LU2 . . . . **124** B8
Crawley Green Rd
Luton LU4 . . . . **124** A8
Luton, Wigmore LU2 . . . . . **117** C1
Crawley Rd
Cranfield MK43 . . . . **59** C3
Luton LU1 . . . . **123** D8
Woburn MK17 . . . . **82** A1
Crayton Rd MK45 . . . . **84** E8
Crecy Ct PE19 . . . . **22** C5
Crediton Cl MK40 . . . . **38** E2
Creran Wlk LU7 . . . . **110** C7
Crescent Cl LU5 . . . . **105** F5
Crescent Ct
Lidlington MK43 . . . . **72** B3
Toddington LU5 . . . . **105** F5
Crescent Rd LU2 . . . . **123** F8
Crescent Rise LU2 . . . . . . **123** F8
Crescent The
Ampthill MK45 . . . . **84** E7
Bedford MK40 . . . . **38** B1
Beeston SG19 . . . . **54** B5
Caddington LU1 . . . . **122** E3
Cotton End MK45 . . . . **63** D7
Henlow SG16 . . . . **89** C4
Hitchin SG5 . . . . **100** D1
Moggerhanger MK44 . . . . . **53** C8
Shortstown MK42 . . . . **51** A3
Stanford SG18 . . . . **78** A7
Stewartby MK43 . . . . **61** C1
St Neots, Eaton Socon PE19 **22** C3
St Neots, PE19 . . . . **22** F6
Toddington LU5 . . . . **105** F5
Wharley End MK43 . . . . **58** F2
Cressener Terr ⁵ PE19 . . . . **22** F5
Cresta Cl LU5 . . . . **115** A2
Cresta Ho ³ LU1 . . . . **123** D7
Crest The
Dunstable LU5 . . . . **114** E1
Luton LU3 . . . . **116** B7

Criccieth Way PE19 . . . . . . **22** F1
Cricket Cl MK41 . . . . **39** A2
Cricketer's Rd SG15 . . . . . . **90** A4
Cricket La MK41 . . . . **39** A2
Crocus Way NN10 . . . . **8** B7
Croft Cl ⁴ AL5 . . . . **131** B1
Croft Gn LU6 . . . . **120** F8
Crofton Cl MK41 . . . . **38** C4
Croft Rd LU2 . . . . **117** B3
Croft Stewart SG19 . . . . . . **56** C6
Crofts The
Sharnbrook MK44 . . . . **16** E4
Stotfold SG5 . . . . **90** F6
Croft The
Bedford MK41 . . . . **39** A2
Flitwick MK45 . . . . **84** E3
Luton LU3 . . . . **115** D8
Cromer Way
Luton, Stopsley Common
LU2 . . . . **116** E6
Luton, Warden Hill LU2 . . . **116** D7
Cromwell Ct
Kempston MK42 . . . . **49** E4
St Neots PE19 . . . . **22** F3
Cromwell Hill LU2 . . . . . . **116** D1
Cromwell Rd
Barton-le-C MK45 . . . . **97** C3
Bedford MK40 . . . . **38** B1
Luton LU3 . . . . **116** D1
St Neots PE19 . . . . **22** F3
Cromwell Way SG5 . . . . **99** D4
CROOK CORNER **11** A3
Crosby Cl
Dunstable LU6 . . . . **121** C6
Luton LU4 . . . . **116** A2
CROSS END **18** E1
Cross End MK44 . . . . **18** E1
Cross End La MK44 . . . . **18** E2
Crosshall
Crosshall Inf Sch PE19 . . . . **22** C6
Crosshall Jun Sch PE19 . . . . **22** C6
Cross Hall Rd PE19 . . . . **22** D6
Cross Keys Mall ⁸ PE19 . . . . **22** E5
Crosslands LU1 . . . . **122** E3
Crossleys SG6 . . . . **90** F2
Crosspaths AL5 . . . . **130** C5
Cross St N ² LU6 . . . . **114** A1
Cross St
Bedford MK40 . . . . **38** B1
Covington PE28 . . . . **2** D2
Letchworth SG6 . . . . **101** F7
Luton LU2 . . . . **123** E8
Cross The SG19 . . . . **44** D5
Crossway LU7 . . . . **111** D7
Cross Way AL5 . . . . **131** C3
Crossways LU5 . . . . **114** C5
Crossways Cl SG16 . . . . **78** D1
Crossways Pk SG15 . . . . . . **89** F2
Cross Way The LU1 . . . . . . **123** C5
Crowe Rd MK40 . . . . **50** A8
Crow La
Husborne Crawley MK43 . . . **82** B4
Woburn Sands MK17 . . . . . **81** B8
Crowland Rd LU2 . . . . **117** C5
Crown La SG18 . . . . **78** F6
Crown Lodge SG15 . . . . **90** A4
Crown Pl MK42 . . . . **50** B7
Crown Quay MK40 . . . . **50** B7
Crown Wlk PE19 . . . . **22** B4
Crowther Ct SG18 . . . . **66** F7
Croxden Way MK42 . . . . **50** D3
Croxley Ct LU7 . . . . **110** F7
Croxton Cl ³ LU3 . . . . **116** A7
Croyland Dr MK42 . . . . **50** D3
Cryselco Pl MK42 . . . . **49** D2
Cubbington Cl LU3 . . . . . . **116** A7
Cuckoo Cl SG19 . . . . **42** B2
Cuckoo's Nest LU2 . . . . . . **124** A7
Cuffley Ct LU3 . . . . **115** F4
Culloden Cl PE19 . . . . **22** C5
Culver Ho MK40 . . . . **38** A2
Culverhouse Rd LU3 . . . . . **116** C3
Culworth Ct LU1 . . . . **122** E3
Cumberland St
Houghton Regis LU5 . . . . . **114** B4
Luton LU1 . . . . **123** E6
Cumberland Way PE19 . . . . **22** F1
Cumbria Cl LU5 . . . . **114** E5
Cunningham Way PE19 . . . . **22** A2
Curlew Cl SG6 . . . . **90** E1
Curlew Cres MK41 . . . . **38** B4
Curlew Rd LU2 . . . . **117** C5
Curzon Cl LU3 . . . . **116** C1
Cusworth Way LU6 . . . . . . **113** E1
Cusworth Wlk LU6 . . . . . . **113** E1
Cutcliffe Gdns MK40 . . . . . **49** F8
Cutcliffe Gr MK40 . . . . **49** F8
Cutcliffe Pl MK40 . . . . **49** F8
Cutenhoe Rd LU1 . . . . **123** E4
Cutlers Gn LU2 . . . . **117** F2
Cutlers Way LU2 . . . . **117** F2
Cut Throat Ave HP4, LU6 . . **126** F2
Cut Throat La MK41 . . . . . . **37** F2
Cygnus Dr LU7 . . . . **111** B8
Cymbeline Ct ⁶ MK40 . . . . . **38** A1
Cynthia Ct MK43 . . . . **61** A6

D

Daffodil Dr NN10 . . . . **8** B7
Dag La MK44 . . . . **10** F2
DAGNALL **126** C6
Dagnall Rd
Dunstable LU6 . . . . **120** D2
Great Gaddesden HP1 . . . . **132** C5
Dagnalls SG6 . . . . **101** F2

Dagnall Sch HP4 . . . . **126** C5
Dahl Cl MK42 . . . . **50** C4
Dahlia Cl LU2 . . . . **117** B4
Dairy Cotts SG5 . . . . **98** B2
Dairy Ct PE19 . . . . **22** F6
Daisy Croft NN10 . . . . **8** C8
Dalby Cl MK42 . . . . **115** B3
Dale Cl
Bedford MK41 . . . . **39** A3
Dunstable LU5 . . . . **114** F1
Toddington LU5 . . . . **105** F5
Dale Rd
Dunstable LU5 . . . . **114** F1
Luton LU1 . . . . **123** C7
Dale The SG6 . . . . **101** E6
Dalewood AL5 . . . . **131** D1
Dalkeith Rd AL5 . . . . **131** C1
Dallas Rd MK42 . . . . **50** A6
Dalling Dr LU5 . . . . **114** C5
Dallow Prim Sch LU1 . . . . **123** C8
Dallow Rd LU1 . . . . **123** B8
Dalroad Ind Est LU1 . . . . . **123** B8
Dalton Cl LU3 . . . . **108** B1
Dame Alice Harpur Sch
MK42 . . . . **50** C7
Dame Alice St MK40 . . . . . . **38** B1
Dammersey Cl AL3 . . . . . . **128** F4
Dane Cl
Harpenden AL5 . . . . **131** C4
Stotfold SG5 . . . . **90** F8
Danefield Rd SG5 . . . . **99** C4
Dane La MK45 . . . . **62** C5
Dane Rd
Barton-le-C MK45 . . . . **97** D3
Luton LU1 . . . . **123** C7
Danesborough Dr MK17 . . . **81** A2
Danescroft SG6 . . . . **91** A1
Dane St MK40 . . . . **50** B8
Danes Way LU7 . . . . **111** D7
Daneswood MK17 . . . . **81** A4
Danvers Dr LU3 . . . . **108** C1
Dapifer Dr SG19 . . . . **54** C8
Dark La SG18 . . . . **66** F6
Darlington Cl SG19 . . . . . . **42** D1
Darlow Dr MK40 . . . . **37** D1
Darrington Ct PE19 . . . . **22** B3
Dart Rd MK41 . . . . **38** C5
Darwin Rd MK42 . . . . **50** C5
Daubeney Ct LU2 . . . . **95** F2
Daubeney Mid Sch MK42 . . **49** F3
Dauphin Cl LU2 . . . . **116** D1
David Evans Ct SG6 . . . . . **101** D7
Davis Cl MK42 . . . . **50** B5
Davis Cres SG5 . . . . **99** D4
Davis' Row SG15 . . . . **90** A4
Dawlish Dr MK40 . . . . **38** E1
Dawlish Rd LU4 . . . . **115** F3
Dawson Cl SG16 . . . . **89** C5
Daysfield MK45 . . . . **74** B8
Day's La MK40 . . . . **37** D1
Deacon Ave MK42 . . . . **49** C3
Deacon Mews MK43 . . . . . . **72** C8
Deacons Ct ⁶ LU2 . . . . **123** D8
Deacons Way SG5 . . . . **100** D1
DEADMAN'S CROSS **76** C8
Deadman's Hill MK45 . . . . . **75** B2
Dean Cl NN10 . . . . **8** A8
Dean St MK40 . . . . **38** F1
Dearmans Cl MK45 . . . . . . **75** C1
Dearne Villas MK40 . . . . . . **50** A8
Dearne Wlk MK41 . . . . **38** C5
DEEPDALE **55** D7
Deepdale SG19 . . . . **55** D7
Deepdale Water Gardens ★
SG19 . . . . **55** D7
Deep Denes LU2 . . . . **117** A2
Deep Spinney MK40 . . . . . . **37** C1
Deeside MK41 . . . . **38** D5
Deethe Cl MK41 . . . . **81** B5
Degray Manor SG16 . . . . . **78** D2
De Grey Mausoleum ★
MK45 . . . . **85** D4
De Havilland Ave MK42 . . . . **51** B2
Delamare Ct SG19 . . . . **42** B1
Delamere Gdns LU7 . . . . . **110** C7
Delamere Wlk MK41 . . . . . . **39** B3
Delco Way LU6 . . . . **113** F2
Delfield Gdns LU1 . . . . **122** E4
Dell Cl AL5 . . . . **131** D1
Dellcot Cl LU2 . . . . **117** B4
Dellfield Ct LU2 . . . . **117** D2
Dellmont Rd LU5 . . . . **114** B5
Dell Rd LU5 . . . . **114** B5
Dells La SG18 . . . . **67** A5
Dells The SG18 . . . . **67** A5
Dell The
Caddington LU1 . . . . **122** E3
Heath and Reach LU7 . . . . **103** B5
Kempston MK42 . . . . **49** B2
Luton LU1 . . . . **117** F1
Markyate AL3 . . . . **128** D5
Delmerend La AL3 . . . . . . **129** C1
Delphine Cl LU1 . . . . **123** B6
De Montfort Ct LU5 . . . . . **105** F4
Denbigh Cl MK43 . . . . **72** D8
Denbigh High Sch LU3 . . . **116** C2
Denbigh Inf Sch LU3 . . . . . **116** B2
Denbigh Jun Sch LU3 . . . . **116** B2
Denbigh Rd LU3 . . . . **116** B2
Denbigh Way MK41 . . . . . . **39** A4
Dencora Way LU3 . . . . **115** B8
Dene Cl MK17 . . . . **81** C4
Denel Cl MK45 . . . . **84** E4
Dene Way SG18 . . . . **66** B8
Denham Cl LU3 . . . . **115** E8
Denmark Cl LU3 . . . . **107** E1

Denmark St MK40 . . . . **50** E8
Dennis Ct MK42 . . . . **49** D2
DENNIS GREEN **44** C4
Dennis Rd MK42 . . . . **49** D2
Denny Cres SG18 . . . . **78** F8
Denton Cl
Irchester NN29 . . . . **7** B8
Kempston MK42 . . . . **49** D6
Luton LU4 . . . . **115** B3
Denton Dr MK43 . . . . **72** C7
Dents Rd MK42 . . . . **50** D5
De Parys Ave MK40 . . . . . . **38** C1
Derby Pl MK40 . . . . **38** B1
Derby Rd LU4 . . . . **115** C2
Derwent Ave
Biggleswade SG18 . . . . . . **67** B4
Luton LU3 . . . . **116** B7
Derwent Cotts MK43 . . . . . **26** B3
Derwent Dr LU6 . . . . **121** C6
Derwent Lower Sch SG16 . . **89** B5
Derwent Pl MK42 . . . . **50** B6
Derwent Rd
Harpenden AL5 . . . . **130** C4
Henlow SG16 . . . . **89** B4
Leighton Buzzard LU7 . . . . **110** B7
Luton LU2 . . . . **124** A8
Derwent Rise MK45 . . . . . . **84** E2
Des Fuller Ct ³ LU1 . . . . . **123** F6
Deverell Way LU7 . . . . **111** C5
Devizes Ave LU3 . . . . **115** B3
Devon Rd
Bedford MK40 . . . . **38** D2
Luton LU2 . . . . **124** B8
Devonshire Rd ⁵ AL5 . . . . **131** B1
Dewlands MK43 . . . . **36** F7
Dew Pond Rd MK45 . . . . . . **84** D3
Dewsbury Rd LU3 . . . . **116** C6
Dexter Cl LU3 . . . . **108** B1
DIAMOND END **24** C6
Dickens Bvd SG5 . . . . **90** C2
Dickens Cl MK43 . . . . **24** F6
Dickens Ct SG18 . . . . **67** A5
Dickens La LU7 . . . . **113** A5
Dickens Rd MK45 . . . . **84** C3
Dickerson Cl SG19 . . . . **44** D6
Digby Ct PE19 . . . . **22** B3
Digby Rd LU7 . . . . **111** A8
Dillock La MK43 . . . . **48** C1
Dimmock Cl LU7 . . . . **111** C4
Dimmock Rd MK43 . . . . . . **60** F7
Dines Cl MK45 . . . . **62** E4
Dingle Dell LU7 . . . . **102** F2
Disbrowe Ct NN9 . . . . **3** C7
Ditchling Cl LU2 . . . . **117** C3
Ditmas Ave MK42 . . . . **49** C2
Ditton Gn LU2 . . . . **117** E3
Docklands SG5 . . . . **99** D4
Dodds Cl MK44 . . . . **11** B3
Doggett St LU2 . . . . **117** A7
Dog Kennel Path LU6 . . . . **114** B1
Dolce Way MK44 . . . . **16** B3
Dolmans Pl ¹² LU6 . . . . . . **121** B8
Dolphin Dr LU5 . . . . **114** E6
Dolphins Way SG19 . . . . . . **44** D6
Don Butler Cl MK45 . . . . . . **86** B3
Donlee Furlong LU7 . . . . . **111** C7
Donnelly Dr MK41 . . . . **39** B1
Dony Field Centre LU2 . . . **116** B8
Doolittle Mill MK45 . . . . . . **84** D5
Dorchester Cl LU5 . . . . . . **114** B1
Dorchester Way MK42 . . . . **50** C3
Dordans Rd LU4 . . . . **115** F4
Dorel Cl LU4 . . . . **116** F2
Dornan Ct LU1 . . . . **123** E5
Dorrington Cl LU3 . . . . . . **116** C1
Dorset Ct ⁴ LU1 . . . . **123** F6
Dorsey Dr MK42 . . . . **50** B5
Dothans Cl MK44 . . . . **40** F5
Doug Harris Way MK45 . . . **86** B3
Douglas Cres LU5 . . . . **114** B2
Douglas Rd
Bedford MK41 . . . . **38** D6
Harpenden AL5 . . . . **130** F2
Luton LU4 . . . . **116** A2
Dove Cl SG19 . . . . **42** C2
Dovedale LU2 . . . . **116** E6
Dovehouse Cl
Bromham MK43 . . . . **36** F2
St Neots PE19 . . . . **22** F6
Dove House Cl LU6 . . . . . . **119** F3
Dove House Dr SG16 . . . . . **78** D1
Dovehouse Hill LU2 . . . . . **117** B1
Dove House La LU6 . . . . . **127** D8
Dove La MK43 . . . . **25** A6
Dover Cl LU3 . . . . **116** A3
Dover Cres MK41 . . . . **39** A5
Dove Rd MK41 . . . . **38** D4
Dovery Down Lower Sch
LU7 . . . . **103** A2
Dove Tree Rd LU7 . . . . **111** C8
Dove Wlk MK45 . . . . **84** E1
Downfield Way MK42 . . . . . **49** E5
Downham Rd MK17 . . . . . . **81** C4
Downlands LU3 . . . . **115** C7
DOWNSIDE **121** E7
Downside MK41 . . . . **38** D4
Downside Gdns SG19 . . . . . **56** A8
Downside Inf Sch LU1 . . . . **115** E1
Downside Jun Sch LU4 . . . **115** E1
Downside Lower Sch
LU5 . . . . **121** E7
Downs Rd
Dunstable LU5 . . . . **121** D8
Luton LU1 . . . . **123** C7
Downs View LU4 . . . . **115** D4
Downton Ct ² LU3 . . . . . . **123** D8
Downview LU4 . . . . **115** B2
Drakeloe Cl MK17 . . . . **92** F8

Drake Rd PE19 . . . . **22** B2
Drakes Ct LU5 . . . . **121** D8
Drapers Mews LU3 . . . . . . **116** C1
Draper Way LU7 . . . . **111** C5
Drayton Cl NN10 . . . . **8** A8
Drayton Rd
Kempston MK42 . . . . **49** D2
Luton LU4 . . . . **115** A3
Drewels La PE19 . . . . **33** E4
Drivers Ct LU7 . . . . **111** D7
Drive The
Harpenden AL5 . . . . **131** A4
Ivinghoe Aston LU6 . . . . . **119** A1
Oakley MK43 . . . . **36** F7
Sharnbrook MK44 . . . . **16** C4
Wharley End MK43 . . . . . . **58** D2
Drove Rd
Biggleswade SG18 . . . . . . **67** B6
Gamlingay SG19 . . . . **44** B7
Drovers Way LU6 . . . . **120** F8
Drummonds The LU4 . . . . **115** C2
Drury Cl LU5 . . . . **114** C5
Drury La LU5 . . . . **114** C5
Dryden Ct PE19 . . . . **22** F5
Dubbs Knoll Rd SG8 . . . . . . **69** F5
Duchess Cl PE19 . . . . **22** A3
Duchess Ct LU5 . . . . **114** C1
Duchess Rd MK42 . . . . **50** F4
Duchy Cl NN9 . . . . **3** B8
DUCK END
MK43 . . . . **36** B6
MK45 . . . . **62** A1
MK45 . . . . **62** E5
MK45 . . . . **85** B8
Duck End Cl MK45 . . . . **62** A1
Duck End La
Biddenham MK40 . . . . **37** B1
Maulden MK45 . . . . **85** B8
Wilstead MK45 . . . . **62** E5
Duck La
Shefford SG17 . . . . **77** C3
St Neots PE19 . . . . **22** F4
Woburn MK17 . . . . **92** F7
Duckmill Cres MK42 . . . . . . **50** C7
Duck Mill La MK42 . . . . **50** C7
DUCK'S CROSS **30** C5
Dudley St MK42 . . . . **49** E3
Dudley St
Bedford MK40 . . . . **50** E8
Leighton Buzzard LU7 . . . . **111** A6
Luton LU2 . . . . **123** E8
Dugdale Ct SG5 . . . . **100** C1
Duke Dr MK41 . . . . **37** D7
Dukeminster Trad Est
LU5 . . . . **114** C1
Dukes Ave LU6 . . . . **126** E8
Dukes Ct
Flitwick MK45 . . . . **85** A2
⁴ Luton LU2 . . . . **123** D6
Dukes Rd
Ampthill MK45 . . . . **84** F8
St Neots PE19 . . . . **22** B4
Dukes Ride
Leighton Buzzard LU7 . . . . **102** F3
¹³ Luton LU2 . . . . **116** D1
Dukes Row PE28 . . . . **6** F5
Duke St
Aspley Guise MK17 . . . . . . **81** D4
Bedford MK40 . . . . **50** C8
Luton LU2 . . . . **123** E8
DULOE **21** F6
Duloe PE19 . . . . **22** A6
Duloe Brook PE19 . . . . **22** B4
Duloe Rd PE19 . . . . **22** B5
Dulverton Ct LU7 . . . . **110** C8
Dumfries Ct ⁸ LU1 . . . . . . **123** D6
Dumfries St LU1 . . . . **123** D6
Duncan Rd MK43 . . . . **58** E2
Duncombe Cl LU3 . . . . **116** C6
Duncombe Ct LU4 . . . . **114** E2
Duncombe Dr
Dunstable LU5 . . . . **114** E2
Leighton Buzzard LU7 . . . . **111** A6
Duncombe St MK42 . . . . . . **49** F4
Duncots Cl SG5 . . . . **100** E3
Dungee Rd NN29, MK43 . . . **14** C4
Dunham Cl MK42 . . . . **50** F5
Dunkirk Cl MK42 . . . . **50** A5
Dunlin SG6 . . . . **90** E1
Dunmow Cl LU3 . . . . **116** D2
Dunraven Ave LU1 . . . . . . **123** A8
Dunsby Rd LU3 . . . . **116** A6
Dunsmore Rd LU1 . . . . . . **123** C6
DUNSTABLE **121** D8
Dunstable Cl
Flitwick MK45 . . . . **84** E2
Luton LU4 . . . . **116** A1
Dunstable Coll LU5 . . . . . . **114** C1
Dunstable Ct LU4 . . . . **115** D3
Dunstable Downs Ctry Pk ★
LU6 . . . . **120** E3
Dunstable Icknield Lower
Sch LU6 . . . . **121** B8
Dunstable Pl ⁵ LU1 . . . . . . **123** D7
Dunstable Rd
Caddington LU1 . . . . **122** C3
Dagnall HP4, LU6 . . . . . . **126** C7
Eaton Bray LU6 . . . . **120** A5
Flamstead AL3 . . . . **129** F1
Flitwick MK45 . . . . **84** E1
Houghton Regis LU5 . . . . . **114** B3
Luton LU4 . . . . **116** B1
Studham LU6 . . . . **127** B6
Tilsworth LU7 . . . . **113** A6
Toddington LU5 . . . . **105** F3
Totternhoe LU6 . . . . **120** D7
Dunstable St MK45 . . . . . . **84** E8
Dunstall Rd MK45 . . . . **97** C2

Dunster Gdns MK41 . . . . . . **39** B5
Dunster Way PE19 . . . . . . **22** F2
DUNTON **68** D5
Dunton La
　Biggleswade SG18 . . . . . . **67** C4
　Biggleswade SG18 . . . . . . **67** E4
Dunton Lower Sch SG18 . . **68** D5
Dunvegan Way MK41 . . . . **38** F5
Durbar Rd LU4 . . . . **116** B1
Durham Cl
　Biggleswade SG18 . . . . . . **67** A4
　Flitwick MK45 . . . . **84** E1
Durham Rd LU2 . . . . . . **124** A7
Durler Ave MK42 . . . . . . **49** C3
Durler Gdns LU1 . . . . . . **123** D5
Durrell Cl LU7 . . . . **110** E7
DUTTER END **44** E6
Dutter End SG19 . . . . . . **44** E5
Duxford Cl LU3 . . . . **116** B7
Dyers Rd LU6 . . . . **119** E7
Dylan Ct LU5 . . . . **114** C5
Dynes Pl MK44 . . . . **53** C7
Dynevor Cl MK43 . . . . . . **36** E2
Dynevor Rd MK40 . . . . . . **38** A1

E

Eagle Centre Way LU4 . . **115** B7
Eagle Cl LU4 . . . . **115** B7
Eagle Ct SG7 . . . . **91** E1
Eagle Dr MK45 . . . . **84** D2
Eagle Farm Rd SG18 . . . . **67** B5
Eagle Gdns MK41 . . . . . . **38** B3
Eagle Way MK43 . . . . . . **24** F6
Earl Cl PE19 . . . . **22** B4
Earls Ct LU5 . . . . **114** C1
Earls Holme MK42 . . . . . **49** D6
Earlsmead SG6 . . . . . . **101** F3
Earls Meade LU2 . . . . . **116** D1
Easby Abbey MK41 . . . . . **51** B8
Easedale Cl LU6 . . . . . . **121** C6
Easingwold Gdns LU1 . . **122** F8
Eastcheap SG6 . . . . . . **101** F6
East Cl SG4 . . . . **101** B1
Eastcote MK42 . . . . **51** A3
Eastcott Cl LU2 . . . . . . **117** D1
EASTCOTTS **51** A4
Eastcotts Rd MK42 . . . . . **50** F5
East Ct
　Bedford MK41 . . . . **39** A2
　2 St Neots PE19 . . . . . . **22** F5
Eastdale Cl MK42 . . . . . . **50** A4
EAST END
　MK43 . . . . **59** C2
　MK44 . . . . **30** B3
East End
　Houghton Regis LU5 . . . **114** C5
　Pavenham MK43 . . . . . . **26** F3
East End La MK44 . . . . . . **30** B3
Eastern Ave
　Dunstable LU5 . . . . . . **121** D8
　Henlow SG16 . . . . **89** C3
Eastern Way
　Heath and Reach LU7 . . **103** D5
　Letchworth SG6 . . . . . . **91** A1
Eastfield Cl LU2 . . . . . . **117** C4
East Hill LU3 . . . . **116** B6
Easthill Rd LU5 . . . . . . **114** C5
East Hills MK43 . . . . **59** B1
EAST HYDE **130** F8
East La SG19 . . . . **44** C6
East Lodge SG17 . . . . . . **77** A2
Eastnor Gdns MK41 . . . . . **39** A4
Easton Cl MK45 . . . . **84** F3
Easton Rd MK45 . . . . **84** F3
East Rd
　Langford SG18 . . . . **78** E8
　Sandy SG19 . . . . **54** D2
　Wharley End MK43 . . . . . **58** D2
East Side SG19 . . . . **54** C5
East Sq MK42 . . . . **51** A3
East St
　Irchester NN29 . . . . **7** B8
　Kimbolton PE28 . . . . **6** F4
　Leighton Buzzard LU7 . . **111** B8
　Lilley LU2 . . . . **109** D2
　St Neots PE19 . . . . **22** F5
Eastville Rd MK42 . . . . . . **50** B5
East Wlk SG18 . . . . **67** B7
EATON BRAY **119** F6
Eaton Bray Lower Sch
　LU6 . . . . **119** F6
Eaton Bray Rd
　Northall LU6 . . . . **119** C5
　Totternhoe LU6 . . . . . . **119** E8
EATON FORD **22** D6
Eaton Ford Gn PE19 . . . . **22** D5
Eatongate Cl LU6 . . . . . **119** F4
Eaton Green Rd LU2 . . . **124** D8
Eaton Pk LU6 . . . . **119** F6
Eaton Pl LU2 . . . . **117** D1
Eaton Rd MK42 . . . . **49** E2
EATON SOCON **22** C3
Eaton Valley Rd LU2 . . . **124** B8
Ebble Mead MK41 . . . . . . **38** D6
Ebenezer St LU1 . . . . . **123** D6
Eddiwick Ave LU5 . . . . . **114** D7
Edens La MK43 . . . . **25** B2
Eden Way
　Bedford MK41 . . . . **38** D5
　Leighton Buzzard LU7 . . **111** B5
Edgcott Cl LU3 . . . . . . **108** B1
Edgcumbe Ct SG19 . . . . . **54** C7
Edgecote Cl LU2 . . . . . **122** E3
Edgehill Gdns LU3 . . . . **115** C8
Edgewood Dr LU2 . . . . . **117** C6

Edinburgh Cl MK42 . . . . . **50** D5
Edinburgh Dr PE19 . . . . . **22** C4
Edison Rd MK41 . . . . . . **39** C3
Edith Cavell Lower Sch
　MK41 . . . . **38** A2
Edkins Cl LU2 . . . . **116** E5
EDLESBOROUGH **119** C6
Edlesborough Sch LU6 . . **119** B3
Edward Arnold Ct MK42 . . **49** D5
Edward Cl SG19 . . . . **54** D7
Edward Peake Mid Sch
　SG19 . . . . **67** C8
Edward Rd
　Bedford MK42 . . . . **50** A6
　Biggleswade SG18 . . . . . **67** B5
　Irchester NN29 . . . . **7** B7
　St Neots PE19 . . . . **22** F2
Edward St
　Dunstable LU5 . . . . . . **114** B1
　Leighton Buzzard LU7 . . **111** A8
　Luton LU2 . . . . **116** F1
EDWORTH **80** A6
Edworth Rd SG18 . . . . . . **79** C5
Egdon Dr LU2 . . . . **116** D6
EGGINGTON **112** B7
Egglestone Cl MK42 . . . . **49** D4
Eighth Ave LU3 . . . . . . **115** D7
Eileen Wade Lower Sch
　PE28 . . . . **5** B4
Eisenhower Pl SG17 . . . . **76** E2
Eisenhower Rd SG17 . . . . **77** C1
Elaine Gdns LU1 . . . . . . **123** A1
Eldefield SG6 . . . . **101** D7
Elderberry Cl LU2 . . . . . **117** B4
Elder Cl SG19 . . . . **54** B6
Eldon Rd LU4 . . . . **115** C1
Eldon Way SG18 . . . . . . **67** A4
Eleanor Cl MK17 . . . . . . **92** F7
Eleanor Ct **4** LU6 . . . . **121** B8
Eleanor's Cross **5** LU6 . **121** B8
Eleanor Wlk MK17 . . . . . **92** F7
Elgar Dr SG17 . . . . **77** D3
Elgar Path LU2 . . . . . . **123** E8
Elger Cl MK40 . . . . **37** D1
Eliot Way SG5 . . . . **90** D3
Elizabeth Ct
　Dunstable LU5 . . . . . . **121** C8
　Henlow SG16 . . . . **78** D1
　9 Luton LU1 . . . . . . **123** D6
　St Neots PE19 . . . . **22** C4
Elizabeth St LU1 . . . . . **123** D6
Elizabeth Way SG19 . . . . **44** C6
Ella Ct LU2 . . . . **116** F1
Ellenhall Cl LU2 . . . . . . **116** C1
Ellenshaw Ct MK45 . . . . . **84** F4
Ellerdine Cl LU3 . . . . . . **116** B4
Ellesmere Cl LU6 . . . . . **120** C6
Ellington Rd MK42 . . . . . **50** B5
Elliot Cres MK41 . . . . . . **39** B3
Ellis Rd MK41 . . . . **38** D3
Elliswick Rd AL5 . . . . . . **131** B2
Elm Ave LU1 . . . . **122** E3
Elm Cl
　Bedford MK41 . . . . **38** E4
　Campton MK17 . . . . **76** F1
　Hargrave NN9 . . . . **1** F2
　Henlow SG16 . . . . **78** D1
Elm Dr MK45 . . . . **86** B5
Elm Farm Cl SG17 . . . . . **78** B2
Elmfield Ct LU2 . . . . . . **117** A1
Elm Gr
　Toddington LU5 . . . . . . **105** F6
　Woburn Sands MK17 . . . . **81** B4
Elm Ho PE19 . . . . **22** F3
Elmhurst Gdns SG5 . . . . . **87** F1
Elm Lodge PE19 . . . . **22** F3
Elmore Rd LU2 . . . . . . **117** A1
Elm Park Cl LU5 . . . . . . **114** D6
Elm Rd
　Biggleswade SG18 . . . . . **67** B5
　Shefford SG17 . . . . **77** D2
Elms Cl MK45 . . . . **84** F7
Elmsdale Rd MK43 . . . . . **61** A8
ELMS FARM **39** C3
Elmside LU6 . . . . **127** E8
Elms Ind Est
　Bedford, Elms Farm MK41 . **39** D3
　Bedford, Goldington MK41 . **39** B3
Elms La MK43 . . . . **63** C4
Elms The
　Kempston MK42 . . . . . . **49** E3
　Leighton Buzzard LU7 . . **110** E7
Elmtree Ave LU2 . . . . . . **117** E3
Elm Tree Gr MK44 . . . . . **19** C7
Elmtree Rd SG19 . . . . . . **54** B8
Elmwood MK43 . . . . **34** E6
Elmwood Cres
　Flitwick MK45 . . . . **84** F2
　Luton LU2 . . . . **116** E3
Elphick Ct SG18 . . . . . . **66** F6
ELSTOW **50** C2
Elstow Lower Sch MK42 . . **50** B4
Elstow Moot Hall Mus★
　MK42 . . . . **50** B4
Elstow Rd
　Bedford MK42 . . . . **50** C5
　Kempston MK42 . . . . . . **49** F4
Elstow Storage Depot
　MK45 . . . . **62** A4
Elveden Cl LU2 . . . . . . **116** E6
Elvington Gdns LU3 . . . . **108** B1
Ely Cl MK45 . . . . **84** E4
Ely Croft SG18 . . . . **67** A4
Ely Way
　Kempston MK42 . . . . . . **49** E6
　Luton LU4 . . . . **115** D4
Embankment The MK40 . . **50** D8
Embla Cl MK41 . . . . **39** E3

Emerald Rd LU4 . . . . . . **115** A3
Emerton Way MK43 . . . . . **60** F8
Emery Pl PE19 . . . . **22** F7
Emmer Gn LU2 . . . . . . **117** E2
Emmerton Rd MK42 . . . . . **49** D5
Empire Cl LU3 . . . . **66** F5
Empress Rd LU3 . . . . . . **115** E4
Emu Cl LU7 . . . . **103** A5
Enderby Rd LU3 . . . . . . **116** C6
Endsleigh Rd MK42 . . . . . **50** B6
Enfield Cl LU5 . . . . **114** D6
Engayne Ave SG19 . . . . . **42** B1
England Ave LU6 . . . . . **113** F3
Englands La LU2 . . . . . **121** C8
Englefield LU2 . . . . . . **116** F3
Englehurst AL5 . . . . . . **131** D1
Ennerdale Ave LU6 . . . . **121** B7
Ennerdale Cl MK42 . . . . . **49** D3
Ennismore Gn LU2 . . . . **117** F1
Enslow Cl LU1 . . . . . . **122** E3
Enterprise Ctr **1** LU2 . . **123** F8
Enterprise Way
　Flitwick MK45 . . . . **84** F3
　Leighton Buzzard LU7 . . **111** A5
　Luton LU3 . . . . **116** B8
Epping Way LU3 . . . . . **107** C1
Epping Wlk MK41 . . . . . . **39** B3
Epsom Cl
　Leighton Buzzard LU7 . . **110** D6
　Rushden NN10 . . . . **8** D8
Ereswell Rd LU3 . . . . . . **116** A7
Eriboll Cl LU7 . . . . **110** B6
Erin Cl LU4 . . . . **116** A2
Erin Ct LU4 . . . . **116** A2
Ermine Pl **8** LU2 . . . . **116** D1
Escarpment Ave HP4,
　LU6 . . . . **126** D8
Eskdale LU4 . . . . **115** C5
Esmonde Ct LU7 . . . . . . **111** D5
Essex Cl LU1 . . . . **123** F6
Essex Ct **7** LU1 . . . . . **123** E6
Essex Gdns MK42 . . . . . . **50** D5
Etonbury Mid Sch SG15 . . **90** C7
Eton Ct MK40 . . . . **38** D2
Ettrick Dr MK41 . . . . . . **39** C4
Eugster Ave MK42 . . . . . **49** C3
Evans Cl LU5 . . . . **114** E4
Evans Yd LU3 . . . . **103** B4
Evedon Cl LU3 . . . . . . **115** F6
Evelyn Rd LU5 . . . . **114** F2
Evelyn Way NN29 . . . . . . **7** C7
Everard Rd MK41 . . . . . . **38** F2
Everest Cl SG15 . . . . . . **90** B5
Evergreen Way LU3 . . . . **116** A8
EVERSHOLT **94** B7
Eversholt Ho LU7 . . . . . **111** A6
Eversholt Lower Sch
　MK17 . . . . **94** A5
Eversholt Rd
　Ridgmont MK43 . . . . . . **82** F4
　Steppingley MK45 . . . . . **83** F3
EVERTON **43** C3
Everton Hill SG19 . . . . . **43** B3
Everton Lower Sch SG19 . **43** C3
Everton Rd
　Gamlingay Great Heath
　　SG19 . . . . **43** E3
　Potton SG19 . . . . **55** F8
　Sandy SG19 . . . . **54** F7
Eves Field MK45 . . . . . . **85** D3
Evesham Abbey MK41 . . . **51** A8
Evesham Ct MK41 . . . . . **38** C5
Exeter Cl SG18 . . . . **67** A4
Exeter Wlk MK41 . . . . . . **39** A5
Exton Ave LU2 . . . . . . **117** A1
Exton Cl MK45 . . . . **85** A8
EYEWORTH **68** F8
Eyeworth Rd SG19 . . . . . **57** B2
Eyncourt Rd LU5 . . . . . **114** D2
EYNESBURY **22** E3
Eynesbury CE Prim Sch
　PE19 . . . . **22** E4
Eynesbury Gn PE19 . . . . **22** F4
Eynsford Rd LU4 . . . . . **115** D3

F

Fairfax Ave LU3 . . . . . . **115** D7
Fairfax Cl SG17 . . . . **78** A2
Fairfax Ct PE19 . . . . **22** F2
Fairfax Rd MK40 . . . . . . **49** F7
Fairfield SG19 . . . . **44** D5
Fairfield Cl
　Dunstable LU5 . . . . . . **114** F1
　Harpenden AL5 . . . . . . **131** D1
Fairfield Rd
　Biggleswade SG18 . . . . . **66** F7
　Dunstable LU5 . . . . . . **114** E1
Fairford Ave LU2 . . . . . **116** E4
Fairgreen Rd LU1 . . . . . **122** F3
Fairground Way SG17 . . . **78** B2
Fairholme
　Bedford MK41 . . . . **38** F3
　Biggleswade SG18 . . . . . **66** F7
Fairlands MK41 . . . . **38** F3
Fairmead Cres NN10 . . . . **7** F8
Fair Oak Cl LU2 . . . . . . **116** F3
Fair Oak Dr LU2 . . . . . . **116** F3
Fair Way MK44 . . . . **40** F5
Fairways The MK45 . . . . . **86** C4
Fairway The MK41 . . . . . **39** A2
Fakeswell La SG16 . . . . . **88** E2
Falcon Cl
　Dunstable LU6 . . . . . . **114** B1
　Sandy SG19 . . . . **42** B1
Falcon Cres MK41 . . . . . **84** E1

Falconers Field AL5 . . . . **130** E3
Falconers Rd LU2 . . . . . **117** B1
Faldo Rd
　Barton-le-C MK45 . . . . . **97** B4
　Bedford MK42 . . . . **50** D6
Fallow Dr PE19 . . . . **22** B5
Fallowfield
　Ampthill MK45 . . . . **84** E7
　Leighton Buzzard LU7 . . **111** C7
　Luton LU3 . . . . **116** C4
Fallows Gn AL5 . . . . . . **131** B3
Falstaff Rd PE19 . . . . . . **22** C3
Falstone Gn LU2 . . . . . **117** E1
FANCOTT **106** B4
Faraday Cl LU4 . . . . . . **115** C1
Faraday Gdns SG5 . . . . . **90** C2
Faraday Rd MK42 . . . . . . **50** C5
Faraday Sq MK42 . . . . . . **50** C5
Farcet Ct PE19 . . . . **22** C6
Fareham Way LU5 . . . . . **114** E5
Faringdon Rd LU4 . . . . . **115** C5
Farley Ct LU1 . . . . **123** C5
Farley Farm Rd LU1 . . . . **123** B5
FARLEY HILL **123** C6
Farley Hill LU1 . . . . . . **123** C6
Farley Jun Sch LU1 . . . . **123** C6
Farley Lodge LU2 . . . . . **123** D5
Farley Way MK43 . . . . . . **36** C7
Farm Ave AL5 . . . . **130** D4
Farmbrook LU2 . . . . . . **116** D5
Farm Cl
　Ampthill MK45 . . . . **84** D7
　Houghton Regis LU5 . . . **114** C5
　Letchworth SG6 . . . . . . **91** A1
　Wyboston MK44 . . . . . . **31** F6
Farm Gn LU1 . . . . **123** C5
Farm Rd LU1 . . . . **130** B7
FARNDISH **7** B4
Farndish Rd NN29 . . . . . . **7** B7
Farnham Dr NN10 . . . . . . **7** F8
Farnham Way MK41 . . . . . **39** A5
Farnley Gr LU2 . . . . . . **124** A7
Farrell Rd MK43 . . . . **60** F7
Farrer St MK42 . . . . **49** E4
Farrer Top AL3 . . . . . . **128** E5
Farriers Cl SG7 . . . . **91** E1
Farrow Cl LU3 . . . . **108** C1
Farrows Cl MK43 . . . . . . **27** A1
Farr's La LU2 . . . . **125** B1
Farsands MK43 . . . . **36** F8
Faulkner's Way LU7 . . . . **110** E7
Faynes Ct LU2 . . . . **54** C7
Fearnhill Sch LU5 . . . . . **101** C5
Fearnley Cres MK42 . . . . **50** A4
Fedden Ho MK43 . . . . . . **58** D3
Felbrigg Cl LU2 . . . . . . **117** F2
Felix Ave LU2 . . . . **117** A2
FELMERSHAM **26** C7
Felmersham Rd LU1 . . . **123** B7
Felmersham Gravel Pits
　Nature Reserve★ MK43 . . **16** C1
Felmersham Rd
　Carlton MK43 . . . . **25** C5
　Luton LU1 . . . . **123** A7
　Radwell MK43 . . . . **26** E7
Felstead Cl LU2 . . . . . . **116** F3
Felstead Way LU2 . . . . . **116** F3
Felton Cl LU2 . . . . **117** D1
Fen End SG5 . . . . **90** F8
FENLAKE **50** E5
Fenlake Rd MK42 . . . . . . **50** D6
Fensome Dr LU5 . . . . . . **114** E5
Fenwick Cl LU3 . . . . . . **116** B5
Fenwick Rd LU5 . . . . . . **114** E5
Feoffee Almshouses
　MK45 . . . . **73** F1
Fermor Cres LU2 . . . . . **117** C1
Fermor Cl LU2 . . . . **117** C1
Ferndale **7** AL5 . . . . . **131** A4
Ferndale Rd LU1 . . . . . **123** B7
Fern Gdns MK45 . . . . . . **84** E3
Fernheath LU3 . . . . . . **108** A1
Fernlea Cl MK40 . . . . . . **49** E7
Fernwood Sch MK17 . . . . **81** B2
Ferrars Ave PE19 . . . . . . **22** E4
Ferrars Cl LU4 . . . . **115** B1
Ferrars Inf Sch LU4 . . . . **115** B3
Ferrars Jun Sch LU4 . . . . **115** B3
Festival Rd SG19 . . . . . . **55** F7
Fetlock Cl MK41 . . . . . . **37** D7
Field Cottage Rd PE19 . . **22** C3
Field End Cl LU2 . . . . . **117** C4
Fieldfare
　Letchworth SG6 . . . . . . **90** E1
　Sandy SG19 . . . . **42** C2
Field Fare Gn LU4 . . . . . **115** A5
Fieldgate Rd LU4 . . . . . **115** D7
Fielding Ct PE19 . . . . . . **22** C7
Field La SG6 . . . . **101** F4
Fieldside MK41 . . . . **39** B3
Fieldside Rd MK45 . . . . . **85** E1
Fields Rd MK43 . . . . **61** A6
Fields The SG18 . . . . . . **66** F1
Fildyke Cl SG17 . . . . . . **88** C5
Fildyke Rd SG17 . . . . . . **88** C5
Filland Ct SG19 . . . . . . **54** B6
Filmer Rd LU4 . . . . **115** E4
Finchale Priory MK41 . . . **51** B8
Finch Cl LU4 . . . . **115** A4
Finch Cres LU7 . . . . . . **110** E5
Finches The
　Bedford MK40 . . . . **38** A1
　Sandy SG19 . . . . **42** C2
Finch Wlk MK45 . . . . . . **84** E1
Finley Rd AL5 . . . . **131** D3
Finn's Villas LU4 . . . . . **106** A6
Finsbury Rd LU4 . . . . . . **115** D5
Finway LU1 . . . . **123** A8
Firbank Cl LU3 . . . . . . **107** C1

Firbank Ct LU7 . . . . . . **111** B5
Firbank Ind Est LU1 . . . . **123** A8
Firbank Rd MK42 . . . . . . **50** C6
Firbank Way LU7 . . . . . **111** A5
Firecrest SG6 . . . . **90** E1
Firs Lower Sch The MK45 . **84** E8
Firs Path LU7 . . . . **103** A1
First Ave LU6 . . . . **121** B7
Firs The
　Harpenden AL5 . . . . . . **131** D2
　Kempston MK42 . . . . . . **49** F3
Fir Tree Cl MK45 . . . . . . **84** E1
Fir Tree Rd MK45 . . . . . . **86** B4
Fisher Cl MK45 . . . . **97** B3
Fishers Cl
　Gravenhurst MK45 . . . . . **87** C4
　Great Barford MK44 . . . . **40** E6
Fishers Yd PE19 . . . . . . **22** E5
Fitzgerald Cl MK42 . . . . . **50** C6
Fitzroy Ave LU3 . . . . . . **116** B3
Fitzwarin Cl LU3 . . . . . **115** E8
Five Oaks LU1 . . . . **122** F4
Five Oaks Mid Sch LU1 . . **122** F3
Five Springs LU3 . . . . . **115** E6
Five Springs Ct LU3 . . . . **115** E6
Five Springs Ct LU3 . . . . **115** F7
FLAMSTEAD **129** B1
Flamstead Sch AL3 . . . . **129** B1
Flanders Cl MK42 . . . . . . **50** A5
Flawn Way PE19 . . . . . . **22** E2
Flax Mews AL3 . . . . . . **128** E5
Fleming Cl MK40 . . . . . . **37** C1
Fleming Dr SG5 . . . . **90** D2
FLEWTON END **27** C5
Flexmore Way SG18 . . . . **78** F5
Flight Path SG16 . . . . . . **89** B3
Flint Cl LU3 . . . . **115** E7
Flint Ct
　Dunstable LU6 . . . . . . **114** A1
　Luton LU1 . . . . **123** D5
Flintings The HP2 . . . . . **132** F8
Flint Way
　Bedford MK41 . . . . **39** B5
　Bedford, Woodside MK41 . **39** A4
　St Neots PE19 . . . . **22** E2
Flintwick Rd MK45 . . . . . **84** A3
FLITTON **85** E4
Flitton Hill MK45 . . . . . . **85** E5
Flitton Rd
　Greenfield MK45 . . . . . . **85** D3
　Pulloxhill MK45 . . . . . . **85** E1
FLITWICK **84** E2
Flitwick Lower Sch MK45 . **84** E2
Flitwick Rd
　Ampthill MK45 . . . . **84** E6
　Flitwick MK45 . . . . **95** E7
　Maulden MK45 . . . . **85** B7
　Steppingley MK45 . . . . . **84** B3
　Westoning MK45 . . . . . . **95** E6
Flitwick Sta MK45 . . . . . **84** E2
Florence Ave LU3 . . . . . **115** D6
Flowerdale Wlk MK41 . . . **39** B4
Flowers Ind Est **11** LU1 . . **123** E6
Flowers Way LU1 . . . . . **123** E7
Folly Farm MK43 . . . . . . **71** A8
Folly La
　Caddington LU1 . . . . . **122** E4
　North Crawley MK16 . . . . **58** B5
Fontwell Cl MK40 . . . . . . **38** D1
Football Cl SG7 . . . . **91** E1
Foot La NN9 . . . . **3** C8
Ford Cl PE19 . . . . **22** D5
Ford End Rd MK40 . . . . . **49** F7
Fordfield Rd MK45 . . . . . **84** B6
Ford La MK44 . . . . **31** E1
Ford The MK41 . . . . **37** E5
Forest Ctr The★ MK43 . . . **72** E8
Foresters' Cl MK45 . . . . . **64** A1
Forge Cl
　Chalton LU4 . . . . **106** E2
　St Neots PE19 . . . . **22** B2
Forge Gdns MK44 . . . . . . **4** A3
Forrest Cres LU2 . . . . . **117** A3
Forty Foot La MK44 . . . . . **9** A1
Foster Ave LU5 . . . . . . **114** C3
Foster Gr SG19 . . . . **54** C6
Foster Hill Rd MK40 . . . . **38** B1
Foster Pl MK42 . . . . **49** E4
Foster Rd
　Harlington LU5 . . . . **95** F2
　Kempston MK42 . . . . . . **49** E5
　Wootton MK43 . . . . **60** F8
Foster St MK40 . . . . **38** B1
Foster Way MK43 . . . . . . **60** F8
Foston Cl LU3 . . . . **115** F6
Foundry La SG5 . . . . **67** A5
Foundry Way PE19 . . . . . **22** B1
Fountaine Ct MK45 . . . . . **73** D1
Fountain Gr MK42 . . . . . **49** D5
Fountains Rd
　Bedford MK41 . . . . **38** F5
　Luton LU3 . . . . **116** D3
Fourth Ave LU3 . . . . . . **115** D7
Fowler Cl MK42 . . . . **49** D5
Fowlers Dr MK43 . . . . . . **88** B6
Foxbrook MK43 . . . . **36** C7
Fox Brook Ct PE19 . . . . . **22** F5
Foxbury Cl LU2 . . . . . . **116** D6
Fox Cl
　Clapham MK41 . . . . **37** C7
　Dunton SG18 . . . . **68** D5
Fox Cnr SG8 . . . . **69** F5
FOX CORNER **103** A7
Foxdell Inf Sch LU1 . . . . **123** A8
Foxdell Jun Sch LU1 . . . **122** E8

Fox Dells LU6 . . . . 121 C5
Foxglove Cl
Rushden NN10 . . . . 8 C8
St Neots PE19 . . . . 22 C5
Foxglove Dr SG18 . . . . 67 C4
Foxglove Way MK42 . . . . 50 E4
Fox Hedge Way MK44 . . . . 16 B3
Foxhill LU2 . . . . 116 E5
Fox Hill SG8 . . . . 69 F5
Fox Hill Rd SG8 . . . . 69 F5
Foxlease MK41 . . . . 38 D5
Frampton Ct MK41 . . . . 38 C5
Frances Ashton Ho 11
LU6 . . . . 121 B8
Frances Ct LU7 . . . . 110 E7
Franciscan Cl NN10 . . . . 7 F8
Francis Cl SG5 . . . . 90 E6
Francis Groves Cl MK41 . . 38 D4
Francis Rd SG7 . . . . 80 C6
Francis St LU1 . . . . 123 D8
Frank Hamel Ct MK45 . . . . 97 C2
Franklin Ave MK45 . . . . 97 B3
Franklin Cl
Marston Moretaine MK43 . . 60 D2
Pirton SG5 . . . . 99 D4
Franklin Gdns SG4 . . . . 101 B1
Franklin Rd
Biggleswade SG18 . . . . 66 F5
Dunstable LU6 . . . . 120 F8
Franklyn Gdns MK40 . . . . 37 C1
Franks Cl SG16 . . . . 89 B5
Fraser Rd MK44 . . . . 51 C6
Frederick St LU2 . . . . 116 E1
Frederick Street Pas
LU2 . . . . 116 E1
Freeman Ave LU3 . . . . 116 B8
Freemans Cl
Hitchin SG5 . . . . 100 D1
Houghton Regis LU5 . . . . 114 A4
Freemantle Ct PE19 . . . . 22 B3
Freewaters Cl SG5 . . . . 100 E4
Frenchmans Cl LU5 . . . . 105 E5
French's Ave LU6 . . . . 113 E2
French's Gate LU6 . . . . 113 F2
Frensham Dr SG4 . . . . 101 C2
Freshwater Cl LU3 . . . . 115 F7
Friars Cl LU1 . . . . 123 B5
Friars Ct LU1 . . . . 123 B5
Friars Way LU1 . . . . 123 B5
Friars Wlk
Dunstable LU6 . . . . 121 B8
Sandy SG19 . . . . 54 D8
Friary Field LU6 . . . . 121 B8
Friday St LU7 . . . . 110 F7
Friendless La AL3 . . . . 128 F2
Friesian Cl LU4 . . . . 115 A3
Frinton Cl NN10 . . . . 7 F8
Friston Gn LU2 . . . . 117 D1
Froghall Rd MK45 . . . . 84 C5
Frome Cl
Bedford MK41 . . . . 38 C5
Luton LU4 . . . . 115 E4
Front St LU1 . . . . 123 C1
FROXFIELD 93 E7
Fuchsia Way NN10 . . . . 8 B7
Fulbourne Cl LU4 . . . . 115 E2
Fulbrook Mid Sch MK17 . . 81 B5
Fullers Ct SG6 . . . . 101 E7
Fulmar Rd MK41 . . . . 38 D4
Fulmore Cl AL5 . . . . 131 D4
Furlay Cl SG6 . . . . 101 D7
Furlong La LU6 . . . . 120 C7
Furlong The MK41 . . . . 38 F4
Furness Ave LU6 . . . . 121 C7
Furness Cl MK41 . . . . 38 F5
Furrows The LU3 . . . . 116 B7
Furze Cl LU2 . . . . 116 D7
Furzedown Ct 18 AL5 . . . . 131 B1
Furzefield MK41 . . . . 38 F3
Furzen Cl LU6 . . . . 121 C5
Furzenhall Rd SG18 . . . . 55 A1
Fyne Dr LU7 . . . . 110 C8

G

Gables The LU7 . . . . 110 E6
Gable Way LU5 . . . . 114 C6
Gaddesden Turn LU7 . . . . 111 E2
Gade Valley Cotts HP1 . . 132 E4
Gadsby St MK40 . . . . 50 C8
Gadsden Cl MK43 . . . . 59 D2
Gainsborough Ave PE19 . . 22 D5
Gainsborough Dr LU5 . . . 114 D5
Gainsborough Rise MK41 . 38 B3
Gainsford Cres SG4 . . . . 101 C2
Gale Ct MK45 . . . . 97 C2
Gales Pl MK45 . . . . 63 D7
Gallery The
Letchworth SG6 . . . . 101 F6
7 Luton LU1 . . . . 123 E7
Galleywood SG5 . . . . 100 D4
Galliard Cl LU3 . . . . 116 B4
Galloway Cl MK42 . . . . 49 C3
Galston Rd LU3 . . . . 115 D8
Gamblingay Village Coll
SG19 . . . . 44 E5
Gamligay Fst Sch SG19 . . . 44 D5
GAMLINGAY 44 E5
GAMLINGAY CINQUES 44 C6
GAMLINGAY GREAT
HEATH 43 E3
Gamlingay Rd
Gamlingay SG19 . . . . 44 D8
Potton SG19 . . . . 44 C1
Garden Cl MK42 . . . . 49 D5
Gardener Pl MK40 . . . . 37 C1
Gardeners Cl
Flitwick MK45 . . . . 85 A3
Maulden MK45 . . . . 85 C8
Gardeners La SG16 . . . . 78 D2
Garden Fields SG19 . . . . 55 F8
Garden Fields Ct NN29 . . . 7 C8
Garden Hedge LU7 . . . . 111 A8
Gardenia Ave LU3 . . . . 116 A4
Garden Leys LU7 . . . . 111 C6
Garden Rd LU6 . . . . 121 C7
Gardens The
Henlow SG16 . . . . 89 D8
Stotfold SG5 . . . . 90 E6
Gardner Ct LU1 . . . . 123 E4
Gardner's Cl LU6 . . . . 120 E7
Garfield Ct LU2 . . . . 117 D3
Garfield St MK41 . . . . 38 B2
Garland Way LU7 . . . . 111 D5
Garner Cl SG18 . . . . 53 E2
Garnith Cl MK42 . . . . 49 F4
Garrett Cl LU6 . . . . 121 E5
Garretts Mead LU2 . . . . 117 B3
Garter Ct 10 LU2 . . . . 116 D1
Garth Rd SG6 . . . . 101 E3
Gas House La MK45 . . . . 73 F2
Gatehill Gdns LU3 . . . . 108 B1
Gateshead Cl SG19 . . . . 42 C1
Gaunts Way SG6 . . . . 91 A2
Gayland Ave LU2 . . . . 124 B8
Gayton Cl LU3 . . . . 116 B4
Gazelle Cl PE19 . . . . 22 B5
Gelding Cl LU4 . . . . 114 F5
Geldonia Ct MK40 . . . . 38 D2
Gelt The MK41 . . . . 38 C7
Gemini Cl LU7 . . . . 111 D8
Gentian Cl NN10 . . . . 8 C8
George Ct
Biggleswade SG18 . . . . 67 A5
Leighton Buzzard LU7 . . . . 111 B7
George Pl PE19 . . . . 22 F2
George St W LU1 . . . . 123 E7
George St
Bedford MK40 . . . . 50 E8
Clapham MK41 . . . . 37 D6
Dunstable LU6 . . . . 114 B1
Leighton Buzzard LU7 . . . . 111 B7
Luton LU1 . . . . 123 E7
Markyate AL3 . . . . 128 E5
Maulden MK45 . . . . 74 C1
Shefford SG17 . . . . 77 C2
Woburn MK17 . . . . 92 F6
Georgetown SG19 . . . . 42 A1
Georgetown Rd SG19 . . . . 42 A1
Georgina Ct SG15 . . . . 90 A3
Gerald Ct MK40 . . . . 37 F1
Gerard Ct 2 AL5 . . . . 131 A2
Gernon Rd SG6 . . . . 101 F5
Gernon Wlk SG6 . . . . 101 F5
Gery Ct PE19 . . . . 22 C5
Gibbards Cl MK44 . . . . 16 B3
Gibbons Rd MK40 . . . . 50 A8
Gibraltar Lodge AL5 . . . . 131 D3
Gibson Dr LU7 . . . . 111 D5
Gifford Rd MK42 . . . . 50 D6
Gig La LU7 . . . . 103 B5
Gilbert Cl MK42 . . . . 49 D6
Gilbert Ct AL5 . . . . 131 B4
Gilbert Inglefield Mid Sch
LU7 . . . . 103 C1
Gilbert Mews 6 LU7 . . . . 111 A8
Gilded Acre LU6 . . . . 121 C5
Gilder Cl LU3 . . . . 116 A8
Gilderdale LU4 . . . . 115 B6
Gillam St LU2 . . . . 123 E8
Gillan Way LU5 . . . . 114 E5
Gillespie Cl MK42 . . . . 50 C6
Gilpin Cl
Houghton Regis LU5 . . . . 114 D5
Stanford SG18 . . . . 78 A7
Gilpin Gn AL5 . . . . 131 C1
Gilpin St LU6 . . . . 114 A2
Gilwell Cl MK41 . . . . 38 E5
Gipping Cl MK41 . . . . 38 D7
Gipsy La
Luton LU1 . . . . 124 A6
Slapton LU7 . . . . 118 D8
Girdle Rd SG4 . . . . 101 A2
GIRTFORD 54 A8
Girtford Cres SG19 . . . . 54 B7
Glade The
Bromham MK43 . . . . 36 C3
Letchworth SG6 . . . . 101 F3
Gladstone Ave LU1 . . . . 123 C7
Gladstone Cl SG18 . . . . 67 A6
Gladstone St MK41 . . . . 38 B2
Glaisdale LU4 . . . . 115 C5
Glamis Ct PE19 . . . . 22 E2
Glamis Wlk MK41 . . . . 39 A4
Glastonbury Abbey MK41 . 51 B8
Glebe Ave
Arlesey SG15 . . . . 90 A7
Flitwick MK45 . . . . 84 E2
Glebe Cl
Sandy SG19 . . . . 54 B8
Thurleigh MK44 . . . . 18 C2
Glebe Gdns LU5 . . . . 95 F2
Glebe Ho MK40 . . . . 38 C2
Glebe Rd
Ampthill MK45 . . . . 84 E7
Bedford MK40 . . . . 38 C1
Biggleswade SG18 . . . . 67 B7
Sandy SG19 . . . . 54 C8
Glebe Rise MK44 . . . . 16 C4
Glebe The
Campton SG17 . . . . 76 F1
Clapham MK41 . . . . 37 C7
Glebe The *continued*
Gravenhurst MK45 . . . . 87 C5
Lavendon MK46 . . . . 34 A8
Glebe Way MK45 . . . . 74 A7
Glemsford Cl LU4 . . . . 115 B6
Glemsford Dr AL5 . . . . 131 D2
Glenariff PE19 . . . . 22 E4
Glenavon Rd MK41 . . . . 39 C4
Gleneagles Dr LU2 . . . . 116 E6
Glenfield Rd LU3 . . . . 116 C6
Glen Miller Mus★ MK41 . . 27 F2
Glenrose Ave MK41 . . . . 38 E6
Glen The
Caddington LU1 . . . . 122 E3
Kempston MK42 . . . . 49 D3
Glenwood Sch LU6 . . . . 121 E5
Globe Cl AL5 . . . . 131 B1
Globe La LU7 . . . . 102 E1
Glossop Way SG15 . . . . 90 B7
Gloucester Ct MK45 . . . . 84 E8
Gloucester Rd
Bedford MK42 . . . . 50 C5
1 Luton LU1 . . . . 123 F6
Glovers Ct SG5 . . . . 100 F1
Godfrey La MK44 . . . . 16 E4
Godfreys Cl LU1 . . . . 123 B6
Godfreys Ct LU1 . . . . 123 B6
Godso Cl MK41 . . . . 38 F4
Godwin Cl MK43 . . . . 36 F2
Godwin Way MK43 . . . . 36 F2
Gold Crest Cl LU4 . . . . 115 A5
Goldcrest Way MK41 . . . . 38 B4
Golden Riddy LU7 . . . . 110 E8
GOLDINGTON 39 B2
Goldington Ave MK40 . . . . 38 D1
Goldington Gn MK41 . . . . 39 A2
Goldington Green Lower Sch
MK41 . . . . 39 B1
Goldington Mid Sch MK41 38 F2
Goldington Rd MK41 . . . . 39 A1
Gold La MK40 . . . . 37 B1
Gold St
Podington NN29 . . . . 7 E2
Riseley MK44 . . . . 10 F2
Goldstone Cres LU5 . . . . 114 E2
Goodhall Cres MK45 . . . . 86 C8
Good Intent LU6 . . . . 119 E4
Goodman Dr LU7 . . . . 111 B5
Goodman Rd MK42 . . . . 50 B5
Goodmayes Cl MK42 . . . . 50 F6
Goodrich Ave MK41 . . . . 39 B4
Goodwins Yd MK44 . . . . 41 A5
Goodwood Cl MK45 . . . . 86 C8
Gooseberry Hill LU3 . . . . 116 B7
Goose Gn LU7 . . . . 104 D2
Gordon St LU1 . . . . 123 D7
Gorham Pl PE19 . . . . 22 D4
Gorham Way LU5 . . . . 114 F2
Gorst Cl SG6 . . . . 101 E5
Gosforth Cl SG19 . . . . 42 C2
Goshawk Cl LU4 . . . . 115 A4
GOSSARD'S GREEN 59 C4
Gostwick Pl MK44 . . . . 52 C8
Gostwick Rd MK42 . . . . 50 C4
GOSWELL END 95 F3
Goswell End Rd LU5 . . . . 95 F2
Gothic Mede Lower Sch
SG15 . . . . 90 A5
Gothic Way SG15 . . . . 90 B5
Goulsbra Rd NN10 . . . . 8 D8
Gower Dr MK40 . . . . 37 C1
Graces Cl MK43 . . . . 59 C3
Grafton Rd MK40 . . . . 50 A8
Graham Gdns LU3 . . . . 116 C4
Graham Rd LU5 . . . . 121 E7
Grampian Way LU3 . . . . 115 C8
Granary La AL5 . . . . 131 C1
Granby Ave AL5 . . . . 131 D2
Granby Ct AL5 . . . . 131 D2
Granby Rd LU4 . . . . 115 E2
Granet Cl MK40 . . . . 37 F1
Grange Ave LU4 . . . . 115 D4
Grange Cl
Houghton Conquest MK45 . . 74 A7
Irchester NN29 . . . . 7 B7
Leighton Buzzard LU7 . . . . 110 D6
Markyate AL3 . . . . 128 D6
Oakley MK43 . . . . 37 A8
Grange Ct
Bromham MK43 . . . . 36 E3
Heath and Reach LU7 . . . . 103 A6
Letchworth SG6 . . . . 91 A1
Grange Dr SG5 . . . . 90 F5
Grange Farm Cl MK45 . . . . 97 B3
Grange Gdns
Beeston SG19 . . . . 54 B5
Campton SG17 . . . . 76 F1
Heath and Reach LU7 . . . . 103 B6
Sharnbrook MK44 . . . . 16 C4
Toddington LU5 . . . . 105 F5
Grange Jun Sch SG6 . . . . 91 A2
Grange La
Bromham MK43 . . . . 36 F3
Cople MK44 . . . . 52 A5
Grange Rd
Ampthill MK45 . . . . 84 E7
Barton-le-C MK45 . . . . 97 B3
Bedford MK41 . . . . 39 A1
Blunham MK44 . . . . 41 E5
Felmersham MK43 . . . . 26 C8
Letchworth SG6 . . . . 101 F8
Toddington LU5 . . . . 105 F6
Grange Specl Sch MK42 . . 49 E5
Grange St SG17 . . . . 78 A3
Grange The
Lower Caldecote SG18 . . . . 54 D2
Toddington LU5 . . . . 105 F5
Grangeway
Houghton Regis LU5 . . . . 114 E6
Rushden NN10 . . . . 8 A8
Grange Way
Irchester NN29 . . . . 7 B7
Willington MK44 . . . . 52 C8
Grange Wlk LU5 . . . . 105 F6
Gransden Cl LU3 . . . . 116 A7
Grant Gdns AL5 . . . . 131 B2
Grantham Rd LU4 . . . . 116 B1
Granville Rd
Hitchin SG4 . . . . 101 C1
Luton LU1 . . . . 123 B8
Granville St MK42 . . . . 50 A6
Graphic Cl LU6 . . . . 121 D6
Grasmere Ave
Harpenden AL5 . . . . 131 C1
Luton LU3 . . . . 116 B7
Grasmere Cl
Dunstable LU6 . . . . 121 B7
Flitwick MK45 . . . . 84 E2
Kempston MK42 . . . . 49 E3
Grasmere Rd
Biggleswade SG18 . . . . 67 A4
Luton LU3 . . . . 116 C7
Grasmere Way LU7 . . . . 110 D7
Grasmere Wlk LU5 . . . . 114 C6
Grass Yd PE28 . . . . 6 F4
Gratton Rd MK40 . . . . 49 F8
Gravel Pit Rd MK45 . . . . 84 F2
Gravenhurst Lower Sch
MK45 . . . . 87 C4
Gravenhurst Rd
Campton SG17 . . . . 87 F8
Shillington SG5 . . . . 87 E4
Graylings The MK41 . . . . 38 F4
Grays Cl MK45 . . . . 97 C3
Grays Gr MK44 . . . . 13 B2
Gray's Rd SG19 . . . . 44 D6
Gray St NN29 . . . . 7 A7
Graze Hill MK44 . . . . 28 C2
Great Aldens MK41 . . . . 38 F4
GREAT BARFORD 40 F4
Great Barford Lower Sch
MK44 . . . . 40 F5
Great Bramingham La
LU3 . . . . 108 B2
GREAT BRICKHILL 102 C8
GREAT DENHAM 49 C8
Great Farm Cl MK43 . . . . 72 C3
Greatfield Cl AL5 . . . . 130 C4
GREAT GADDESDEN 132 D3
Great Gaddesden CE Prim
Sch HP1 . . . . 132 D3
Great Gn SG5 . . . . 99 D4
Great Hill SG17 . . . . 77 C4
Great La MK45 . . . . 75 D4
Great Marlings LU2 . . . . 117 C7
Great Northern Rd LU5 . . 121 D8
Great North Rd
St Neots PE19 . . . . 22 B2
Wyboston MK44 . . . . 32 A6
Great Portway MK40 . . . . 49 B6
GREAT STAUGHTON 13 F6
Great Staughton Prim Sch
PE19 . . . . 13 F6
Greaves Way LU7 . . . . 111 D6
Grebe Cl MK45 . . . . 84 D2
Greenacre Dr
Rushden NN10 . . . . 8 B7
Rushden NN10 . . . . 8 B8
Greenacres MK41 . . . . 38 E4
Green Acres
Gamlingay SG19 . . . . 44 C5
Lilley LU2 . . . . 109 D2
Green Bushes LU4 . . . . 115 D6
Green Cl
Luton LU4 . . . . 115 C5
Stanbridge LU7 . . . . 112 D5
Green Ct 6 LU4 . . . . 115 C5
Green Dragon Ct 8 LU1 . 123 F6
GREEN END
MK44 . . . . 13 A3
MK44 . . . . 40 E6
MK44 . . . . 49 A3
Green End
Gamlingay SG19 . . . . 44 C5
Little Staughton MK44 . . . . 13 A3
Workhouse End MK41 . . . . 40 A5
Green End Rd
Great Barford MK44 . . . . 40 E6
Kempston MK43 . . . . 49 A4
GREENFIELD 85 C2
Greenfield Ave SG5 . . . . 100 D4
Greenfield CE Lower Sch
MK45 . . . . 85 D2
Greenfield Cl LU6 . . . . 113 E1
Greenfield La SG5 . . . . 100 E4
Greenfield Rd
Flitton MK45 . . . . 85 D3
Flitwick MK45 . . . . 85 A2
Pulloxhill MK45 . . . . 85 D1
Westoning MK45 . . . . 95 F6
Greenfields SG5 . . . . 87 E1
Greenfield Way SG18 . . . . 68 D5
Green Gables PE19 . . . . 22 D4
Greengate LU3 . . . . 115 C8
Greenhill LU7 . . . . 103 A1
Greenhill Ave LU2 . . . . 116 E3
Greenhill St 12 MK40 . . . . 50 B8
Green La
Aspley Guise MK17 . . . . 81 E4
Clapham MK41 . . . . 37 F6
Dunstable LU6 . . . . 120 E8
Eaton Bray LU6 . . . . 119 D7
Everton SG19 . . . . 43 C3
Great Staughton PE19 . . . . 13 F6
Hitchin SG4 . . . . 101 B1
Green La *continued*
Kensworth LU6 . . . . 127 E8
Letchworth SG6 . . . . 91 B1
Luton LU2 . . . . 117 C4
Markyate AL3 . . . . 128 F5
Renhold MK41 . . . . 39 B6
Swineshead MK44 . . . . 11 C8
Greenlands LU7 . . . . 111 C8
Greenleas Lower Sch
LU7 . . . . 110 C7
Green Milverton LU3 . . . . 116 A7
Green Oaks LU2 . . . . 116 F3
Greenriggs LU2 . . . . 117 F2
Greensand Ridge MK43 . . . 72 B2
Greens Cl SG19 . . . . 54 C7
Greenshields Rd MK40 . . . 50 E8
Greenside Pk LU2 . . . . 116 E3
Green The
Bromham MK43 . . . . 36 F3
Cardington MK44 . . . . 51 D4
Chelveston NN9 . . . . 3 C8
Edlesborough LU6 . . . . 119 F4
Great Staughton PE19 . . . . 13 F7
Harrold MK43 . . . . 25 A6
Houghton Regis LU5 . . . . 114 C4
Luton LU4 . . . . 115 C5
Marston Moretaine MK43 . . 72 D7
Newnham SG7 . . . . 91 E7
Peters Green LU2 . . . . 125 C3
Stotfold SG5 . . . . 90 F7
Turvey MK43 . . . . 34 E5
Wharley End MK43 . . . . 58 E2
Greenview Cl MK42 . . . . 49 C3
Greenway SG17 . . . . 77 A1
Greenways
Eaton Bray LU6 . . . . 119 D7
Flitwick MK45 . . . . 84 F3
Luton LU2 . . . . 117 B5
Gregories Cl LU3 . . . . 116 D1
Gregory Cl SG17 . . . . 88 B5
Greig Cl SG17 . . . . 77 D3
Grenadier Cl MK41 . . . . 38 C7
Grenidge Way MK43 . . . . 36 F8
Grenville Way PE19 . . . . 22 B2
Gresham Cl LU2 . . . . 124 D8
Gresham Ct MK40 . . . . 38 D2
Gresham Way SG17 . . . . 77 C4
Greskine Cl MK41 . . . . 39 C4
Greycote MK42 . . . . 51 A2
Greyfriars MK40 . . . . 50 B8
Greys Education Ctr
MK42 . . . . 49 D4
Greystoke Wlk MK41 . . . . 38 F4
Grimaldi Ave LU3 . . . . 116 A3
Grisedale Ct MK42 . . . . 49 E2
Groat La SG19 . . . . 44 D8
Grosvenor Gdns
Biggleswade SG18 . . . . 67 B6
St Neots PE19 . . . . 22 E6
Grosvenor Rd
Baldock SG7 . . . . 91 F1
Luton LU3 . . . . 116 B5
Grosvenor Rd W SG7 . . . . 91 F1
Grosvenor St MK42 . . . . 50 C6
GROVE 111 A1
Grovebury Cl LU6 . . . . 121 D6
Grovebury Ct MK43 . . . . 60 F7
Grovebury Place Est
LU7 . . . . 111 A6
Grovebury Rd
Leighton Buzzard LU7 . . . . 111 A4
Leighton Buzzard LU7 . . . . 111 A5
Grovebury Road Ind Est
LU7 . . . . 111 A5
Grovebury Turn LU7 . . . . 111 C1
Grove Ct
Arlesey SG15 . . . . 90 A8
Turvey MK43 . . . . 34 E6
Grove End LU1 . . . . 123 B5
Grove Ho SG4 . . . . 101 A2
Grovelands Ave SG4 . . . . 101 C2
Groveland Way SG5 . . . . 91 A5
Grove Park Rd LU1 . . . . 123 B3
Grove Pl
2 Bedford MK40 . . . . 50 C8
Leighton Buzzard LU7 . . . . 111 A6
Grove Rd
Dunstable LU5 . . . . 121 D7
Hitchin SG4 . . . . 100 F1
Houghton Regis LU5 . . . . 114 C7
Leighton Buzzard LU7 . . . . 111 A6
Luton LU1 . . . . 123 D7
Slip End LU1 . . . . 123 B2
Turvey MK43 . . . . 34 E6
Groveside SG16 . . . . 78 D2
Grove The
Bedford MK40 . . . . 38 C1
Biggleswade SG18 . . . . 67 B5
Houghton Conquest MK45 . . 74 A7
Lidlington MK43 . . . . 72 C3
Luton LU1 . . . . 123 B5
Silsoe MK45 . . . . 86 B5
St Neots PE19 . . . . 22 E6
Westoning MK45 . . . . 95 D6
Woburn Sands MK17 . . . . 81 B5
Guardian Ind Est LU1 . . . 123 C8
Guernsey Cl LU4 . . . . 115 A3
GUILDEN MORDEN 69 F4
Guilden Morden CE Prim Sch
SG8 . . . . 69 F5
Guildford St LU1 . . . . 123 E7
Guinness Pl MK41 . . . . 51 A8
Guise Ct MK17 . . . . 81 F4
Gulliver Cl MK42 . . . . 49 D5
Gunnersbury Pk MK41 . . . 39 B1
Gurney Ct LU6 . . . . 119 F6
Gurney's La SG5 . . . . 100 B7
Guru Ravidass La MK40 . . 50 A8

Gwyn Ct 2 MK40 50 B8
Gwyn St 5 MK40 38 B1
Gypsy La
Aspley Guise MK17 81 F3
Biggleswade SG18 66 D5

H

Hackett Pl MK16 58 A6
Haddon Cl NN10 8 A8
Haddon Ct 20 AL5 131 B1
Haddon Rd LU2 123 F8
Haden Cl MK41 38 A3
Hadfield Ct MK42 50 B6
Hadleigh Cl MK41 39 A4
Hadley Ct LU3 116 D1
Hadlow Down Cl LU3 116 A5
Hadrian Ave LU5 114 E2
Hadrian Lower Sch LU5 114 E2
Hagdell Rd LU1 123 C5
Hailes Cl MK41 38 E5
Halegate MK43 60 F8
Hale Lodge MK40 38 C2
Hales Mdw AL5 131 A2
Halesowen Dr MK42 50 D3
Half Moon La
Dunstable LU5 121 D7
Pepperstock LU1 129 C8
Half Moon Pl LU6 121 D7
Halfway Ave LU4 115 D1
Halifax Rd MK42 51 A2
Hallards The PE19 22 C6
Hall Ave NN10 8 A8
Hall Cl
Harrold MK43 25 A6
Sharnbrook MK44 16 C4
HALL END
MK43 60 D8
MK45 86 A8
Hall End Cl MK45 86 B8
Hall End Rd MK43 60 E7
Halley's Way LU5 114 D4
Hall La PE28 6 C8
Hall Mead SG6 101 D6
Hall Rd PE19 22 E3
Hallside SG18 68 C5
Hall Way MK45 63 D7
Hallwicks Rd LU2 117 B3
Hallworth Dr SG5 90 E6
Hallworth Ho SG5 90 E6
Halsey Rd MK42 49 E5
Halyard Cl LU3 116 B6
Halyard High Sch LU4 114 F3
Hamble Rd MK41 38 D7
Hambling Pl LU6 120 F8
Hambridge Way SG5 99 D4
Hambro Cl LU2 130 F7
Hamer Ct LU2 116 D8
Hamilton Cl HP4 126 C5
Hamilton Ct 4 LU7 111 A7
Hammerdell SG6 101 D7
Hammersmith Cl LU5 114 C5
Hammersmith Gdns LU5 114 C5
Hammond Ct LU1 123 C1
Hammond Rd MK41 39 D4
Hampden Cl MK45 84 E1
Hampden Ct MK40 37 B1
Hampden Rd
Flitwick MK45 84 E1
Hitchin SG4 101 C1
Hampshire Way LU3 107 E1
Hampton Cl MK45 62 F4
Hampton Rd LU4 123 B8
Hamsterley Cl MK41 39 B4
Hancock Dr LU2 116 E5
Handcross Rd LU2 117 D2
Handley Page Cl MK43 58 E2
Hanover Cl PE19 22 D5
Hanover Ct
Leighton Buzzard LU7 110 D7
Luton LU4 115 D5
Wootton MK43 60 F8
Hanover Pl MK45 97 C4
HANSCOMBE END 98 D8
Hanscombe End Rd SG5 98 D7
Hanswick Cl LU2 117 B2
Hanworth Cl LU2 116 D7
Harbrook La SG17 78 A2
Harbury Dell LU3 116 B7
Harcourt Cl LU7 110 E7
Harcourt St LU1 123 E5
Hardenwick Ct 4 AL5 131 A2
Harding Cl
Bedford MK42 50 E6
Luton LU3 115 E7
Harding Ct AL5 131 B4
Harding Par 8 AL5 131 B1
HARDMEAD 46 D4
Hardmead Rd MK43 34 A3
Hardwick Cl SG17 77 C3
Hardwick Gn LU3 116 B7
Hardwick Hill MK45 61 F7
Hardwick Mews MK17 81 B3
Hardwick Pl MK17 81 B4
Hardwick Rd
Bedford MK42 50 C6
St Neots PE19 22 E3
Woburn Sands MK17 81 B4
Hardy Pl PE19 22 D6
Harefield Ave MK42 50 A4
Harefield Ct LU1 122 F8
Harefield Rd LU1 122 F8
Harepark Terr SG16 88 E3
Harewelle Way MK43 25 A7
Harewood Rd MK42 50 C4
Hargood Ct PE19 22 B3
HARGRAVE 1 E2
Hargreaves Ct MK42 50 C4
Harkness Ct SG4 101 B1
Harkness Way SG4 101 C2
Harland Rd PE19 22 F6
Harlech Ct PE19 22 F2
Harlech Rd MK41 38 F4
Harlestone Cl LU3 108 A1
Harling Rd LU6 120 B4
HARLINGTON 95 F1
Harlington Lower Sch
LU5 95 F2
Harlington Rd
Sharpenhoe MK45 96 C3
Toddington LU5 106 B7
Upper Sundon LU3 107 B5
Harlington Sta LU5 95 E1
Harlington Upper Sch
LU5 95 F3
HARLINGTON WOOD
END 95 B3
Harmill Ind Est LU7 111 A5
Harmony Row LU7 111 E5
Harold Rd MK45 97 C3
HARPENDEN 130 D2
Harpenden Cl MK41 39 A1
Harpenden Memorial Hospl
AL5 131 B2
Harpenden Prep Sch
AL5 130 F2
Harpenden Rise AL5 130 F3
Harpenden Sta AL5 131 B1
Harps Hill AL3 128 E5
Harpur Ctr 8 MK40 50 B8
Harpur Sq 15 MK40 50 B8
Harpur St MK40 50 B8
Harrier Cl SG18 66 F4
Harriers The SG19 42 B1
Harrier Way MK42 49 E2
Harrington Dr MK41 38 E4
Harrington Hts LU5 114 A5
Harris Cl MK42 49 E4
Harris Ct MK45 97 B4
HARROLD 24 F6
Harrold Lower Sch MK43 24 F6
Harrold Odell Country Park★
MK43 25 B7
Harrold-Odell Visitor Ctr★
MK43 25 B6
Harrold Priory MK41 39 B1
Harrold Priory Mid Sch
MK43 24 F6
Harrold Rd MK46 24 C1
HARROWDEN 51 A3
Harrowden Ct LU2 124 C8
Harrowden La
Bedford MK42 50 E4
Harrowden MK42, MK44 51 B4
Harrowden Mid Sch MK42 50 E5
Harrowden Rd
Bedford MK42 50 F4
Luton LU2 124 C8
Harrow Piece MK45 85 C8
Harrow Rd LU7 111 B5
Harry Scott Ct LU4 115 C6
Harter Ave MK43 71 B7
Harter Rd MK42 49 D2
HART HILL 117 A1
Hart Hill Dr LU2 123 F8
Hart Hill La LU2 123 F8
Hart Hill Prim Sch LU2 123 F8
Hartington St MK41 38 B2
Hart La LU2 124 A8
Hartland Ave MK40 38 E1
Hartley Rd LU2 123 F8
Hartop Cl MK41 38 F4
Hartsfield JMI Sch SG7 91 F1
Hartsfield Rd LU2 117 B2
Hartshill MK41 38 E3
Hartwell Cres LU7 111 B7
Hartwell Dr MK42 49 E6
Hartwell Gdns AL5 130 E1
Hartwell Gr LU7 111 A7
Hart Wlk LU2 117 A1
Hartwood 3 LU2 123 F8
Harvest Ct LU4 115 A3
Harvester Ct LU7 111 D7
Harvey Cl SG18 66 C8
Harvey Rd
Bedford MK41 39 A2
Dunstable LU6 120 D7
Rushden NN10 8 B7
Harvey's Hill LU2 116 F5
Harvey St PE19 22 E4
Haselfoot SG6 101 E6
Hasketon Dr LU4 115 B6
Haslingden Cl AL5 130 D3
Hassett St MK40 50 B8
Hastingbury Upper Sch &
Com Coll MK42 49 C2
Hastings Rd
Barton-le-C MK45 97 C3
Kempston MK42 49 D2
Hastings St LU1 123 D6
HATCH 53 F4
Hatch Comm SG19 53 F4
HATCH END 19 A7
Hatch La MK44 19 A6
Hat Factory The LU1 123 E7
Hatfield Ave MK43 71 B7
Hatfield Cl MK45 84 F3
Hatfield Cres
Bedford MK41 38 F1
Flitwick MK45 84 F3
Hatfield Rd MK45 84 F3
Hathaway Cl
Luton LU4 115 B2
St Neots PE19 22 C3
HATLEY END 57 B5
Hatley Rd
Gamlingay SG19 45 B4
Potton SG19 56 E7
HATLEY ST GEORGE 45 F3
Hatters Way LU1 123 B8
Havelock Cl
Gamlingay SG19 44 C5
Sandy SG19 42 B1
Havelock Rd
Biggleswade SG18 67 A7
Luton LU2 116 E1
Havelock Rise LU2 116 E1
Havelock St MK40 50 A7
Haven The SG5 90 F6
Haverdale LU4 115 C4
Hawes Cl MK45 84 E3
Hawesmere Cl SG18 67 A4
Hawk Cl MK45 84 D2
Hawk Dr
Bedford MK41 38 B6
Sandy SG19 42 B2
Hawker Cl LU7 111 D5
Hawkesford Way PE19 22 F7
Hawkfield SG6 101 E8
Hawkfields LU2 116 E6
Hawkins Rd MK42 50 C5
Hawthorn Ave LU2 117 B4
Hawthorn Cl
Ampthill MK45 84 F7
Biggleswade SG18 66 F8
Dunstable LU6 121 C7
Turvey MK43 34 E6
Hawthorn Cres LU1 122 E3
Hawthorne Ave MK40 49 F7
Hawthorne Cl LU7 110 E8
Hawthorne Ct MK45 75 E1
Hawthorn End SG19 44 C5
Hawthorn Hill SG6 101 F7
Hawthorn Park Lower Sch
LU5 114 D6
Hawthorn Rd PE19 22 E6
Hawthorns The
Cranfield MK43 59 B1
Henlow SG16 78 D3
Hawthorn Way
Lower Stondon SG16 88 F2
Silsoe MK45 86 B4
Hay Cl NN10 8 B8
Haycroft
Luton LU2 116 E6
Wootton MK43 61 A6
Hayes Cl LU2 117 C5
Hayhurst Rd LU4 115 B1
Hay La AL5 131 A1
Haylands Way MK41 38 F2
Hayley Ct LU5 114 C6
Hayling Dr LU2 117 D3
Haylock Cl MK42 49 D2
Haymarket Rd LU4 114 E4
Haymoor SG6 101 E7
HAYNES 64 A1
HAYNES CHURCH END 75 C7
Haynes Lower Sch MK45 64 A1
Haynes Rd MK42 50 C5
HAYNES WEST END 74 F5
Hayton Cl LU3 108 B2
Hazelbury Cres LU1 123 C8
Hazelbury Ct LU1 123 C8
Hazel Cl SG17 77 B2
Hazeldene Lower Sch
MK41 38 E3
Hazel Gr SG5 90 E5
Hazel Wlk SG18 66 F8
Hazelwood Cl LU2 117 B4
Hazelwood La MK45 73 E3
Hazelwood Rd MK42 50 D5
Heacham Cl LU4 115 B4
HEATH AND REACH 103 B5
Heath Cl
Luton LU1 123 B6
Woburn Sands MK17 81 C3
Heathcliff Ave SG5 90 B2
Heath Ct LU7 102 F3
Heather Dr SG18 67 C4
Heather Gdns MK41 39 B1
Heather Mead LU6 119 E4
Heathermere SG6 90 F1
Heathfield MK41 39 A3
Heathfield Cl LU1 122 F4
Heathfield Lower Sch
LU1 122 E4
Heathfield Rd
Hitchin SG5 100 F1
Luton LU3 116 C4
Heath Gn LU7 103 A5
Heath La MK17 81 A2
Heath Park Dr LU7 103 A2
Heath Park Rd LU7 103 A3
Heath Rd
Gamlingay SG19 44 B4
Leighton Buzzard LU7 103 A2
Heath The LU7 102 E4
Heathwood Cl LU7 103 A3
Heathwood Lower Sch
LU7 103 B3
Heaton Dell LU2 117 E1
Hebden Cl LU4 115 B4
Hedgerow The LU4 115 D6
Hedley Rise LU2 117 F2
Hedley Way MK45 86 B8
Heights The LU3 115 E5
Helen Ho MK42 50 B6
Helford Cl MK41 38 D6
Helmsley Ave MK41 39 A5
Helmsley Cl LU4 115 C5
Hemel Hempstead Rd
HP4 126 F1
Hemingford Dr LU2 116 D6
Hempsals PE19 22 C6
Hen Brook PE19 22 F4
Henderson Way MK42 49 F4
Henge Way LU3 115 E7
Henley Cl LU5 114 E5
Henley Rd MK40 50 A8
HENLOW 78 D1
HENLOW CAMP 89 A3
Henlow Ind Est SG16 89 B4
Henlow Mid Sch SG16 78 D1
Henry Ct LU6 121 A8
Henson Cl MK43 58 E2
Henstead Pl LU2 117 D1
Herbrand Rd MK42 51 A4
Hercules Cl LU7 111 C8
Hereford Gr SG18 67 A4
Hereford Rd
Bedford MK42 50 E4
Luton LU4 115 A3
Hermitage Gdns MK45 63 D7
Hermitage The SG15 90 B8
Herne Cl LU5 105 F7
Heron Cl
Biggleswade SG18 66 F4
Sandy SG19 54 B6
Shefford SG17 77 C2
Heron Dr LU2 116 E6
Heron Hts MK41 39 A2
Heron Quay MK40 50 B8
Heron Rd MK45 84 E1
Heronscroft MK41 38 F2
Herons Mead MK43 36 F2
Heron Trad Est LU3 115 C7
Heron Way SG5 90 E6
HERRING'S GREEN 63 D6
Heswall Ct 5 LU1 123 F6
Hever Cl NN10 8 C8
Hewlett Rd LU3 115 E5
HEXTON 98 B2
Hexton JMI Sch SG5 98 A1
Hexton Rd
Barton-le-C, Church End
MK45 97 D2
Barton-le-C MK45 97 C2
Lilley LU2 109 C4
Heywood Dr LU2 116 F2
Hibberts Ct SG6 101 E7
Hibbert St LU1 123 E6
Hibbert Street Almshouses
13 LU1 123 E6
Hickling Cl
Bedford MK40 49 E7
Luton LU2 117 D1
Hickling Way AL5 131 C3
Hickman Ct LU3 115 D8
Hicks Rd AL3 128 F6
Higham Dr LU2 117 D1
HIGHAM GOBION 98 A6
Higham Park Rd NN10 9 A5
Higham Rd
Barton-le-C MK45 97 D4
Chelveston NN9 3 B7
High Ave SG6 101 E4
High Banks LU7 112 C5
High Beeches Prim Sch
AL5 131 D1
High Beech Rd LU3 115 D7
Highbury Gr MK41 37 E6
Highbury Rd LU3 116 C1
Highbush Rd SG5 90 E5
Highcroft LU7 111 C6
High Dane SG4 101 A2
High Elms MK43 25 A1
HIGHER BERRY END 83 A1
HIGHER RADS END 94 C6
Highfield
Bedford MK41 38 C5
Letchworth SG6 101 E4
Highfield Cres MK43 71 C1
Highfield Oval AL5 131 A4
Highfield Parc MK43 27 B1
Highfield Rd
Flitton MK45 85 E4
Kempston MK42 49 E3
Leighton Buzzard LU7 111 C6
Luton LU4 116 B1
Oakley MK43 27 B1
Highfields MK45 95 E6
Highfield Sch The SG6 101 D4
Highfields Cl LU5 115 A2
Highfields Ct MK45 95 E6
Highlands MK45 84 E3
Highlands Lodge Art Ctr
SG17 87 D7
High Mead LU3 116 A3
Highmoor AL5 131 A4
Highover Cl LU2 117 B1
Highover JMI Sch SG4 101 C1
Highover Rd SG6 101 D5
Highover Way SG4 101 B1
High Point 14 LU1 123 D6
High Rd
Beeston SG19 54 B5
Broom SG18 66 D3
Cotton End MK45 63 D5
Shillington SG5 98 E8
High Rd The
Felmersham MK43 26 C8
Harrowden MK42 51 A4
High Ridge
Harpenden AL5 130 E3
Luton LU2 117 C1
High St N LU6 114 A1
High St S LU6 121 C7
High St
Arlesey SG15 90 A5
Bedford MK40 50 C8
Biggleswade SG15 67 A6
High St *continued*
Blunham MK44 41 E3
Broom SG18 66 C3
Carlton MK43 25 A3
Chelveston NN9 3 C8
Clophill MK45 75 D1
Cranfield MK43 59 B2
Dunton SG18 68 D5
Eaton Bray LU6 119 E6
Edlesborough LU6 119 E3
Eggington LU7 112 B7
Elstow MK42 50 B4
Eyeworth SG19 68 F8
Flamstead AL3 129 B2
Flitton MK45 85 D4
Flitwick MK45 84 E3
Gravenhurst MK45 87 C4
Great Barford MK44 41 A4
Greenfield MK45 85 C2
Guilden Morden, Eyeworth
SG19 69 A8
Guilden Morden SG8 69 F4
Harpenden AL5 131 A1
Harrold MK43 24 F6
Henlow SG16 78 D2
Hinxworth SG7 80 D6
Houghton Conquest MK45 74 B8
Houghton Regis LU5 114 B4
Irchester NN29 7 B8
Kempston MK42 49 C3
Kimbolton PE28 6 F4
Langford SG18 78 F6
Leighton Buzzard LU7 111 A7
Lidlington MK43 72 C2
Lower Dean PE28 5 C7
Luton LU4 115 C4
Markyate AL3 128 E5
Meppershall SG17 88 B5
North Crawley MK16 58 B6
Oakley MK43 36 F8
Odell MK43 25 C8
Pavenham MK43 26 B3
Pirton SG5 99 D4
Podington NN29 7 E2
Pulloxhill MK45 85 E1
Ridgmont MK43 82 F5
Riseley MK44 11 A2
Roxton MK44 31 E2
Sandy SG19 54 C7
Sharnbrook MK44 16 D4
Shefford SG17 77 C3
Silsoe MK45 86 C4
Souldrop MK44 16 B8
Stagsden MK43 48 A6
St Neots, Eynesbury PE19 22 E5
St Neots PE19 22 B8
Stotfold SG5 90 F6
Sutton SG19 56 A3
Swineshead MK44 11 D8
Thurleigh MK44 18 C2
Tilbrook PE28 6 B6
Tingrith MK17 94 F5
Toddington LU5 105 F6
Turvey MK43 34 E5
Upper Dean PE28 5 B4
Westoning MK45 95 E6
Wilden MK44 29 F3
Woburn Sands MK17 81 B4
Wrestlingworth SG19 57 B3
Wymington NN10 8 B5
Yelden MK44 4 A2
High Street Mews LU7 111 A6
High Top Barns MK44 4 A2
HIGH TOWN 122 E8
High Town Rd LU2 116 F1
High View
Bedford MK41 39 A3
Markyate AL3 128 E5
Highway The MK42 51 A3
High Wood Cl LU1 122 F7
Hillary Cl LU3 115 D7
Hillary Cres LU1 123 C6
Hillary Rise SG15 90 B5
Hillborough Cres LU5 114 C7
Hillborough Inf Sch LU1 123 C6
Hillborough Jun Sch
LU1 123 C6
Hillborough Rd LU1 123 D6
Hillbrow SG6 101 D5
Hill Cl
Harpenden AL5 131 C4
Luton LU3 116 C7
Wingfield LU7 105 E1
Hill Cres MK43 71 C1
Hillcrest MK43 59 C2
Hillcrest Ave LU2 116 C8
Hillcrest Sch (Regis
Education Ctr) LU5 114 E6
Hillcroft LU6 113 E1
Hill Croft Cl LU4 115 C6
Hilldene Cl MK45 84 E3
Hill End House La MK43 72 B2
Hillesden Ave MK42 50 B4
Hillfield Ave SG4 101 A2
HILLFOOT END 87 E1
Hillfoot Rd SG5 87 E1
Hillgate SG4 101 A3
Hillgrounds Rd MK42 49 D6
Hill La
Biggleswade SG18 66 F7
Ickwell SG18 65 F6
Upper Caldecote SG18 66 C7
Hill Milford AL5 131 D3
Hill Pickford AL5 131 D4

Hill Rise
Bedford MK41 . . . . 38 B2
Kempston MK42 . . . . 49 B2
Luton LU3 . . . . 115 D7
Hills Cl MK44 . . . . 31 E1
Hillside
Chelveston NN9 . . . . 3 B8
Houghton Regis LU5 . . . . . 114 B6
Hillside Cl SG5 . . . . 87 E1
Hillside Rd
Dunstable LU5 . . . . 121 D7
Harpenden AL5 . . . . 130 F3
Leighton Buzzard LU7 . . . 103 A2
Luton LU3 . . . . 116 D1
Shillington SG5 . . . . 87 E1
Upper Stondon SG16 . . . . . 88 E3
Hills Lower Sch The
MK41 . . . . 38 E3
Hillson Cl MK43 . . . . 72 D8
Hills View LU3 . . . . 107 B4
Hill The MK44 . . . . 41 E3
Hilltop Ct LU1 . . . . 123 C7
Hilltop View SG17 . . . . 88 B6
Hill View SG19 . . . . 54 C5
Hillview Cres LU1 . . . . . . 116 C8
Hill View La LU7 . . . . 111 D2
Hillway MK17 . . . . 81 A6
Hillyfields LU6 . . . . 121 C6
Hilton Ave LU6 . . . . 121 B6
Himley Gn LU7 . . . . 110 D6
Hindburn Cl MK41 . . . . 38 D6
Hine Way SG5 . . . . 100 C1
Hinksley Rd MK45 . . . . 84 F3
Hinton Cl LU7 . . . . 111 D7
Hinton Wlk LU5 . . . . 114 E6
HINWICK 14 D7
Hinwick Cl SG15 . . . . 90 B7
Hinwick Hall Coll of F Ed
NN29 . . . . 7 C1
Hinwick Rd NN29 . . . . 7 A2
HINXWORTH 80 C5
Hinxworth Rd
Hinxworth SG7 . . . . 80 C3
Hinxworth SG7 . . . . 80 F4
HITCHIN 101 B2
Hitchin Bsns Ctr The
SG4 . . . . 101 A3
Hitchin La SG17 . . . . 78 B2
Hitchin Rd
Arlesey SG15 . . . . 90 A2
Henlow SG16 . . . . 89 C6
Hexton SG5 . . . . 98 E1
Letchworth SG6 . . . . 101 E3
Luton LU2 . . . . 117 A4
Pirton SG5 . . . . 99 E2
Shefford SG17 . . . . 77 E1
Stotfold SG5 . . . . 90 E5
Upper Caldecote SG18 . . . . 66 B7
Hitchin Road Ind & Bsns Ctr
SG15 . . . . 90 A3
Hitchin Road Ind Est
LU2 . . . . 116 F1
Hitchin St SG18 . . . . 66 F5
Hitchmead Rd SG18 . . . . . . 67 B6
Hitchmead Spec Sch
SG18 . . . . 67 C6
Hitherfield La MK41 . . . . 131 A2
Hives The PE19 . . . . 22 D4
Hockley Ct
Hockliffe LU7 . . . . 104 E2
Marston Moretaine MK43 . . 72 D8
HOCKLIFFE 104 F2
Hockliffe Bsns Pk LU7 . . 104 F1
Hockliffe Ho LU7 . . . . . . 111 E1
Hockliffe Lower Sch
LU7 . . . . 104 E3
Hockliffe Rd
Bedford MK42 . . . . 50 D6
Hockliffe LU7, MK17 . . . . 104 F6
Leighton Buzzard LU7 . . . 111 C7
Tebworth LU7 . . . . 105 B1
Hockliffe St LU7 . . . . 111 A7
Hockwell Ring LU4 . . . . . 115 C4
Hodder Rd MK41 . . . . 38 C7
Hogarth Cl MK41 . . . . 38 B2
Hogarth Pl PE19 . . . . 22 D5
Hog Hall La HP4 . . . . 126 A5
Holcroft Rd AL5 . . . . 131 C3
Holden Cl MK40 . . . . 37 C1
Holford Way LU3 . . . . 108 B3
Holgate Dr LU4 . . . . 115 B3
Holkham Ct LU4 . . . . 115 A4
Holland Ct LU3 . . . . 116 C2
Holland Rd
Ampthill MK45 . . . . 84 E7
Luton LU3 . . . . 116 B2
Hollick's La LU6 . . . . 121 D2
Hollies Ct LU7 . . . . 110 E7
Hollies The
Kempston MK42 . . . . 49 F3
Shefford SG17 . . . . 77 C3
Hollies Wlk MK43 . . . . 60 F8
HOLLINGTON 85 E6
Hollis La MK44 . . . . 29 F2
Holliwick Rd LU4 . . . . . . 114 E2
Hollowell Cl NN10 . . . . 8 D8
Hollybush Hill SG5 . . . . . 109 F1
Hollybush La
Flamstead AL3 . . . . 129 B3
Harpenden AL5 . . . . 131 A3
Hollybush Rd
Flitwick MK45 . . . . 84 F2
Luton LU2 . . . . 117 C1
Holly Cl SG18 . . . . 67 A8
Holly Farm Cl LU1 . . . . . 122 E3

Holly La AL5 . . . . 131 E6
Holly St LU1 . . . . 123 E6
Holly Street Trad Est [12]
LU1 . . . . 123 E6
Holly Wlk
Harpenden AL5 . . . . 131 D1
Silsoe MK45 . . . . 86 B4
Woburn Sands MK17 . . . . . 81 B2
Holmbrook Ave LU3 . . . . 116 C5
HOLME 65 C3
Holme Cl MK43 . . . . 72 D8
Holme Court Ave SG18 . . . 67 B3
Holme Cres SG18 . . . . 67 A5
HOLME GREEN 66 B2
Holmedale Mid Sch
SG18 . . . . 67 B4
Holme St MK42 . . . . 50 B7
Holmewood Rd MK45 . . . . . 85 D2
Holmfield Cl
Luton LU1 . . . . 123 D5
Toddington LU5 . . . . 105 E5
Holm Oak Gn MK44 . . . . . . 51 D4
Holmscroft Rd LU3 . . . . . 115 F6
Holmwood Cl LU5 . . . . . . 114 D2
Holt Row MK42 . . . . 50 B7
Holts Ct LU6 . . . . 114 B1
Holtsmere Cl LU2 . . . . . . 117 D1
HOLWELL 100 B7
Holwell Rd
Holwell SG5 . . . . 100 C7
Pirton SG5 . . . . 99 E6
HOLYWELL 127 B6
Holywell CE Mid Sch
MK43 . . . . 59 B1
Holywell Cl LU6 . . . . 127 C6
Holywell Rd LU3 . . . . 116 B4
Holywell Rd LU6 . . . . 127 B6
Homebrook Ho MK42 . . . . . 50 C7
Home Cl
Houghton Conquest MK45 . 74 A8
Luton LU4 . . . . 115 C4
Renhold MK41 . . . . 39 B6
Sharnbrook MK44 . . . . 16 D3
Stotfold SG5 . . . . 90 F7
Wilstead MK45 . . . . 62 E3
Homedale Dr LU4 . . . . . . 115 D2
Homedell Ho AL5 . . . . . . 130 E3
Home Farm Cl SG19 . . . . . 42 B8
Home Farm Ct LU2 . . . . . 117 D5
Home Farm Way MK45 . . . 95 E5
Homefield SG7 . . . . 80 D6
Homefield Mdw MK44 . . . . 31 E5
Home Rd MK43 . . . . 48 F3
Homerton Rd LU3 . . . . . . 116 A6
Homestead Way LU1 . . . . 123 C5
HONEYDON 21 B2
Honeydon Ave PE19 . . . . . . 22 C5
Honeydon Rd MK44 . . . . . . 20 C2
Honeygate LU2 . . . . 116 E4
Honey Hill SG19 . . . . 44 D4
Honey Hill Gdns MK40 . . . 49 E2
Honey Hill Rd MK40 . . . . . 49 E2
Honeysuckle Ave MK45 . . . 62 F2
Honeysuckle Cl SG18 . . . . . 67 C4
Honeysuckle Way MK41 . . . 39 B1
HONEYWICK 119 E8
Honeywick La LU6 . . . . . 119 E8
Honiton Mews LU3 . . . . . 115 E6
Honiton Way MK40 . . . . . . 38 E2
Hoo Cl MK43 . . . . 60 F8
Hooked La MK45 . . . . 63 A5
Hookhams La MK41 . . . . . . 39 B6
Hoo La MK43 . . . . 60 E3
Hooper Cl MK42 . . . . 49 C2
Hoo Rd SG17 . . . . 88 D6
Hoo St LU1 . . . . 123 E5
Hoo The MK42 . . . . 49 B2
Hoover Pl SG17 . . . . 76 E2
Hope Rd MK42 . . . . 50 B7
Horace Brightman Cl
LU3 . . . . 116 A7
Horace Gay Gdns SG6 . . . 101 E6
Hornbeam Cl
Leighton Buzzard LU7 . . . 111 C8
Podington NN29 . . . . 7 E2
Hornbeams The MK42 . . . . 49 F4
Horne La
Bedford MK40 . . . . 50 B8
Potton SG19 . . . . 56 A7
Hornes End Rd MK45 . . . . 84 E1
Hornsby Cl LU2 . . . . 117 C1
Horsefair La MK43 . . . . . . 25 C8
Horsepool La MK43 . . . . . . 82 A3
Horseshoe Cl
Dunton SG18 . . . . 68 D5
Marston Moretaine MK43 . . 60 E1
Horseshoe Ct MK42 . . . . . . 49 D3
Horseshoe The MK42 . . . . . 50 B7
Horsham Cl LU2 . . . . 117 D2
Horsler Cl MK45 . . . . 97 C2
Horslow St SG19 . . . . 56 A7
HORTON 118 B3
Horton Rd
Horton LU7 . . . . 118 A2
Slapton LU7 . . . . 118 C6
Hospital Rd SG15 . . . . 90 A4
Hotch Croft MK43 . . . . 59 C3
Houghton Cl MK45 . . . . . . 84 E7
HOUGHTON CONQUEST . . 74 B7
Houghton Conquest Lower
Sch MK45 . . . . 74 B8
Houghton House (rems of) ★
MK45 . . . . 73 F4
Houghton Mews [11] LU1 . 123 D6
Houghton Par LU6 . . . . . . 114 A2
HOUGHTON PARK 114 E6
Houghton Park Rd LU5 . . 114 E6

Houghton Rd
Bedford MK42 . . . . 50 B6
Houghton Regis LU5 . . . . 114 A3
HOUGHTON REGIS 114 B6
Houghton Regis Lower Sch
LU5 . . . . 114 A4
House La SG15 . . . . 90 A7
Howard Ave MK40 . . . . 49 F8
Howard Cl
Cardington MK44 . . . . 51 E4
Haynes MK45 . . . . 63 F1
Luton LU3 . . . . 116 A4
Stotfold SG5 . . . . 90 E5
Wilstead MK45 . . . . 62 E3
Howard Ct MK45 . . . . 84 E1
Howard Ctr [7] MK40 . . . . . 50 B8
Howard Pl
Bedford MK40 . . . . 49 F8
Dunstable LU5 . . . . 121 D7
Howard Rd PE19 . . . . 22 C1
Howard Road Ind Est
PE19 . . . . 22 C1
Howard's Cl SG18 . . . . 67 A5
Howards Mews MK45 . . . . . 86 C8
Howard St
Bedford MK40 . . . . 50 C8
Kempston MK42 . . . . 49 F4
Howberry Gn SG15 . . . . . . 90 A3
Howbury St MK40 . . . . 50 D8
Howden Gdns MK40 . . . . . . 37 C1
HOWELLBURY 89 B1
HOW END 73 E6
How End Rd MK45 . . . . 73 E5
Howes Dr MK43 . . . . 72 C7
Howes La MK45 . . . . 95 E6
How Field AL5 . . . . 130 E3
Howitt's Gdns PE19 . . . . . . 22 F2
Howitt's La PE19 . . . . 22 F3
Howkin Cl MK43 . . . . 36 E2
Howland Pl MK17 . . . . 92 F7
Hoylake Ct LU1 . . . . 123 F5
Hubbard Cl MK45 . . . . 84 E1
Huckleberry Cl LU3 . . . . . 116 A8
Hucklesby Way LU2 . . . . . 123 D8
Huddleston Way MK41 . . . . 51 A8
HUDNALL CORNER 132 B7
Hudnall Rd HP4 . . . . 132 A7
Hudson Cl MK43 . . . . 72 B3
Hudson Rd MK41 . . . . 39 C3
HULCOTE 70 E2
Hulme Cl
Clapham MK41 . . . . 37 C7
Kempston MK42 . . . . 49 E4
Humber Ave MK41 . . . . 38 D5
Humberley Cl PE19 . . . . . . 22 F3
Humberstone Cl LU4 . . . . 115 E2
Humberstone Rd LU4 . . . . 115 E2
Humphrey Talbot Ave
LU6 . . . . 126 F7
Humphrys Rd LU5 . . . . . . 114 E3
Hunston Cl LU4 . . . . 115 B5
Hunter Cl MK42 . . . . 51 A2
Hunters Cl SG5 . . . . 90 E6
Hunter's Cl MK41 . . . . 37 C6
Hunters Way PE28 . . . . 6 F5
Hunters Yd MK44 . . . . 11 B3
Huntingdon Rd
Kempston MK42 . . . . 49 D3
St Neots PE19 . . . . 22 F7
Huntingdonshire Regional
Coll (St Neots Ctr) PE19 . 22 F6
Huntingdon St PE19 . . . . . 22 F6
Hunting Gate SG4 . . . . . . 101 A3
Hunting Hall LU2 . . . . . . 124 C8
Hunts Cl LU1 . . . . 123 C6
Hunts Field MK44 . . . . 40 F5
Hunts La MK43 . . . . 26 B8
Hunts Path MK43 . . . . 37 A8
Hurlock Cl LU6 . . . . 121 A6
Hurlock Way LU4 . . . . 115 C5
Hurst Gr
Bedford MK40 . . . . 49 F8
Lidlington MK43 . . . . 72 B3
Hurst Way LU3 . . . . 115 F5
HUSBORNE CRAWLEY 82 B4
Husborne Crawley Lower Sch
MK43 . . . . 82 B4
Hutton Way MK17 . . . . 81 B5
Hyacinth Way NN10 . . . . . . 8 B7
Hyde Ave SG5 . . . . 90 E5
Hyde Cl AL5 . . . . 131 B4
Hyde Ho [5] LU2 . . . . 123 F8
Hyde La LU1 . . . . 125 C2
Hyde Rd LU1 . . . . 122 F4
Hyde The LU5 . . . . 114 C6
Hyde View Rd AL5 . . . . . . 131 B4
Hydrus Dr LU7 . . . . 111 D8

Ibbet La SG19 . . . . 55 F7
Ibbett Cl MK43 . . . . 49 A2
Ibbetts Yd [4] PE19 . . . . . . 22 E5
ICKLEFORD 100 E4
Ickleford Bury SG5 . . . . . 100 E3
Ickleford Gate SG5 . . . . . 100 D3
Ickleford Prim Sch SG5 . . 100 E4
Ickleford Rd SG5 . . . . 100 F1
Ickley Cl LU4 . . . . 115 B5
Icknield Cl SG5 . . . . 100 E4
Icknield Gn SG6 . . . . 101 E6
Icknield High Sch LU3 . . 116 C5
Icknield Ho LU7 . . . . 111 A6
Icknield Inf Sch SG6 . . . 101 D6
Icknield Prim Sch LU3 . . 116 B5

Icknield Rd LU3 . . . . 115 F4
Icknield St LU6 . . . . 121 B8
Icknield Villas [10] LU6 . . 121 B8
Icknield Way
Baldock SG7 . . . . 91 E1
Dunstable LU6 . . . . 120 B1
Dunstable, Well Head LU6 120 D5
Letchworth SG6 . . . . 101 E6
Luton LU3 . . . . 116 B7
Icknield Way E SG7 . . . . . 91 F1
Icknield Way Farm Cotts
LU6 . . . . 120 D3
ICKWELL 65 E7
ICKWELL GREEN 65 E8
Ickwell Rd
Northill SG18 . . . . 65 C8
Upper Caldecote SG18 . . . 66 A8
Iddesleigh Rd MK40 . . . . . 49 F7
Idenbury Ct LU1 . . . . 123 C7
Ilford Cl LU2 . . . . 117 D3
Imberfield LU4 . . . . 115 C3
Index Ct LU6 . . . . 121 D7
Index Dr LU6 . . . . 121 D7
Ingles Ct PE19 . . . . 22 F6
Ingram Cl MK43 . . . . 72 C8
Ingram Gdns LU2 . . . . . . 116 D7
Inkerman Rise PE19 . . . . . 22 C5
Inkerman St LU1 . . . . 123 D7
Inns La MK45 . . . . 86 B3
Instow Ct MK40 . . . . 38 E2
Interchange Ret Pk MK42 49 F2
IRCHESTER 7 B7
Irchester Prim Sch NN29 . . 7 A8
Irchester Rd NN29 . . . . 7 A4
IRELAND 77 A7
Ireton Cl PE19 . . . . 22 F3
Irthing Cl MK41 . . . . 38 D6
Irvine Ct MK41 . . . . 38 D5
Irwin Rd MK40 . . . . 38 E1
Isis Rd MK41 . . . . 38 C5
Isis Wlk LU7 . . . . 103 B3
Isle Of Wight La LU6 . . . 121 A3
Ison Cl MK40 . . . . 49 D8
Itchen Cl MK41 . . . . 38 C5
Ivel Bury SG18 . . . . 66 F7
Ivel Cl
Barton-le-C MK45 . . . . 97 D3
Bedford MK41 . . . . 38 D6
Langford SG18 . . . . 78 E5
Shefford SG17 . . . . 77 D2
St Neots PE19 . . . . 22 C4
Ivel Cotts SG18 . . . . 66 F1
Iveldale Dr SG17 . . . . 77 D3
Ivel Gdns SG18 . . . . 66 F6
Ivel Rd
Sandy SG19 . . . . 54 C6
Shefford SG17 . . . . 77 D2
Ivel View SG19 . . . . 54 D6
Ivel Way
Flitwick MK45 . . . . 85 A3
Stotfold SG5 . . . . 90 F8
Ivester Ct LU7 . . . . 110 E6
IVINGHOE ASTON 119 E4
Ivinghoe Bsns Ctr LU5 . . 114 B3
Ivinghoe Way LU4 . . . . . . 119 C1
Ivy Cl
Dunstable LU6 . . . . 113 E1
Tempsford SG19 . . . . 42 B8
Ivy Ct LU1 . . . . 123 B8
Ivy La
Heath and Reach MK17 . . 102 C8
Wilstead MK45 . . . . 63 A4
Ivy Rd
Bedford MK42 . . . . 50 D6
Luton LU1 . . . . 123 C8

Jacey Ct MK42 . . . . 49 D6
Jackman Cl MK43 . . . . 36 F1
Jack's La MK43 . . . . 34 F5
Jackson Pl SG17 . . . . 76 E2
Jacksons Cl LU6 . . . . 119 E4
Jackson St SG7 . . . . 91 E1
Jacobs Cl SG19 . . . . 56 A8
Jacques La MK45 . . . . 75 E1
James Ct
Luton LU4 . . . . 115 B2
[14] Luton, New Town LU1 123 E6
St Neots PE19 . . . . 22 F2
James Foster Ho SG5 . . . 100 E1
James Marshall Commercial
Ctr AL5 . . . . 131 A1
Jameson Rd AL5 . . . . 131 B4
James St
[9] Bedford MK40 . . . . 50 B8
Irchester NN29 . . . . 7 B7
Jansel Ho LU2 . . . . 117 B4
Jardine Way LU5 . . . . 121 E7
Jasmine Cl
Bedford MK41 . . . . 39 C4
Biggleswade SG18 . . . . 67 C4
Jasmine Ct SG5 . . . . 90 F7
Jasmine Gdns NN10 . . . . . . 8 B7
Jay Cl SG6 . . . . 101 E8
Jays The SG19 . . . . 42 C2
Jaywood LU2 . . . . 117 C6
Jeans Way LU5 . . . . 114 F1
Jellicoe Pl PE19 . . . . 22 A2
Jenkins Cl PE19 . . . . 22 B2
Jenkyn Rd MK43 . . . . 60 E6
Jennings Ave PE19 . . . . . . 22 E2
Jennings Cl SG19 . . . . 55 F8
Jeremiah Cl MK45 . . . . 97 C3
Jerrard Ct LU7 . . . . 111 C6
Jersey Rd LU4 . . . . 115 A3
J F Kennedy Dr SG17 . . . . 76 E2

Jillifer Rd LU4 . . . . 115 A2
JOCKEY END 132 F8
Joes Cl MK45 . . . . 85 C2
John Barker Pl SG5 . . . . . 100 C1
John Bunyan Cl MK45 . . . . 85 B8
John Bunyan Upper Sch &
Com Coll MK42 . . . . 50 E4
John Donne CE Lower Sch
MK44 . . . . 41 E3
John Howland Cl SG16 . . . 78 D1
Johnson Cl
Biddenham MK40 . . . . 37 C1
Marston Moretaine MK43 . . 72 C8
Johnson Ct LU5 . . . . 114 D5
Johnson Dr LU7 . . . . 111 C4
John St LU1 . . . . 123 E7
Joint The SG17 . . . . 78 B2
Jordan Cl SG16 . . . . 78 D2
Jowitt Ave MK42 . . . . 49 F4
Jubilee Cl
Clifton SG5 . . . . 78 B2
Lower Stondon SG16 . . . . . 89 B3
St Neots PE19 . . . . 22 E4
Jubilee Cotts MK43 . . . . . . 72 D6
Jubilee Cres SG15 . . . . 90 A2
Jubilee Ct
[3] Dunstable LU6 . . . . . . 114 A1
Harpenden AL5 . . . . 131 C3
Jubilee Gdns
Biggleswade SG18 . . . . 67 B7
Rushden NN10 . . . . 8 C8
Jubilee La SG18 . . . . 78 F6
Jubilee Pl SG17 . . . . 77 C4
Jubilee St LU2 . . . . 116 F1
Judges La LU7 . . . . 110 F6
Judith Gdns
Kempston MK42 . . . . 49 D3
Potton SG19 . . . . 56 B8
Julia Ct LU3 . . . . 116 B4
Julius Gdns LU3 . . . . 115 F7
Juniper Cl
Luton LU4 . . . . 115 E2
Silsoe MK45 . . . . 86 C4
Juniper Wlk MK42 . . . . 49 F2
Jupiter Dr LU7 . . . . 111 D8
Jutland Rise PE19 . . . . 22 C5

K

Karen Ho SG16 . . . . 89 A4
Katherine Dr LU5 . . . . . . 114 F2
Katherine's Ct MK45 . . . . . 84 E8
Katherine's Gdn MK45 . . . . 84 E8
Kathie Rd MK42 . . . . 50 D5
Kayser Ct SG18 . . . . 66 F4
Keaton Cl LU5 . . . . 114 D5
Keats Cl MK40 . . . . 37 F2
Keats Ct PE19 . . . . 22 C6
Keats Ho [15] AL5 . . . . . . 131 B1
Keats Rd MK45 . . . . 84 D3
Keeble Cl LU2 . . . . 117 E1
Keeley Farm Ct MK43 . . . . 48 F1
KEELEY GREEN 48 F1
Keeley La MK43 . . . . 48 E1
Keepers Cl LU2 . . . . 117 C2
Kelling Cl LU2 . . . . 116 C8
Kelvin Ave LU5 . . . . 50 C5
Kelvin Cl LU1 . . . . 123 E6
Kempsey Cl LU2 . . . . 117 D2
Kempster Cl MK40 . . . . 50 A8
KEMPSTON 49 C4
KEMPSTON CHURCH
END 49 B4
Kempston Ct MK43 . . . . . . 61 E5
KEMPSTON HARDWICK . . 61 D5
Kempston Hardwick Gypsy
Site MK45 . . . . 61 F5
Kempston Hardwick Sta
MK43 . . . . 61 D6
Kempston Rd MK42 . . . . . . 50 A6
Kempston Rural Lower Sch
MK43 . . . . 49 B4
KEMPSTON WEST END . . . 48 C4
Kendal Cl LU3 . . . . 115 D7
Kendal Dr MK45 . . . . 84 E2
Kendale Rd LU4 . . . . 115 B2
Kendal Gdns LU7 . . . . 110 C7
Kendall Dr SG17 . . . . 76 F3
Kendall Rd MK42 . . . . 49 D3
Kenilworth Cl PE19 . . . . . . 22 C3
Kenilworth Rd LU1 . . . . . 123 C8
Kenilworth Wlk MK41 . . . . 39 A4
Kennedy Ct LU7 . . . . 110 F7
Kennedy Rd MK42 . . . . 50 C5
Kennel La AL5 . . . . 130 A5
Kennell Hill MK44 . . . . 16 D3
Kennesbourne Ct AL5 . . . 130 D4
Kenneth Rd LU2 . . . . 117 A1
Kenneth Way MK45 . . . . . . 62 B6
Kennet Rise MK41 . . . . 38 C6
Kennington Rd LU3 . . . . . 116 B3
Kensington Cl LU5 . . . . . . 114 E4
KENSWORTH 127 E8
KENSWORTH COMMON . . 121 D1
Kensworth Cl LU3 . . . . . . 115 B3
Kensworth Gate LU6 . . . . 121 C7
Kensworth Lower Sch
LU6 . . . . 127 F8
KENSWORTH LYNCH 122 A1
Kensworth Rd LU6 . . . . . . 127 D4
Kent Ave MK42 . . . . 50 C5
Kent Cl MK45 . . . . 95 E5
Kentmere Cl MK42 . . . . . . 49 D3
Kent Rd
Houghton Regis LU5 . . . . 114 D7
Luton LU1 . . . . 122 F8
Kentwick Sq LU5 . . . . 114 D7

Kenworth Ct MK41 . . . . **38** B2
Kenwyn Cl MK41 . . . . **39** C5
Kernow Ct LU2 . . . . **117** A1
Kerrison Cl MK43 . . . . **72** C3
Kershaw Cl LU3 . . . . **116** A8
Kershope Cl MK41 . . . . **39** C3
Kestrel Rd
  Bedford MK41 . . . . **38** C4
  Flitwick MK45 . . . . **84** D1
Kestrel Way
  Luton LU4 . . . . **115** A5
  Sandy SG19 . . . . **42** B2
Keswick Cl LU6 . . . . **121** B7
Ketton Cl LU2 . . . . **124** A7
Ketton Ct LU2 . . . . **124** A7
Keymer Ct LU2 . . . . **117** C3
KEYSOE **12** B2
Keysoe Rd
  Riseley MK44 . . . . **11** B1
  Thurleigh MK44 . . . . **18** D3
KEYSOE ROW **19** C7
Keysoe Row E MK44 . . . . . **19** D8
Keysoe Row W MK44 . . . . **19** B7
Keyston Rd PE28 . . . . **2** D2
Kidner Cl LU2 . . . . **116** E5
Kielder Path 6 MK41 . . . . **39** B4
Kilby Rd LU7 . . . . **104** F2
Kilmarnock Dr LU2 . . . . . **116** E5
Kiln La MK45 . . . . **75** D2
Kiln Rd MK45 . . . . **61** E4
Kiln Way LU5 . . . . **115** A1
Kilpin Cl MK42 . . . . **50** D6
Kilpin Gn MK16 . . . . **58** B6
Kimberley Cl SG6 . . . . **90** F2
Kimberley Ct LU4 . . . . . . **114** E3
Kimberwell Cl LU5 . . . . . **105** F4
Kimble Dr MK41 . . . . **51** A8
KIMBOLTON **6** F6
Kimbolton Ave MK40 . . . . **38** D2
Kimbolton Cl MK41 . . . . . **38** E3
Kimbolton Ct MK41 . . . . . **38** E3
Kimbolton Prep Sch PE28 . .**6** E5
Kimbolton Rd
  Bedford MK40, MK41 . . . . **38** D4
  Chelveston NN9 . . . . **3** D8
  Pertenhall MK44 . . . . **12** D7
  St Neots PE19 . . . . **22** A8
  Wilden MK44 . . . . **19** D4
Kimbolton Sch PE28 . . . . . . **6** F4
Kimpton Bottom AL5,
  SG4 . . . . **131** E7
Kimpton Rd
  Luton LU1, LU2 . . . . **124** A6
  Peters Green LU2, SG4 . . . . **125** E2
King Cup Cl NN10 . . . . **8** C7
King Edward Rd MK41 . . . . **39** A1
Kingfisher Bsns Pk MK42 . **50** C6
Kingfisher Cl
  Bedford MK41 . . . . **38** D3
  Biggleswade SG18 . . . . . . **66** F5
  Sandy SG19 . . . . **42** C2
Kingfisher Rd
  Flitwick MK45 . . . . **84** D1
  Shefford SG17 . . . . **77** C2
King George Cl SG18 . . . . **78** F7
King Georges Cl SG5 . . . . **100** D1
Kinghamway LU2 . . . . **116** E1
Kingsbrook Rd MK42 . . . . . **50** C7
Kingsbury Ave LU5 . . . . . **114** E1
Kingsbury Ct LU5 . . . . . . **121** C8
Kingsbury Gdns LU5 . . . . **114** F1
Kings Cl MK44 . . . . **10** F2
Kingscroft Ave LU5 . . . . . **114** C1
Kings Ct
  Dunstable LU5 . . . . **114** C1
  Flitwick MK45 . . . . **84** F2
Kingsdown Ave LU2 . . . . . **116** D5
Kings Hedges SG5 . . . . . **100** C3
Kings Houghton Mid Sch
  LU5 . . . . **114** D7
Kingsland Cl LU4 . . . . . . **114** E4
Kingsland Ct 7 LU1 . . . . **123** F6
Kingsland Rd LU1 . . . . . . **123** F6
Kingsley Ave SG5 . . . . **90** C3
Kingsley Ct SG19 . . . . **54** B8
Kingsley Rd
  Bedford MK40 . . . . **50** E8
  Luton LU3 . . . . **116** A5
Kings Mead LU6 . . . . **119** E3
Kingsmead Pk Mobile Home
  Pk NN10 . . . . **8** C7
Kingsmede SG17 . . . . **77** C3
Kingsmoor MK45 . . . . **84** F3
Kingsmoor Lower Sch
  MK45 . . . . **84** F3
King's Pl MK42 . . . . **50** B6
Kings Pond Cl SG18 . . . . . **68** D5
Kings Rd
  Maulden MK45 . . . . **74** C1
  St Neots PE19 . . . . **22** B3
King's Rd
  Broom SG18 . . . . **66** C3
  Flitwick MK45 . . . . **84** F2
  Sandy SG19 . . . . **54** C7
  St Neots PE19 . . . . **22** F6
King St
  Clapham MK41 . . . . **37** D6
  Dunstable LU5 . . . . **121** C8
  Houghton Regis LU5 . . . . **114** B4
  Kempston MK42 . . . . **49** E4
  Leighton Buzzard LU7 . . . **111** A8
  Luton LU1 . . . . **123** E7
  Markyate AL3 . . . . **128** E5
  Potton SG19 . . . . **56** A7
Kingston Cl MK42 . . . . **49** E6
Kingston Ct MK42 . . . . **50** A6
Kingston Rd LU2 . . . . **116** F1

Kingsway
  Bedford MK42 . . . . **50** C7
  Dunstable LU5 . . . . **114** C1
  Luton LU4 . . . . **116** A1
  Stotfold SG5 . . . . **90** F7
Kingsway Gdns SG5 . . . . . **90** F7
Kingsway Ind Est LU1 . . . **123** A8
Kingswood Ave SG4 . . . . . **101** D1
Kingswood Cl MK45 . . . . . **74** B7
King's Wood National Nature
  Reserve★ LU7 . . . . **103** A8
Kingswood Way MK40 . . . . **49** B6
King William Cl
  Barton-le-C MK45 . . . . **97** D4
  Kempston MK42 . . . . **49** D4
King William Rd MK42 . . . **49** C4
Kinloch Ct 6 AL5 . . . . . . **131** B1
Kinmoor Cl LU3 . . . . **107** D1
Kinross Cres LU3 . . . . **115** D8
Kinsbourne Cl AL5 . . . . . **130** C4
Kinsbourne Cres AL5 . . . . **130** D4
Kinsbourne Ct AL5 . . . . . **130** F3
KINSBOURNE GREEN **127** C5
Kinsbourne Green La
  AL5 . . . . **130** B3
Kipling Cl PE19 . . . . **22** D5
Kipling The LU3 . . . . **116** B6
Kipling Way AL5 . . . . **131** B1
Kirby Dr LU3 . . . . **116** A8
Kirby Rd LU6 . . . . **121** A8
Kirkdale Ct 8 LU1 . . . . . **123** E6
Kirkdale Rd AL5 . . . . **131** C4
Kirkman Cl MK42 . . . . **50** D6
Kirkstall Ct MK42 . . . . **50** C3
Kirkstone Dr LU6 . . . . . . **121** B6
Kirkwick Ave AL5 . . . . . . **131** A1
Kirkwood Rd LU4 . . . . . . **114** F3
Kirton Way LU5 . . . . **114** E6
Kitchener Pl MK43 . . . . **61** D1
Kitelands Rd SG18 . . . . . . **67** C4
Kiteleys Gn LU7 . . . . **111** C8
Kite Way SG6 . . . . **101** E8
Kittiwake Cl SG18 . . . . . . **66** F4
Kiwi Cl MK45 . . . . **100** F1
Klondyke AL5 . . . . **130** D4
Knaresborough Ct PE19 . . . **22** F1
Knarsdale Wlk 5 MK41 . . . **39** B4
Knaves Hill LU7 . . . . **110** D8
Kneller Cl MK41 . . . . **38** A2
Knights Ave MK41 . . . . **37** D7
Knights Cl
  Eaton Bray LU6 . . . . **119** F5
  St Neots PE19 . . . . **22** B4
Knights Ct LU6 . . . . **119** E5
Knights Field LU2 . . . . . . **116** D1
Knoll Rise LU6 . . . . **116** E4
Knolls The SG19 . . . . **54** B5
Knolls View
  Northall LU6 . . . . **119** B5
  Tottenhoe LU6 . . . . **112** F1
Knolls Way SG17 . . . . **77** F2
Knoll The
  Maulden MK45 . . . . **85** D8
  Woburn Sands MK17 . . . . **81** A1
KNOTTING **9** E3
KNOTTING GREEN **9** F1
Knotting La MK44 . . . . **10** C1
Knotting Rd MK44 . . . . **10** C7
Knotts Cl LU6 . . . . **121** C5
Knowl Piece SG4 . . . . **101** A3
Kymbrook Lower Sch
  MK44 . . . . **19** C7
Kym Rd PE19 . . . . **22** C4
Kynance Cl LU2 . . . . **117** A2

L

Laburnam Rd SG18 . . . . . . **67** B7
Laburnham Ave MK45 . . . . **62** E2
Laburnum Ave MK40 . . . . . **49** F7
Laburnum Cl LU3 . . . . . . **116** C7
Laburnum Gr LU3 . . . . . . **116** B7
Laburnum Lower Sch
  SG19 . . . . **54** B8
Laburnum Rd SG19 . . . . . . **54** B7
Lachbury Cl LU1 . . . . **123** A6
Ladybridge Terr MK43 . . . . **34** E5
Ladyhill LU5 . . . . **115** B6
Lady Way PE19 . . . . **22** B4
Lady Zia Wernher Special
  Sch LU2 . . . . **117** B3
Lakefield Cl LU5 . . . . **105** F5
Lakes Cl SG18 . . . . **78** C5
Lake St LU7 . . . . **111** A6
Lakeview MK43 . . . . **60** E1
Lalleford Rd LU2 . . . . **117** D1
Lamb Mdw AL5 . . . . **90** A3
Lambourn Dr LU2 . . . . . . **116** E6
Lambourn Gdns LU4 . . . . **130** F3
Lambourn Way MK41 . . . . . **38** D6
Lambs Cl LU5 . . . . **114** F1
Lamers Rd LU2 . . . . **117** B2
Lammas Mead SG5 . . . . . **100** E2
Lammas Way
  Ampthill MK45 . . . . **84** E6
  Letchworth SG6 . . . . **101** F8
  St Neots PE19 . . . . **22** F6
Lammas Wlk LU1 . . . . **111** A7
Lammerside MK41 . . . . **39** C5
Lamorna Cl LU3 . . . . **115** F6
Lamsey Ct 1 LU7 . . . . . . **111** A8
Lancaster Ave
  Bedford MK42 . . . . **50** C5
  Luton LU2 . . . . **116** C8
Lancaster Cl MK45 . . . . . . **97** D4
Lancaster Pl SG17 . . . . **77** C1

Lancaster Rd MK42 . . . . . . **51** A2
Lanchester Cl MK41 . . . . . **37** E6
Lanchester Rd MK43 . . . . . **58** D2
Lancing Rd LU2 . . . . **117** D3
Lancot Ave LU6 . . . . **120** F8
Lancot Cl LU6 . . . . **120** F8
Lancot Lower Sch LU6 . . . **120** E8
Lancot Pl LU6 . . . . **120** E8
Landrace Rd LU4 . . . . **114** E4
Landseer Wlk MK41 . . . . . . **38** A2
Lane's End LU7 . . . . **103** A4
Lane The
  Chalton LU4 . . . . **106** E1
  Tebworth LU7 . . . . **105** B3
  Wyboston MK44 . . . . **31** F6
Langdale MK41 . . . . **38** E3
Langdale Ave AL5 . . . . . . **131** D2
Langdale Cl LU6 . . . . **121** C7
Langdale Rd LU6 . . . . **121** B6
LANGFORD **78** E6
Langford Dr LU2 . . . . **117** A3
LANGFORD END **42** C8
Langford Lower Sch SG18 . **78** F7
Langford Mill SG18 . . . . . . **78** E7
Langford Rd
  Biggleswade SG18 . . . . . . **66** F2
  Henlow SG16 . . . . **78** D4
Langham Cl LU2 . . . . **116** D7
Langham Ho 8 LU1 . . . . . **123** D8
Langlands Rd MK41 . . . . . . **39** B4
Langley Gdns SG19 . . . . . . **55** E7
Langley St LU1 . . . . **123** E6
Langley Terrace Ind Pk 10
  LU1 . . . . **123** E6
Langridge Ct LU6 . . . . . . **113** F1
Langwood Cl PE19 . . . . . . **22** C6
Lansbury Cl PE19 . . . . **22** C4
Lansdowne Rd
  Bedford MK40 . . . . **38** A1
  Luton LU3 . . . . **116** D1
Lansdowne Terr 7 MK40 . . **38** A1
Lanthony Ct SG15 . . . . **90** A4
Laporte Way LU4 . . . . . . **115** F1
Lapwing Rd LU4 . . . . **115** A4
Larch Cl NN29 . . . . **7** A7
Larches The
  Kempston MK42 . . . . **49** F3
  Luton LU2 . . . . **116** D1
Larkins Cl SG7 . . . . **91** F1
Lark Rise Lower Sch
  LU6 . . . . **121** B6
Larkspur Gdns LU4 . . . . . **115** F2
Larks Rise SG19 . . . . **42** C2
Larkway
  Bedford MK41 . . . . **38** D4
  Flitwick MK45 . . . . **84** D2
Latimer Rd LU1 . . . . **123** E6
Launton St LU3 . . . . **108** B1
Laurel Cl PE19 . . . . **22** F4
Laurel Mews SG7 . . . . **91** F1
Laurel View 2 SG18 . . . . . **67** A6
Laurel Way SG5 . . . . **100** E3
Laurel Wlk MK42 . . . . **50** A3
Lavender Cl LU2 . . . . **116** E7
Lavender Ct
  Ampthill MK45 . . . . **84** E7
  Baldock SG7 . . . . **91** E1
Lavender Way
  Biggleswade SG18 . . . . . . **67** C5
  Rushden NN10 . . . . **8** C3
LAVENDON **34** A8
Lavenham Dr MK40 . . . . . . **37** C1
Lawford Cl LU1 . . . . **123** C7
Lawn Gdns LU1 . . . . **123** E6
Lawnside SG18 . . . . **67** B6
Lawnside Lower Sch
  SG18 . . . . **67** B6
Lawns The LU3 . . . . **43** C3
Lawrence End Rd LU2 . . . **125** D4
Lawrence Rd
  Biggleswade SG18 . . . . . . **67** A6
  St Neots PE19 . . . . **22** C5
Lawrence St MK40 . . . . **49** F7
Lawrence Way LU6 . . . . . **113** F2
Laws Cl MK43 . . . . **34** E6
Laxton Cl
  Luton LU2 . . . . **117** E1
  St Neots PE19 . . . . **22** C4
Laycock Abbey MK41 . . . . . **51** B8
Layham Dr LU2 . . . . **117** E1
Lea Bank AL5 . . . . **131** B6
Lea Bank Ct LU3 . . . . **116** E6
Leacroft AL5 . . . . **131** D3
Lea Ct AL5 . . . . **131** A3
Leafield LU3 . . . . **115** F4
Leafield Ct MK45 . . . . **84** E8
Leafields LU5 . . . . **114** C5
Leaf Rd LU5 . . . . **114** B6
Leagrave High St LU3 . . . **115** B3
Leagrave Prim Sch LU4 . . **115** C4
Leagrave Rd LU4 . . . . **116** B2
Leagrave Sta LU4 . . . . . . **115** E5
Lealands High Sch LU3 . . **115** C8
Lea Manor High Sch LU3 . **116** A7
Lea Manor Recn Ctr LU3 . **115** F8
Leamington Rd LU4 . . . . . **116** A7
Lea Prim Sch The AL5 . . . **131** A4
Lea Rd
  Ampthill MK45 . . . . **84** F8
  Harpenden AL5 . . . . **131** B3
  Luton LU1 . . . . **123** F7
Lime Gr
  Leighton Buzzard LU7 . . . **110** E8
  St Neots PE19 . . . . **22** F6

Leaside LU5 . . . . **114** E6
Leaside Ct AL5 . . . . **131** C3
Leasway MK41 . . . . **38** F3
Leathwaite Cl LU3 . . . . . . **116** A6
LEA VALLEY **131** F2
Lea Wlk AL5 . . . . **131** C4
Leck Rd 10 LU7 . . . . **111** A7
LEDBURN **110** C1
Ledburn Rd LU7 . . . . **110** E6
Ledgemore La HP2 . . . . . **132** F5
Ledwell Rd LU1 . . . . **122** F3
Lee Bridge Cnr LU2 . . . . . **130** F7
Lee Cl MK40 . . . . **37** C1
Lee Ct PE19 . . . . **22** E5
LEEDON **111** D7
Leedon Lower Sch LU7 . . **111** C6
Leeds Smith Dr SG19 . . . . **54** C8
Lee Farm Cotts MK44 . . . . **15** C4
Lees Cl SG18 . . . . **68** D5
Leghorn Cres LU4 . . . . . . **115** A3
Leicester Rd LU4 . . . . **115** E1
Leigh Cl LU5 . . . . **105** F6
Leigh St MK40 . . . . **38** B1
Leighfield Cl MK41 . . . . . . **39** C3
LEIGHTON BUZZARD **111** E6
Leighton Buzzard Narrow
  Gauge Railway★ LU7 . . . **103** C1
Leighton Buzzard Rd
  HP1 . . . . **132** E2
Leighton Buzzard Sta
  LU7 . . . . **110** E6
Leighton Ct
  Bedford MK40 . . . . **38** C5
  Dunstable LU5 . . . . **121** A8
Leighton Mid Sch LU7 . . **110** F6
Leighton Rd
  Ascott LU7 . . . . **110** A3
  Eggington LU7 . . . . **112** A7
  Heath and Reach LU7 . . . **103** B4
  Leighton Buzzard, Eggington
    LU7 . . . . **112** B8
  Leighton Buzzard LU7 . . . **102** B1
  Northall LU6 . . . . **119** C4
  Stanbridge LU7 . . . . **112** B5
  Toddington LU5 . . . . **105** E5
Leighton St MK17 . . . . **92** E6
Leith Rd MK42 . . . . **50** F5
Lely Cl MK41 . . . . **38** A3
Lennon Cl LU2 . . . . **123** D7
Lennox Gn LU2 . . . . **117** F2
Leopold Rd LU7 . . . . **110** D7
Lesbury Cl LU2 . . . . **117** E1
Leston Cl LU6 . . . . **121** D5
LETCHWORTH **101** C5
Letchworth La SG6 . . . . . **101** C5
Letchworth Mus & Art Gall★
  SG6 . . . . **101** F5
Letchworth Rd LU3 . . . . . **116** A4
Letchworth Sta SG6 . . . . **101** F6
Levellers La PE19 . . . . **22** F5
Leven Cl LU7 . . . . **110** B7
Levendale LU4 . . . . **115** C5
Leven Wlk MK41 . . . . **38** C7
Lewens Croft MK16 . . . . . . **47** A3
Lewes Gdns MK41 . . . . **39** A5
Lewis La SG15 . . . . **90** A6
LEWSEY FARM **114** E4
Lewsey Park Ct LU4 . . . . . **115** A4
Lewsey Rd LU4 . . . . **115** B2
Leyburne Rd LU3 . . . . **116** B6
Leydene Pl SG17 . . . . **76** F3
Leygreen Cl LU2 . . . . **124** A8
Leyhill Dr LU1 . . . . **123** B4
Leys Ave SG6 . . . . **101** F6
Ley Side MK43 . . . . **36** F2
Leys Rd PE19 . . . . **22** E6
Leys The
  Ampthill MK45 . . . . **84** F7
  Langford SG18 . . . . **78** F6
  Woburn Sands MK17 . . . . **81** A4
Leyton Gn AL5 . . . . **131** A5
Leyton Rd AL5 . . . . **131** A5
Library Rd LU1 . . . . **123** E7
Library Wlk MK41 . . . . **38** F4
Lichfield SG18 . . . . **67** A4
Lichfield Cl MK42 . . . . **49** E5
Liddel Cl LU3 . . . . **116** B3
Liddell Way LU7 . . . . **111** D5
Lidgate Cl LU4 . . . . **115** B6
LIDLINGTON **72** B2
Lidlington Sta MK43 . . . . . **72** B3
Life Cl LU4 . . . . **114** F4
Lighthorne Rise LU3 . . . . **116** A7
Lilac Ave MK45 . . . . **62** F2
Lilac Cl
  Biggleswade SG18 . . . . . . **67** C5
  Luton LU3 . . . . **107** C1
  Rushden NN10 . . . . **8** B7
Lilac Wlk MK42 . . . . **49** F3
Lilleshall Dr MK42 . . . . . . **50** C3
LILLEY **109** C2
Lilley Bottom LU2 . . . . . . **117** E8
Lilleyhoo La LU2, SG5 . . . **109** F2
Lily Cl MK42 . . . . **50** F4
Limbersey La MK43 . . . . . . **74** D3
LIMBURY **115** F5
Limbury Rd LU3 . . . . **115** F4
Lime Ave
  Beeston SG19 . . . . **54** B6
  Luton LU4 . . . . **115** C5
Lime Cl
  Barton-le-C MK45 . . . . **97** C3
  Bromham MK43 . . . . **36** E1
  Flitwick MK45 . . . . **84** F2

Lime Gr continued
  Woburn Sands MK17 . . . . **81** B4
Lime St MK40 . . . . **50** B8
Limes The
  Arlesey SG15 . . . . **90** A8
  Luton LU1 . . . . **123** E5
Limetree Ave LU5 . . . . . . **130** A7
Lime Tree Cl LU3 . . . . . . **107** C1
Lime Tree Dr SG18 . . . . . . **68** C5
Lime Tree Rd SG17 . . . . . . **78** A3
Lime Tree Wlk SG18 . . . . . **67** A7
Lime Wlk
  Dunstable LU5 . . . . **121** D8
  Henlow SG16 . . . . **78** D2
Linacres LU4 . . . . **115** D4
Linbridge Way LU2 . . . . . **117** C3
Linclare Pl PE19 . . . . **22** C4
Lincoln Cl
  Dunstable LU5 . . . . **121** F6
  Flitwick MK45 . . . . **84** E4
Lincoln Cres SG18 . . . . . . **67** A4
Lincoln Ct MK40 . . . . **50** E8
Lincoln Rd
  Kempston MK42 . . . . **49** D2
  Luton LU4 . . . . **116** B1
  Shortstown MK42 . . . . **51** A2
Lincoln Way LU5 . . . . **96** A2
Lincombe Slade LU7 . . . . **110** E8
Lincroft
  Cranfield MK43 . . . . **59** B1
  Oakley MK43 . . . . **37** A7
Lincroft Mid Sch MK43 . . . **37** A7
Linden Cl LU5 . . . . **114** F1
Linden Cres SG6 . . . . **91** A1
Linden Ct
  Bedford MK40 . . . . **38** A2
  4 Luton LU2 . . . . **123** F8
Linden Rd
  Bedford MK40 . . . . **38** A1
  Dunstable LU5 . . . . **114** F2
  Luton LU4 . . . . **115** E4
Lindens The LU5 . . . . **114** B4
Lindisfarne Cl
  Sandy SG19 . . . . **54** C8
  St Neots PE19 . . . . **22** F1
Lindisfarne Priory MK41 . . **51** B8
Lindler Ct LU7 . . . . **111** A6
Lindley Cl AL5 . . . . **131** A4
Lindsell Cres SG18 . . . . . . **67** A7
Lindsey Rd LU2 . . . . **117** D1
Link Rd NN10 . . . . **8** B7
Links The MK42 . . . . **49** E3
Links Way LU2 . . . . **116** D8
Link The
  Houghton Regis LU5 . . . . **114** B5
  Letchworth SG6 . . . . **91** A1
Linkway MK41 . . . . **39** A2
Link Way SG17 . . . . **78** A2
Linley Dell LU2 . . . . **117** D2
Linley Rd PE19 . . . . **22** E3
Linmere Wlk LU5 . . . . . . **114** E6
Linnet Cl
  Letchworth SG6 . . . . **101** E8
  Luton LU4 . . . . **115** A4
  Sandy SG19 . . . . **42** C2
Linnet Way MK41 . . . . **38** C4
Linnins Pond AL3 . . . . . . **129** B1
LINSLADE **110** D7
Linslade Lower Sch LU7 . **110** D7
Linslade Mid Sch LU7 . . **110** E5
Linslade Rd LU7 . . . . **102** F4
Linton Cl PE19 . . . . **22** A3
Linwood Gr LU7 . . . . **111** B6
Lippitts Hill LU2 . . . . **116** E5
Lipscombe Dr MK45 . . . . . **84** E1
Liscombe Rd LU5 . . . . . . **121** E8
Liston Cl LU4 . . . . **115** B5
Litchfield MK44 . . . . **11** A2
LITTLE BARFORD **32** E6
Little Beeches MK41 . . . . . **66** F7
Little Berries LU3 . . . . . . **115** F4
LITTLE BILLINGTON **111** D1
Littlebury Cl SG5 . . . . **91** A5
Little Church Rd LU2 . . . . **117** B3
LITTLE CRAWLEY **58** A7
Littledale St MK42 . . . . . . **49** F5
LITTLE END **22** B1
Little End Rd PE19 . . . . . . **22** B1
Little End Road Ind Est
  PE19 . . . . **22** B2
Littlefield Rd LU2 . . . . . . **117** B2
Littlegreen La LU1 . . . . . **122** E3
Little Grove Pl MK40 . . . . . **50** C8
Little Headlands MK41 . . . . **38** F4
LITTLE HEATH **44** C3
Little Heath SG19 . . . . **44** C4
Little Hill LU7 . . . . **111** E2
Little La
  Clophill MK45 . . . . **75** D1
  Hockliffe LU7 . . . . **104** E1
  Pirton SG5 . . . . **99** D5
LITTLE ODELL **25** B7
Little Portway MK40 . . . . . **49** B6
Little Spinney MK43 . . . . . **59** C3
LITTLE STAUGHTON **13** A2
Little Staughton Airfield
  MK44 . . . . **20** D8
Little Staughton Rd MK44 **20** C3
Little Townsend Cl MK42 . . **50** B4
Little Wood Croft LU3 . . . **115** E7
LITTLEWORTH **63** A4
LITTLE WYMINGTON **8** A7
Liverpool Rd LU1 . . . . . . **123** D7
Livingstone Lower Sch
  MK41 . . . . **38** A2

Loake Cl MK41 . . . . 37 C7
Locarno Ave LU4 . . . . . . 115 C6
Lochy Dr LU7 . . . . 110 C7
Lockhart Cl LU6 . . . . 121 E6
Lockington Cres LU5 . . . 114 F2
Lodge Ave MK42 . . . . 49 C3
Lodge Cl MK44 . . . . 16 C4
Lodge Ct SG5 . . . . 100 E3
Lodge Gdns AL5 . . . . 131 A2
Lodge Rd
  Cranfield MK43 . . . . 71 A7
  Rushden NN10 . . . . 8 A8
  Sharnbrook MK44 . . . . . 16 C4
Lodge The MK41 . . . . 37 D6
Lodge The Nature Reserve★
  SG19 . . . . 54 F4
Loftus Cl LU4 . . . . 115 B3
Lollard Cl LU4 . . . . 114 E3
Lombard St MK43 . . . . . . 72 C3
Lombardy Cl MK41 . . . . . 38 E4
Lomond Dr LU7 . . . . 110 C8
London End
  Irchester NN29 . . . . 7 B8
  Milton Ernest MK44 . . . . 27 B4
  Woburn MK17 . . . . 92 F6
London La MK45 . . . . 74 D6
London Luton Airport
  LU2 . . . . 124 D7
London Rd
  Astwick SG18 . . . . 79 E7
  Bedford MK42 . . . . 50 D6
  Biggleswade SG18 . . . . . 67 C4
  Dunstable LU6 . . . . 121 D6
  Luton LU1 . . . . 129 F7
  Luton, New Town LU1 . . 123 E4
  Markyate AL3 . . . . 128 F5
  Sandy SG19 . . . . 54 B7
  Woburn MK17 . . . . 93 B3
London Road Ind Est
  SG19 . . . . 42 A1
London Road Trad Est
  SG18 . . . . 67 C3
London Row SG15 . . . . . . 90 A3
Longborns MK43 . . . . 59 C2
Longbrooke LU5 . . . . 114 D4
Long Cl
  Lower Stondon SG16 . . . . 88 E2
  Luton LU2 . . . . 117 C3
Longcroft Ave AL5 . . . . . 130 F1
Longcroft La MK43 . . . . . 72 D8
Longcroft Rd MK45 . . . . . 97 B2
Long Croft Rd LU1 . . . . . 123 A7
Longden Cl MK45 . . . . . . 64 A1
Long Dr MK45 . . . . 76 A5
Longfellow Ave PE19 . . . . 22 D5
Longfield Ct SG6 . . . . . . 101 D7
Longfield Dr LU4 . . . . . . 115 D1
Longfield Rd SG19 . . . . . 54 B8
Long Hedge LU5 . . . . . . 114 D5
Longholme Way MK40, MK41,
  MK42 . . . . 50 E7
Long La
  Gamlingay SG19 . . . . . . 45 B6
  Tingrith LU5 . . . . 95 A2
Longleat MK41 . . . . 39 B1
Longleat Cl MK45 . . . . . . 84 D1
Long Mdw
  Dunstable LU6 . . . . 121 A8
  Markyate AL3 . . . . 128 F5
Longmead SG6 . . . . 101 E7
Long Mead LU5 . . . . 114 B6
Longmeadow LU5 . . . . . . 114 E5
Longmeadow Dr
  Ickleford SG5 . . . . 100 F5
  Wilstead MK45 . . . . 62 E2
Long Twitchell SG18 . . . . 66 F6
Long Wlk SG17 . . . . 76 D3
Lonsdale Cl LU3 . . . . 116 B5
Lords Cl LU7 . . . . 112 E5
Lord's Hill LU5 . . . . 105 F1
Lordsmead MK43 . . . . . . 59 C2
Lords Mead LU6 . . . . 119 E6
Lords Pl 12 LU2 . . . . 116 D1
Lords Terr LU6 . . . . 119 E6
Loring Rd
  Dunstable LU6 . . . . 113 F1
  Sharnbrook MK44 . . . . . 16 B4
Lorraine Ct MK41 . . . . . . 39 A1
Lorraine Rd MK43 . . . . . . 60 F8
Lorrimer Cl LU2 . . . . 116 E6
Loseby Cl NN10 . . . . 8 A8
Lothair Rd LU2 . . . . 117 A4
Lottings Way PE19 . . . . . 22 C6
Lovat Wlk MK42 . . . . 49 E3
Lovell Memorial Homes
  MK43 . . . . 37 B6
Lovell Rd
  Bedford MK42 . . . . 50 F5
  Oakley MK43 . . . . 37 B6
Lovent Dr LU7 . . . . 111 B7
Loveridge Ave MK42 . . . . 49 D6
Lovers' Wlk LU5 . . . . 121 C8
Lovet Rd MK45 . . . . 84 E1
Lovett Gn MK45 . . . . 96 C3
Lovett Way LU5 . . . . 114 D3
LOWER BERRY END 94 A8
LOWER CALDECOTE 54 D2
LOWER DEAN 5 C7
LOWER END
  LU6 . . . . 112 C1
  MK17 . . . . 81 C8
Lower End Rd MK17 . . . . 81 A8
Lower Farm Cotts SG18 . 80 B7
Lower Farm Rd MK43 . . . 37 C4

LOWER GRAVENHURST . . . 87 C3
LOWER GREEN 100 E5
Lower Harpenden Rd LU1,
  LU2 . . . . 124 C3
Lower Luton Rd AL5 . . . 131 C3
LOWER RADS END 94 D6
LOWER SHELTON 60 C2
Lower Shelton Rd MK43 . 60 D2
LOWER STONDON 88 F2
LOWER SUNDON 107 C3
Lowry Dr LU5 . . . . 114 D5
Lowry Rd PE19 . . . . 22 C6
Lowsdon La MK44 . . . . . 10 F1
Lowther Rd
  Bedford MK41 . . . . 38 E5
  Dunstable LU6 . . . . 121 D5
Loyne Cl LU7 . . . . 110 C8
Lucas Ct MK40 . . . . 37 C1
Lucas Gdns LU3 . . . . 116 B8
Lucas Way LU3 . . . . 116 C4
Lucerne Way LU3 . . . . . . 116 C4
Ludlow Ave LU1 . . . . 123 E4
Ludlow Wlk MK41 . . . . . . 39 A4
Ludun Cl LU5 . . . . 121 E8
Luffenham Pl SG17 . . . . . 76 D3
Luke Pl MK42 . . . . 50 C4
Luke St PE19 . . . . 22 E4
Lullington Cl LU2 . . . . . . 117 C3
Lunedale Cl MK42 . . . . . . 49 E3
Lune Wlk MK41 . . . . 38 C5
Lurke St MK40 . . . . 50 C8
LUTON 123 D4
Luton Airport Parkway Sta
  LU1 . . . . 124 B5
Luton Dr The LU1 . . . . . 124 B3
Luton & Dunstable Hospl
  LU4 . . . . 115 C3
Luton & Dunstable Hospl
  (Faringdon Wing) LU4 . 115 C3
Luton Ent Pk LU3 . . . . . 115 B8
Luton Ind Coll LU1 . . . . 123 E7
Luton La AL3 . . . . 130 B1
Luton Maternity Hospl
  LU4 . . . . 115 C2
Luton Mus & Art Gall★
  LU3 . . . . 116 D2
Luton Rd
  Barton-le-C MK45 . . . . . 97 B1
  Caddington LU1 . . . . . . 123 A4
  Chalton LU4, LU5 . . . . . 106 C3
  Cockernhoe LU2 . . . . . . 117 E3
  Dunstable LU5 . . . . 114 E1
  Harpenden AL5 . . . . . . 130 D4
  Luton LU4 . . . . 115 A7
  Markyate AL3 . . . . 128 F7
  Peters Green SG4 . . . . . 125 F2
  Streatley LU3 . . . . 108 A6
  Wilstead MK45 . . . . 62 E3
Luton Regional Sports Ctr
  LU2 . . . . 117 A5
Luton Ret Pk LU1 . . . . . 124 A6
Luton Sixth Form Coll
  LU2 . . . . 116 E4
Luton Sta LU2 . . . . 123 E8
Luton Town FC LU1 . . . . 123 C8
Luton White Hill LU2 . . . 117 F8
Luxemborg Cl LU3 . . . . . 115 D8
Lyall Cl MK45 . . . . 84 F2
Lyall Ct MK45 . . . . 85 A4
Lychmead SG17 . . . . 78 B3
Lydds Hill MK43 . . . . 82 E5
Lydekker Mews 1 AL5 . . 131 A2
Lydford Cl MK40 . . . . 38 E1
Lye Hill SG4 . . . . 125 D7
Lygetun Dr LU3 . . . . 115 F7
Lymans Rd SG15 . . . . . . 90 A6
Lyme Rd MK45 . . . . 84 E8
Lymington Gdns MK41 . . 39 C4
Lynch Hill LU6 . . . . 128 A8
Lyndhurst Cl AL5 . . . . . . 131 C2
Lyndhurst Dr AL5 . . . . . 131 C2
Lyndhurst Rd LU1 . . . . . 123 C7
Lyneford Way NN10 . . . . . 7 F8
Lyneham Rd LU2 . . . . . . 117 C1
Lynn Cl MK42 . . . . 50 C2
Lynton Ave SG15 . . . . . . 90 A5
Lynton Gr MK42 . . . . 50 B4
Lynwood Ave LU2 . . . . . 117 A3
Lynwood Lodge 6 LU6 . . 114 A1
Lyon Cl MK42 . . . . 49 E2
Lypsitt Comm SG17 . . . . 88 C6
Lyra Gdns LU7 . . . . 111 D8
Lytham Pl MK40 . . . . 49 B6
Lytton Ave SG6 . . . . 101 F5
Lywood Rd LU7 . . . . 111 C6

M

Mabel Rd MK42 . . . . 50 B5
MacAulay Rd LU4 . . . . . 115 A2
MACKERYE END 131 F4
Maddison Ho PE19 . . . . . 22 E6
Magdalene Cl SG18 . . . . 68 D5
Magnolia Ave LU6 . . . . . 114 F1
Magnolia Dr NN10 . . . . . . 8 B7
Magnolia Pl SG18 . . . . . . 67 C4
Magpie Ave MK43 . . . . . . 61 C1
Magpies The
  Luton LU2 . . . . 116 E6
  Maulden MK45 . . . . 74 C1
Mags La MK17 . . . . 93 E1
Mahew Ct MK42 . . . . 49 D5
Maia Cl MK41 . . . . 51 A8
Maidenbower Ave LU6 . . 113 F1
Maidenhall Inf Sch LU4 . 116 A2
Maidenhall Jun Sch LU4 116 A2
Maidenhall Rd LU4 . . . . 116 A2

Main Rd
  Astwood MK16 . . . . 47 A3
  Biddenham MK40 . . . . . . 49 C8
Main Rd N HP4 . . . . 126 A6
Main Rd S HP4 . . . . 126 D4
Main St SG19 . . . . 45 F3
Maitland St MK40 . . . . . . 50 B8
Malakand Rd MK42 . . . . . 50 A5
Malcote Cl MK40 . . . . . . 37 C1
Malden Ho PE19 . . . . 22 E6
Maldon Cl AL5 . . . . 131 B2
Malham Cl
  Flitwick MK45 . . . . 84 E2
  Luton LU4 . . . . 115 F2
Mallard Cl SG17 . . . . 77 C2
Mallard Gdns LU3 . . . . . 116 A5
Mallard Hill MK41 . . . . . 38 C4
Mallard La PE19 . . . . 22 F4
Mallow The LU3 . . . . 115 F3
Mall The LU5 . . . . 114 C1
Malmesbury Abbey MK41 51 A8
Malms Cl MK41 . . . . 121 D1
Malthouse Gn LU2 . . . . . 117 F1
Malthouse La SG5 . . . . . . 91 A7
Malting Cl MK43 . . . . 59 A1
Maltings Cl MK43 . . . . . . 59 A1
Maltings Orch SG5 . . . . . 99 D3
Maltings Pl SG19 . . . . . . 44 D5
Maltings The
  Ampthill MK45 . . . . 73 E1
  Dunstable LU6 . . . . 114 A1
  Henlow SG16 . . . . 78 D1
  Leighton Buzzard LU7 . . 111 B6
  Letchworth SG6 . . . . . . 91 C1
  Shefford SG17 . . . . 77 C3
  St Neots PE19 . . . . 22 C5
Maltings Way MK44 . . . . 41 A5
Malvern Ave MK41 . . . . . 38 F2
Malvern Cl MK45 . . . . . . 84 D2
Malvern Dr LU7 . . . . 110 C8
Malvern Rd LU1 . . . . 123 B7
Malzeard Ct 17 LU3 . . . . 116 D1
Malzeard Rd LU3 . . . . . . 116 D1
Manchester Pl LU5 . . . . 114 B1
Manchester St LU1 . . . . 123 E7
Mancroft Rd LU5 . . . . . . 122 E2
Mander Cl LU5 . . . . 105 F6
Mandrell Cl LU5 . . . . . . 114 A4
MANGROVE GREEN 117 E4
Mangrove Rd
  Cockernhoe LU2 . . . . . . 117 E4
  Luton LU2 . . . . 117 C2
Manland Ave LU5 . . . . . . 131 B3
Manland Prim Sch AL5 . . 131 B3
Manland Way AL5 . . . . . 131 C3
Manning Ct LU5 . . . . 114 C5
Manning Pl LU2 . . . . 117 E2
Mannock Way LU7 . . . . . 111 D5
Manor Ave LU7 . . . . 104 C4
Manorbier Rd MK41 . . . . 38 F5
Manor Cl
  Bromham MK43 . . . . 37 A4
  Carlton MK43 . . . . 25 A3
  Clifton SG17 . . . . 78 A3
  Great Staughton PE19 . . 13 F6
  Harlington LU5 . . . . 95 F2
  Ickleford SG5 . . . . 100 E3
  Irchester NN29 . . . . 7 B8
  Kempston MK42 . . . . . . 49 D4
  Langford SG18 . . . . 78 F6
  Letchworth SG6 . . . . . . 101 F3
  Salford MK17 . . . . 70 D3
  Westoning MK45 . . . . . . 95 E5
  Wilden MK44 . . . . 29 F3
Manor Ct
  Caddington LU1 . . . . . . 122 F4
  Leighton Buzzard LU7 . . 102 F2
  Marston Moretaine MK43 72 C7
  Rushden NN10 . . . . 8 C8
Manor Dr MK42 . . . . 49 F8
Manor Farm Bsns Pk SG5 98 A6
Manor Farm Cl
  Barton-le-C MK45 . . . . . 97 C3
  Luton LU4 . . . . 115 C3
Manor Farm Way MK44 . . 16 C3
Manor Gdns MK45 . . . . . 95 D6
Manor Hospl MK45 . . . . . 49 B8
Manor House Cl PE19 . . . 22 C2
Manor La NN10 . . . . 8 A5
Manor Lodge MK42 . . . . 49 D4
Manor Park Dr MK45 . . . 95 D6
Manor Pk 114 C4
Manor Pl SG18 . . . . 66 B8
Manor Rd
  Barton-le-C MK45 . . . . . 97 D3
  Bedford MK41 . . . . 39 A2
  Biddenham MK40 . . . . . . 49 B8
  Caddington LU1 . . . . . . 122 F2
  Gamlingay SG19 . . . . . . 44 D6
  Henlow SG16 . . . . 78 C1
  Kempston Hardwick MK43 61 D6
  Lea valley LU4 . . . . 131 F2
  Lower Sundon LU3 . . . . 107 C3
  Luton LU1 . . . . 123 F6
  Marston Moretaine MK43 72 C7
  Rushden NN10 . . . . 8 B8
  Sandy SG19 . . . . 54 B8
  Toddington LU5 . . . . . . 105 F6
  Wootton MK43 . . . . 61 A7
Manor The SG19 . . . . 56 B8
Manor Way
  Cotton End MK45 . . . . . 63 D7
  Flitwick MK45 . . . . 84 D2
  Letchworth SG6 . . . . . . 101 F3
  Potton SG19 . . . . 56 B8
Manse Ct AL3 . . . . 128 F5
Mansfield Rd LU4 . . . . . 116 B1

Manshead CE Upper Sch
  LU1 . . . . 121 F5
Manshead Ct LU1 . . . . . 121 D6
Mansion La MK43 . . . . . . 24 F6
Manton Cl MK45 . . . . 84 F8
Manton Ctr The MK41 . . 38 A3
Manton Dr LU2 . . . . 116 D3
Manton La MK41 . . . . . . 38 A3
Manton Rd LU6 . . . . 120 D5
Manx Cl LU1 . . . . 116 A2
Maple Cl
  Biggleswade SG18 . . . . . 67 A7
  Clifton SG17 . . . . 77 F2
  Greenfield MK45 . . . . . . 85 D2
  Lower Stondon SG16 . . . . 88 E2
Maple Ct
  Gamlingay SG19 . . . . . . 44 C5
  Luton LU1 . . . . 123 D6
Maple Dr SG17 . . . . 77 C2
Maple Flats AL5 . . . . . . 131 A3
Maple Gdns MK44 . . . . . 11 A3
Maple Gr MK17 . . . . 81 B4
Maple Rd
  Harpenden AL5 . . . . . . 130 F1
  Sandy SG19 . . . . 42 C1
Maple Rd E LU4 . . . . . . 123 B8
Maple Rd W LU4 . . . . . . 123 B8
Maples The
  Kempston MK42 . . . . . . 49 E3
  Silsoe MK45 . . . . 86 B4
Maple Tree Lower Sch
  SG19 . . . . 42 B2
Maple Way
  Cranfield MK43 . . . . 71 A8
  Kensworth LU6 . . . . . . 127 E8
Maple Wood NN10 . . . . . . 8 B7
Marbury Pl LU3 . . . . 115 F4
Marchioness Way PE19 . . 22 B4
Mardale Ave LU6 . . . . . . 121 C6
Mardale Cl MK42 . . . . . . 49 E4
Mardle Cl LU1 . . . . 122 E2
Mardle Rd LU7 . . . . 110 E6
Maree Cl LU7 . . . . 110 C7
Maresfield Ave SG17 . . . 76 F2
Mareth Rd MK42 . . . . . . 50 E6
Margaret Beaufort Mid Sch
  MK44 . . . . 11 B3
Margetts Rd MK42 . . . . . 49 F4
Margrett La MK45 . . . . . . 96 F6
Marigold Way MK42 . . . . 50 F4
Marina Ct MK42 . . . . 50 A6
Marina Dr LU6 . . . . 120 E7
Market Mews 8 LU7 . . . 111 A7
Market Pl
  Ampthill MK45 . . . . 73 E1
  Woburn MK17 . . . . 92 F7
Market Sq
  Bedford MK40 . . . . 50 B8
  Biggleswade SG18 . . . . . 67 A6
  Leighton Buzzard LU7 . . 111 A7
  Luton LU1 . . . . 123 B6
  Potton SG19 . . . . 56 F7
  Sandy SG19 . . . . 54 C7
  St Neots PE19 . . . . 22 E5
  Toddington LU5 . . . . . . 105 F6
Markfield Cl LU3 . . . . . . 116 C7
Markham Cres LU5 . . . . 114 F2
Markham Rd LU3 . . . . . . 116 C8
Mark Rutherford Rd
  MK42 . . . . 50 D6
Mark Rutherford Upper Sch
  & Com Coll MK41 . . . . . 39 A5
MARKYATE 128 E6
Markyate Rd LU1 . . . . . . 123 B1
Markyate Village Sch
  AL3 . . . . 128 D6
Marlborough Ct LU1 . . . 123 D7
Marlborough Lower Sch
  MK40 . . . . 49 F8
Marlborough Pk MK42 . . 49 F6
Marlborough Pl LU5 . . . 105 F6
Marlborough Rd
  Bedford MK40 . . . . 49 F8
  Luton LU3 . . . . 116 D1
Marley Fields LU7 . . . . . 111 D6
Marlin Cl LU4 . . . . 114 E4
Marlin Rd LU4 . . . . 114 E3
Marlow Ave LU1 . . . . . . 123 A8
Marlow Ct PE19 . . . . 22 B6
Marlow Way MK41 . . . . . 38 C6
Marlowe Ct PE19 . . . . . . 22 B6
Marmet Ave SG6 . . . . . . 101 E6
Marne St MK42 . . . . 50 A5
Marquis Cl
  Harpenden AL5 . . . . . . 131 D2
  St Neots PE19 . . . . 22 B4
Marquis Ct
  9 Luton LU2 . . . . 116 D1
  Woburn MK17 . . . . 92 F7
Marquis Hill SG5 . . . . . . 88 A1
Marquis La AL5 . . . . 131 D2
Marriott Rd LU3 . . . . . . 116 B6
Marriotts Cl MK43 . . . . . 26 B8
Marschefield SG5 . . . . . . 90 E6
Marshall Cl MK42 . . . . . . 49 D5
Marshall Ct MK41 . . . . . 39 A1
Marshall Rd
  Luton LU2 . . . . 117 C2
  St Neots PE19 . . . . 22 F5
Marshalls Ave SG5 . . . . . 87 F1
Marshalls Way AL4 . . . . 131 F2
MARSH FARM 115 E7
Marsh Ho LU3 . . . . 115 F4
Marsh La MK44 . . . . 27 B5
Marsh Leys Ind Est MK43 61 D8
Marsh Rd LU3 . . . . 115 F4
Marsh The MK43 . . . . . . 25 A3
Marsom Gr LU3 . . . . 116 B8
Marston Gdns LU2 . . . . . 116 D4

Marston Hill MK43 . . . . . 59 F2
MARSTON MORETAINE . . 72 D8
Marston Rd MK43 . . . . . . 72 C3
Marston Thrift (Nature
  Reserve)★ MK43 . . . . . 71 E8
Marston Vale Mid Sch
  MK43 . . . . 61 C1
Marston Vale Millennium
  Country Pk★ MK43 . . . . 72 E7
Marston Vale Millennium
  Ctry Pk★ MK43 . . . . . . 60 F1
Martham Cl MK40 . . . . . . 49 D7
Martham Ct AL5 . . . . . . 131 C3
Martin Cl MK41 . . . . 38 D4
Martin Rd MK45 . . . . 84 D1
Martindales The LU2 . . . 123 F7
Martin Way SG6 . . . . . . 101 D5
Martins Dr The LU7 . . . . 102 F1
Mary Bassett Lower Sch
  LU7 . . . . 110 F7
Mary Brash Ct LU2 . . . . 117 C3
Maryland Coll MK17 . . . . 92 E6
Maryport Rd LU4 . . . . . . 116 A2
Maryville Rd MK42 . . . . . 50 B5
Marywells SG17 . . . . 88 B5
Masefield Ave PE19 . . . . 22 C6
Masefield Ct AL5 . . . . . . 131 B4
Masefield Rd AL5 . . . . . 131 B4
Maskell Dr MK41 . . . . . . 39 C5
Massey Cl MK42 . . . . 49 E4
Masters Cl LU1 . . . . 123 B5
Matlock Cres LU4 . . . . . 115 C1
Matthew St LU6 . . . . 121 B8
Mattocke Rd SG5 . . . . . 100 C1
MAULDEN 74 C1
Maulden Cl LU2 . . . . 117 C1
Maulden Lower Sch
  MK45 . . . . 85 D8
Maulden Rd MK45 . . . . . 85 A4
Maulden Road Ind Est
  MK45 . . . . 85 A4
Maule Cl PE19 . . . . 22 E1
Maundsey Cl LU6 . . . . . 121 D5
Maurice Cl PE28 . . . . 6 F5
May Cl
  Eaton Bray LU6 . . . . . . 119 E6
  Rushden NN10 . . . . 8 C7
Maycroft SG6 . . . . 91 A1
Maye Dicks Rd NN10 . . . . 8 C8
Mayer Way LU5 . . . . 114 A3
Mayes Cl MK44 . . . . 29 F2
Mayfield Cl
  Harpenden AL5 . . . . . . 130 E3
  Kempston MK42 . . . . . . 49 E5
Mayfield Cres SG16 . . . . 88 E2
Mayfield Ct SG19 . . . . . . 54 B7
Mayfield Rd
  Dunstable LU5 . . . . 121 D7
  Luton LU1 . . . . 117 B4
Mayfields SG17 . . . . 77 D3
Mayhew Cl MK41 . . . . . . 36 E1
Maynards The SG18 . . . . 66 C3
Mayne Ave LU4 . . . . 115 C4
May Rd MK43 . . . . 34 E6
May St LU1 . . . . 123 E5
Mead End SG18 . . . . 67 B5
Meadhook Dr MK45 . . . . 97 B3
Mead Open Farm & Rare
  Breeds★ LU7 . . . . 112 A2
Meadowbank SG4 . . . . . 101 B1
Meadow Cl
  Beeston SG19 . . . . 54 B5
  St Neots PE19 . . . . 22 F5
Meadow Croft LU1 . . . . . 122 F4
Meadow Farm Rd MK43 . 48 B2
Meadow La
  Bedford MK44 . . . . 51 D7
  Gamlingay SG19 . . . . . . 44 D3
  Houghton Regis LU5 . . . 114 B5
Meadow Piece MK45 . . . 76 A8
Meadow Rd
  Luton LU3 . . . . 116 B4
  Toddington LU5 . . . . . . 105 F5
Meadows The
  Flitwick MK45 . . . . 84 D5
  Stewartby MK43 . . . . . . 61 C1
  Wingfield LU7 . . . . 105 E1
Meadowsweet
  Lower Stondon SG16 . . . . 88 F2
  St Neots PE19 . . . . 22 B6
Meadowsweet Dr MK42 . 50 E4
Meadow Sweet Rd NN10 . . 8 C7
Meadow View MK17 . . . . 81 D6
Meadowview Rd MK42 . . 49 C3
Meadow Way
  Ampthill MK45 . . . . 84 D7
  Caddington LU1 . . . . . . 122 E4
  Leighton Buzzard LU7 . . 111 D7
  Letchworth SG6 . . . . . . 101 F5
  Stotfold SG5 . . . . 90 F6
Meadow Wlk SG16 . . . . . 78 D1
Meads Cl LU5 . . . . 114 C5
Mead's Cl MK17 . . . . 93 E2
Meads Prim Sch The
  LU3 . . . . 116 A6
Meads The
  Eaton Bray LU6 . . . . . . 119 E5
  Letchworth SG6 . . . . . . 101 E6
  Luton LU3 . . . . 116 A3
Mead The SG5 . . . . 100 F2
Meadway
  Bedford MK41 . . . . 39 A2
  Dunstable LU6 . . . . 121 A7
  Harrold MK43 . . . . 25 A7
  Leighton Buzzard LU7 . . 111 C6
Meadway Ct LU6 . . . . . . 120 F7
Medallion Ct 4 PE19 . . . 22 F5
Medbury La MK42 . . . . . . 50 C2

Medina Rd LU4 . . . . 116 A1
Medley Cl LU6 . . . . 119 F5
Medlows AL5 . . . . 130 E2
Medmenham Ave SG17 . . . 76 F2
Medusa Way SG19 . . . . 42 B1
Medway Cl MK45. . . . . 84 D2
Medway Ct MK41 . . . . 38 D5
Mees Cl LU3. . . . . 107 F1
Meeting Cl MK45. . . . . 63 D7
Meeting House La SG7 . . . 91 E1
Meeting La SG19. . . . . 56 A7
Melbourn Cl SG5. . . . . 90 F6
Melbourne St MK42 . . . . . 50 B7
MELCHBOURNE 10 D8
Melchbourne Rd MK44 . . . . 9 F4
Melford Cl 3 LU2. . . . . . 117 D1
Melfort Dr LU7 . . . . 110 B6
Melrose Dr MK42 . . . . 50 C3
Melson Sq 9 LU1 . . . . 123 E7
Melson St LU1 . . . . 123 E7
Melton Ct LU6 . . . . 120 F7
Melton Wlk LU5 . . . . 114 E6
Memorial La
Bletsoe MK44 . . . . 17 C1
Felmersham MK43. . . . . . . 26 C8
Memorial Rd LU3 . . . . 115 F4
Mendham Way MK45. . . . . 86 C8
Mendip Cl MK45 . . . . 84 D2
Mendip Cres MK41 . . . . . . 38 F3
Mendip Way LU3. . . . . . . 107 C1
Mentmore Cl MK40. . . . . . 49 B6
Mentmore Cres LU6. . . . . 121 C5
Mentmore Gdns LU7 . . . . 110 E5
Mentmore Rd LU7 . . . . . . 110 E5
Mentone Ave MK17 . . . . . 81 D4
Mepham Rd MK43. . . . . . . 60 F8
MEPPERSHALL. 88 B5
Meppershall CE Lower Sch SG17. . . . . 88 B5
Meppershall Rd
Meppershall SG17, SG5. . . . 88 A3
Upper Stondon SG16 . . . . . 88 D4
Merchant La
Cranfield MK43 . . . . 59 A1
Wharley End MK43 . . . . . . 58 F2
Mercury Pl SG17. . . . . 76 D3
Mercury Way LU7 . . . . . . 111 D8
Merlin Dr SG19 . . . . 42 B2
Merlin Gdns MK41 . . . . . . 38 C4
Merlins Ct LU7. . . . . 111 A7
Mersey Cl MK45. . . . . 84 D2
Mersey Pl 1 LU1 . . . . . . 123 D7
Mersey Way MK41 . . . . . . 38 C5
Merton Ho MK40. . . . . 38 B1
Merton Rd MK40 . . . . 38 D2
Mews The
3 Harpenden AL5 . . . . . . 131 B1
Letchworth SG6. . . . . 91 C1
Meyrick Ave LU1. . . . . . . 123 C6
Meyrick Ct LU1 . . . . 123 D6
Mickle Hill PE28 . . . . 2 D7
MIDDLE END. 120 A8
Middlefield Com Prim Sch PE19. . . . . 22 F2
Middlefield Ind Est SG19 . 54 D8
Middlefield La SG16. . . . . 89 C7
Middlefields SG6 . . . . 90 F1
Middlefields Ct SG6. . . . . 90 F1
Middle Gn LU7. . . . . 111 C8
Middleham Cl SG19 . . . . . . 54 C8
Middlemarch SG5. . . . . 90 C3
Middlesex Univ (Bedford) MK40 . . . . 38 A1
Middleton Rd LU2. . . . . . . 117 D4
Middleton Way LU7 . . . . . 111 D5
Midhurst SG6. . . . . 101 F8
Midhurst Gdns LU3 . . . . . 116 C4
Midland Cl SG17 . . . . 77 C2
Midland Cotts SG4 . . . . . . 101 A1
Midland Rd
Bedford MK40 . . . . 50 B8
Luton LU2 . . . . 123 E8
Sandy SG19 . . . . 54 B8
Midland Way SG16 . . . . . . 89 B3
Midway LU7 . . . . 111 C7
Milburn Cl LU3 . . . . 108 B1
Milburn Rd MK41 . . . . 39 B4
Milebush LU7. . . . . 110 C8
Mile Rd MK42. . . . . 50 D4
Miles Ave LU7 . . . . 111 B7
Miles Dr SG17 . . . . 78 B2
Milestone Rd SG5. . . . . . . 100 D2
Miletree Cres LU6 . . . . . . 121 D6
Miletree Ct LU7. . . . . 111 B8
Mile Tree Rd LU7 . . . . . . 103 E4
Milford Hill AL5. . . . . 131 D4
Milford Park Hospl MK44 . 31 E6
Millards Cl
Cranfield MK43 . . . . 59 C2
Flitwick MK45 . . . . 84 D3
Millard Way SG4 . . . . 101 C1
Millbank
Bedford MK40 . . . . 50 D8
Leighton Buzzard LU7 . . . 110 F8
MILLBROOK 73 A2
Millbrook Rd MK42. . . . . . 50 B6
Millbrook Sta MK45 . . . . . . 72 F6
Mill Cl
Biggleswade SG18. . . . . 66 F5
Henlow SG16. . . . . 78 D3
Stotfold SG5 . . . . 91 A6
Mill End Cl LU6 . . . . 119 F4
Miller Cl MK41. . . . . 37 C6
Miller Rd MK42 . . . . 50 B5
Millers Cl LU7 . . . . 111 D7
Millers Ct SG18 . . . . 66 F6
Millers Lay LU5 . . . . 114 F2
Millers Way LU5 . . . . 114 A4
Mill Est NN10. . . . . 8 B7
Millfield MK43 . . . . 36 F2
Millfield Cl
Cranfield MK43 . . . . 59 B2
Flitwick MK45 . . . . 85 A2
Millfield La AL3, LU1 . . . . 122 D2
Millfield Mews LU1 . . . . . 122 D2
Millfield Rd LU3 . . . . 116 B3
Millfield Way LU1. . . . . . . 122 D3
Mill Hill
Keysoe MK44. . . . . 12 B2
Thurleigh MK44 . . . . 18 B1
Mill Hill Rd PE19. . . . . 22 C5
Milliners Way LU3 . . . . . . 116 C1
Mill La
Arlesey SG15. . . . . 89 F4
Astwick SG5. . . . . 79 F1
Barton-le-C MK45 . . . . 97 C3
Biggleswade SG18. . . . . 66 F5
Campton SG17. . . . . 88 A8
Clophill MK45. . . . . 75 C1
Everton SG19. . . . . 43 D1
Flamstead AL3. . . . . 129 A1
Greenfield MK45 . . . . 85 C3
Hexton SG5 . . . . 98 C3
Houghton Conquest MK45. . 62 B1
Hulcote MK17 . . . . 70 E1
Kempston MK42 . . . . 49 C4
Keysoe MK44. . . . . 12 B2
Langford SG18. . . . . 78 E7
Odell MK43 . . . . 25 D8
Pavenham MK43 . . . . 26 B3
Potton SG19. . . . . 55 F8
Salford MK17. . . . . 70 C3
Sandy SG19 . . . . 54 B6
St Neots PE19 . . . . 22 F8
Stotfold SG5 . . . . 91 A6
Tempsford SG19 . . . . 42 A7
Turvey MK43 . . . . 34 D5
Woburn Sands MK17. . . . . . 81 C5
Mill Mdw SG18. . . . . 78 E7
MILLOW. 68 C4
Mill Rd
Colmworth MK44. . . . . 30 C7
Cranfield MK43 . . . . 59 C2
Houghton Regis LU5 . . . . . 114 A4
Husborne Crawley MK43. . . 82 D5
Leighton Buzzard LU7 . . . . 111 A8
Sharnbrook MK44 . . . . 16 F3
Slapton LU7. . . . . 118 D7
Stanbridge LU7 . . . . 112 C6
Stanford SG18 . . . . 78 B7
Thurleigh MK44 . . . . 28 B7
Mill Rise MK43. . . . . 34 D5
Mill St
Bedford MK40 . . . . 50 C8
Gamlingay SG19 . . . . 44 D5
Luton LU1 . . . . 123 D8
Millstream Cl SG4 . . . . . . 101 A1
Millstream Ct SG17 . . . . . . 77 D3
Millstream Way LU7. . . . . 110 F7
Mills Wlk SG19 . . . . 54 C8
Mill Tower LU6 . . . . 119 E6
Mill Vale Mid Sch LU5. . . 114 E2
Mill View Ct PE19 . . . . 22 C2
Mill Way MK17. . . . . 81 D5
Millwood Ct SG5. . . . . 90 F6
Millwright Way MK45 . . . . 84 D4
Milner Ct LU2. . . . . 123 E8
Milne Row MK40. . . . . 37 F1
Milton Ave PE19 . . . . 22 D6
MILTON BRYAN 93 E1
Milton Ct 12 AL5 . . . . 131 B1
MILTON ERNEST 27 A5
Milton Ernest Lower Sch MK44 . . . . 27 B5
Milton Rd
Bedford MK40 . . . . 37 F1
Clapham MK41. . . . . 37 C7
Flitwick MK45 . . . . 84 D3
Harpenden AL5 . . . . 131 B1
Luton LU1 . . . . 123 C6
Milton Way LU5. . . . . 114 D4
Milton Wlk LU5 . . . . 114 D4
Milverton Gn LU3 . . . . . . 116 A7
Minden Cl MK45 . . . . 84 E4
Minden Ct PE19. . . . . 22 C5
Minorca Way LU4 . . . . 115 A3
Miss Joans Ride HP4, LU6 . . . . 126 E7
Mistletoe Ct LU2 . . . . 124 C8
Mistletoe Hill LU2. . . . . . 124 C8
Mitchell Ct MK42 . . . . 51 A3
Mitchell Rd MK43 . . . . 58 E2
Mitford Cl MK41 . . . . 39 A4
Mitre Cl MK41 . . . . 39 B1
Mixes Hill Ct LU2 . . . . . . 117 A4
Mixes Hill Rd LU2. . . . . . . 116 F4
Mixies The SG5 . . . . 90 E6
Moakes The LU3 . . . . 115 E7
Moat Farm Cl
Greenfield MK45 . . . . 85 B2
Marston Moretaine MK43 . . 72 C7
Moat La LU3. . . . . 116 B4
Mobbs Cl MK42 . . . . 49 D5
Mobley Gn LU2 . . . . 117 B3
MOGGERHANGER 53 C6
Moggerhanger Lower Sch MK44 . . . . 53 C7
Moira Cl LU3 . . . . 115 D7
Molescroft AL5 . . . . 130 D4
Molivers La MK43 . . . . 36 F3
Molly Moore Ave MK42 . . . 49 D3
Monarch Hall LU2. . . . . . . 124 C8
Monarch Rd PE19. . . . . 22 B4
Monklands SG6. . . . . 101 D6
Monks Cl
Dunstable LU5. . . . . 114 E1
Monks Cl *continued*
Letchworth SG6. . . . . 101 C6
Monkshill MK41. . . . . 39 A3
Monks Row MK43. . . . . 26 B3
Monmouth Cl
Bedford MK42 . . . . 50 D5
Toddington LU5 . . . . 105 E6
Monmouth Rd LU5 . . . . 95 F2
Monoux Pl SG19 . . . . 54 C7
Monoux Rd MK43 . . . . 61 A6
Montagu Ct PE19 . . . . 22 E4
Montague Ave LU4. . . . . . 115 C6
Montagu Gdns PE28. . . . . 6 F5
Montagu Ho PE19. . . . . 22 E4
Montagu Sq PE19 . . . . 22 E4
Montagu St PE19 . . . . 22 E4
Montgomery Ave SG17 . . . 77 C1
Montgomery Cl
Leighton Buzzard LU7 . . . . 103 B1
Stewartby MK43 . . . . 61 C1
Montgomery Ct MK42 . . . . 50 A5
Montgomery Way SG18 . . 67 D3
Monton Cl LU3. . . . . 115 F6
Montrose Ave LU3 . . . . . . 116 C3
Moore Cres LU5 . . . . 114 C4
Moor End LU6 . . . . 119 F5
Moor End Cl LU6. . . . . 119 F4
Moor End La
Eaton Bray LU6 . . . . 119 F5
Felmersham MK43. . . . . 16 F1
Moor End Rd MK43. . . . . . . 26 F8
Moore's Cl MK45. . . . . 86 C8
Moores Wlk 7 PE19 . . . . . . 22 E5
Moorhouse Path LU7. . . . 111 D5
Moorhouse Way LU7 . . . . 111 D5
Moor La
Bedford MK42 . . . . 50 D4
Flitwick MK45 . . . . 85 A2
Maulden MK45. . . . . 85 C8
Moorland Cl MK45 . . . . 85 D3
Moorland Gdns LU2. . . . . 123 D8
Moorland Rd AL5 . . . . 131 B4
Moorlands Sch LU4 . . . . . . 115 C3
Moor Pond Piece MK45 . . 73 D1
Moor Rd PE19 . . . . 13 E1
Moor St LU1 . . . . 123 C8
Moors View MK45. . . . . 85 B2
Moor The MK43. . . . . 25 A4
Morar Cl LU7 . . . . 110 C7
Morcambe Cl LU4. . . . . . . 115 B3
Morcom Rd LU5 . . . . 121 E6
Mordaunt Cl MK43 . . . . 34 E6
Moreteyne Rd MK43. . . . . . 72 D8
Moreton Ave AL5 . . . . 130 F2
Moreton End Cl AL5. . . . . 130 F2
Moreton End La AL5 . . . . 130 F2
Moreton Pk LU2 . . . . 117 A2
Moreton Pl AL5. . . . . 130 F3
Moreton Rd N LU2 . . . . . . 117 A2
Moreton Rd S LU2 . . . . . . 117 A2
Morgan Cl LU4. . . . . 115 E3
Morgans Cl MK45 . . . . 62 F3
Moriston Rd MK41 . . . . 38 C6
Morland Cl LU6 . . . . 121 A6
Morland Way MK41 . . . . . . 38 B3
Morrell Cl LU3. . . . . 116 A7
Morris Cl
Henlow SG16. . . . . 89 C5
Luton LU3 . . . . 115 E8
Morris Gdns MK45 . . . . 84 D7
Morris Wlk MK44 . . . . 31 F6
Mortimer Cl LU1 . . . . 123 A7
Mortimer Rd MK42. . . . . . . 49 D6
Mossbank Ave LU2. . . . . . 124 C8
Mossdale Ct 3 LU4 . . . . . 115 C5
Moss La MK42 . . . . 50 C1
Mossman Dr LU1 . . . . 122 E4
Moss Way SG5. . . . . 100 C1
Mostyn Rd LU3 . . . . 115 E4
Moulton Ave MK42 . . . . 50 E6
Moulton Rise LU2. . . . . . . 123 F8
Mountbatten Ct PE19 . . . . 22 C4
Mountbatten Dr SG18 . . . . 67 B7
Mountbatten Gdns LU7. . . 103 B1
Mountbatten Pl MK41 . . . . 39 B1
Mountbatten Way SG17 . . 76 E4
Mount Dr MK41 . . . . 39 A3
Mountfield Rd LU2. . . . . . 116 E2
Mountfort Cl PE19 . . . . 22 F3
Mount Grace Rd LU2 . . . . 117 C6
Mountjoy SG4 . . . . 101 C1
MOUNT PLEASANT 61 A8
Mount Pleasant
Aspley Guise MK17 . . . . 81 F4
Ridgmont MK43. . . . . 82 F5
Mount Pleasant Ave LU5 105 F4
Mount Pleasant Cl LU5 . . 105 F4
Mount Pleasant Rd
Clapham MK41. . . . . 37 D6
Luton LU3 . . . . 115 E5
Mount The
Aspley Guise MK17 . . . . 81 D4
4 Luton LU2. . . . . 123 D8
Mountview Ave LU5 . . . . . 121 E6
Mowbray Cl MK43. . . . . 36 E3
Mowbray Cres SG5. . . . . . . 90 F7
Mowbray Dr LU7. . . . . 110 D7
Mowbray Pl MK44. . . . . 40 C1
Mowbray Rd MK42 . . . . 50 C4
Mowhills MK43 . . . . 24 F6
Moxes Wood LU3 . . . . 115 E7
Muddy La SG6 . . . . 101 F3
Muirfield
Biddenham MK40. . . . . 49 B6
Luton LU2 . . . . 116 E6
Mulberry Cl
Biggleswade SG18. . . . . 66 F8
Luton LU1 . . . . 123 B7
Mulberry Cl *continued*
Stotfold SG5 . . . . 90 F5
Mulberry Way SG5 . . . . . . 100 D2
Mulberry Wlk MK42 . . . . . . 49 F3
Mullein Cl PE19. . . . . 22 C5
Mullion Cl LU2. . . . . 117 B5
Mullway SG6 . . . . 101 C6
Muntjac Cl PE19 . . . . 22 B5
Murdock Rd MK41 . . . . 38 A4
Murfitt Way SG19. . . . . 44 D6
Murrell Cl PE19. . . . . 22 F7
Murrell Ct PE19. . . . . 22 F7
Murrell La SG5 . . . . 91 A5
Musgrave Way 6 PE19 . . . 22 F5
Mussons Path LU2 . . . . . . 116 E1
Muswell Cl LU3 . . . . 116 B6
Muswell Rd MK42 . . . . 50 B5
Mutford Croft 2 LU2. . . . . 117 D1
Myers Rd SG19 . . . . 56 A8
Myrtle Rd MK42. . . . . 50 D5

N

Nagshead La MK44. . . . . . . 32 A5
Nags Head La NN9 . . . . 1 F2
Napier Ct LU1 . . . . 123 D7
Napier Hall LU2. . . . . 124 C8
Napier Rd
Bedford MK41 . . . . 39 D3
Luton LU1 . . . . 123 D7
Nappsbury Rd LU4 . . . . . . 115 D5
Narrow Path MK17 . . . . 81 B3
Naseby Pl MK45. . . . . 84 E4
Naseby Rd LU1 . . . . 123 B7
Nash Cl LU5 . . . . 114 D5
Nash Rd MK42 . . . . 50 E6
Navigation Wharf PE19. . . 22 E5
Nayland Cl LU2 . . . . 117 E1
Naylor Ave MK42. . . . . 49 E2
Neale Rd MK43 . . . . 60 F8
Neale Way MK43 . . . . 60 F8
Neath Abbey MK41. . . . . . . 51 B8
Nebular Ct LU7 . . . . 111 C8
Needham Rd LU4 . . . . 115 B6
Needwood Rd MK41. . . . . . 39 C3
Nelson Rd
Chicksands SG17. . . . . 76 E4
Dagnall HP4. . . . . 126 C5
Leighton Buzzard LU7 . . . 103 B1
St Neots PE19 . . . . 22 B2
Nelson St MK40 . . . . 49 F7
Nene Rd
Flitwick MK45 . . . . 84 D2
Henlow SG16. . . . . 89 B4
St Neots PE19 . . . . 22 C4
Neotsbury Ct MK45. . . . . . . 84 F8
Neotsbury Rd MK45 . . . . . . 84 F8
Neptune Cl LU5 . . . . 114 E6
Neptune Gdns LU7 . . . . . . 111 D8
Neptune Sq LU5 . . . . 114 E6
Nethercroft Cl LU2. . . . . . 117 C1
Netherstones SG5 . . . . 90 F7
Nettle Cl LU4 . . . . 114 E4
NETTLEDEN 132 B1
Nettleden Rd HP1. . . . . . . 132 C1
Nettleton Cl LU7 . . . . 111 C6
Nevell's Gn SG6. . . . . 101 F6
Nevells Rd SG6 . . . . 101 F6
Nevern Gdns MK40. . . . . . . 37 C1
Neville Cl MK43. . . . . 36 E2
Neville Cres MK43 . . . . 36 F2
Neville Rd LU3. . . . . 116 A5
Neville Road Pas LU3 . . . 116 A5
Nevis Cl LU7. . . . . 110 C7
Newark Ave MK41. . . . . 39 A5
Newark Rd LU4 . . . . 116 A2
New Barn Farm La LU5 . . 106 B2
New Bedford Rd
Luton LU1 . . . . 123 D8
Luton LU3 . . . . 116 D3
Newbold Rd LU3 . . . . 116 B7
Newbury Cl
Kempston MK42 . . . . 49 D4
Luton LU4 . . . . 115 E2
Silsoe MK45. . . . . 86 B5
Newbury Ct MK45. . . . . 86 B5
Newbury Ho MK40 . . . . 38 D2
Newbury La MK45. . . . . 86 B5
Newbury Rd LU5 . . . . 114 E6
New Cl MK44 . . . . 28 F1
Newcombe Rd LU1. . . . . . 123 C7
New Cotts AL3. . . . . 128 E6
New Inn Rd SG7 . . . . 80 D5
Newis Cres SG17. . . . . 78 B2
Newlands Rd
Luton LU1 . . . . 123 C3
Westoning MK45. . . . . 95 E6
Newmans Dr AL5 . . . . 130 F2
Newman Way LU7 . . . . . . 111 B7
NEW MILL END. 124 D1
NEWNHAM 91 E8
Newnham Ave MK41 . . . . . 50 F8
Newnham Cl LU2 . . . . 117 D1
Newnham Mid Sch MK41. 38 E2
Newnham Rd
Bedford MK40 . . . . 50 C8
Newnham SG7. . . . . 91 E6
Newnham St MK40 . . . . 50 C8
Newport Pagnell Rd MK43 . . . . 47 D5
Newport Rd
Hardmead MK16 . . . . 46 C2
Woburn MK17 . . . . 92 F8
Woburn Sands MK17. . . . . . 81 A6
New Rd
Bromham MK43. . . . . 36 E1
Clifton SG17. . . . . 78 A1
New Rd *continued*
Colmworth MK44. . . . . 29 F8
Great Barford MK44 . . . . . . 41 B5
Harrold MK43 . . . . 24 E6
Leighton Buzzard LU7 . . . . 110 E7
Maulden MK45. . . . . 85 C6
Sandy SG19 . . . . 54 D5
New St
Irchester NN29 . . . . 7 B8
Luton LU1 . . . . 123 E6
Shefford SG17 . . . . 77 C2
Slip End LU1 . . . . 123 C1
St Neots PE19 . . . . 22 E5
Newstead Way MK41 . . . . . 38 F5
New Street Ct NN29. . . . . . . 7 B8
NEWTON 68 B5
NEWTON BLOSSOMVILLE. 34 A4
Newton Blossomville CE First Sch MK43 . . . . 34 B4
NEWTON BROMSWOLD 9 D8
Newtondale LU4 . . . . 115 C5
Newton Rd
Bedford MK42 . . . . 50 C5
Chelveston NN10. . . . . 3 B3
Rushden NN10. . . . . 8 F8
Turvey MK43 . . . . 34 E5
Newton Way
Leighton Buzzard LU7 . . . . 111 D6
Sandy SG19 . . . . 54 C8
NEW TOWN. 123 E5
Newtown
Henlow SG16. . . . . 78 D3
Kimbolton PE28 . . . . 6 F5
Potton SG19. . . . . 55 F7
St Neots PE19 . . . . 22 B8
Newtown Ct SG18. . . . . 67 B7
Newtown La PE28. . . . . 6 F5
New Town Rd 9 LU1. . . . . 123 E6
New Town St LU1. . . . . . . 123 E6
NEW WATER END 94 B8
New Wlk
Shillington SG5 . . . . 87 E1
Shillington SG5 . . . . 87 F1
New Woodfield Gn LU5. . 121 E6
Nicholas Way 6 LU5 . . . . 121 B8
Nicholls Cl
Barton-le-C MK45 . . . . 97 C3
Marston Moretaine MK43 . . 72 C8
Nicholls Rd MK42 . . . . 50 D6
Nichols Cl LU2. . . . . 117 C2
Nicholson Dr LU7 . . . . . . 111 D5
Nickleby Way SG5 . . . . 90 C2
Nightingale Ave MK41. . . . 38 C5
Nightingale Cl LU2. . . . . . 117 C6
Nightingale Ct LU3. . . . . . 123 C8
Nightingale Mews SG17 . . 77 C2
Nightingale Terr SG15. . . . 90 A3
Nightingale Way MK44 . . . 16 B4
Nimbus Pk LU5 . . . . 114 C3
Nimrod Dr SG17 . . . . 76 E4
Ninelands LU7. . . . . 104 F2
Ninfield Ct LU2 . . . . 117 C3
Ninth Ave LU3 . . . . 115 D7
Nith Wlk MK41. . . . . 38 C7
Nodders Way MK40 . . . . . . 37 C1
Noke Shot AL5. . . . . 131 C4
Norcott Cl LU5. . . . . 121 D7
Norfolk Cl MK41 . . . . 38 D6
Norfolk Rd
Dunstable LU5. . . . . 121 F6
Luton LU2 . . . . 124 A7
Turvey MK43 . . . . 34 E6
Norman Cl MK44. . . . . 40 F5
Normandy Cl MK42. . . . . . . 50 A5
Normandy La SG18. . . . . . . 67 D3
Norman Rd
Barton-le-C MK45 . . . . 97 D4
Luton LU3 . . . . 116 B2
Sharnbrook MK44 . . . . 16 D3
Normans Cl SG6 . . . . 90 F1
Norman Way
Dunstable LU6. . . . . 120 E8
Irchester NN29 . . . . 7 C8
Norse Rd MK41 . . . . 39 D4
NORTHALL 119 B6
Northall Cl LU6 . . . . 119 D6
Northall Rd LU6. . . . . 119 D6
Northampton Rd
Bromham MK43. . . . . 36 B3
Bromham MK43. . . . . 36 E3
North Area Pupil Referral Unit SG6 . . . . 101 D3
Northbridge St SG17 . . . . . 77 C3
Northbridge Wharf SG17 . 77 C3
Northcliffe LU6 . . . . 119 E6
Northcote MK41 . . . . 39 A3
Northcourt LU7. . . . . 103 A1
NORTH CRAWLEY 58 A6
North Crawley CE Fst Sch MK16 . . . . 58 B6
Northcroft SG19 . . . . 54 C7
North Ct AL3 . . . . 128 E5
Northdale Cl MK42. . . . . . . 50 A4
North Dr MK42. . . . . 51 A3
North Drift Way LU1 . . . . 123 B6
NORTH END
MK43. . . . . 47 D8
MK44. . . . . 17 D3
North End MK42 . . . . 51 A3
Northern Ave SG16. . . . . . . 89 C3
Northfield Cl
Gamlingay SG19 . . . . 44 D6
Henlow SG16. . . . . 78 D2

Northfield Rd
Guilden Morden SG7 . . . **69** C2
Harpenden AL5 . . . . . **131** C4
Wyboston MK44 . . . . **21** F1
Northfields
Biggleswade SG18 . . . . . **67** A7
Dunstable LU5 . . . . . . **114** A3
Letchworth SG6 . . . . **90** F1
Northfields Inf Sch SG6 . . **90** F1
Northfields Tech Coll
LU5 . . . . **114** A3
North Hertfordshire Coll
SG6 . . . . **101** F5
NORTHILL **53** E2
Northill CE Lower Sch
SG18 . . . . **53** D2
Northill Rd
Cople MK44 . . . . **52** D3
Ickwell SG18 . . . . **65** D8
North La
Gamlingay SG19 . . . . . . **44** B6
Haynes MK45 . . . . **63** F1
North Luton Ind Est LU4 . **115** B7
North Par 2 MK40 . . . . . **38** B1
North Pl SG5 . . . . **100** D1
North Rd SG7 . . . . **91** C2
North St
Leighton Buzzard LU7 . . **111** A7
Luton, High Town LU2 . . **123** E8
Luton LU2 . . . . **116** E1
North Star Dr LU7 . . . . . **111** C8
North Station Way LU6 . . **114** A2
Northview Rd
Houghton Regis LU5 . . . **114** A2
Luton LU2 . . . . **116** E1
Northway Ct MK42 . . . . . **50** D6
Northwell Dr LU3 . . . . . **115** F7
Northwood End Rd MK45 . **76** B7
Northwood La MK45 . . . . **63** A4
NORTON **91** C1
NORTON BURY **91** C2
Norton Bury La SG6 . . . . **91** C2
Norton Ct LU6 . . . . . . **121** B8
Norton Mill La SG6 . . . . **91** D3
Norton Rd
Letchworth SG6 . . . . **91** C2
Luton LU3 . . . . **115** F4
Stotfold SG5 . . . . **91** A4
Norton Road Prim Sch
LU3 . . . . **115** F4
Nunnery La LU3 . . . . . . **116** B5
Nurseries The LU6 . . . . **119** E6
Nursery Cl
Biggleswade SG18 . . . . . **67** B8
Clophill MK45 . . . . **86** B8
Dunstable LU6 . . . . . . **121** A8
Potton SG19 . . . . **55** E2
Nursery Dr SG19 . . . . . . **54** A8
Nursery Gdns MK41 . . . . **38** D4
Nursery Par LU3 . . . . . **115** E5
Nursery Rd
Luton LU3 . . . . **115** F5
St Neots PE19 . . . . **22** F4
Nutleigh Gr SG5 . . . . . **100** D1
Nutwood Cl MK41 . . . . . **39** C3
Nymans Cl LU2 . . . . . . **117** D3

O

Oak Ave MK45 . . . . **62** F2
Oak Bank Dr LU7 . . . . . **103** A3
Oak Bank Special Sch
LU7 . . . . **103** A3
Oak Cl
Dunstable LU5 . . . . . . **121** D8
Harlington LU5 . . . . **95** F1
Irchester NN29 . . . . **7** A7
Sandy SG19 . . . . **54** B8
Westoning MK45 . . . . . . **95** E6
Wootton MK43 . . . . **61** A8
Oak Cres
Biggleswade SG18 . . . . . **67** B4
Potton SG19 . . . . **55** F7
Upper Caldecote SG18 . . **66** B8
Oakcroft MK43 . . . . **48** A6
Oak Dr
Greenfield MK45 . . . . . . **85** D2
Henlow SG16 . . . . **78** D1
Oaken Pin Cl MK43 . . . . **71** B8
Oak Gdns MK43 . . . . **72** C2
Oakham Cl NN10 . . . . **8** A8
Oaklands Rd MK40 . . . . . **38** D2
OAKLEY **37** A7
Oakley Cl LU4 . . . . **115** D4
Oakley Gn LU7 . . . . . . **103** B1
Oakley Lower Sch MK43 . . **37** A7
Oakley Rd
Bromham MK43 . . . . **37** A4
Clapham MK41 . . . . **37** C6
Luton LU4 . . . . **115** E3
Oak Rd
Bedford MK42 . . . . **50** E5
Flitwick MK45 . . . . **84** E4
Luton LU4 . . . . **123** C8
Oakridge Pk LU7 . . . . . **111** B5
Oaks The
Heath and Reach LU7 . . **103** A5
Silsoe MK45 . . . . **86** C4
Slip End LU1 . . . . **123** C1
Oak Tree Cl SG6 . . . . . **101** E4
Oaktree Rd MK45 . . . . . . **84** F7
Oak Tree Row LU2 . . . . . **117** A2
Oakway LU6 . . . . **127** B7
Oakwell Rd LU6 . . . . . . **120** F7

Oakwood Ave LU5 . . . . . **121** E7
Oakwood Dr LU3 . . . . . . **115** C8
Oakwood Rd SG17 . . . . . **77** D2
Oasis Pool MK42 . . . . . . **50** E7
Oatfield Cl LU4 . . . . . . **114** F4
Oatfield Gdns LU7 . . . . **111** D7
Oban Terr LU1 . . . . **123** B8
Oberon Ct MK41 . . . . . . **38** A1
Ockendon Cl PE19 . . . . . **22** B3
ODELL **25** C8
Odell Cl MK42 . . . . **49** D6
Odell Rd
Odell MK43 . . . . **25** A8
Sharnbrook MK44 . . . . . **16** B2
Odin Cl MK41 . . . . **39** D4
Offa Rd MK42 . . . . **50** B5
Old Allotments The MK44 . **13** A2
Old Bakery Yd SG18 . . . . **68** D5
Old Barn Cl SG16 . . . . . **78** D2
Old Barns The MK40 . . . . **49** B8
Old Bedford Rd
Luton LU2 . . . . **116** D6
Luton LU2 . . . . **116** E4
Potton SG19 . . . . **55** F7
Old Brewery Cl SG5 . . . . **90** F7
Old Bridge Ct SG17 . . . . **77** C2
Old Bridge Way SG17 . . . **77** C2
Old Chapel Mews LU7 . . **111** A6
Old Chapel The PE19 . . . . **22** B2
Old Church Path MK45 . . . **75** E1
Old Dairy Cl LU5 . . . . . **114** F2
Old Farm Cl LU1 . . . . . **118** A3
Oldfield Farm Rd
Henlow SG16 . . . . **89** B4
Henlow SG16 . . . . **89** C4
Oldfield Rd MK40 . . . . . **49** E8
Old Ford End Rd MK40 . . **49** E7
Old Hale Way SG5 . . . . **100** E3
Old Harrowden Rd MK42 . **51** A3
Old Hat Factory The 1
LU2 . . . . **116** D1
Oldhill LU6 . . . . **121** D6
OLDHILL WOOD **127** D6
Oldhill Wood LU6 . . . . . **127** D6
Old Kiln La MK45 . . . . . . **75** C2
OLD LINSLADE **102** D2
Old Linslade Rd LU7 . . . . **102** D3
Old Main Rd MK45 . . . . . . **75** A6
Old Market Ct PE19 . . . . **22** E5
Old Mews MK41 . . . . **38** A2
Old Mill Cl SG18 . . . . . . **78** E7
Old Mill La MK45 . . . . . . **87** D4
Old Milton Rd MK44 . . . . **28** A8
Old Oak Cl SG15 . . . . . . **90** A8
Old Orch LU1 . . . . **123** D5
Old Orchard The SG18 . . . **67** B6
Old Rd
Barton-le-C MK45 . . . . . **97** C1
Leighton Buzzard LU7 . . **110** E7
Old Rd The MK43 . . . . . . **16** D1
Old Rectory Cl AL5 . . . . **131** A2
Old School Ct
Clifton SG17 . . . . **78** B2
Eaton Bray LU6 . . . . . . **119** E6
Hockliffe LU7 . . . . **104** C2
2 Leighton Buzzard LU7 . **111** A7
Old School Gdns
Barton-le-C MK45 . . . . . **97** C3
St Neots PE19 . . . . **22** C2
Wootton MK43 . . . . **60** F7
Old School La SG18 . . . . **78** A7
Old School Wlk
Arlesey SG15 . . . . **90** A4
Slip End LU1 . . . . **123** C1
Old School Yd PE19 . . . . **22** F4
Old Silsoe Rd MK45 . . . . **86** C8
Old Station Ct MK45 . . . . **41** D2
Old Station Way SG17 . . . **77** C3
Old Vicarage Gdns
Henlow SG16 . . . . **78** D2
Markyate AL3 . . . . **128** D6
OLD WARDEN **65** B4
Old Watling St AL3 . . . . **129** B3
Old Way MK41 . . . . **17** C1
Oldways Rd MK44 . . . . . . **28** F1
Oliver Ct MK40 . . . . **38** B1
Oliver's La SG5 . . . . **90** F7
Oliver St MK45 . . . . **84** F7
Olivier Way SG17 . . . . . . **78** B2
Olma Rd LU5 . . . . **114** A2
Olyard Ct LU1 . . . . **123** B6
Olympic Cl LU3 . . . . **107** E1
Olympus Rd SG16 . . . . . . **89** B4
Ombersley Rd MK42 . . . . **50** B6
Omega Cl LU7 . . . . **111** C8
Omega Ctr The SG18 . . . . **67** D3
Onley Ct SG19 . . . . **54** D6
Onslow Rd LU4 . . . . **115** D5
Openshaw Way SG16 . . . **101** F6
Orchard Ave AL5 . . . . . **130** F1
Orchard Cl
Barton-le-C MK45 . . . . . **97** C1
Bedford MK41 . . . . **38** E3
Biggleswade SG18 . . . . . **67** B6
Bromham MK43 . . . . **37** A4
Caddington LU1 . . . . . . **122** E4
Cranfield MK43 . . . . **59** A1
Gravenhurst MK45 . . . . . **87** C4
Houghton Regis LU5 . . . **114** B3
Letchworth SG6 . . . . . . **101** F8
Meppershall SG17 . . . . . **88** C6
Potton SG19 . . . . **56** A7
St Neots PE19 . . . . **22** C4
Toddington LU5 . . . . . . **105** F6
Orchard Dr
Chicksands SG17 . . . . . . **76** F2
Leighton Buzzard LU7 . . **110** D6
Wilstead MK45 . . . . **62** E3

Orchard End LU6 . . . . . **119** E4
Orchard Est LU7 . . . . . . **112** A7
Orchard Ho LU5 . . . . **95** F2
Orchard La MK43 . . . . . . **24** F7
Orchard Pl NN29 . . . . **7** A8
Orchard Rd
Baldock SG7 . . . . **91** E1
Beeston SG19 . . . . **54** C5
Hitchin SG4 . . . . **101** B1
Pulloxhill MK45 . . . . **96** E8
St Neots PE19 . . . . **22** C4
Orchard St MK42 . . . . . . **49** F3
Orchards The
Eaton Bray LU6 . . . . . . **119** E7
Silsoe MK45 . . . . **86** C4
Slip End LU1 . . . . **123** C2
Orchard Way
Cranfield MK43 . . . . **59** A1
Eaton Bray LU6 . . . . . . **119** F5
Flitwick MK45 . . . . **84** F2
Great Barford MK44 . . . . **41** A4
Letchworth SG6 . . . . . . **101** F8
Lower Stondon SG16 . . . . **89** B3
Luton LU4 . . . . **115** C4
North Crawley MK16 . . . . **58** A6
Stanbridge LU7 . . . . . . **112** D5
Orchid Cl
Dunstable LU6 . . . . . . **113** E1
St Neots PE19 . . . . **22** C6
Ordelmere SG6 . . . . **90** F1
Oregon Way LU3 . . . . . . **116** A8
Orion Way LU7 . . . . **111** D8
Ormesby Way MK40 . . . . **49** E7
Ormsby Cl LU1 . . . . **123** E5
Orpington Cl LU4 . . . . . **115** A3
Orwell Cl MK41 . . . . **38** C5
Osborn Cres SG17 . . . . . **77** C2
Osborne Ave SG17 . . . . . **76** E2
Osborne Ct 9 LU1 . . . . **123** F6
Osborne Rd
Dunstable LU6 . . . . . . **121** B7
Luton LU1 . . . . **123** F6
Osborn Ho 1 LU6 . . . . . **121** B8
Osborn Rd MK45 . . . . . . **97** C2
Osier Ct PE19 . . . . **22** C6
Osier Link MK45 . . . . . . **84** F7
Osprey Cl
Kempston MK42 . . . . . . **49** E2
Sandy SG19 . . . . **42** B2
Osprey Rd
Biggleswade SG18 . . . . . **66** F5
Flitwick MK45 . . . . **84** E2
Osprey Wlk LU4 . . . . . . **115** A5
Ossory Pl MK45 . . . . **84** E8
Ossory Way MK42 . . . . . . **50** B6
Othello Cl MK40 . . . . . . **37** F2
Otterton Cl AL5 . . . . . . **130** F3
Otter Way PE19 . . . . **22** B5
Otter Wlk MK41 . . . . **38** C5
Oulton Rise MK45 . . . . . **131** C3
Our Lady RC Prim Sch
SG5 . . . . **100** E2
Ouseland Rd MK40 . . . . . **49** E7
Ouseley Cl LU4 . . . . . . **115** D3
Ouse Rd
Bedford MK41 . . . . **39** A2
St Neots PE19 . . . . **22** C4
Oval The SG16 . . . . **89** C3
Overdale MK41 . . . . **39** A3
Overend Green La LU7 . . **103** C6
Overfield Rd LU2 . . . . . **117** C1
Overhills Prim Sch PE28 . . **6** F5
Overlord Cl SG17 . . . . . . **77** C1
Overstone Rd
Harpenden AL5 . . . . . . **131** C1
Luton LU4 . . . . **115** D1
Overtrees AL5 . . . . **130** F3
Oving Cl LU2 . . . . **117** D2
Owen Cl
Kempston MK42 . . . . . . **49** D3
Marston Moretaine MK43 . **72** C8
Owen Jones Cl SG16 . . . . **89** C5
Owlswood SG19 . . . . **42** B2
Oxendon Cl LU7 . . . . . . **102** F2
Oxen Rd LU2 . . . . **116** F1
Oxford Rd 2 LU1 . . . . . **123** E6
Oxford St NN10 . . . . **8** A7
Ox La AL5 . . . . **131** B3

P

Padbury Ho 4 MK40 . . . . **38** A1
Paddlers Ct MK40 . . . . . . **49** E7
Paddock Cl
Clapham MK41 . . . . **37** D7
Letchworth SG6 . . . . . . **101** F5
Luton LU4 . . . . **114** F5
Paddocks The
Bromham MK43 . . . . **36** F1
Flitwick MK45 . . . . **84** D5
Leighton Buzzard LU7 . . **110** F8
Potton SG19 . . . . **55** F7
Toddington LU5 . . . . . . **106** A5
Paddock The
Biddenham MK40 . . . . . . **49** D8
Lidlington MK43 . . . . . . **72** C2
St Neots PE19 . . . . **22** D5
Page's Almshouses 5
LU7 . . . . **111** A8
Page's Ind Pk LU7 . . . . . **111** B5
Paignton Cl LU4 . . . . . . **115** D4
Paines Mill PE19 . . . . . . **22** E6
Paisley Cl LU4 . . . . **115** D3
Palace St SG18 . . . . **67** A5
Palgrave Rd MK42 . . . . . **50** B7
Palma Cl LU6 . . . . **113** F3

Palmer Cl SG17 . . . . **77** C3
Palmerston St MK41 . . . . **38** B2
Palmerston Way SG5 . . . . **90** C2
Parade The
1 Dunstable LU6 . . . . **114** A1
Letchworth SG6 . . . . **90** F1
Luton LU3 . . . . **115** C7
Paradine Rd MK42 . . . . . **50** D6
Parish Cl MK41 . . . . **39** B4
Park Ave
Bedford MK40 . . . . **38** C2
Houghton Regis LU5 . . . **114** C5
Luton LU3 . . . . **115** C7
Totternhoe LU6 . . . . . . **120** B8
Park Ave N AL5 . . . . . . **130** F1
Park Avenue Trad Est
LU3 . . . . **115** C7
Park Ave S AL5 . . . . . . **130** F1
Park Cl
Markyate AL3 . . . . **128** D5
Moggerhanger MK44 . . . . **53** B6
Park Cres MK43 . . . . **61** C1
Park Ct
Luton LU2 . . . . **116** D1
Sandy SG19 . . . . **54** C6
PARK END **36** D7
Parker Cl
Letchworth SG6 . . . . . . **101** E4
St Neots PE19 . . . . **22** E2
Parkers La SG7 . . . . **80** D5
Park Farm LU7 . . . . **105** B2
Park Farm Cl SG16 . . . . . **89** D8
Park Farm Ct MK41 . . . . . **37** F6
Parkfield AL3 . . . . **128** D5
Parkfields Mid Sch LU5 . . **105** F7
Park Hill
Ampthill MK45 . . . . **73** E1
Harpenden AL5 . . . . . . **130** F1
Toddington LU5 . . . . . . **105** F7
Park La
Blunham MK44 . . . . **41** E3
Eaton Bray LU6 . . . . . . **119** D6
Gamlingay SG19 . . . . . . **44** C5
Henlow SG16 . . . . **78** D1
Kimbolton MK44, PE19 . . . **6** F2
Sharnbrook MK44 . . . . . **16** E5
Parkland MK43 . . . . **36** D3
Parkland Dr LU1 . . . . . . **123** D5
Parklands MK41 . . . . **38** E2
Park Lane Cres SG16 . . . . **78** D2
Park Leys LU5 . . . . **95** F1
Parkmead 6 LU1 . . . . . **123** F6
Park Meadow MK45 . . . . . **97** B3
Park Mews
Leighton Buzzard LU7 . . **111** A6
Sandy SG19 . . . . **54** C7
Park Mount AL5 . . . . . . **130** F3
Park Palings Wlk MK45 . . **75** F8
Park Rd
Dunstable LU5 . . . . . . **121** C7
Kempston MK42 . . . . . . **49** F5
Melchbourne MK44 . . . . . **10** D8
Moggerhanger MK44 . . . . **53** B7
Roxton MK44 . . . . **31** E2
Sandy SG19 . . . . **54** C7
Stevington MK43 . . . . . . **36** D6
St Neots PE19 . . . . **22** F7
Toddington LU5 . . . . . . **105** D7
Westoning MK45 . . . . . . **95** E5
Wilstead MK45 . . . . **62** E2
Park Rd N
Bedford MK41 . . . . **38** B2
Houghton Regis LU5 . . . **114** D4
Park Rd W MK41 . . . . . . **38** B2
Park Rise AL5 . . . . **130** E3
Park Rise Cl AL5 . . . . . **130** E3
Park St W LU1 . . . . **123** E7
PARKSIDE **114** D5
Parkside
Gravenhurst MK45 . . . . . **87** B4
Milton Ernest MK44 . . . . **27** B5
Parkside Cl LU5 . . . . . . **114** D5
Parkside Dr LU5 . . . . . . **114** D6
Parkside Flats LU6 . . . . **121** C8
Park Sq LU2 . . . . **123** E7
Park St
Ampthill MK45 . . . . **73** E1
Dunstable LU6 . . . . . . **114** A1
Luton LU1 . . . . **123** F6
Woburn MK17 . . . . **93** A7
Parkstone Cl MK41 . . . . . **38** E6
Park Terr 2 LU1 . . . . . **123** F6
PARK TOWN **123** F6
Park Viaduct LU1 . . . . . **123** F6
Park View MK44 . . . . **41** D3
Park View Cl LU3 . . . . . **115** D6
Park View Dr
Leighton Buzzard LU7 . . **110** E7
St Neots PE19 . . . . **22** D5
Park View Dr AL3 . . . . . **128** D6
Parkview La LU7 . . . . . . **105** C2
Parkway
Houghton Regis LU5 . . . **114** E6
Woburn Sands MK17 . . . . **81** A6
Park Way PE19 . . . . **22** F7
Parkway Rd LU1 . . . . . . **116** B5
Parmiter Way MK45 . . . . **84** D7
Parrish Cl MK43 . . . . **72** D8
Parrot Cl LU5 . . . . **114** E1
Parsonage Cl MK43 . . . . . **37** A7
Parson's Cl AL3 . . . . . . **129** B1
Parsons Rd NN29 . . . . **7** B8
Partridge Cl LU4 . . . . . . **115** A5
Partridge La MK43 . . . . . **36** D1
Partridge Piece
Cranfield MK43 . . . . **59** C3
Sandy SG19 . . . . **42** B2
Parys Rd LU3 . . . . **116** B6

Pascomb Rd LU6 . . . . . **120** F8
Pashley Ct PE19 . . . . . . **22** E2
Pasture La SG4 . . . . . . **125** E8
Pasture Rd SG6 . . . . . . **101** E3
Pastures Ct LU4 . . . . . . **115** A3
Pastures The
Edlesborough LU6 . . . . **119** F3
Lower Stondon SG16 . . . . **88** E3
Stewartby MK43 . . . . . . **61** C1
Upper Caldecote SG18 . . **66** B8
Pastures Way LU4 . . . . . **115** A4
Pathway The MK45 . . . . . **74** B1
Patterdale Rd LU6 . . . . . **121** B7
Patteshull Ct 1 MK40 . . . **50** B8
Paula Radcliffe Way MK41,
MK43 . . . . **37** C5
Paulsons Cl MK44 . . . . . . **11** A2
Paul Waller Ave MK42 . . . **51** B3
PAVENHAM **26** B4
Pavenham Rd
Felmersham MK43 . . . . . **26** C7
Pavenham MK43 . . . . . . **26** C7
Stevington MK43 . . . . . . **25** D4
Pax Hill MK41 . . . . **38** E4
Payne Rd MK43 . . . . **60** F7
Paynes Cl SG6 . . . . **91** A1
Peach Ct LU1 . . . . **123** F6
Peach's Cl MK45 . . . . . . **25** A6
Peacock Mews 6 LU7 . . . **111** A7
Peacock Rd MK43 . . . . . . **36** E2
Peakes End MK45 . . . . . . **84** A3
Pearcey Rd MK42 . . . . . . **50** C5
Pearmain Cl MK41 . . . . . **38** F1
Pearson Cl PE19 . . . . . . **22** E2
Peartree Cl
Shefford SG17 . . . . **77** E2
Toddington LU5 . . . . . . **105** E5
Pear Tree Cl
Bromham MK43 . . . . **36** D1
Lower Stondon SG16 . . . . **89** B3
Pear Tree La LU7 . . . . . **111** A8
Peartree Rd LU2 . . . . . . **117** C4
Pear Tree View MK42 . . . **50** C2
Peashill La MK44 . . . . . . **40** F6
Pebblemoor LU6 . . . . . . **119** F3
Pebbles The SG7 . . . . . . **91** C4
Peck Ct MK45 . . . . **97** B4
Peckworth Ind Est SG16 . . **89** A4
Peddars La LU7 . . . . . . **112** D4
Pedley Hill HP4, LU6 . . . **127** C1
Pedley La SG17 . . . . **77** F3
Peel Pl 7 LU1 . . . . **123** D7
Peel's Pl SG19 . . . . **54** D7
Peel St
7 Bedford MK40 . . . . . **38** B1
Houghton Regis LU5 . . . **114** B5
6 Luton LU1 . . . . **123** D7
Peer Rd PE19 . . . . **22** B4
Peers Dr MK17 . . . . **81** E3
Pegasus Ct SG18 . . . . . . **66** F7
Pegasus Dr SG18 . . . . . . **67** D3
Pegasus Mews SG18 . . . . **67** D3
Pegasus Rd LU7 . . . . . . **111** D8
PEGSDON **98** D1
Pegsdon Cl LU3 . . . . . . **116** B7
Pegsdon Way SG5 . . . . . **98** E1
Pelican Way SG6 . . . . . . **90** F1
Pemberley Ave MK40 . . . . **38** C2
Pemberley La MK40 . . . . **38** C1
Pembroke Ave
Luton LU4 . . . . **115** F3
St Neots PE19 . . . . **22** F2
Pembroke Cl MK45 . . . . . **72** D8
Pembroke Rd MK45 . . . . . **74** B7
Pembroke St MK40 . . . . . **50** D8
Penda Cl LU3 . . . . **115** F7
Pendennis Rd MK41 . . . . **39** A4
Penfold Cl SG17 . . . . . . **77** A2
Penhill LU3 . . . . **115** E6
Penhill Ct LU3 . . . . **115** E6
Penlee Cl MK41 . . . . **38** F1
Penley Way LU7 . . . . . . **111** A5
Pennine Ave LU3 . . . . . . **115** D8
Pennine Rd MK41 . . . . . . **38** E3
Pennine Rise MK45 . . . . . **84** D2
Pennivale Cl LU7 . . . . . . **111** A8
Pennyfarthers Cl MK45 . . **86** B8
Penrith Ave LU6 . . . . . . **121** B7
Penrwyn Ct PE19 . . . . . . **22** F1
Penshurst Cl AL5 . . . . . **130** D4
Pentelowes The PE28 . . . . **2** D2
Pentland Cl SG19 . . . . . . **54** B8
Pentland Rise MK45 . . . . **38** E3
Penwright Cl MK42 . . . . . **49** D5
Penwrights La MK44 . . . . **40** F5
Peppercorns La PE19 . . . . **22** C2
PEPPERSTOCK **123** C1
Peppiatts The LU6 . . . . . **119** B5
Pepsal End Rd LU1 . . . . **129** C7
Percheron Dr LU4 . . . . . **115** A3
Percival Way LU2 . . . . . **124** C7
Peregrine Rd LU4 . . . . . **115** A4
Periwinkle La
Dunstable LU6 . . . . . . **121** C7
Hitchin SG5 . . . . **100** F1
Periwinkle Terr LU6 . . . . **121** C7
Perkins Rd MK41 . . . . . . **39** C2
Perring Cl MK44 . . . . **16** C4
PERRY GREEN **124** C3
Perrymead LU2 . . . . **117** F2
Perry Mead LU6 . . . . . . **119** B6
Pershore Cl MK41 . . . . . . **38** E5
PERTENHALL **12** C8
Pertenhall Rd MK44 . . . . **12** B4
Petard Ct LU4 . . . . **114** A2
Petersfield Gdns LU3 . . . **107** E1
PETERS GREEN **125** C3
Petley Cl MK45 . . . . **84** E1

Petteril Wlk MK41 38 C7
Petunia Ct LU3 116 C1
Pevensey Cl LU2 117 D4
Pevensey Gr MK45 84 E1
Pevensey Rd MK41 39 A3
Pheasant Wlk MK45 84 D2
Philip Gdns PE19 22 F2
Philip Larkin Ho MK40 50 A8
Phillips Mdws MK44 4 A3
Phillpotts Ave MK40 38 E1
Phipps Cl MK45 62 F3
Phoenix Cl LU7 111 D8
Phoenix Sq PE19 22 E6
Pickering Cl SG19 54 C8
Pickford Hill AL5 131 C3
Pickford Rd AL3 128 C3
Pie Cnr AL3 129 B1
Pie Gdn AL3 129 C1
Pietley Hill AL3 129 A1
Pigeonwick AL5 131 B3
Piggottshill La AL5 131 E1
Piggotts La LU4 115 D4
Pilcroft St MK42 50 C7
Pilgrim Ctr MK41 38 D3
Pilgrims Cl
– Bedford MK42 50 C4
– Flitwick MK45 84 E3
– Harlington LU5 95 F1
Pilgrims Pre-Prep Sch MK41 38 C3
Pilgrims Way MK42 50 C4
Pillinge Rd MK43 61 C1
Pinchmill Cl MK44 16 C3
Pinchmill Lower Sch MK43 26 C8
Pinchmill Way MK44 16 C3
Pine Cl
– Biggleswade SG18 67 A7
– Irchester NN29 7 A7
– Leighton Buzzard LU7 103 A2
– Rushden NN10 8 A8
Pine Crest Mews LU7 110 E6
Pine Gr MK17 81 A4
Pinemead SG17 77 E2
Pines The
– Ampthill MK45 84 E8
– Kempston MK42 49 F3
Pine View Pk MK45 86 B7
Pinewood Cl LU3 107 C1
PINFOLDPOND 92 E6
Pinford Dell 4 LU2 117 D1
Pinkle Hill Rd LU7 103 A5
Pinsent Ave MK43 36 E1
Pioneer Pk MK42 50 B5
Pipers Croft LU6 120 F7
Pipers Hill HP1 132 D3
Pipers La AL3, LU1 122 F1
Pipit Cl MK45 84 E2
Pipit Gr SG19 42 B2
Pipit Rise MK41 38 D4
PIRTON 99 E4
Pirton Hill Inf Sch LU4 115 B6
Pirton Hill Jun Sch LU4 115 B6
Pirton Rd
– Holwell SG5 100 A7
– Luton LU4 115 D5
Pirton Sch SG5 99 D4
Pitsdean Rd PE19 33 F3
Pitsford Terr LU2 117 A1
Pix Ct SG15 90 A8
Pixmore Way SG6 101 F5
Pix Rd SG5 90 E5
Place Theatre The MK40 38 E1
Plaiters Cl MK43 26 B3
Plaiters Way LU5 114 A5
Planes The MK42 49 E3
Plane Tree Cl SG19 44 C6
Plantation Rd
– Leighton Buzzard LU7 102 F3
– Luton LU3 115 D7
Platt Cl LU4 115 D4
Platz Ho LU5 114 D5
Playfield Cl SG18 67 B5
Playford Sq LU4 115 D5
Pleasance The AL5 130 D4
Pleasent Pl SG19 54 C7
Plewes Cl LU6 127 E8
Plough Cl
– Cranfield MK43 71 A8
– Luton LU4 114 E4
Plough Ct LU4 114 E4
Ploversfield SG19 42 B2
Plover Way MK41 38 B4
Plummer Haven LU7 103 A1
Plummers La
– Haynes MK45 75 F8
– Peters Green LU2 125 C2
Plumpton Cl LU2 117 D3
Plum Tree La LU7 111 A8
Plum Tree Rd SG16 89 B2
Plymouth Cl LU2 117 B1
PODINGTON 7 E2
Podington Prim Sch NN29 7 E1
Podington Rd NN10 8 A4
Poets Ct AL5 131 B1
Poets Gn LU4 115 A2
Pokas Cotts NN9 3 C8
Polam Sch MK40 38 A1
Polegate LU2 117 D2
Polhill Ave MK40, MK41 38 E2
Pollards Cl MK45 62 E3
Pollards Way
– Lower Stondon SG16 89 A3
– Pirton SG5 99 D4
Polo Field Way MK42 50 A2
Polzeath Cl LU2 124 C8
Pomeroy Gr LU2 116 E6
Pomfret Ave LU2 116 F1
Pond Cl LU4 115 B5
Pondwick Rd AL5 130 E2
Pondwicks Rd LU1 123 F7
Pope Cl MK45 84 E1
Pope Rd PE19 22 E4
Popes Ct LU2 116 D1
Popes Way MK43 60 E7
Popham Cl PE19 22 A3
Poplar Ave
– Bedford MK41 38 E4
– Luton LU3 116 C8
– Wilstead MK45 62 F2
Poplar Cl
– Biggleswade SG18 67 A8
– Irchester NN29 7 A7
– Leighton Buzzard LU7 103 A2
– Roxton MK44 31 E1
– Rushden NN10 8 A8
– Silsoe MK45 86 C4
Poplar Dr SG5 90 F7
Poplar Gr SG19 54 B7
Poplar Rd LU6 127 E8
Poplars Cl LU2 117 B3
Poplars The
– Ampthill MK45 84 F8
– Arlesey SG15 90 A8
– Ickleford SG5 100 F5
Poppy Cl NN10 8 C8
Poppy Field SG18 67 C5
Poppyfields MK41 39 C4
Porlock Dr LU2 117 C1
Porters Hill AL5 131 C4
Portland Cl
– Bedford MK41 39 A2
– Houghton Regis LU5 114 B4
Portland Ct LU4 116 A1
Portland Ind Est SG15 90 A3
Portland Rd LU4 116 A1
Portland Ride LU5 114 B2
Portman Cl SG5 100 D2
Portnall Pl MK43 59 B1
Portobello Cl MK45 97 C2
Porz Ave LU5 114 D3
Postley Rd MK42 49 E2
POTSGROVE 104 A8
Potten End Hill HP1 132 F1
Potters Cross MK43 61 A8
POTTER'S END 94 A5
Potter Way MK42 50 C4
Pottery Cl LU3 115 F7
POTTON 56 B7
Potton Lower Sch SG19 55 F7
Potton Rd
– Biggleswade SG18 67 A7
– Biggleswade SG18 67 B8
– Everton SG19 43 D2
– Gamlingay Great Heath SG19 43 F3
– Gamlingay SG19 44 D3
– Guilden Morden SG8 69 F6
– Sandy SG19 55 B6
– St Neots PE19 22 F2
– Wrestlingworth SG19 57 B4
Poulter Cl 6 MK40 50 B8
Pound Cl
– Blunham MK44 41 E4
– Langford SG18 78 F7
– Upper Caldecote SG18 54 B1
Pound Gn SG8 69 F5
Pound La
– Kimbolton PE28 6 F4
– North Crawley MK16 58 B7
Pounds Cl MK43 59 B1
Pound The MK45 95 E6
Powells Rd SG17 77 C3
Power Ct LU1 123 F7
Powers Cl SG19 42 B1
Powis Mews MK45 84 D1
Powis Pl PE19 22 F1
Powis Rd MK41 39 B4
Poynters Rd LU4 114 E3
Prebendal Dr LU1 123 B2
Prebend St MK40 50 B7
Prentice Gdns MK42 49 F6
Prentice Way LU2 124 D7
Presentation Ct LU1 123 F6
Preservine Wlk MK41 37 E5
President Way LU2 124 D8
Preslent Cl SG5 87 F1
Preston Cl MK45 84 E8
Preston Gdns LU2 116 F2
Preston Path LU2 116 F2
Preston Rd
– Bedford MK40 49 F8
– Toddington LU5 106 A5
Prestwick Cl LU2 116 E5
Prestwick Rd MK40 49 B8
Priestleys LU1 123 A7
Primary Way SG15 90 A4
Primrose Cl
– Arlesey SG15 90 A4
– Biggleswade SG18 67 C4
– Flitwick MK45 84 D2
– Marston Moretaine MK43 72 C7
Primrose Ct LU6 121 A8
Primrose La SG15 90 A4
Prince Andrew Dr SG5 91 A6
Prince Charles Ave SG5 91 A6
Prince Cl PE19 22 B5
Prince Edward Way SG5 91 A6
Prince Harry Cl SG5 91 A5
Prince Philip Ave MK43 58 D2
Princes Ct
– Dunstable LU5 114 C1
– Leighton Buzzard LU7 110 F8
Princes Pl 15 LU2 116 D1
Princes Rd MK43 36 E2
Princess Cl MK45 84 F2
Princess St
– Clapham MK41 37 D6
– Luton LU1 123 D7
Princes St
– 9 Bedford MK40 38 B1
– Dunstable LU6 121 A8
– Toddington LU5 106 A5
Prince's St SG5 90 F7
Prince Way LU2 124 D8
Prinknash Rd MK41 38 E5
Printers Ct MK45 73 F1
Printers Way LU6 114 B1
Prior Cl MK41 37 C6
Priors Cl NN10 7 F8
Priors Hill SG5 99 C4
Priory Bsns Pk MK44 51 C6
Priory Cl
– Harrold MK43 25 A6
– Turvey MK43 35 B5
Priory Ct
– 1 Bedford MK40 38 B1
– Dunstable LU5 121 C8
Priory Ctry Pk* MK41 51 A7
Priory Gate SG17 77 A2
Priory Gdns LU2 116 D4
Priory La PE19 22 E5
Priory Lower Sch MK40 50 A8
Priory Mall 2 PE19 22 E5
Priory Mews PE19 22 E6
Priory Mid Sch LU5 121 C8
Priory Orch AL3 129 B2
Priory Park Inf Sch PE19 22 F6
Priory Rd
– Campton SG17 76 F1
– Dunstable LU5 121 C8
– St Neots PE19 22 E6
Priory Sch The SG5 100 E2
Priory St MK40 50 B8
Priory Terr 4 MK40 38 B1
Priory The PE19 22 E5
Proctor Cl MK42 49 D5
Proctor Way LU2 124 C7
Progress Pk MK42 50 A2
Progress Way
– Elstow MK42 50 B4
– Luton LU4 115 B7
Prospect Ave NN29 7 A7
Prospect Rd SG18 78 F6
Prospect Row 3 PE19 22 F5
Prospect Way LU2 124 C7
Provost Way LU2 124 C8
Prudden Cl MK42 50 B4
Prudence Cl LU5 95 F1
Puddephat's La AL3 128 C1
Pulford Rd LU7 110 F6
Pulford's CE Lower Sch LU7 111 A6
PULLOXHILL 85 E1
Pulloxhill Bsns Pk MK45 85 D2
Pulloxhill Lower Sch MK45 96 E8
Pulloxhill Rd MK45 85 D2
Purbeck Cl MK41 39 A2
Purcell Rd LU4 114 F3
Purcell Way SG17 77 E3
Purley Ctr LU3 115 E7
Purway Cl LU3 115 E7
Purwell Wlk LU7 103 B3
PUTNOE 38 E3
Putnoe Hts MK41 38 F4
Putnoe La MK41 38 E4
Putnoe Lower Sch MK41 39 A3
Putnoe St MK41 39 A4
Putteridge High Sch LU2 117 C5
Putteridge Jun & Inf Sch LU2 117 C5
Putteridge Par LU2 117 B4
Putteridge Rd LU2 117 C4
Putteridge Recn Ctr LU2 117 C5
Putterills The AL5 131 A1
Pyghtle Ct LU1 123 A7
Pyghtle The
– Luton LU1 123 A7
– Turvey MK43 34 E6
– Westoning MK45 95 E5
Pyms Cl MK44 40 F5
Pym's Way SG19 42 B1
Pynders La LU5 114 E2
Pytchley Cl LU2 116 E5

Q

Quadrant The
– Houghton Regis LU5 114 C5
– Letchworth SG6 101 F6
Quantock Cl
– Bedford MK41 38 E2
– Luton LU3 116 B8
Quantock Rise LU3 108 B1
Quantocks The MK45 84 D2
Quantrelle Ct MK42 51 A3
Quarry Wlk LU6 121 A7
Queen Alexandra Rd MK41 39 A1
Queen Anne's Cl SG5 90 F5
Queen Elizabeth Cl SG17 77 D2
Queensbury Cl MK40 49 F8
Queensbury Upper Sch LU6 121 B7
Queens Cl
– Flitwick MK45 84 F2
– 4 Luton LU1 123 E6
– Northill SG18 53 E1
– Oakley MK43 36 F8
Queen's Cl MK40 37 D1
Queens Cres MK41 37 D7
Queen's Cres MK41 38 F3
Queens Ct
– Dunstable LU5 114 C1
– 14 Luton LU2 116 D1
– Shefford SG17 77 D2
– St Neots PE19 22 B3
Queen's Ct 12 MK40 38 B1
Queen's Dr MK41 38 F3
Queens Gdns PE19 22 B4
QUEEN'S PARK 49 F8
Queens Park Lower Sch MK40 49 F8
Queens Rd
– Ampthill MK45 84 F8
– Colmworth MK44 20 B2
Queen's Rd SG19 54 B7
Queen St
– Bedford MK40 38 B1
– Houghton Regis LU5 114 B4
– Leighton Buzzard LU7 110 F8
– Stotfold SG5 91 A6
Queensway
– Dunstable LU5 114 B1
– St Neots PE19 22 F7
Queen's Way SG18 78 F8
Queensway Dr SG4 101 C1
Quenby Way MK43 36 F1
Quickswood LU3 116 A7
Quilter Cl LU3 115 F4

R

Raban Ct SG7 91 F1
Race Meadows Way MK42 49 F2
Rackman Dr LU3 116 C5
Radburn Ct LU6 114 A1
Radnor Rd LU4 114 F4
Radnor Wlk MK41 39 B3
Radstone Pl LU2 117 E1
RADWELL
– MK43 26 E8
– SG7 91 C4
Radwell La SG7 91 C4
Radwell Rd
– Felmersham MK43 26 D8
– Milton Ernest MK43, MK44 26 F6
Raglan Cl LU4 114 F3
Raglan Gn MK41 39 A4
Railton Rd MK42 49 D1
Railway Cotts
– Kempston Hardwick MK45 61 F4
– Oakley MK43 37 A8
Railway View 1 SG18 67 A6
Rainbow Special Sch MK43 36 D3
Raleigh Cl PE19 22 A2
Raleigh Gr LU4 115 D1
Raleigh St MK40 49 F7
Rally The SG15 90 A7
Ramerick Gdns SG15 90 A2
Ramillies Cl MK42 49 F5
Ramridge Prim Sch LU2 117 B2
Ramridge Rd LU2 117 A2
Ramsay Cl MK41 38 B3
Ramsey Cl
– Kempston MK42 49 D2
– Luton LU4 114 F3
Ramsey Ct LU4 114 F3
Ramsey Manor Lower Sch MK45 97 D2
Ramsey Rd MK45 97 C3
Ram Yd MK40 50 C8
Randall Dr LU5 105 F5
Randalls Cl MK43 36 F2
Rand's Cl SG5 100 B7
Rand's Cotts SG5 100 B7
Rand's Mdw SG5 100 B7
Rannock Gdns LU7 110 C7
Ranock Cl LU3 115 D8
Ranworth Wlk MK40 49 D7
Rapper Ct LU3 123 D8
Raunds Rd NN9 3 C8
Ravenbank Rd LU2 117 C5
Ravenhill Way LU4 115 B4
Ravensburgh Cl MK45 97 B3
Ravenscourt LU6 113 F3
RAVENSDEN 29 B1
Ravensden CE Lower Sch MK44 29 B1
Ravensden Rd
– Renhold MK41 39 B7
– Wilden MK44 29 D3
Ravensthorpe LU2 117 B4
Raven Wlk MK45 84 E2
Raymond Cotts SG5 100 E4
Raynham Way LU2 117 D1
Raynsford Lower Sch SG16 78 D1
Ray's Cl MK42 50 C7
Reach Gn LU7 103 A6
Reach La LU7 103 B5
Readers Cl LU6 114 B2
Readshill MK45 86 C8
Ream Cl PE19 22 E2
Reaper Cl LU4 114 E4
Recreation Rd LU5 114 C6
Recreation Rise MK45 87 C4
Rectory Cl
– Carlton MK43 25 A4
– Clifton SG17 78 B3
– Slapton LU7 118 D6
Rectory Ct SG19 54 D7
Rectory Farm Bsns Pk SG16 88 D4
Rectory La
– Ampthill MK45 73 F1
– Cranfield MK43 71 B8
Rectory La *continued*
– Houghton Conquest MK45 74 A7
– Lilley LU2 109 D2
Rectory Rd
– Campton SG17 76 F1
– Meppershall SG17 88 B5
– Steppingley MK45 83 F3
Redborne Upper Sch & Com Coll MK45 84 E6
Red Cedar Rd MK43 36 C4
Reddall Cl MK42 50 F5
Redding Cl NN10 8 A7
Reddings La AL3 129 F1
Rede Cl MK41 38 C6
Redferns Cl LU1 123 A6
Redferns Ct LU1 123 A6
Redfield Cl LU6 120 E8
Redgrave Gdns LU3 115 F7
Redhill Rd SG5 100 D1
Redhoods Way E SG6 101 E7
Redhoods Way W SG6 101 E6
Red Lion Cl MK43 59 B1
Redman Gdns SG18 67 A7
Redmire Cl LU4 115 B6
Red Oak Cl MK43 36 C4
Redoubt Cl SG4 101 A1
Red Rails LU1 123 C5
Red Rails Ct LU1 123 C5
Redwald Cl MK42 49 E4
Redwood Cl NN29 7 A7
Redwood Dr LU3 115 C8
Redwood Glade LU7 103 A3
Redwood Gr MK42 50 C6
Reed Pl AL5 130 F3
Reedsdale LU2 117 F2
Reeve Cl LU7 111 C5
Reeves Ave LU3 116 B4
Regency Court Park Homes SG16 88 E2
Regency Ct LU6 121 C7
Regent Cl
– Bedford MK41 38 C6
– St Neots PE19 22 B4
Regent Ct
– 1 Bedford MK40 38 A1
– Stotfold SG5 90 F7
Regents Mews MK40 49 C8
Regent St
– Dunstable LU6 114 B1
– Leighton Buzzard LU7 111 B7
– Luton LU1 123 E7
– Stotfold SG5 90 F7
Reginald St LU2 116 E1
Regis Rd LU4 114 E4
Rendlesham Wlk MK41 39 C3
RENHOLD 39 E6
Renhold Lower Sch MK41 39 D6
Renhold Rd MK44 29 E1
Renshaw Cl LU2 117 E2
Repton Cl
– Bedford MK41 38 F4
– Luton LU3 115 F6
Repton Rd SG17 76 E4
Reston Path LU2 117 E2
Restormel Cl MK41 38 F5
Retreat The LU5 114 F1
Reynes Cl MK43 72 D7
Reynes Dr MK43 37 A8
Reynolds SG6 90 F1
Reynolds Cl
– Bedford MK41 38 A2
– Biggleswade SG18 67 A7
– Wharley End MK43 58 E2
Reynolds Ct PE19 22 D6
Rhineland Way MK41 38 D6
Ribble Way MK41 38 C6
Ribocon Way LU4 115 B7
Richards Cl LU1 123 B6
Richard's Cres SG18 65 A4
Richards Ct LU1 123 B5
Richbell Ct MK40 38 B1
Richmond Cl PE19 22 F1
Richmond Ct LU2 116 F1
Richmond Hill LU2 116 F2
Richmond Hill Sch LU2 116 E2
Richmond Rd
– Bedford MK40 38 D1
– Leighton Buzzard LU7 111 C6
– Westoning MK45 95 E6
Rickyard Cl LU2 117 B3
Rickyard The SG6 91 C1
Riddy La LU3 116 C5
Ride The LU6 120 B6
Ridge Ave AL5 130 E4
Ridge Ct LU2 117 A1
Ridgeley Dr LU7 111 C5
Ridge Rd MK42 49 B2
Ridgeway
– Harpenden AL5 130 E4
– Kensworth LU6 127 E8
– St Neots PE19 22 F3
Ridgeway Ave LU5 114 D2
Ridgeway Bsns Pk The SG19 53 E8
Ridgeway Dr LU5 114 E1
Ridgeway Sch MK42 49 C2
Ridgeway The
– Bedford MK41 39 A4
– Blunham MK44 53 E8
– Flitwick MK45 84 E4
– Potton SG19 56 A7
Ridgewood Dr AL5 130 E4
Ridgewood Gdns AL5 130 E4
RIDGMONT 82 E5

Ridgmont Lower Sch MK43 .... 82 F4
Ridgmont Rd MK43 .... 82 D4
Ridgmont Sta MK43 .... 82 C7
Ridgmount St MK42 .... 50 B6
Ridgway MK17 .... 81 B6
Ridgway Rd
  Brogborough MK43 .... 71 C1
  Luton LU2 .... 116 F1
Ridings The
  Luton LU3 .... 116 C1
  Markyate AL3 .... 128 E6
Riglen Cl MK43 .... 72 C3
Ringmer Ct LU2 .... 117 C3
RINGSHALL 126 B1
Ringshall Rd HP4 .... 126 B3
Ringwood Cl MK42 .... 49 F4
Ringwood Rd LU2 .... 116 D7
Ripley Rd LU4 .... 115 C1
Ripon Cl MK42 .... 49 E6
Ripon Ct SG18 .... 67 A4
Risborough Ct MK41 .... 38 F1
Risborough Rd MK41 .... 38 F1
RISELEY 11 A2
Riseley CE Lower Sch MK44 .... 10 F2
Riseley Rd MK44 .... 12 A3
Risings The MK41 .... 39 A3
Rival Houses MK45 .... 97 C4
Riverbanks Cl AL5 .... 131 C4
River Ct SG5 .... 100 F4
Riverfield Dr MK41 .... 39 B1
Riverford Cl AL5 .... 131 B4
Riverhead Gdns SG19 .... 54 B6
River Hill AL3 .... 129 B2
River La MK44 .... 27 B4
River Mead SG5 .... 100 C4
Rivermead Ct SG18 .... 78 E5
River Rd PE19 .... 22 C4
River Row MK43 .... 26 B3
Riverside
  Leighton Buzzard LU7 .... 111 A8
  Shefford SG17 .... 77 C3
Riverside Cl MK42 .... 50 A4
Riverside Est AL5 .... 131 C4
Riverside Gdns SG18 .... 78 E5
Riverside Rd LU3 .... 116 A5
Riverside View MK44 .... 27 A5
Riversmead PE19 .... 22 E6
River St MK40 .... 50 B8
River Terr
  St Neots, Eynesbury PE19 .... 22 E4
  St Neots PE19 .... 22 E5
Riverview Way MK42 .... 49 C4
River Way LU3 .... 115 E5
Robert Allen Ct 3 LU1 .... 123 E6
Robert Bloomfield Mid Sch SG17 .... 77 B2
Robert Bruce Mid Sch MK42 .... 49 D4
Robert Hunt Gdns SG19 .... 54 B4
Robert Peel Lower Sch SG19 .... 54 C8
Robert Saunders Ct SG6 .... 101 E4
Roberts Cl PE19 .... 22 B2
Roberts Dr MK43 .... 60 E2
Robertson Cnr LU6 .... 120 F4
Robin Cl
  Flitwick MK45 .... 84 E2
  Sandy SG19 .... 42 B1
Robin Ct AL5 .... 131 B4
Robin Hill MK41 .... 38 C4
Robins Folly MK44 .... 28 E7
Robinson Cres LU5 .... 95 F2
Robinson Ct SG19 .... 44 B3
Robinson Pool★ MK40 .... 38 B2
Robinswood LU2 .... 116 B5
Robinswood Cl LU7 .... 102 F2
Rochdale Cl 6 LU1 .... 123 E4
Rochester Ave LU2 .... 117 C4
Rochester Mews LU7 .... 110 F7
Rochford Dr LU2 .... 117 E2
Rockbeck Cl MK42 .... 49 E4
Rock Cl LU7 .... 110 D6
Rockingham Ct NN10 .... 8 A8
Rockingham Wlk MK41 .... 39 B5
Rock La LU7 .... 110 D7
Rockleigh Ct LU7 .... 110 E7
Rockley Rd LU1 .... 123 A7
Rodean Ct MK40 .... 38 D2
Rodeheath LU4 .... 115 D3
Rodney Ct LU4 .... 114 F3
Roebuck Cl LU1 .... 123 B6
Roe Cl SG5 .... 90 E5
Roecroft Lower Sch SG5 .... 90 F6
Roedean Cl LU2 .... 117 D3
Roe End La AL3 .... 128 E4
Roe Gn PE19 .... 22 B5
Roff Ave MK41 .... 38 B2
Rogate Rd LU2 .... 117 C5
Roise Ct 3 MK40 .... 38 B1
Roise St MK40 .... 38 B1
Roman Ct 2 LU5 .... 114 B4
Roman Gdns LU5 .... 114 B4
Roman Paddock MK43 .... 25 A6
Roman Rd
  Barton-le-C MK45 .... 97 D3
  Luton LU2 .... 115 D4
Roman View SG19 .... 54 D6
Roman Way
  Flitwick MK45 .... 84 F4
  Irchester NN29 .... 7 B7
  Markyate AL3 .... 128 E6
Romany Cl SG6 .... 101 C6
Romney Ct PE19 .... 22 C5

Romney Wlk MK41 .... 38 B3
Romsey Way MK42 .... 50 C3
Ronald Cl MK42 .... 49 E2
Rondini Ave LU3 .... 116 B3
Rookery Dr LU2 .... 116 E6
Rookery Rd MK44 .... 31 F8
Rookery The SG19 .... 42 C2
Rookery Wlk SG17 .... 78 B2
Rooksmead MK41 .... 38 C4
Rook Tree Cl SG5 .... 91 A6
Rook Tree La SG5 .... 91 A6
Rooktree Way MK45 .... 64 A1
Roosevelt Ave
  Leighton Buzzard LU7 .... 111 B8
  Shefford SG17 .... 77 C1
ROOTHAM'S GREEN 30 A7
Ropa Cl LU2 .... 110 F7
Rope Wlk MK42 .... 50 C7
Ropkins Cl MK45 .... 95 F6
Rosamond Rd MK40 .... 38 E1
Rosata Cl SG17 .... 76 E4
Rosebay Cl MK45 .... 84 D3
Rosebery Ave
  Harpenden AL5 .... 130 F1
  Leighton Buzzard LU7 .... 110 E7
Rosebery Ct LU7 .... 110 F7
Roseby Way MK41 .... 51 A8
Rose Cotts SG15 .... 90 A4
Rose Ct
  Eaton Bray LU6 .... 119 D6
  Irchester NN29 .... 7 B8
  St Neots PE19 .... 22 C4
Rosedale LU5 .... 114 E5
Rosedale Cl LU3 .... 115 C7
Rosedale Way MK42 .... 49 E4
Rose La SG18 .... 67 A6
Rosemary Dr MK43 .... 36 F2
Rosemont Cl SG6 .... 101 E6
Rose Wlk
  Ampthill MK45 .... 73 E1
  Houghton Regis LU5 .... 114 E6
  Toddington LU5 .... 105 F5
Rose Wood Cl LU2 .... 116 F3
Roslyn Way LU5 .... 114 A5
Ross Cl LU1 .... 123 B6
Rossendale Wlk 1 MK41 .... 39 B4
Rossfold Rd LU3 .... 115 D8
Rosslyn Cres LU3 .... 116 C5
Rossway LU1 .... 123 B1
Rothamsted Ave AL5 .... 131 A1
Rothamsted Ct AL5 .... 131 A1
Rothbury Cl SG19 .... 42 C2
Rothbury Ct 3 MK41 .... 39 B4
Rotheram Ave LU1 .... 123 B5
Rother Cl MK41 .... 38 D5
Rother Field LU2 .... 117 D3
Rotherwood Cl LU6 .... 113 E1
Rothesay Rd LU1 .... 123 D7
Rothsay Gdns MK40 .... 38 D1
Rothsay Pl MK40 .... 50 D8
Rothsay Rd MK40 .... 50 D8
Rothschild Rd LU7 .... 110 E8
Rotten Row MK44 .... 10 F2
Roundel Dr LU7 .... 111 D5
Roundfield Ave AL5 .... 131 D3
ROUND GREEN 116 F2
Roundmead MK41 .... 39 A2
Roundwood Cl SG4 .... 101 C2
Roundwood Ct AL5 .... 130 D3
Roundwood Gdns AL5 .... 130 E2
Roundwood La AL5 .... 130 D3
Roundwood Park Sch AL5 .... 130 E2
Roundwood Pk AL5 .... 130 E3
Roundwood Prim Sch AL5 .... 130 E2
Rousbury Rd MK43 .... 61 C1
Rowallan Dr MK41 .... 38 E5
Rowan Cl LU1 .... 123 B7
Rowan Cres
  Biggleswade SG18 .... 67 B7
  Letchworth SG6 .... 101 E7
Rowan Ct SG19 .... 54 B8
Rowan Gdns SG19 .... 44 C5
Rowans The
  Kempston MK42 .... 49 B3
  Silsoe MK45 .... 86 C4
Rowan Way MK43 .... 71 A8
Rowelfield LU2 .... 117 C1
Rowington Cl LU2 .... 117 E2
Rowlandson Way MK41 .... 38 A3
Rowlands The SG18 .... 67 C4
Rowland Way SG6 .... 101 F6
Rowley Furrows LU5 .... 110 E8
Rowney Forest Walk★ SG17 .... 76 F5
Roxhill Rd MK43 .... 59 F3
ROXTON 31 F1
Roxton CE Lower Sch MK44 .... 31 E2
Roxton Rd
  Great Barford MK44 .... 41 B7
  Roxton MK44 .... 31 E4
Royal Ct PE19 .... 22 B4
Royal Oak Cl SG18 .... 66 F7
Royal Oak La SG5 .... 99 D4
Royal Wlk LU6 .... 121 C7
Royce Cl LU6 .... 120 F7
Royce Ct PE19 .... 22 D5
Royce Rd MK43 .... 58 D3
Roydon Cl LU4 .... 115 A4
Royle Gdns MK42 .... 50 F5
Royston Cl SG19 .... 56 A7
Royston Rd SG7 .... 91 F1
Royston St SG19 .... 56 A7
Rudyard Cl LU4 .... 115 D2
Rueley Dell Rd LU2 .... 109 D2
Ruffs Furze MK43 .... 36 F7

Runfold Ave LU3 .... 116 A5
Runham Cl LU4 .... 115 A4
Runley Rd LU1 .... 122 F7
Runnalow SG6 .... 101 E7
Rushall Gn LU2 .... 117 E2
Rushbrook Cl MK45 .... 73 F1
RUSHDEN 8 D8
Rushden Hospl NN10 .... 8 B8
Rushden Rd
  Milton Ernest MK44 .... 27 B5
  Newton Bromswold NN10 .... 9 C7
  Wymington NN10 .... 8 A6
RUSHMERE 102 F4
Rushmoor Sch MK40 .... 37 F2
Rushmore Cl LU1 .... 122 E4
Rusper Gn LU2 .... 117 D3
Russel Ctr MK45 .... 84 E2
Russell Ave MK40 .... 50 E8
Russell Cl LU6 .... 127 E8
Russell Cres MK45 .... 85 D8
Russell Ct PE19 .... 22 F6
Russell Dr
  Ampthill MK45 .... 84 F7
  Willington MK44 .... 40 C1
Russell Gr MK45 .... 73 B2
Russell Lower Sch MK45 .... 84 F8
Russell Rd LU5 .... 105 F5
Russell Rise LU1 .... 123 D6
Russell St
  Luton LU1 .... 123 D6
  St Neots PE19 .... 22 E6
  Woburn Sands MK17 .... 81 C4
Russell Way
  Leighton Buzzard LU7 .... 111 D7
  Wootton MK43 .... 60 F6
Russet Cl
  Bedford MK41 .... 38 C7
  Stewartby MK43 .... 61 B1
Russett Cl MK45 .... 73 E1
Ruthin Cl LU1 .... 123 D5
Rutland Cres LU2 .... 124 A7
Rutland Ct LU2 .... 124 A7
Rutland Gdns SG19 .... 54 D7
Rutland Hall LU2 .... 124 A7
Rutland Rd MK40 .... 50 A8
Ryans Cl LU2 .... 116 F1
Rycroft Ave PE19 .... 22 F6
Rydal Cres SG18 .... 67 A4
Rydal Way LU3 .... 115 F5
Ryder Ave SG5 .... 100 D3
Ryder Way SG5 .... 100 D3
Rye Cl
  Harpenden AL5 .... 131 B4
  Leighton Buzzard LU7 .... 111 D7
  Rushden NN10 .... 8 C8
  St Neots PE19 .... 22 F1
Rye Cres MK42 .... 52 A6
Ryecroft Way LU2 .... 117 A4
Ryefield LU3 .... 108 A1
Rye Hill
  Harpenden AL5 .... 131 B4
  2 Luton LU2 .... 116 D1
Rye The LU6 .... 119 C8
Rylands Heath LU2 .... 117 F2
Rylands Mews LU7 .... 111 A6
Ryley Cl SG16 .... 89 B5
Ryswick Rd MK42 .... 50 A5
Ryton Cl
  Bedford MK41 .... 38 C6
  Luton LU1 .... 123 B6

S

Sabel Cl SG18 .... 67 C3
Sacombe Gn LU3 .... 108 B1
Sacred Heart Jun & Inf Schs LU2 .... 117 A3
Saddle Cl MK41 .... 37 C7
Saddlers Mews AL3 .... 128 E5
Sadleirs Gn MK17 .... 81 B5
Saffron Cl
  Arlesey SG15 .... 90 A7
  10 Bedford MK40 .... 38 D7
  Luton LU2 .... 116 D7
Saffron Ct SG18 .... 67 A5
Saffron Hill SG6 .... 101 E6
Saffron Rd SG18 .... 67 A5
Saffron Rise LU6 .... 119 E6
St Alban Rd MK40 .... 38 D2
St Albans Cl MK45 .... 84 E4
St Albans Rd AL5 .... 131 B1
St Aldates Ct LU3 .... 116 B3
St Andrew's Ave AL5 .... 130 F1
St Andrews CE Lower Sch SG18 .... 66 F6
St Andrews Cl
  Biggleswade SG18 .... 66 F5
  Flitwick MK45 .... 84 E4
  Leighton Buzzard LU7 .... 111 A7
St Andrew's Cl
  Ampthill MK45 .... 73 E1
  Slip End LU1 .... 123 B1
St Andrews Ct SG18 .... 66 F6
St Andrews La
  Houghton Regis LU5 .... 114 C5
  Kimbolton PE28 .... 6 F4
St Andrews Mews LU3 .... 116 A4
St Andrews Rd MK40 .... 38 C2
St Andrew's Sch MK40 .... 38 C2
St Andrew's St
  Biggleswade SG18 .... 66 F6
  Leighton Buzzard LU7 .... 111 A8
St Andrew's Way SG18 .... 78 F8
St Andrews Wlk LU1 .... 123 C1
St Ann's Rd LU2 .... 123 F7

St Anselm Pl PE19 .... 22 E6
St Augustine Ave LU3 .... 116 C3
St Augustine's Rd MK40 .... 38 D2
St Bede's RC Mid Sch MK40 .... 38 A1
St Bernard's Cl LU3 .... 116 A3
St Catherines Ave LU3 .... 116 B3
St Christopher Sch SG6 .... 101 F3
St Christopher's Cl LU5 .... 114 F1
St Christopher's Lower Sch LU5 .... 114 F2
St Cuthberts St 3 MK40 .... 50 C8
St Cuthbert's St 1 MK40 .... 50 C8
St David's Way LU1 .... 114 D6
St Dominics Sq LU4 .... 114 F4
St Edmond Rd MK40 .... 38 D2
St Ethelbert Ave LU3 .... 116 C4
St Faiths Cl SG4 .... 101 B1
St Francis Coll LU1 .... 101 E4
St Francis Ct SG17 .... 77 C3
St Francis Way SG17 .... 77 C2
St George's Cl
  Leighton Buzzard LU7 .... 111 B8
  Toddington LU5 .... 105 F6
St George's Lower Sch LU7 .... 111 B8
St George's Rd MK40 .... 38 C2
St George's Sch LU5 .... 131 B2
St Georges Sq 10 LU1 .... 123 E7
St Georges Tower SG19 .... 45 F3
St Gregory's RC Mid Sch MK40 .... 37 E1
St Helena Rd MK42 .... 50 D5
St Helenas Gdn MK42 .... 50 B8
St Hilda's Sch AL5 .... 130 F3
St Ives Cl LU3 .... 116 B3
St James CE Lower Sch MK40 .... 37 C1
St James Cl
  Houghton Regis LU5 .... 114 E4
  Pulloxhill MK45 .... 96 E8
St James St MK40 .... 38 C2
St James Rd AL5 .... 131 B4
St James' Rd LU3 .... 116 B3
St James's Ct AL5 .... 131 B3
St John Cl LU1 .... 123 B5
St John Rigby RC Lower Sch MK41 .... 38 E2
St John's Ave MK42 .... 49 D3
St Johns Cl LU7 .... 112 C5
St Johns Cl LU1 .... 123 B5
St Johns Ctr MK42 .... 50 C7
St John's Homes MK42 .... 49 D4
St John's Rd
  Arlesey SG15 .... 90 A4
  Moggerhanger MK44 .... 53 C7
St John's Sch MK42 .... 49 F6
St John's St
  Bedford MK42 .... 50 C7
  Biggleswade SG18 .... 67 A7
  Kempston MK42 .... 49 D3
St John's Terr MK42 .... 50 C7
St John's Wlk MK42 .... 49 D3
St Joseph's Cl LU3 .... 116 A4
St Joseph's RC Inf Sch LU3 .... 116 A4
St Joseph's RC Jun Sch LU3 .... 116 A4
St Joseph's RC Lower Sch MK40 .... 49 E8
St Katharines Cl SG5 .... 100 D3
St Kilda Rd LU4 .... 114 A4
St Lawrence Lower Sch NN10 .... 8 A5
St Lawrences Ave LU3 .... 116 C3
St Lawrence Wlk NN10 .... 8 B5
St Leonard's Ave MK42 .... 50 C6
St Leonard's Cl LU7 .... 103 B3
St Leonards St MK42 .... 50 B6
St Leonard's-Heath and Reach Lower Sch LU7 .... 103 A5
St Leonard's St MK42 .... 50 C6
St Leonard's Way LU6 .... 119 E1
St Loyes St 17 MK40 .... 50 B8
St Luke's Cl LU2 .... 115 E2
St Margaret of Scotland RC Inf Sch LU1 .... 123 B5
St Margaret of Scotland RC Jun Sch LU1 .... 123 B5
ST MARGARET'S 132 C3
St Margarets Ave LU3 .... 116 B3
St Margarets Cl
  Lidlington MK43 .... 72 C3
  Streatley LU3 .... 108 A6
St Margarets Gdns SG18 .... 67 C4
St Marks Cl MK45 .... 84 F4
St Mark's Cl MK40 .... 50 D1
St Martin de Porres RC Prim Sch LU4 .... 115 A4
St Martin's Ave LU2 .... 116 F2
St Martins Bsns Ctr MK42 .... 51 B5
St Martins AL5 .... 131 C4
St Martins Way MK42 .... 51 A5
St Mary's SG19 .... 44 E5
St Mary's Ave SG5 .... 90 F6
St Marys Cl
  Bletsoe MK44 .... 17 C1
  Elstow MK42 .... 50 A5
  Marston Moretaine MK43 .... 72 D7
St Mary's Cl
  Felmersham MK43 .... 26 C8
  Letchworth SG6 .... 101 F2
  Pirton SG5 .... 99 D4
  Tebworth LU7 .... 105 C2
St Mary's (Clophill) Lower Sch MK45 .... 75 D1
St Marys Ct PE19 .... 22 C3

St Mary's Ct
  8 Dunstable LU6 .... 121 B8
  Leighton Buzzard LU7 .... 110 D8
  St Neots PE19 .... 22 E4
St Mary's Gate LU6 .... 121 B8
St Mary's Glebe LU6 .... 119 E4
St Mary's Nursing Ctr LU1 .... 123 D7
St Mary's Pl SG17 .... 88 B5
St Mary's RC Lower Sch LU1 .... 121 F6
St Marys Rd MK43 .... 60 F7
St Mary's Rd LU1 .... 123 F7
St Mary's St
  Bedford MK40 .... 50 C7
  St Neots PE19 .... 22 E4
St Mary's (Stotfold) Lower Sch SG5 .... 91 A6
St Mary's Way LU7 .... 110 E8
St Mary's Wlk SG19 .... 43 C3
St Mathews Cl MK42 .... 49 D3
St Matthews Cl LU2 .... 123 E8
St Matthew's Inf Sch LU2 .... 116 E1
St Mellion Dr MK42 .... 49 B7
St Michaels Ave LU5 .... 114 B4
St Michael's Cres LU3 .... 116 D3
St Michael's Cts MK40 .... 38 D2
St Michael's Rd MK40 .... 38 D2
St Mildreds Ave LU3 .... 116 C3
St Minver Rd MK40 .... 38 D2
St Monicas Ave LU3 .... 116 B3
ST NEOTS 22 B6
St Neots Com Coll PE19 .... 22 E2
St Neots L Ctr PE19 .... 22 E2
St Neots Mus★ PE19 .... 22 E5
St Neots Rd
  Bedford MK41 .... 40 B3
  Bolnhurst MK44 .... 19 E4
  Little Barford PE19 .... 33 F7
  Sandy SG19 .... 54 B8
  St Neots PE19 .... 22 D4
St Nicholas CE Prim Sch
  Harpenden AL5 .... 131 A1
  Letchworth SG6 .... 91 C1
St Nicholas Cl MK17 .... 94 F5
St Nicholas Ct AL5 .... 130 F3
St Ninian's Ct 7 LU2 .... 123 D8
St Olam's Cl LU3 .... 116 B6
St Olives SG6 .... 90 E6
St Pauls Cl MK45 .... 84 F3
Saint Paul's Gdns LU1 .... 123 E5
St Paul's Rd
  Bedford MK40 .... 49 F7
  Luton LU1 .... 123 E5
St Paul's Sq MK40 .... 50 B8
St Peters Ave SG15 .... 90 A7
St Peter's Cl MK45 .... 84 F4
St Peters Ct MK44 .... 16 C4
St Peters Cl SG19 .... 56 A8
St Peters Rd LU5 .... 121 C8
St Peter's St MK40 .... 38 C1
St Saviours's Cres LU1 .... 123 D6
St Swithuns Lower Sch SG19 .... 54 C7
St Swithun's Way SG19 .... 54 D7
St Thomas More RC Prim Sch SG6 .... 101 D4
St Thomas More RC Sch MK41 .... 38 C6
St Thomas's Cl LU2 .... 117 A4
St Thomas's Rd LU2 .... 117 A4
St Vincent Gdns LU4 .... 115 D3
St Vincents MK17 .... 81 C4
St Vincent's RC Lower Sch LU5 .... 114 C4
St Winifreds Ave LU3 .... 116 C3
Salcombe Cl MK40 .... 38 E1
Sale Dr SG7 .... 91 F1
SALFORD 70 C3
Salford Rd
  Aspley Guise MK17 .... 81 D7
  Brogborough MK43 .... 82 B8
Salisbury Ave AL5 .... 131 A1
Salisbury Cl SG5 .... 90 D2
Salisbury Ho 8 MK40 .... 38 A1
Salisbury Rd
  Baldock SG7 .... 91 F1
  Flitwick MK45 .... 84 E4
  Harpenden AL5 .... 131 D3
  Luton LU1 .... 123 D6
Salisbury St MK41 .... 38 B2
Sallowsprings LU6 .... 120 F2
SALPH END 39 B6
Saltash Cl MK40 .... 38 E2
Saltdean Cl LU2 .... 117 D4
Salters Way LU6 .... 113 F3
Saltfield Cres LU4 .... 115 C4
Sambar Cl PE19 .... 22 B5
Sampshill Rd MK45 .... 95 E5
Samuel Whitbread Com Coll SG17 .... 77 B7
Sandalwood Cl LU3 .... 116 B7
Sandell Cl LU2 .... 116 F2
Sanderling Cl SG6 .... 101 E8
Sanders Cl MK42 .... 49 D6
Sanderson Cl MK45 .... 95 E6
Sanderson Rd MK45 .... 95 E6
Sanders Way MK41 .... 60 F8
Sandfields Rd PE19 .... 22 F5
Sandford Rise SG19 .... 54 A7
Sandgate Rd LU4 .... 115 D2
Sandhill Cl MK45 .... 73 A1
Sandhills LU7 .... 103 B1
Sandhouse Cotts LU7 .... 103 D8
Sandhurst Pl MK42 .... 50 B6
Sandhurst Rd MK42 .... 50 B6

Sand La
Barton-le-C MK45 . . . . 97 B8
Biggleswade SG18 . . . . . . 67 A6
Northill SG18 . . . . 53 E1
Sandy SG19 . . . . 54 E7
Sandland Cl LU6 . . . . . . 114 A1
Sandleford Dr MK42 . . . . 50 E3
Sandon Cl SG19 . . . . 54 C8
Sandpiper Cl SG18 . . . . . 66 F5
Sandpiper Way LU7 . . . . 111 C5
Sand Rd MK45 . . . . 85 E3
Sandringham Dr LU5 . . . . 114 E4
Sandringham Rd MK45 . . . 84 D1
SANDY 54 C6
Sandy Acres MK45 . . . . . 74 B1
Sandy Bsns Pk SG19 . . . . 42 C2
Sandye La MK44 . . . . 11 D8
Sandye Place Mid Sch
SG19 . . . . 54 C6
Sandy La
Chicksands SG17 . . . . 76 E5
Husborne Crawley MK17 . . 82 D3
Leighton Buzzard LU7 . . . 103 A3
Tilbrook PE28 . . . . 6 C6
Woburn Sands MK17 . . . . . 81 B2
Sandy Rd
Bedford MK41 . . . . 39 A1
Everton SG19 . . . . 43 B2
Potton SG19 . . . . 55 E7
Willington MK44 . . . . 52 E8
Sandy Sta SG19 . . . . 54 D6
Sandy Upper Sch & Com Coll
SG19 . . . . 42 A1
Sandy View SG18 . . . . . . 67 B8
Sanfoin Rd LU4 . . . . 115 A4
San Remo Rd MK17 . . . . . 81 F4
Santa Pod Raceway NN29 . 15 C6
Santingfield N LU1 . . . . . 123 B6
Santingfield S LU1 . . . . . 123 B6
Sarum Rd LU3 . . . . 115 F4
Saturn Cl LU7 . . . . 111 D8
Saucey Ave
Harpenden AL5 . . . . 131 B3
Harpenden AL5 . . . . 131 C1
Saucey Wood AL5 . . . . . 131 E4
Saucey Wood La AL5 . . . 131 E6
Saucey Wood Prim Sch
AL5 . . . . 131 D4
Saunders Gdns MK40 . . . 49 E4
Saunders Piece MK45 . . . 84 F8
Savannah Cl MK42 . . . . . 49 F5
Savernake Wlk MK41 . . . . 39 B3
Savile's Cl PE19 . . . . 22 D7
Saville Ct MK44 . . . . 41 A5
Sawtry Cl LU3 . . . . 116 A6
Sawyers Cres NN9 . . . . . . 3 B8
Sax Ho SG6 . . . . 90 E1
Saxon Cl
Dunstable LU6 . . . . 120 E8
Flitwick MK45 . . . . 84 F4
Harpenden AL5 . . . . 131 C4
Letchworth SG6 . . . . 90 F1
Roxton MK44 . . . . 31 E1
Saxon Cres MK45 . . . . . . 97 C4
Saxon Ctr MK42 . . . . 49 E4
Saxon Pl PE19 . . . . 22 F4
Saxon Pool & L Ctr SG18 . 67 C5
Saxon Rd LU3 . . . . 116 C2
Saxon Rise NN29 . . . . 7 C8
Saxons LU7 . . . . 111 C7
Saxtead Ct LU2 . . . . 117 C1
Saywell Rd LU2 . . . . 117 B1
SCALD END 28 C3
Scawsby Cl LU6 . . . . 113 E4
Sceptre Sch LU5 . . . . . . 114 E1
School Cl SG19 . . . . 44 D5
School Hill NN29 . . . . 7 B8
School House Mews
MK45 . . . . 86 C4
School La
Bolnhurst MK44 . . . . 19 D4
Carlton MK43 . . . . 25 A2
Colmworth MK44 . . . . . . 20 A2
Eaton Bray LU6 . . . . 119 F6
Great Barford MK44 . . . . . 41 A5
Greenfield MK45 . . . . 85 C2
Husborne Crawley MK43 . . 82 B4
Irchester NN29 . . . . 7 A8
Luton LU4 . . . . 115 D4
Podington NN29 . . . . 7 F2
Roxton MK44 . . . . 31 F2
Shefford SG17 . . . . 77 B2
Southill SG18 . . . . 65 D1
Stewartby MK43 . . . . 61 C1
St Neots, Eynesbury PE19 . 22 E4
St Neots PE19 . . . . 22 C2
Wootton MK43 . . . . 60 F7
School Rd NN29 . . . . 7 A8
Scotchbrook Rd MK43 . . . 72 D7
Scotfield Ct LU2 . . . . 117 D3
Scott Ave MK42 . . . . 51 A4
Scott Ct LU5 . . . . 114 C1
Scott Lower Sch MK41 . . . 38 C5
Scott Rd LU3 . . . . 115 C7
Seabrook LU4 . . . . 115 B3
Seaford Cl LU2 . . . . 117 C3
Seal Cl LU4 . . . . 115 D3
Seamons Cl LU6 . . . . . . 121 D6
Sears Ct SG17 . . . . 78 B3
Sears The LU6 . . . . 119 B5
Seaton Dr MK40 . . . . 38 E2
Seaton Rd LU4 . . . . 115 F3
Sebright Rd AL3 . . . . 128 E5
Sedbury Ct LU3 . . . . 116 A6
SEDDINGTON 54 C3
Sedgwick Rd LU4 . . . . . . 115 B7
Seebohm Cl SG5 . . . . . . 100 C1

Segenhoe Cl MK43 . . . . . 82 F5
Selbourne Rd LU4 . . . . . 116 A2
Selina Cl LU3 . . . . 115 C7
Selsey Dr LU2 . . . . 117 C6
Selsey Way MK41 . . . . . . 38 E2
Sergeants Way MK41 . . . . 39 C2
Servite Ho LU4 . . . . 115 C3
Setchel PE19 . . . . 22 C6
Severalls The LU2 . . . . . . 117 B3
Severn Cl MK45 . . . . 84 D2
Severn Way MK41 . . . . . . 38 C5
Severn Wlk LU7 . . . . 103 B3
SEVICK END 29 E1
SEWELL 113 D2
Sewell La LU6 . . . . 113 D3
Sexton Ave MK42 . . . . . . 50 A4
Seymour Ave LU1 . . . . . . 123 F5
Seymour Rd LU1 . . . . . . 123 F5
Shackleton Lower Sch
MK42 . . . . 50 C5
Shady Wlk PE19 . . . . 22 F5
Shaftesbury Ave
Bedford MK40 . . . . 50 E8
St Neots PE19 . . . . 22 F5
Shaftesbury Dr SG5 . . . . . 90 C3
Shaftesbury Rd LU4 . . . . 116 B1
Shakespeare Dr SG18 . . . 66 C8
Shakespeare Rd
Bedford MK40 . . . . 38 A1
Harpenden AL5 . . . . 131 C1
Luton LU4 . . . . 115 B2
St Neots PE19 . . . . 22 C3
Shaldon Ct MK40 . . . . . . 38 E2
Shanklin Cl LU3 . . . . 116 A7
Shannon Cl
Lower Stondon SG16 . . . . 88 F2
Sandy SG19 . . . . 42 B1
Shannon Ct SG19 . . . . . . 54 C7
Shannon Pl SG19 . . . . . . 55 F7
SHARNBROOK 16 B4
Sharnbrook Ct MK44 . . . . 16 D3
Sharnbrook John Gibbard
Lower Sch MK44 . . . . . . 16 D4
Sharnbrook Rd MK44 . . . . 16 B7
Sharnbrook Upper Sch &
Com Coll MK44 . . . . 16 B3
Sharnside MK44 . . . . 16 D4
Sharose Ct AL3 . . . . 128 E5
Sharp Cl MK45 . . . . 86 B7
SHARPENHOE 96 E2
Sharpenhoe Clappers★
LU3 . . . . 107 F7
Sharpenhoe Rd
Barton-le-C MK45 . . . . 97 B2
Streatley LU3 . . . . 107 F7
Sharples La LU3 . . . . . . 116 B8
Sharps Way SG4 . . . . . . 101 A1
Shay La PE28 . . . . 5 B4
Shearley Cl MK40 . . . . . . 38 C7
Sheepcote Cres LU7 . . . . 103 A5
Sheepfold Hill MK45 . . . . 84 F3
Sheeplands MK41 . . . . . . 39 B3
SHEEPLANE 92 C2
Sheeplane MK17 . . . . 92 C2
SHEEPTICK END 72 A3
Sheeptick End MK43 . . . . 72 B3
Sheepwalk Cl SG19 . . . . . 56 B6
Sheep Wlk SG18 . . . . 67 A2
Sheffield Cl SG19 . . . . . . 56 A7
SHEFFORD 77 D3
Shefford Bsns Pk SG17 . . 77 D3
Shefford Ind Pk SG17 . . . 77 C2
Shefford Lower Sch SG17 . 77 B2
Shefford Rd
Clifton SG17 . . . . 77 F7
Clophill MK45 . . . . 76 A2
Meppershall SG17 . . . . . . 88 C7
Sheldon Ct MK17 . . . . . . 81 B4
Sheldon La MK44 . . . . . . 20 B3
Shelley Ct [16] AL5 . . . . . 131 B1
Shelley Pl PE19 . . . . 22 C6
Shelley Rd LU4 . . . . 115 B2
Shelton Ave LU5 . . . . . . 105 F4
Shelton Cl LU5 . . . . 105 F4
Shelton Ct MK44 . . . . 40 F5
Shelton Lower Sch MK43 . 60 C3
Shelton Rd
Hitchin SG5 . . . . 100 F2
Leighton Buzzard LU7 . . . 103 A1
Shelton Way LU2 . . . . . . 117 A3
Shenley Cl LU7 . . . . 103 B3
Shenley Hill Rd LU7 . . . . 103 C3
Shepherd Rd LU4 . . . . . . 114 F4
Shepherds Cl LU5 . . . . . . 95 F1
Shepherds Mead
Hitchin SG5 . . . . 100 F2
Leighton Buzzard LU7 . . . 103 A1
Shepherds Way AL5 . . . . 130 D4
Sherborne Ave LU2 . . . . 116 D6
Sherbourne Way MK41 . . . 38 F5
Sherd Cl LU3 . . . . 115 F7
Sheridan Rd LU3 . . . . . . 116 C1
Sheriden Cl LU6 . . . . 114 B1
Sheringham Cl LU2 . . . . . 116 C7
Sherwood SG6 . . . . 101 F8
Sherwood Rd LU4 . . . . . 116 A2
Sherwood Terr NN29 . . . . . 7 B8
Sherwood Wlk MK41 . . . . 39 B3
SHILLINGTON 87 F1
Shillington Lower Sch
SG5 . . . . 87 E1
Shillington Rd
Gravenhurst MK45 . . . . . . 87 D4
Lower Stondon SG5 . . . . . 88 C2
Meppershall SG17 . . . . . . 88 C3
Pirton SG5 . . . . 99 B5
Shingle Cl LU3 . . . . 116 A8
Ship Rd LU7 . . . . 110 E6

Shirdley Rd PE19 . . . . . . 22 F4
Shire La MK16 . . . . 58 E4
Shires The LU2 . . . . 116 D1
Shirley Rd LU1 . . . . 123 C8
Shortcroft Ct MK45 . . . . . 97 B2
Shortmead St SG18 . . . . . 66 F6
Short Path LU5 . . . . 114 C6
Shorts Ave MK42 . . . . . . 51 A2
Short St MK40 . . . . 49 F7
SHORTSTOWN 51 A2
Shortstown Lower Sch
MK42 . . . . 50 F2
Shrubbery La MK44 . . . . . 29 C4
Shuttleworth Collection Mus
The★ SG18 . . . . 65 D6
Shuttleworth College
SG18 . . . . 65 D5
Shuttleworth Ct SG18 . . . 67 A6
Shuttleworth Ct Bsns Pk
MK41 . . . . 39 C3
Shuttleworth Rd MK41 . . . 39 C3
Sibley Cl LU2 . . . . 117 B3
Sibton Abbey MK42 . . . . . 51 B8
Sidings The MK42 . . . . . . 50 C6
Sidmouth Cl MK40 . . . . . 38 E2
Sidney Rd
Ampthill MK45 . . . . 84 E7
Bedford MK40 . . . . 37 F1
Signal Cl SG16 . . . . 89 B3
Silbury Ct MK45 . . . . 86 B5
Silecroft Rd LU2 . . . . 124 B8
SILSOE 86 B4
Silsoe CE Lower Sch
MK45 . . . . 86 C4
Silsoe Rd
Flitton MK45 . . . . 85 E3
Maulden MK45 . . . . 85 E7
Silverbirch Ave SG5 . . . . 90 F8
Silverbirches LU1 . . . . . . 81 B2
Silver Birches The MK42 . 49 F2
Silverburn Cl MK41 . . . . . 39 C5
Silverdale St MK42 . . . . . 49 F4
Silver End Rd MK45 . . . . . 63 F1
Silver St
Bedford MK40 . . . . 50 B8
Great Barford MK44 . . . . . 40 F5
Guilden Morden SG8 . . . . 69 F4
Luton LU1 . . . . 123 E7
Stevington MK43 . . . . 36 B7
St Neots PE19 . . . . 22 F4
Silverweed PE19 . . . . 22 C5
Simdims MK43 . . . . 59 A1
Simpkin Cl LU4 . . . . 115 D2
Simpkins Dr MK45 . . . . . 97 C4
Simpson Cl LU4 . . . . 115 D2
Singer Cl MK42 . . . . 49 D2
Singer Way MK42 . . . . . . 49 D2
Singlets La AL3 . . . . 129 C2
Sir Herbert Janes Village
The LU4 . . . . 115 D4
Sir John Lawes Sch AL5 . 131 C3
Sir Malcolm Stewart Homes
MK43 . . . . 73 C8
Sir Peter's Way HP4 . . . . 126 E6
Skegsbury La SG4 . . . . . 125 F1
Skelton Cl LU3 . . . . 108 B1
Skerne Pas MK41 . . . . . . 38 C7
Skimpot Rd LU4 . . . . 115 A1
Skipton Cl SG19 . . . . 54 C8
Skua Cl LU4 . . . . 115 A5
Slade The
Clapham MK41 . . . . 37 E6
Clophill MK45 . . . . 75 C1
Wrestlingworth SG19 . . . . 57 B3
SLAPTON 118 D6
Slapton La LU6 . . . . 118 F6
Slate Hall LU3 . . . . 107 A4
Slater Cl MK42 . . . . 49 D5
Slate Row MK44 . . . . 16 A8
Slickett's La LU6 . . . . 119 F3
SLIP END 123 B1
Slip End Lower Sch LU1 . . 123 B1
Slip The MK43 . . . . 26 C7
Slype The AL5 . . . . 131 F6
Smithcombe Cl MK45 . . . 97 C3
Smiths Lane Mall [5] LU1 . 123 E7
Smiths Sq [6] LU1 . . . . . 123 E7
Snagge Ct MK43 . . . . . . 60 E1
SNAILSWELL 100 E6
Snailswell La SG5 . . . . . . 100 E6
Snowdrop Wlk SG18 . . . . 67 C5
Snowford Cl [1] LU3 . . . . 116 A7
Snow Hill LU4 . . . . 74 B1
Sollershott E SG6 . . . . . . 101 E4
Sollershott Hall SG6 . . . . 101 E4
Sollershott W SG6 . . . . . . 101 E4
Solway N LU3 . . . . 116 A4
Solway Rd S LU3 . . . . . . 116 A3
Someries Jun & Inf Sch
LU2 . . . . 117 C3
Someries AL5 . . . . 131 C4
Somersby Cl LU1 . . . . . . 123 E5
Somerset Ave LU2 . . . . . 117 A1
Somerton Cl MK41 . . . . . 39 A5
Sopwith Way MK42 . . . . . 51 A2
Sorrel Cl LU3 . . . . 116 B8
Souberie Ave SG6 . . . . . 101 C5
Soulbury Rd LU7 . . . . . . 110 D7
SOULDROP 16 B8
Souldrop Rd MK44 . . . . . 16 B8
Southampton Gdns LU3 . . 107 D1
South Ave MK42 . . . . 50 C1
Southbridge St SG17 . . . . 77 C3
Southcott Lower Sch
LU7 . . . . 110 D7
Southcott Village LU7 . . . 110 D6
Southcourt Ave LU7 . . . . 110 D6
Southcourt Rd LU7 . . . . . 110 D7

Southcroft Ho LU7 . . . . . 110 D7
Southdown Rd AL5 . . . . . 131 B1
South Dr MK42 . . . . 51 A2
South Drift Way LU1 . . . . 123 B5
SOUTH END 50 B5
South End Jun & Inf Schs
NN10 . . . . 8 B8
South End La LU1 . . . . . . 119 B4
Southern Ave SG16 . . . . . 89 C3
Southern Rise LU2 . . . . . 130 F7
Southern Way
Letchworth SG6 . . . . 101 E8
Studham LU6 . . . . 127 C4
Southfield Jun & Inf Schs
LU4 . . . . 114 F4
Southfields
Letchworth SG6 . . . . 90 F1
Roxton MK44 . . . . 31 E1
Shefford MK42 . . . . 77 E2
Southfields Ct SG17 . . . . 77 E2
Southfields Rd
Dunstable LU6 . . . . 121 D6
Kempston MK42 . . . . 50 A3
Southgate Ct [3] AL5 . . . . 131 A2
South Gr NN10 . . . . 8 B5
SOUTHILL 77 E8
Southill Lower Sch SG18 . 65 D1
Southill Rd
Broom SG18 . . . . 66 B2
Cardington MK44 . . . . 51 E2
Shefford MK42 . . . . 77 E2
Southland Rise SG18 . . . . 78 F5
Southlands Lower Sch
SG18 . . . . 67 B4
South Luton High Sch
LU1 . . . . 123 F5
Southlynn Ho [2] LU2 . . . 123 F8
South Rd
Luton LU1 . . . . 123 D6
Sandy SG19 . . . . 54 B7
South St
Leighton Buzzard LU7 . . . 111 B7
St Neots PE19 . . . . 22 E5
Southview MK44 . . . . 40 F5
South View
Biggleswade SG18 . . . . . . 67 A5
Letchworth SG6 . . . . 101 F5
Southview Gdns LU7 . . . . 111 B6
Southview Rd AL5 . . . . . . 131 D3
Southville Rd MK42 . . . . . 50 B5
Southway MK42 . . . . 50 E5
South Wlk SG18 . . . . 67 B7
Southwood Rd LU5 . . . . . 121 E6
Sovereign Pk LU4 . . . . . . 115 F1
Sovereigns Quay MK40 . . 50 B8
Sowerby Ave LU2 . . . . . . 117 C3
Spa Ho PE19 . . . . 22 F5
Sparhawke MK42 . . . . . . 91 A1
Sparkesfield SG16 . . . . . . 78 D2
Sparrow Cl LU4 . . . . 115 A4
Sparrow Hall Bsns Pk
LU6 . . . . 119 D3
Spayne Cl LU3 . . . . 116 B8
Spear Cl LU3 . . . . 115 E6
SPEEDWELL 93 C5
Speedwell Cl LU3 . . . . . . 116 A8
Spencer Cl
Potton SG19 . . . . 56 A8
St Neots PE19 . . . . 22 D6
Spencer Ct LU7 . . . . 103 B1
Spencer Ho SG5 . . . . 90 F6
Spencer Rd
Luton LU3 . . . . 116 C2
Sandy SG19 . . . . 54 D6
Spencers The MK44 . . . . 41 A5
Spenser Ct MK40 . . . . . . 37 F1
Spenser Rd
Bedford MK40 . . . . 37 F1
Harpenden AL5 . . . . 131 C1
Spensley Rd MK45 . . . . . 95 C5
Spinney Bglws LU7 . . . . . 118 C6
Spinney Cres LU6 . . . . . . 120 F8
Spinney La MK17 . . . . . . 81 F4
Spinney Rd
Chawston MK44 . . . . 31 E4
Luton LU3 . . . . 115 D7
Spinney The
Bedford MK41 . . . . 39 B3
Harpenden AL5 . . . . 130 E4
Spire Harpenden Hospl
(private) AL5 . . . . 131 A4
Spitfire Rd SG17 . . . . 77 C1
Spittlesea Rd LU2 . . . . . . 124 C7
Spoondell LU6 . . . . 121 A6
Spratts La LU6 . . . . 121 C5
Spreckley Cl SG16 . . . . . 89 B5
Spriggs Cl MK41 . . . . 37 C7
Springbrook PE19 . . . . . . 22 F4
Spring Cl
Ampthill MK45 . . . . 84 F7
Biggleswade SG18 . . . . . . 67 B6
Springfield SG18 . . . . 68 C5
Springfield Ave MK42 . . . 49 E4
Springfield Cres AL5 . . . . 131 B5
Springfield Ct LU7 . . . . . 110 E7
Springfield Ctr MK42 . . . . 49 F3
Springfield Dr MK43 . . . . 36 E3
Springfield Lower Sch
MK42 . . . . 49 F3
Springfield Rd
Dunstable LU6 . . . . 120 D5
Leighton Buzzard LU7 . . . 110 E7
Luton LU3 . . . . 116 C6
Rushden NN10 . . . . 8 D8
Springfield Way MK43 . . . 59 C2
Spring Gdns MK42 . . . . . 50 A4
Spring Gr
Sandy SG19 . . . . 54 B7
Woburn Sands MK17 . . . . 81 B5

Spring Hill MK44 . . . . 13 A3
Spring La
Stagsden MK43 . . . . 48 C6
Yelden MK44 . . . . 4 A3
Spring Pl [5] LU1 . . . . . . 123 D6
Spring Rd
Clifton SG17 . . . . 78 A2
Harpenden AL5 . . . . 130 A4
Kempston MK42 . . . . 50 A4
Letchworth SG6 . . . . 101 E4
Letchworth SG6 . . . . 101 E6
Springshott SG6 . . . . 101 E5
Springside LU7 . . . . 110 E7
Spruce Wlk MK42 . . . . . . 49 F3
Spurcroft LU3 . . . . 108 C1
Square The
Aspley Guise MK17 . . . . . 81 E4
Dunstable LU6 . . . . 121 B8
Wilstead MK45 . . . . 62 E4
Squires Cl SG17 . . . . 77 E2
Squires Ct PE19 . . . . 22 C4
Squires Pl LU5 . . . . 105 F6
Squires Rd
Marston Moretaine MK43 . . 72 D7
Wootton MK43 . . . . 60 F6
Stables The
Ampthill MK45 . . . . 84 F7
Leighton Buzzard LU7 . . . 110 D6
Stadium Est The LU4 . . . . 115 B1
Stafford Rd MK42 . . . . . . 50 A6
STAGSDEN 48 A7
Stagsden Rd MK43 . . . . . 36 E2
Staines Sq LU6 . . . . 121 C7
Stainmore Rd MK41 . . . . 39 C4
Stakers Ct AL5 . . . . 131 B1
STANBRIDGE 112 C5
Stanbridge Crossing
LU7 . . . . 112 B3
STANBRIDGEFORD 112 C5
Stanbridge Lower Sch
LU7 . . . . 112 D5
Stanbridge Rd
Billington LU7 . . . . 111 F1
Leighton Buzzard LU7 . . . 111 C6
Tilsworth LU7 . . . . 112 F5
Totternhoe, Lower End
LU6 . . . . 112 E2
Totternhoe, Stanbridgeford
LU7 . . . . 112 E3
Stanbridge Road Terr
LU7 . . . . 111 B6
Stanbridge View MK45 . . . 97 C2
Stanbridge Way MK45 . . . 74 B8
Stanbrook Way MK44 . . . . 4 A3
Stancliffe Rd MK41 . . . . . 38 E3
Standalone Farm★ SG6 . . 101 D7
Standalone Warren MK45 . 76 C7
STANFORD 78 A7
Stanford La SG17 . . . . . . 78 A3
Stanford Rd
Clifton SG17, SG18 . . . . . . 78 A5
Luton LU2 . . . . 117 A1
Shefford SG17 . . . . 77 D3
Southill SG18 . . . . 77 F8
Stanhope Rd MK41 . . . . . 38 E4
Stanley Cl MK45 . . . . 96 E8
Stanley Livingstone Ct [2]
LU1 . . . . 123 D6
Stanley Rd LU3 . . . . 108 A5
Stanley St
Bedford MK42 . . . . 38 B2
Kempston MK42 . . . . 49 F4
Luton LU1 . . . . 123 D6
Stanmore Cres LU3 . . . . 115 F4
Stannard Way MK44 . . . . 51 C6
Stanton Rd
Kempston MK42 . . . . 49 D5
Luton LU4 . . . . 115 C1
Stapleford Rd LU2 . . . . . 117 C4
Stapleton Rd MK42 . . . . . 50 D4
STAPLOE 21 D6
Staploe Rd MK44 . . . . . . 21 D2
Starey Cl MK43 . . . . 27 B5
Starling Cl SG19 . . . . 42 B1
Starling Way MK41 . . . . . 38 C4
Startpoint LU1 . . . . 123 C7
Stately Ct LU3 . . . . 116 D1
Statham Cl LU3 . . . . 108 B1
Station App AL5 . . . . 131 B1
Station Cres MK43 . . . . . 72 B3
Station Ct SG19 . . . . 55 F7
Station Par SG6 . . . . 101 F6
Station Pl SG6 . . . . 101 F6
Station Rd
Ampthill MK45 . . . . 84 C7
Ampthill MK45 . . . . 84 D7
Arlesey SG15 . . . . 90 A4
Baldock SG7 . . . . 91 F1
Bedford MK42 . . . . 50 C7
Biggleswade SG18 . . . . . . 67 A5
Blunham MK44 . . . . 41 D2
Cheddington LU7 . . . . 118 A1
Dunstable LU5 . . . . 121 D8
Flitwick MK45 . . . . 84 F2
Gamlingay SG19 . . . . 44 F4
Hargrave NN9 . . . . 1 B7
Harlington SG5 . . . . 95 F1
Harpenden AL5 . . . . 131 C2
Irchester NN29 . . . . 7 C8
Langford SG18 . . . . 78 F6
Leighton Buzzard LU7 . . . 110 E7
Letchworth SG6 . . . . 101 F6
Lidlington MK43 . . . . 72 B3
Lower Stondon SG16 . . . . 88 F3
Luton, High Town LU1 . . . 123 E8

Station Rd *continued*
Luton, Leagrave LU4 . . . **115** E5
Marston Moretaine MK43 . . **72** D6
Oakley MK43 . . . . **37** A8
Potton SG19. . . . . **55** F7
Ridgmont MK43 . . . . **82** E6
Sandy SG19 . . . . **54** D6
Sharnbrook MK44 . . . . . . **16** E4
Stanbridge LU7 . . . . **112** D4
Tempsford SG19 . . . . **42** C8
Tilbrook PE28 . . . . **6** C7
Toddington LU5 . . . . **106** A7
Turvey MK43 . . . . **35** B5
Willington MK44 . . . . **52** C8
Woburn Sands MK17 . . . . **81** B5
Station Sq MK45 . . . . . . **84** E2
Station Way SG6 . . . . . . **101** E6
Staughton Pl PE19 . . . . . **22** C4
Staughton Rd MK44 . . . . **12** D5
Staunton Ho MK17 . . . . . **92** F7
Staveley Rd
Dunstable LU6 . . . . **121** B6
Luton LU4 . . . . **115** C1
Stephens Gdns LU2 . . . . **117** A3
Stephenson Cl LU7 . . . . **110** E6
Stephenson Lower Sch
MK42 . . . . **50** E5
STEPPINGLEY **84** A3
Steppingley Hospl MK45 . . **84** A4
Steppingley Rd MK45 . . . **84** D3
Steppingley Road Trad Est
MK45 . . . . **84** E3
Steppingstone Pl LU7 . . . **111** B6
Stepping Stones The
LU3 . . . . **115** E5
Stevenson Ct PE19 . . . . . **22** D6
STEVINGTON **36** B7
Stevington Windmill★
MK43 . . . . **36** C6
STEWARTBY **61** C1
Stewartby Sta MK43 . . . . **61** B1
Stewartby Way MK43 . . . . **61** C1
Stewart Cl MK43 . . . . . . **37** A4
Stewart Clark Ct 4 LU4 . . **114** A1
Stewart Ct MK43 . . . . . . **61** A6
Stewart Rd AL5 . . . . **131** B2
Stileman Way MK44 . . . . **16** C4
Stile The LU7 . . . . **103** A5
Stillitters Farm Rd MK43 . **70** E8
Stipers Cl LU6 . . . . **121** E5
STIPERS HILL **121** D5
Stirling Cl SG19 . . . . **42** B1
Stirling Rd MK42 . . . . . . **51** A2
Stivers Way LU5 . . . . . . **95** F3
Stockbridge Rd SG17 . . . **78** C3
Stockdale LU5 . . . . **105** F5
Stocker Way PE19 . . . . . **22** E2
Stockgrove Ctry Pk★
LU7 . . . . **102** F7
Stockgrove Park Ho LU7 **102** F8
Stockholm Way LU3 . . . . **115** E8
Stockingstone Rd LU2 . . **116** E3
Stocks La SG19 . . . . **44** D5
Stockton End SG19 . . . . . **54** D8
Stockwell Farm Rd LU5 . . **106** C4
Stockwood Craft Mus &
Gdns★ LU1 . . . . **123** D4
Stockwood Cres LU1 . . . . **123** D6
Stockwood Ct 16 LU1 . . . **123** D6
Stockwood Pk★ LU1 . . . . **123** D3
Stoke Albany Mews 3
MK40 . . . . **38** A1
Stoke Rd LU7 . . . . **102** D1
Stokesay Cl MK41 . . . . . **39** A4
Stondon Lower Sch SG16 . **88** E3
Stondon Rd SG17 . . . . . . **88** C4
Stondon Transport
Museum★ SG16 . . . . . . **88** F3
Stone Cl MK40 . . . . **49** B6
Stonecroft SG19 . . . . . . **54** D7
Stonedale Rd MK42 . . . . **50** A4
Stonehenge Works Sta★
LU7 . . . . **103** E3
Stonehill JMI Sch SG6 . . . **90** E1
Stoneland Ave SG18 . . . . **67** A7
Stoneleigh Cl LU3 . . . . . **116** B7
Stoneley SG6 . . . . **90** F1
Stonemason Cl AL5 . . . . **131** A3
Stone Pine Rd MK43 . . . . **36** D3
Stonesdale LU3 . . . . **115** C4
Stoneways Cl LU4 . . . . . **115** C6
Stoneygate Rd LU4 . . . . **115** D3
Stonnells Cl SG6 . . . . . . **101** F8
STOPSLEY **117** B4
STOPSLEY COMMON **116** F6
Stopsley Com Prim Sch
LU2 . . . . **117** A4
Stopsley High Sch LU2 . . **116** F4
Stopsley Way LU2 . . . . . **117** A3
Stormont Rd SG5 . . . . . . **100** F1
STOTFOLD **90** E7
STOTFOLD COMMON **79** E1
Stotfold Ho SG5 . . . . . . **90** F6
Stotfold Rd
Arlesey SG5 . . . . **90** C7
Hinxworth SG7 . . . . **80** C1
Letchworth SG4, SG6 . . **101** C4
Letchworth SG6 . . . . . . **90** D1
Stour Way MK41 . . . . . . **38** C5
Stow Rd PE28 . . . . **6** F5
Strafford Cl LU5 . . . . . . **95** F1
Strand The MK45 . . . . . . **75** C1
Strangers Way LU4 . . . . **115** C4
STRATFORD **54** E4
Stratford Cl LU5 . . . . . . **105** E6

Stratford Ct MK40 . . . . . . **38** A2
Stratford Pl PE19 . . . . . . **22** C3
Stratford Rd
Luton LU4 . . . . **116** B1
Sandy SG19 . . . . **54** E5
Stratford Way MK43 . . . . **60** D2
Strathconon Rd MK41 . . . **39** C4
Strathmore Ave
Hitchin SG5 . . . . **100** F1
Luton LU1 . . . . **123** F6
Strathmore Ct SG5 . . . . **100** F1
Strathmore Inf Sch SG5 . **100** E2
Strathmore Wlk LU1 . . . **123** F6
Stratton Bsns Pk SG18 . . **67** D3
Stratton Ct 7 SG18 . . . . . **67** A6
Stratton Gdns LU2 . . . . **116** D4
Stratton Mews LU7. . . . . **111** B7
Stratton Pk SG18 . . . . . . **67** D4
Stratton Upper Sch & Com
Coll SG18 . . . . **67** C6
Stratton Way
Bedford MK41 . . . . **39** D3
Biggleswade SG18 . . . . **67** B7
Strawberry Field LU3 . . . **115** E7
Strawberry Hill Cotts MK44 **9** F2
Straw Plait SG15 . . . . . . **89** F4
STREATLEY **108** C3
Streatley Rd LU3 . . . . . . **107** D4
Street Cl MK43. . . . . **25** A3
Streetfield Mid Sch LU5 . **121** F6
Stringfellow Cl MK43. . . . **58** E2
Stronnell Cl LU2 . . . . . . **117** B3
Stuart Cl SG19 . . . . **42** B8
Stuart Pl 8 LU1 . . . . . . **123** D7
Stuart St
Dunstable LU6 . . . . . . **114** A1
Luton LU1 . . . . **123** D7
Stubbs Cl LU5 . . . . **114** D5
STUDHAM **127** C4
Studham CE Lower Sch
LU6 . . . . **127** B4
Studham La
Dagnall HP4 . . . . **126** D4
Whipsnade LU6 . . . . . . **127** A7
Studio Ho MK40 . . . . **50** A8
Studley Rd
Luton LU3 . . . . **116** D1
Wootton MK43 . . . . **60** E1
Sturgeon's Rd SG4 . . . . **101** B2
Styles Cl LU2 . . . . **117** C2
Sudbury Rd LU4 . . . . . . **115** B6
Sudeley Wlk MK41 . . . . . **39** B4
Suffield Ho 1 PE19 . . . . **22** F5
Suffolk Cl LU4 . . . . **115** A3
Suffolk Rd LU5 . . . . **121** D5
Sugden Ct LU6 . . . . **121** A8
Sullivan Cl SG17 . . . . . . **77** D3
Summerfield Dr MK43. . . . **60** F6
Summerfield Rd LU1 . . . **122** F8
Summerleys LU6 . . . . . . **119** E4
Summers Lo SG6 . . . . . **101** D5
Summers Rd LU2 . . . . . **117** C1
Summer St
Leighton Buzzard LU7 . . **111** B7
Slip End LU1 . . . . **123** C1
Summer Wlk AL3 . . . . . . **128** C5
Sunbeam Rd MK42 . . . . . **49** D1
Sunbower Ave LU6. . . . . **113** E3
Suncote Ave LU6. . . . . . **113** E3
Suncote Cl LU6 . . . . **113** E3
Sundew Cl
Bedford MK42 . . . . **50** F4
St Neots PE19 . . . . **22** B6
Sundon Hills Ctry Pk★
LU3 . . . . **107** C6
Sundon La LU5 . . . . **114** C5
Sundon Lower Sch LU3 . . **107** B4
SUNDON PARK **115** B8
Sundon Park Jun Sch
LU3 . . . . **115** C8
Sundon Park Rd LU3 . . . **115** C7
Sundon Rd
Chalton LU4 . . . . **107** A2
Harlington LU5 . . . . . . **107** A8
Houghton Regis LU5 . . . **114** D7
Streatley LU3 . . . . **107** F5
Sundown Ave LU5 . . . . . **121** D7
Sunrise Est LU2 . . . . . . **117** A2
Sunset Dr LU2 . . . . **116** F3
Sun St
Biggleswade SG18 . . . . **66** F7
Potton SG19. . . . . **56** A7
Surrey St LU1 . . . . **123** E6
Surrey Street Prim Sch
LU1 . . . . **123** F6
Sursham Ct AL3 . . . . . . **128** C5
Sussex Cl LU4 . . . . **114** F4
Sussex Pl LU2 . . . . **117** D2
Sutherland Pl LU1 . . . . . **123** D5
SUTTON **56** A3
Sutton Ave SG18 . . . . . . **67** B6
Sutton CE Lower Sch
SG19 . . . . **56** A3
Sutton Cross Roads SG19. **55** E4

Sutton Gdns
Caddington LU1 . . . . . . **122** D3
Luton LU2 . . . . **115** D6
Sutton Mill Rd SG19. . . . . **55** F6
Sutton Rd
Eyeworth SG18 . . . . . . **68** F8
Potton SG19. . . . . **56** C7
Sutton SG19. . . . . **56** B3
Swaden SG19 . . . . **54** E6
Swaffield Cl MK41 . . . . . **73** E1
Swale Path MK41 . . . . . . **38** C7
Swales Dr LU7 . . . . **111** D6
Swallow Cl
Flitwick MK45 . . . . **84** D2
Luton LU4 . . . . **115** A4
Shefford SG17 . . . . **77** C2
Swallow Crest SG19. . . . . **42** B2
Swallowfield
Upper Caldecote SG18 . . **66** D8
Wyboston MK44. . . . . . . **31** F6
Swallowfield Lower Sch
MK17 . . . . **81** B5
Swamsholme Garden Ct
SG19 . . . . **54** C7
Swanbourne Cl SG18. . . . **67** B5
Swan Cl LU7. . . . . **119** A1
Swan Ct
Dunstable LU6 . . . . . . **121** B8
Milton Ernest MK44. . . . . **27** C5
Swan La
Guilden Morden SG8 . . . **69** F4
Sandy SG19 . . . . **54** B7
Swan Mead LU4 . . . . . . **115** B4
Swannells Wood LU6. . . . **127** C4
Swansholme Gdns SG19. . **54** C6
Swansons LU6 . . . . **119** F3
Swanston Grange LU4. . . **115** B2
Swasedale Rd LU3 . . . . . **116** A6
Swift Cl
Bedford MK41 . . . . **38** B4
Flitwick MK45 . . . . **84** D2
Letchworth SG6. . . . . . **101** E8
Sandy SG19 . . . . **42** C2
Swifts Green Cl LU2. . . . . **117** B5
Swifts Green Rd LU2 . . . . **117** B5
Swinburne Ave SG5 . . . . **100** C1
Swindale MK41 . . . . **38** D6
SWINESHEAD **11** D8
Swiss Garden★ SG18 . . **65** D6
Sworder Cl LU3 . . . . . . **107** F1
Sybil's Way MK45 . . . . . . **74** A7
Sycamore Cl
Biggleswade SG18 . . . . **67** A8
Flitwick MK45 . . . . **84** F2
Luton LU3 . . . . **107** C1
Potton SG19. . . . . **55** F7
Sycamore Rd LU5 . . . . . **114** C6
Sycamores The
Baldock SG7 . . . . **91** E1
Kempston MK42 . . . . . . **49** F3
Silsoe MK45 . . . . **86** B5
St Neots PE19 . . . . **22** F6
Sylam Cl LU3 . . . . **115** E7
Sylmond Gdns NN10 . . . . . **8** A7
Sylvester St LU7 . . . . . . **103** A5
Symonds Cl MK43. . . . . . **36** F1
Syon Path MK45 . . . . **84** D1

T

Tabor Cl LU5 . . . . **95** F2
Taddy Cl SG18 . . . . **66** B8
Tadlow Rd SG19 . . . . **57** C3
Taft Pl SG17 . . . . **76** E2
Talbot Cl LU7 . . . . **111** A8
Talbot Rd
Bedford MK40 . . . . **38** E1
Luton LU2 . . . . **116** F1
Talbot Way SG6 . . . . **91** B1
Talisman Cl SG19 . . . . . . **42** B1
Tallents Cres AL5 . . . . . **131** D3
Tall Pines LU7 . . . . **102** F2
Tamar Rd MK41 . . . . **38** D5
Tamar Wlk LU2 . . . . **103** B3
Tameton Cl LU2 . . . . . . **117** F2
Tamworth Rd MK41 . . . . . **39** A5
Tancred Rd LU2 . . . . . . **117** A4
Tandys Cl
Pavenham MK43 . . . . . . **26** C4
Turvey MK43 . . . . **34** E5
Tanfield Gn LU2 . . . . . . **117** E1
Tanglewood AL5 . . . . . . **130** F2
Tannery La MK43 . . . . . . **36** E1
Tanqueray Ave MK45 . . . . **86** C8
Tansur Ct PE19 . . . . **22** F8
Tansy Cl
Bedford MK42 . . . . **50** F4
St Neots PE19 . . . . **22** B5
Tan Yd PE19 . . . . **22** E5
Tarnside Cl LU6. . . . . . . **121** B6
TARTLETT END. **71** B8
Taskers Row LU6 . . . . . . **119** F4
Taskers Row Cotts LU6 . . **119** F4
Taunton Cl MK41. . . . . . . **39** A5
Taunton Rd LU2 . . . . . . **117** B1
Tavistock Ave MK45. . . . . **84** D6
Tavistock Cl MK17 . . . . . **81** B6
Tavistock Cres LU1 . . . . **123** E5
Tavistock Ct PE19 . . . . . . **22** E6
Tavistock Pl MK40 . . . . . **38** B1
Tavistock St
Bedford MK40 . . . . **38** B1
Dunstable LU6 . . . . . . **114** A2
Luton LU1 . . . . **123** E6
Taylors Cl SG17 . . . . **88** B5
Taylors End MK45 . . . . . **74** B1

Taylor's Rd SG5 . . . . **80** A1
Taylor's Ride LU7 . . . . . **102** F2
Taylor St LU7 . . . . **123** F8
Teal Rd SG18 . . . . **66** F5
Teasel Cl
Rushden NN10 . . . . **8** C7
St Neots PE19 . . . . **22** C5
TEBWORTH **105** C2
Tebworth Rd
Tebworth LU7 . . . . **105** A1
Wingfield LU5 . . . . **105** E1
Tedder Ave SG16 . . . . . . **89** B5
Teesdale LU4 . . . . **115** C5
Telford Way
Bedford MK42 . . . . **51** B5
Luton LU1 . . . . **123** D8
Telmere Ind Est 16 LU1 . **123** E6
Telscombe Way LU2 . . . . **117** C3
Templars Way MK44 . . . . **16** E4
Temple Cl LU2 . . . . **116** E5
Temple Way MK45 . . . . . **84** E2
TEMPSFORD **42** B8
Tempsford Rd
Everton SG19 . . . . **42** E5
Sandy SG19 . . . . **42** A3
Sutton SG19. . . . . **43** C3
Tempsford SG19. . . . . . **41** F5
Tempsford St MK42 . . . . . **49** E4
Tenby Dr LU4 . . . . **115** F3
Tenby Mews LU4. . . . . . **115** E3
Tenby Way PE19 . . . . **22** F1
Tennyson Ave
Biggleswade SG18 . . . . **67** A5
Houghton Regis LU5 . . . **114** D4
Tennyson Ho LU1 . . . . . **123** E5
Tennyson Pl PE19 . . . . . . **22** D6
Tennyson Rd
Bedford MK40 . . . . **50** E8
Flitwick MK45 . . . . **84** D3
Harpenden AL5 . . . . . . **131** A2
Luton LU1 . . . . **123** E5
Tennyson Road Prim Sch
LU1 . . . . **123** E5
Tenth Ave LU3 . . . . **115** C7
Tenzing Gr LU1 . . . . . . **123** C6
Terrace The MK17 . . . . . **81** E5
Test Cl MK41 . . . . **38** D7
TETWORTH **43** F7
Tetworth Hill SG19. . . . . . **44** A8
Teversham Way PE19 . . . **22** C6
Tewkesbury Dr NN10 . . . . . **8** D8
Tewkesbury Rd MK42 . . . . **50** D3
Thames Cl MK45 . . . . . . **84** D2
Thames Ct LU3 . . . . **116** B3
Thames Ind Est LU6 . . . . **121** B8
Thatch Cl LU4 . . . . **114** F4
Thaxted Cl LU2 . . . . **117** F2
THE CITY **20** C3
The Furlong MK43 . . . . . **27** A1
The Granary SG15 . . . . . **90** A5
The Hawthorns MK45 . . . **84** E3
Thelby Cl LU3 . . . . **115** F6
Theobald Bsns Ctr SG4. . **101** A3
The Orchard
Barton-le-Clay MK45 . . . **97** A7
Houghton Conquest MK45. **74** A8
Therfield Wlk LU5 . . . . . **114** E6
The Rickyard MK43 . . . . **60** D2
Thetford Cl MK42 . . . . . . **49** F4
Thetford Gdns LU2 . . . . **116** E6
Theydon Ave MK17 . . . . . **81** B4
Thickthorn La MK45. . . . . **62** A3
Thinnings The MK45 . . . . **84** E3
Third Ave LU3 . . . . **115** D7
Thirlestone Rd LU4 . . . . **115** D1
Thirlmere Cl SG18 . . . . . **67** B4
Thirlmere Gdns MK45 . . . **84** E2
Thirlmere Rd MK42 . . . . . **49** C3
Thistle Rd LU1 . . . . **123** F7
Thistley La MK43. . . . . . . **36** E1
Thomas Johnson Lower Sch
MK43 . . . . **72** B3
Thomas St LU7 . . . . **103** A5
Thomas Whitehead CE Sch
LU5 . . . . **114** B5
Thompsons Cl LU3 . . . . **131** A1
Thompsons Mdw SG8 . . . **69** F4
Thomson Ave MK42 . . . . . **51** A2
Thor Dr MK41 . . . . **39** D3
THORN **113** E8
Thornage Cl LU2 . . . . . . **117** F2
Thornbridge Cl NN10 . . . . . **8** A8
Thornbury
Dunstable LU5 . . . . . . **114** F2
Harpenden AL5 . . . . . . **131** D1
Thornbury Ct LU5 . . . . . **114** C7
THORNCOTE GREEN **53** E4
Thorncote Rd SG18, SG19 . **53** E4
Thorneycroft Cl LU3 . . . . **115** F4
Thornhill Cl LU5 . . . . . . **114** D7
Thornhill Lower Sch
LU5 . . . . **114** D7
Thornhill Rd LU4 . . . . . . **115** D7
Thorn Rd LU5 . . . . **113** E6
Thorntondale 5 LU4 . . . . **115** C5
Thornton St MK42 . . . . . . **49** F5
Thorn View Rd LU5 . . . . **114** B5
Thorpe Cl MK40. . . . . . . **37** B1
Thorpe Way MK43 . . . . . **60** F8
Thrales Cl LU3 . . . . **115** E7
THRALES END. **127** D5
Thrales End Rd AL5 . . . . **130** C5
Thrapston Rd PE28 . . . . . . **6** F5
Threave Cl MK41 . . . . . . **38** F5

Three Closes SG5 . . . . . . **99** C4
Thresher Cl LU4 . . . . . . **114** F4
Threshers Ct LU7 . . . . . **111** D7
Thricknells Cl LU3 . . . . . **115** E7
Thrift Rd LU7 . . . . **103** A5
Thrift St NN29 . . . . **7** A7
Thrift View MK43 . . . . . . **59** C2
Thrupp End MK43 . . . . . . **72** B3
THURLEIGH. **18** C1
Thurleigh Airfield Bsns Pk
MK44 . . . . **17** F3
Thurleigh Lower Sch
MK44 . . . . **18** C2
Thurleigh Rd
Bolnhurst MK44 . . . . . . **19** C2
Milton Ernest MK44. . . . **27** D5
Ravensden MK44 . . . . . **28** E2
Thurlestone Cl MK40 . . . . **38** F1
Thurlow Cl LU4 . . . . **114** F4
Thurlow St 11 MK40 . . . . **50** B8
Thurne Way MK41 . . . . . . **38** D7
Tibbett Cl LU6 . . . . **121** D7
Tiberius Rd LU3 . . . . . . **115** F6
Tidbury Cl MK17 . . . . . . **81** A4
Tiddenfoot L Ctr LU7 . . . **110** E5
Tilbrook **6** B7
Tilbrook Rd PE28 . . . . **6** D6
Tilgate LU2 . . . . **117** D3
Tiller Ct LU7 . . . . **111** D7
TILSWORTH **112** F5
Tilsworth Rd LU7 . . . . . **112** D5
Timber La MK17 . . . . **92** F7
Timbers Ct AL5 . . . . **130** F2
Times Cl SG5 . . . . **100** D2
Timworth Cl LU2 . . . . . . **117** D1
Tindall Ave LU7 . . . . . . **103** B1
Tingey's Cnr SG18 . . . . . **54** E1
TINGRITH **94** F5
Tingrith Rd MK17 . . . . . . **94** D6
Tinker's Cnr MK43 . . . . . **48** E1
Tinkers Hill MK42 . . . . . . **51** A3
Tinsley Cl
Clapham MK41. . . . . . . **37** C7
Luton LU1 . . . . **123** B5
Tintagel Cl LU3 . . . . **116** B4
Tintagel Ct PE19 . . . . **22** F2
Tintagel Wlk MK41 . . . . . **39** B5
Tintern Abbey MK41 . . . . **51** A8
Tintern Cl AL5 . . . . **130** C4
Tipcat Cl MK42 . . . . **50** B4
Tippett Dr SG17 . . . . **77** D3
Titan Ct LU4 . . . . **115** F1
Titchfield Dr MK42 . . . . . **50** C3
Tithe Barn MK43 . . . . . . **26** C8
Tithe Barn Rd MK43 . . . . **60** F7
TITHE FARM **114** C6
Tithe Farm Cl SG18 . . . . **78** F7
Tithe Farm Lower Sch
LU5 . . . . **114** B6
Tithe Farm Rd LU5 . . . . **114** B6
Tithe Rd MK43 . . . . **48** E4
Tithe The MK43 . . . . **26** C8
Tiverton Rd MK40 . . . . . . **38** E2
TODDINGTON **105** E6
Toddington Manor★
LU5 . . . . **105** E8
Toddington Rd
Harlington LU5 . . . . . . **95** D2
Luton LU4 . . . . **115** C6
Tebworth LU7 . . . . **105** C3
Toddington St George
Lower Sch LU5 . . . . . . **105** F6
Toland Cl LU4 . . . . **115** C1
Tolkien Cl MK41 . . . . . . **39** E3
Tollers Mews PE19 . . . . . **22** E5
Tollfield PE28. . . . . **6** F4
Tollgate Cl MK43. . . . . . . **36** E1
Tomlinson Ave LU4 . . . . **114** F4
Tompions End SG18 . . . . **65** E8
TOP END
MK40 . . . . **10** F1
MK44 . . . . **13** B1
Top End MK43 . . . . **39** F6
Topham Ct PE19 . . . . **22** F7
Top Row MK44 . . . . **17** C1
Tornay Ct LU7 . . . . **118** D6
Torquay Dr LU4 . . . . . . **115** D4
Torre Abbey MK41 . . . . . **51** B8
Torridge Rise MK41 . . . . **38** C5
Torrington Cl SG19 . . . . . **55** F8
Totnes Cl MK40 . . . . **38** E1
TOTTERNHOE **120** B7
Totternhoe Knolls Nature
Reserve★ LU6 . . . . . . **120** B8
Totternhoe Lower Sch
LU6 . . . . **120** B7
Totternhoe Rd
Dunstable LU6 . . . . . . **120** E7
Eaton Bray LU6 . . . . . **119** D7
Tower Ct LU2 . . . . **117** A1
Tower Rd LU2 . . . . **124** A8
Tower Way LU2 . . . . . . **124** A8
Town Cl MK45 . . . . **62** E4
Town Farm Cl SG8 . . . . . **69** F4
Town Farm Ct SG16 . . . . **78** D1
Townfield Rd MK45 . . . . . **84** F1
Town Lot La MK43 . . . . . **26** B8
Town Meadow Dr SG17. . . **77** C3
Townsend Cl
Cranfield MK43 . . . . . . **71** A8
Harpenden AL5 . . . . . . **130** F1
Townsend Ctr The LU4 . . **114** B3
Townsend Farm Rd LU5 . **114** B3
Townsend Ind Est LU5. . . **114** B4
Townsend La AL5 . . . . . **130** F1
Townsend Rd AL5 . . . . . **131** A2
Towns End Rd MK44 . . . . **16** C4
Townsend Terr LU5 . . . . **114** A4

Town Shott MK45 . . . . 75 E1
Townside LU6 . . . . 119 F3
Townsley Cl LU1 . . . . 123 E6
Town The PE19 . . . . 13 E6
Townwell La NN29 . . . . .7 B8
Tracey Ct 15 LU1 . . . . 123 E6
Trafalgar Dr MK45 . . . . 84 E4
Trafalgar Rd PE19 . . . . 22 C5
Trailly Cl MK44 . . . . 4 A3
Trefoil Cl
  Luton LU4 . . . . 114 F4
  Rushden NN10 . . . . 8 C7
Trenchard Ave SG17 . . . . 76 D4
Trenchard La SG17 . . . . 76 E4
Trent Ave MK45 . . . . 84 D2
Trent Rd
  Bedford MK41 . . . . 38 D5
  Luton LU3 . . . . 116 B4
Trent Way LU7 . . . . 111 C5
Trescott Cl LU2 . . . . 117 E2
Trevor Dr MK43 . . . . 36 E2
Trevor St MK40 . . . . 38 A1
Trident Dr LU5 . . . . 114 E6
Triggs Way LU2 . . . . 117 E3
Trilley Fields MK45 . . . . 86 B8
Trimley Cl LU4 . . . . 115 B5
Tring Rd
  Dunstable LU6 . . . . 120 C4
  Dunstable LU6 . . . . 120 E7
Trinity Cl
  Biggleswade SG18 . . . . 66 F6
  Felmersham MK43 . . . . 26 C8
  Roxton MK44 . . . . 31 E2
Trinity Rd
  Bedford MK40 . . . . 49 F7
  Luton LU3 . . . . 116 A4
  Stotfold SG5 . . . . 90 F7
Tristram Rd SG4 . . . . 101 B2
Triumph Way MK42 . . . . 49 E2
Troon Cl MK41 . . . . 38 E5
Troon Gdns LU2 . . . . 116 E7
Trowbridge Gdns LU2 . . . . . 116 E3
Trow Cl MK45 . . . . 63 C7
Trowley Hill Rd AL3 . . . . 129 B1
Trowley Hts AL3 . . . . 129 B2
Truemans Rd SG5 . . . . 100 D2
Truman Pl SG17 . . . . 76 E2
Truncals LU1 . . . . 123 D6
Trunk Furlong Est MK17 . . 81 D6
Truro Gdns
  Flitwick MK45 . . . . 84 E4
  Luton LU3 . . . . 116 C5
Trust Cotts HP4 . . . . 126 A1
Tudor Cl
  Barton-le-C MK45 . . . . 97 C4
  Bedford MK40 . . . . 38 A1
  Bromham MK43 . . . . 36 F3
Tudor Ct
  Dunstable LU6 . . . . 114 A2
  Kimbolton PE28 . . . . .6 F5
  Leighton Buzzard LU7 . . . . 110 F7
Tudor Dr LU5 . . . . 114 E4
Tudor Rd LU3 . . . . 116 B2
Tudors The MK44 . . . . 20 B2
Tuffnells Way AL5 . . . . 130 D4
Tulip Cl SG18 . . . . 67 C5
Tulip Dr NN10 . . . . .8 B7
Tulip Tree Cl MK43 . . . . 36 C6
Tunstall Wlk MK41 . . . . 39 C3
Turnberry Wlk MK41 . . . . . 38 E5
Turner Cl LU5 . . . . 114 D5
Turner Rd PE19 . . . . 22 C6
Turners Cl AL5 . . . . 131 C4
Turners Rd N LU2 . . . . 117 A2
Turners Rd S LU2 . . . . 117 A2
Turner Way MK41 . . . . 38 A2
Turnham Dr LU7 . . . . 111 C5
Turnpike Cl LU6 . . . . 121 C6
Turnpike Cl MK17 . . . . 81 A5
Turnpike Dr LU3 . . . . 108 C1
Turnpike La SG5 . . . . 100 E3
Turnpike Rd MK43 . . . . 82 B3
Turnpike Way MK41 . . . . . . 39 B3
TURVEY 34 F6
Turvey Lower Sch MK43 . . 34 E6
Turvey Mill MK43 . . . . 34 D5
Turvey Rd
  Astwood MK16 . . . . 46 F6
  Carlton MK43 . . . . 24 E2
Tweedsmuir Rd MK41 . . . . . 38 F4
Twigden Ct LU3 . . . . 115 E5
Twinwood Arena MK41 . . . 27 E2
Twinwood Rd MK41 . . . . 37 C7
Twinwoods Bsns Pk MK44 27 E5
Twyford Dr LU2 . . . . 117 D1
Tyburn La
  Pulloxhill MK45 . . . . 96 D8
  Westoning MK45 . . . . 95 E6
Tydeman Cl MK41 . . . . 38 C7
Tylecote Cl MK43 . . . . 72 C7
Tylers AL3 . . . . 131 D1
Tylers Mead LU2 . . . . 116 E5
Tyne Cl MK45 . . . . 84 D2
Tyne Cres MK41 . . . . 38 C6
Tyne Rd SG19 . . . . 42 C2
TYRELLS RD 94 A6
Tythe Barn Cl MK45 . . . . . . 95 E6
Tythe Cl
  Flitwick MK45 . . . . 85 A2
  Sharnbrook MK44 . . . . 16 E3
Tythe Mews LU6 . . . . 119 E3
Tythe Rd LU4 . . . . 115 C6

U

Ullswater Cl
  Biggleswade SG18 . . . . 67 B4
  Flitwick MK45 . . . . 84 D2
  Kempston MK42 . . . . 49 E3
Ullswater Dr
  Bedford MK41 . . . . 49 E3
Ullswater Dr LU7 . . . . 110 C7
Ullswater Rd LU6 . . . . 121 B6
Ulverston Rd LU6 . . . . 121 A6
Underwood Cl LU3 . . . . 107 F1
Union Chapel Ho 1 LU1. 123 E6
Union St
  Bedford MK40 . . . . 38 A1
  Dunstable LU6 . . . . 114 A1
  Luton LU1 . . . . 123 E6
University Way SG18 . . . . . 58 D1
Univ of Bedfordshire
  Bedford MK41 . . . . 38 F1
  Luton LU1 . . . . 123 F7
Univ of Bedfordshire
(Lansdowne Campus)
  MK40 . . . . 38 A1
Univ of Bedfordshire,
  Putteridge Bury LU2 . . 117 D6
Unwin Cl SG6 . . . . 101 E4
Uplands
  Bedford MK41 . . . . 38 F4
  Luton LU3 . . . . 115 D8
Uplands Ct LU1 . . . . 123 E4
UPPER CALDECOTE 66 B7
Upper Coombe LU7 . . . . . . 110 E8
UPPER DEAN 5 A4
Upper George St LU1 . . . . 123 D7
UPPER GRAVENHURST . . . 87 D5
UPPER SHELTON 60 C3
Upper Shelton Rd MK43 . . 60 C3
UPPER STAPLOE 21 C4
UPPER STONDON 88 D4
Upperstone Cl SG5 . . . . 90 F6
UPPER SUNDON 107 A4
Upton Cl LU2 . . . . 116 D6
Upton Ct MK41 . . . . 38 C5
UPTON END 87 F2
Upton End Rd SG5 . . . . 87 F2
Upwell Rd LU2 . . . . 117 B2
Urban Hive LU1 . . . . 115 C7
Urban Way SG18 . . . . 67 A7
Ursula Taylor Lower Sch
  MK41 . . . . 37 E5
Ursula Taylor Wlk MK41 . 37 E5
Usher Cl MK42 . . . . 50 B7

V

Vadis Cl LU3 . . . . 115 E7
Valarian Cl PE19 . . . . 22 C6
Vale Cl AL5 . . . . 130 D4
Vale Cl MK43 . . . . 59 D2
Valence End LU6 . . . . 121 D6
Valentine Gdns PE28 . . . . . .6 F5
Valiant Cl LU5 . . . . 95 F1
Valley Cl
  Studham LU6 . . . . 127 B4
  Whipsnade HP4 . . . . 126 E7
Valley La AL3 . . . . 128 E1
Valley Rd
  Letchworth SG6 . . . . 101 D7
  Studham LU6 . . . . 127 B3
Valley Rise AL4 . . . . 131 F2
Vanbrugh Dr LU5 . . . . 114 D5
Vandyke Cl MK17 . . . . 81 B6
Vandyke Rd LU7 . . . . 103 C2
Vandyke Upper Sch & Com
  Coll LU7 . . . . 103 C1
Vanguard Cl MK42 . . . . 49 D6
Varna Cl LU3 . . . . 116 A3
Vaughan Rd
  Harpenden AL5 . . . . 131 B1
  Stotfold SG5 . . . . 90 E7
Vauxhall Rd LU1, LU2 . . . . 124 B5
Vauxhall Way LU2 . . . . 117 B1
Venetia Rd LU2 . . . . 117 A4
Ventnor Gdns LU3 . . . . 116 A7
Verey Rd LU5 . . . . 114 C2
Verne Dr MK45 . . . . 84 F8
Vernon Pl LU5 . . . . 114 B1
Vernon Rd LU1 . . . . 123 C8
Verulam Gdns LU3 . . . . . . 115 F6
Vespers Cl LU4 . . . . 115 A2
Vestry Cl LU1 . . . . 123 D7
Viaduct Cotts LU1 . . . . 130 F8
Vicarage Cl
  Arlesey SG15 . . . . 90 A8
  Langford SG18 . . . . 78 E8
  Ravensden MK44 . . . . 29 B1
  Shillington SG5 . . . . 98 F8
Vicarage Gdns
  Flamstead AL3 . . . . 129 B1
  Leighton Buzzard LU7 . . . . 110 E6
Vicarage Gn MK44 . . . . 18 C1
Vicarage Hill MK45 . . . . . . 84 E1
Vicarage La
  Podington NN29 . . . . 7 E2
  Wilstead MK45 . . . . 62 E3
Vicarage Rd
  Houghton Regis LU5 . . . . 114 B5
  Leighton Buzzard LU7 . . . . 110 E6
  Silsoe MK45 . . . . 86 C4
Vicarage St
  Luton LU1 . . . . 123 F7
  Woburn Sands MK17 . . . . . 81 C4
Vicarage Wlk PE19 . . . . 13 F6
Vicars Cl MK40 . . . . 49 C8
Vicars Wlk MK41 . . . . 39 B2
Viceroy Cl PE19 . . . . 22 A3

Viceroy Ct LU6 . . . . 121 C8
Victor Cl MK42 . . . . 51 A2
Victoria Cl
  Langford SG18 . . . . 78 E6
  Wrestlingworth SG19 . . . . 57 B4
Victoria Cotts LU5 . . . . 114 A6
Victoria Ct 5 SG18 . . . . . . 67 A6
Victoria Dr
  Houghton Conquest MK45 . 74 A8
  Stotfold SG5 . . . . 91 A5
Victoria Pl SG18 . . . . 67 A5
Victoria Rd
  Bedford MK42 . . . . 50 B6
  7 Harpenden AL5 . . . . . . 131 B1
  Leighton Buzzard LU7 . . . . 110 E6
  Shefford SG17 . . . . 77 D2
Victoria St
  Dunstable LU6 . . . . 114 A1
  Dunstable LU6 . . . . 121 D6
  Luton LU1 . . . . 123 E6
Victoria Terr LU7 . . . . 111 D7
Viking Gr MK42 . . . . 49 D6
Viking Ind Est MK41 . . . . . 39 D4
Villa Ct 5 LU2 . . . . 123 D8
Village Ct LU7 . . . . 110 D6
Village Rd MK43 . . . . 36 F3
Villa Park (Mobile Home Pk)
  MK43 . . . . 70 F7
Villa Rd LU2 . . . . 123 D8
Villiers Cl LU4 . . . . 115 D3
Vimy Ct LU7 . . . . 110 F7
Vimy Rd LU7 . . . . 110 F7
Vincent Rd LU4 . . . . 115 D5
Vinegar Hill SG19 . . . . 54 A3
Vines The SG5 . . . . 90 E6
Vineyard Way MK42 . . . . . . 49 E5
Violet Cl
  Bedford MK42 . . . . 50 F4
  Biggleswade SG18 . . . . 67 C4
Violets Cl MK16 . . . . 58 B6
Virginia Cl LU2 . . . . 116 F3
Viscount Cl LU3 . . . . 116 A5
Viscount Ct
  11 Luton LU2 . . . . 116 D1
  St Neots PE19 . . . . 22 B4
Voyce Way MK42 . . . . 50 D6
Vulcan St MK42 . . . . 50 C6
Vulcan Way PE19 . . . . 22 B1
Vyne Cl MK42 . . . . 49 D5

W

Waddesdon Cl LU2 . . . . 117 D2
Wadhurst Ave LU3 . . . . 116 C4
Wagstaffe Cl MK41 . . . . 38 E6
Walcot Ave LU2 . . . . 117 B1
Walcourt Rd MK42 . . . . 50 A5
Waldeck Rd LU3 . . . . 123 C8
Waldegrave Pk AL5 . . . . . . 131 D1
Waleys Cl LU5 . . . . 115 E8
Walgrave Rd LU5 . . . . 114 F2
Walkers Cl SG17 . . . . 77 C3
Walk House Cl MK43 . . . . . . 59 B1
Walkley Rd LU5 . . . . 114 B4
Wallace Dr LU6 . . . . 119 E6
Wallace Mews LU6 . . . . . . 119 E6
Wallace Way SG4 . . . . 101 A2
Waller Ave
  Luton LU5 . . . . 115 F2
  Luton LU4 . . . . 115 F3
Waller Street Mall 3
  LU1 . . . . 123 E7
Wallis Way MK42 . . . . 51 B4
Walmsley House Sch
  MK40 . . . . 38 D2
Walnut Acre LU5 . . . . 105 F6
Walnut Cl
  Biggleswade SG18 . . . . 66 F8
  Blunham MK44 . . . . 41 D3
  Bromham MK43 . . . . 36 D1
  Luton LU2 . . . . 117 B4
  Pavenham MK43 . . . . 26 B3
  Stotfold SG5 . . . . 90 F6
Walnut Gr MK43 . . . . 72 B3
Walnuts The LU7 . . . . 103 B2
Walnut Tree Rd SG5 . . . . . . 99 D3
Walnut Way SG5 . . . . 100 E4
Walnut Wlk MK42 . . . . 49 F3
Walsingham Cl LU2 . . . . . . 116 D7
WALSWORTH 101 A1
Waltham Cl MK41 . . . . 38 F5
Waltham Cl LU2 . . . . 117 C3
Waltham Dr MK42 . . . . 50 D3
Walton Cl SG17 . . . . 77 E3
Wandon Cl LU2 . . . . 117 C4
Wansbeck Rd MK41 . . . . . . 38 C5
Wantage Pl NN29 . . . . .7 B8
Wantage Rd NN29 . . . . .7 B8
WARDEDGES 85 F4
Warden Abbey MK41 . . . . . 39 B1
Warden Ct 5 LU1 . . . . 123 E8
WARDEN HILL 116 D7
Warden Hill LU5 . . . . 43 C3
Warden Hill Cl LU2. . . . . . . 116 C8
Warden Hill Gdns LU2 . . . 116 C8
Warden Hill Inf Sch LU3 116 C7
Warden Hill Jun Sch
  LU3 . . . . 116 C7
Warden Hill Rd LU2 . . . . . 116 C8
Warden Rd SG18 . . . . 65 D7
WARDEN STREET 64 F5
Wardhedges Rd MK45 . . . . 85 E4
Wardown Cres LU2 . . . . . . 116 A3
Wardown Ct LU3 . . . . 116 D2
Ware Rd PE19 . . . . 22 E6
Waresley Rd SG19 . . . . 44 D7
Warkworth Cl SG19 . . . . . . 54 C8

Warminster Cl LU2 . . . . 117 F1
Warneford Way LU7 . . . . . . 111 C5
Warren Cl
  Biggleswade SG18 . . . . 67 A7
  Irchester NN29 . . . . 7 C7
  Letchworth SG6 . . . . 101 D7
  Toddington LU5 . . . . 105 F7
Warren Dr The LU1 . . . . . . 124 C1
Warren Rd
  Ampthill MK45 . . . . 84 F7
  Luton LU1 . . . . 122 F8
Warren The MK41 . . . . 37 E5
Warton Gn LU2 . . . . 117 E2
Warwick Ave MK40 . . . . 38 A1
Warwick Cl MK45 . . . . 84 D1
Warwick Ct
  Luton LU4 . . . . 123 B8
  St Neots PE19 . . . . 22 C3
Warwick Ho MK40 . . . . 38 A2
Warwick Rd E LU4 . . . . 123 B8
Warwick Rd W LU4. . . . . . . 123 B8
Washbank Rd PE19 . . . . . . 22 E4
Washbrook Cl MK45 . . . . . . 97 C1
Washburn Cl MK41 . . . . 38 D6
Washingleys MK43 . . . . 59 C2
Washington Ave SG17 . . . . 76 E3
Waterborne Wlk 7 LU7 . 111 A7
Waterdell LU7 . . . . 111 C7
WATER END
  HP1 . . . . 132 F2
  MK17 . . . . 94 C7
  MK44 . . . . 52 A4
  MK45 . . . . 86 A7
  SG19 . . . . 57 B3
Water End
  Cople MK44 . . . . 52 B4
  Workhouse End MK41 . . . . 40 A4
  Wrestlingworth SG19 . . . . 57 B3
Water End La LU4 . . . . 106 C2
Water End Rd MK45 . . . . . . 85 F7
WATERHALL 70 C2
Water La
  Chelveston NN9 . . . . 3 B8
  Flitwick MK45 . . . . 85 A2
  Hitchin SG5 . . . . 100 F1
  Kempston MK42 . . . . 49 C3
  Leighton Buzzard LU7 . . . . 110 F7
Waterloo Cl MK45 . . . . 84 E4
Waterloo Dr PE19 . . . . 22 F3
Waterloo La SG5 . . . . 100 A6
Waterloo Rd
  Bedford MK40 . . . . 50 D8
  Leighton Buzzard LU7 . . . . 110 E6
Waterlow Chapel 5 LU6 114 A1
Waterlow Rd LU6 . . . . 114 A1
Watermead Rd LU3 . . . . . . 115 F6
Waters End SG5 . . . . 90 E6
Waterside LU6 . . . . 119 F4
Waterslade Gn LU3 . . . . . . 116 B6
Watery La AL3 . . . . 129 E3
Watkin Wlk SG18 . . . . 66 F7
Watling Ct
  Dunstable LU6 . . . . 114 A2
  1 Houghton Regis LU5. . 114 B4
Watling Gdns LU6. . . . . 121 D6
Watling Lower Sch LU6 . 121 C7
Watling Pl LU5 . . . . 114 B4
Watling St LU6 . . . . 113 E4
Watson Rd MK45 . . . . 62 C6
Watson Way MK43 . . . . 72 D8
Waulud Prim Sch LU3 . . . 115 E7
Waulds Bank Dr LU3 . . . . . 115 E7
Wavell Cl MK43 . . . . 61 C1
Wavendon Ho MK17 . . . . . 81 A8
Wavendon House Dr
  MK17 . . . . 81 B8
Wavendon Rd MK17 . . . . . 70 C2
Waveney Ave MK41 . . . . . . 38 D5
Waveney Rd AL5 . . . . 131 C3
Waverly Ave SG19 . . . . 42 B1
Waverly Pre-Prep Sch
  MK45 . . . . 84 E3
Wayside LU6 . . . . 121 D5
Wear The MK41 . . . . 38 C7
Weatherby LU6 . . . . 120 E8
Weatherby Rd LU4 . . . . 115 C2
Weathercock Cl MK17 . . . . 81 C4
Weathercock La MK17 . . . . 81 C4
Weatherfield Sch LU6 . . . 113 E1
Weaver Cl MK41 . . . . 38 D6
Weavers Gn SG19 . . . . 42 C2
Weavers La MK43 . . . . 26 C4
Weavers Orch SG15 . . . . . . 90 A4
Webber Cl SG17 . . . . 77 D3
Webbs Cl MK43 . . . . 36 F3
Wedgewood Rd LU4 . . . . . . 114 F4
Wedgwood Rd MK41 . . . . . 38 B3
Weedon Cl SG16 . . . . 89 C5
Welbeck Gdns MK41 . . . . . 38 F5
Welbeck Rd 3 LU2 . . . . . 123 E8
Welbourne Gdns MK42 . . . 50 F5
Welbury Ave LU2 . . . . 116 C7
Weldon Cl LU2 . . . . 117 C1
Welland Ct
  Bedford MK41 . . . . 38 D5
  St Neots PE19 . . . . 22 C4
Wellfield Ave LU3 . . . . 115 C8
Wellgate Rd LU4 . . . . 115 D2
WELL HEAD 120 D5
Well Head Rd LU6 . . . . 120 C6
Wellhouse Cl LU1 . . . . 123 A7
Wellingham Ave SG5 . . . . 100 D1
Wellington Ct 3 LU1. . . . 123 D6
Wellington Dr SG17 . . . . . . 76 F3
Wellington Ho LU7 . . . . . . 103 A4
Wellington Rd MK42 . . . . . 50 F7

Wellington St
  Bedford MK40 . . . . 38 B1
  Luton LU1 . . . . 123 D7
Wellington Terr LU5 . . . . . 121 C8
Well La LU7 . . . . 110 A1
Wellpond Cl MK44 . . . . 16 D3
Wells Ct
  Harpenden AL5 . . . . 130 E4
  Kempston MK42 . . . . 49 E6
Wells Ct 1 LU7 . . . . 111 A7
Wellsfield MK44 . . . . 41 E3
Wells Rd MK44 . . . . 10 F2
Weltmore Rd LU3 . . . . 115 F6
Wendover Cl AL5 . . . . 131 D1
Wendover Ct MK41 . . . . . . 38 F1
Wendover Dr MK41 . . . . . . 39 A1
Wendover Way LU2 . . . . . . 116 F3
Wenlock CE Jun Sch
  LU2 . . . . 124 B8
Wenlock Rd MK42 . . . . 49 C3
Wenlock St LU2 . . . . 123 E6
Wensleydale LU2 . . . . 116 E1
Wentworth Av LU4 . . . . . . 115 C6
Wentworth Cl LU5 . . . . 105 F7
Wentworth Cl LU5 . . . . 95 F1
Wentworth Dr
  Bedford MK41 . . . . 38 F5
  Leighton Buzzard LU7 . . . . 111 A8
Wentworth Gdns LU5 . . . . 106 A6
Werth Dr MK17 . . . . 81 B2
Wesley Cl SG15 . . . . 90 A4
Wesley Rd
  Markyate AL3 . . . . 128 E5
  Sandy SG19 . . . . 42 C1
West Arc 13 MK40 . . . . . . 50 B8
Westbourne Rd
  Bedford MK40 . . . . 49 F7
  Luton LU4 . . . . 116 B1
Westbury Cl LU5 . . . . 114 B3
Westbury Ct
  Ampthill MK45 . . . . 84 F8
  Bedford MK41 . . . . 38 C5
Westbury Gdns LU2 . . . . . 116 E3
Westbury Pl SG6 . . . . 101 E5
Westbury Prim Sch SG6 . 101 E5
West Cl SG4 . . . . 101 B1
West Ct
  Bedford MK41 . . . . 39 A2
  Leighton Buzzard LU7 . . . . 110 F7
Westdale Wlk MK42 . . . . . 49 F4
West Dene HP2 . . . . 132 F8
Westdown Gdns LU6 . . . . 120 F7
West Dr SG15 . . . . 90 B4
WEST END
  MK43 . . . . 36 B8
  MK43 . . . . 70 F8
  MK44 . . . . 13 A2
  MK45 . . . . 86 B4
West End
  Elstow MK42 . . . . 50 B3
  Stevington MK43 . . . . 36 A8
West End La SG19 . . . . 56 A8
West End Rd
  Kempston MK43 . . . . 48 D5
  Silsoe MK45. . . . . 86 B3
Westerdale LU4. . . . . 115 B5
Western Ave SG16 . . . . 89 B3
Western Cl SG6. . . . . 90 E1
Western Rd LU1 . . . . 123 D6
Western St MK40 . . . . 50 B8
Western Way
  Dunstable LU6 . . . . 114 E1
  Letchworth SG6 . . . . 90 E1
  Sandy SG19 . . . . 54 B8
Westfield Ave AL5 . . . . 131 A3
Westfield Dr AL5 . . . . 131 B4
Westfield Gdns SG19 . . . . . 54 B8
Westfield Mid Sch MK40. . 49 B8
Westfield Pl AL5 . . . . 131 B4
Westfield Rd
  Bedford MK40 . . . . 49 F8
  Dunstable LU6 . . . . 113 F1
  Harpenden AL5 . . . . 131 B4
  Henlow SG16 . . . . 78 C1
  Oakley MK43 . . . . 36 E8
  Wyboston MK44. . . . . 31 F8
Westgate Ct LU6 . . . . 121 A8
West Gr MK40 . . . . 49 F8
West Hill
  Aspley Guise MK17 . . . . . . 81 D4
  Dunstable LU6 . . . . 121 C5
West Hill Rd LU1 . . . . 123 C5
Westholme SG6. . . . . 101 F8
West La SG5 . . . . 99 D5
Westlecote Gdns LU2 . . . . 116 A4
West Lodge Cotts LU2. . . 117 D5
WESTMILL 100 C1
Westmill La
  Hitchin SG5 . . . . 100 C2
  Ickleford SG5 . . . . 100 C3
Westmill Lawns SG5 . . . . 100 D1
Westmill Rd SG5. . . . . 100 D1
Westminster Gdns
  Houghton Regis LU5 . . . . 114 D6
  Kempston MK42 . . . . 49 E6
Westmorland Ave LU3. . . . 115 F5
Weston Ave LU7 . . . . 111 C6
Weston Ct PE19 . . . . 22 C4
WESTONING 95 F6
Westoning Lower Sch
  MK45 . . . . 95 E6
Westoning Rd
  Greenfield MK45 . . . . 85 B1
  Harlington LU5 . . . . 95 E3
Westoria Ct MK45 . . . . 95 E5

West Par LU6 . . . . **121** A8
West Rd
  Gamlingay SG19 . . . . **44** C4
  Sandy SG19 . . . . **54** B8
  Wharley End MK43 . . . . . . **58** D2
  Woburn Sands MK17 . . . . . **81** B5
Westrope Way MK41 . . . . **38** D7
Westside
  Leighton Buzzard LU7 . . . . **110** F7
  Leighton Buzzard LU7 . . . . **111** A8
West St
  Dunstable LU6 . . . . **121** A8
  Leighton Buzzard LU7 . . . . **110** F7
  Lilley LU2 . . . . **109** D1
  St Neots PE19 . . . . **22** E5
West View
  Beeston SG19 . . . . **54** B5
  Langford SG18 . . . . **78** F6
  Letchworth SG6 . . . . **101** E4
  Letchworth SG6 . . . . **101** E4
Westway LU2 . . . . **117** C4
West Way
  Harpenden AL5 . . . . **131** C2
  Moggerhanger MK44 . . . . . **53** C7
West Wlk SG6 . . . . **67** B7
Westwood Cl MK42 . . . . . **51** A2
Wetherne Link LU4 . . . . . **115** C5
Wexham Cl LU3 . . . . **115** E8
Weybourne Cl AL5 . . . . . **131** D2
Weybourne Dr LU2 . . . . . **116** C7
Wharfdale 7 LU4 . . . . . . **115** C5
Wharfe The MK41 . . . . . . **38** C6
Wharf Mews SG18 . . . . . **66** F6
WHARLEY END **58** D2
Wheatfield Cl LU7 . . . . . **111** D7
Wheatfield Ct LU4 . . . . . **114** E4
Wheatfield Rd LU4 . . . . . **114** E4
Wheat Hill SG6 . . . . **101** F8
Wheathouse Cl MK41 . . . . **38** F4
Wheatlands Cl MK45 . . . . **85** E8
Wheatsheaf Rd PE19 . . . . **22** C3
Wheel Wright Cl SG5 . . . . **87** F1
Whinnett's Way MK45 . . . **85** E1
Whipperley Ct LU1 . . . . . **123** C5
Whipperley Inf Sch LU1 . **123** A6
Whipperley Ring LU1 . . . . **123** A6
Whipperley Way LU1 . . . . **123** C5
WHIPSNADE **120** F1
Whipsnade Rd LU6 . . . . . **120** F7
Whipsnade Tree Cathedral★
  LU6 . . . . **120** F1
Whipsnade Wild Animal
  Park★ LU6 . . . . **126** E7
Whistler Rd PE19 . . . . . . **22** C5
Whiston Cres SG17 . . . . . **78** B3
Whitbread Ave MK42 . . . . **50** A6
Whitby Rd LU3 . . . . **116** C1
Whitby Way MK42 . . . . . . **50** C3
White Beam Cl MK42 . . . . **49** F2
Whitechurch Cl LU2 . . . . . **117** D2
Whitecroft Rd LU2 . . . . . **124** A8
White Crofts SG5 . . . . . . **90** F6
Whitefield Ave LU3 . . . . . **115** C7
Whitefield Inf Sch LU3 . . **115** E8
Whitefield Jun Sch LU3 . . **115** E8
Whitefriars NN10 . . . .**7** F8
Whitefriars Jun & Inf Schs
  NN10 . . . .**7** F8
Whitehall MK43 . . . . **72** B2
Whitehall Wlk PE19 . . . . . **22** F4
Whitehaven LU3 . . . . **107** F1
Whitehicks SG6 . . . . **91** A1
White Hill Rd MK45 . . . . . **97** C3
White Ho PE19 . . . . **22** C4
White Horse Cl LU7 . . . . . **104** E2
White Horse Ct LU7 . . . . . **111** A7
Whitehorse St SG7 . . . . . **91** F1
Whitehorse Vale LU3 . . . . **107** F1
Whitehouse Cl LU5 . . . . . **114** B4
Whitehurst Ave SG5 . . . . **100** F1
White Lion Ret Pk LU5 . . **114** C1
White Lodge Cl MK42 . . . . **49** C3
Whitethorn Way LU1 . . . . **123** A6
Whitewaybottom La SG4 **125** F5
Whitings MK40 . . . . **49** B6
Whitings Cl AL5 . . . . **131** D4
Whitley Gn LU2 . . . . **117** D2
Whitley Rd MK42 . . . . **51** A3
Whittingham Cl LU2 . . . . **117** F1
Whittingstall Ave MK42 . . **50** A4
Whittle Cl SG16 . . . . **89** B4
Whitwell Cl LU3 . . . . **116** B8
Whitworth Ct
  Kempston MK42 . . . . **49** E4
  Shefford SG17 . . . . **77** C3
Whitworth Jones Ave
  SG16 . . . . **89** C5
Whitworth Way MK45 . . . **62** F3
WICK END **48** B8

Wickets The LU2 . . . . **116** E1
Wick Hill LU6 . . . . **127** F8
Wickmere Cl LU2 . . . . **116** C7
Wickstead Ave LU4 . . . . . **115** E4
WIGMORE **117** E2
Wigmore La LU2 . . . . **117** D2
Wigmore Park Ctr LU2 . . . **117** E1
Wigmore Pl LU2 . . . . **117** E1
Wigmore Prim Sch LU2 . . **117** E2
Wigram Cl MK42 . . . . **50** B4
Wilbury Cl SG6 . . . . **101** C7
Wilbury Dr LU5 . . . . **114** E3
Wilbury Hills Rd SG6 . . . . **101** C7
Wilbury Jun Sch SG6 . . . . **101** D6
Wilbury Rd SG6 . . . . **101** E8
Wilbury Way SG4 . . . . . . **101** A3
Wildber Cl PE19 . . . . **22** F4
Wild Cherry Dr LU1 . . . . . **123** D5
WILDEN **29** F3
Wilden CE Lower Sch
  MK44 . . . . **29** F3
Wilden Rd
  Colmworth MK44 . . . . **30** A6
  Renhold MK41 . . . . **39** C7
Wildflower Way MK42 . . . **50** F4
Wilhamstead Lower Sch
  MK45 . . . . **62** F4
Wilkinson Cl PE19 . . . . . . **22** B3
Willenhall Cl LU3 . . . . . . **116** A7
William Austin Inf Sch
  LU3 . . . . **116** C4
William Austin Jun Sch
  LU3 . . . . **116** C4
William Dr PE19 . . . . **22** F1
Williams Cl SG18 . . . . **67** B8
Williamson Ct MK42 . . . . **49** C2
Williamson Rd MK42 . . . . **49** D2
Williamson St 1 LU1 . . . . **123** E7
William St
  Luton LU1 . . . . **116** E1
  Markyate AL3 . . . . **128** E5
William Sutton Ct
  Bedford MK40 . . . . **50** A8
  Luton LU2 . . . . **117** B5
Williams Way MK45 . . . . . **84** D4
Willian Rd SG4, SG6 . . . . **101** E1
WILLINGTON **52** C8
Willington Lower Sch
  MK44 . . . . **40** C1
Willington Rd MK44 . . . . . **52** A6
Williton Rd LU2 . . . . **117** C2
Willmers Cl MK41 . . . . . . **38** E4
Willmott Rd NN10 . . . . **8** C8
Willoughby Cl
  Dunstable LU6 . . . . **121** C7
  Great Barford MK44 . . . . . **40** F5
Willoughby Rd AL5 . . . . . **131** B4
Willow Bank Wlk LU7 . . . **111** C8
Willow Cl
  Bromham MK43 . . . . **36** F3
  St Neots PE19 . . . . **22** F3
Willow Ct LU3 . . . . **115** E5
Willowfield Lower Sch
  LU1 . . . . **122** F4
Willowgate Trad Est
  LU3 . . . . **115** A8
Willow Gr LU1 . . . . **122** E3
Willow Herb Cl NN10 . . . . .**8** C7
Willow Ho LU7 . . . . **110** E7
Willow Rd
  Bedford MK42 . . . . **50** D5
  Potton SG19 . . . . **56** A7
  Shefford SG17 . . . . **77** D2
  Wilstead MK45 . . . . **62** E2
Willow Rise SG19 . . . . **54** D6
Willows La HP1 . . . . **132** F1
Willow Springs MK43 . . . **71** A4
Willows The
  Edlesborough LU6 . . . . . . **119** F3
  Flitwick MK45 . . . . **84** E3
  Leighton Buzzard LU7 . . . . **111** B6
  Wootton MK43 . . . . **61** A8
Willow Tree Way SG5 . . . **100** F2
Willow Views 1 PE19 . . . **22** E5
Willow Way
  Ampthill MK45 . . . . **84** F7
  Flitwick MK45 . . . . **84** F1
  Harpenden AL5 . . . . **131** C4
  Houghton Regis LU5 . . . . **114** D6
  Luton LU3 . . . . **115** E5
  Toddington LU5 . . . . **105** F5
Willsheres Rd SG18 . . . . . **67** A7
Wilman Ct SG18 . . . . **78** E5
Wilsden Ave LU1 . . . . **123** C6
Wilshere Cres SG4 . . . . . **101** D1
Wilson Ct MK45 . . . . **62** F4
WILSTEAD **62** F3
Wilstead Hill MK45 . . . . . **74** F7
Wilstead Rd
  Elstow MK42 . . . . **50** C2
  Elstow MK42 . . . . **62** C8
  Wilstead MK45 . . . . **63** C5

Wilton Rd SG5 . . . . **100** E1
Wimborne Rd LU1 . . . . . . **123** C8
Wimple Rd LU4 . . . . **115** A2
Winchester Gdns LU3 . . . **107** E1
Winchester Rd
  Bedford MK42 . . . . **50** F4
  Sandy SG19 . . . . **54** C8
Winchfield LU1 . . . . **122** E4
Winch St LU2 . . . . **116** F1
Windermere Cl
  Dunstable LU6 . . . . **121** B7
  Flitwick MK45 . . . . **84** E2
Windermere Cres LU3 . . . **115** F5
Windermere Dr SG18 . . . . **67** A4
Windermere Gdns LU7 . . . **110** C7
Windermere The MK42 . . . **49** D3
Windmill Cl MK41 . . . . . . **39** B3
Windmill Ct MK44 . . . . . . **16** D3
Windmill Hill MK40 . . . . . **37** D2
Windmill Path 5 LU7 . . . **111** A7
Windmill Rd
  Flamstead AL3 . . . . **129** B6
  Flitwick MK45 . . . . **84** D4
  Luton LU1 . . . . **123** F6
Windmill Row 5 PE19 . . . **22** E5
Windmill View SG18 . . . . **67** A4
Windmill Way MK43 . . . . . **59** C3
Windrush Ave MK41 . . . . . **38** C5
Windrush Cl MK45 . . . . . . **84** D2
Windsor Ave LU7 . . . . **110** F7
Windsor Cl
  Flitwick MK45 . . . . **84** D1
  St Neots PE19 . . . . **22** F2
Windsor Ct 10 LU1 . . . . . **123** D6
Windsor Dr LU5 . . . . **114** D4
Windsor Gdns MK40 . . . . **38** D2
Windsor Par MK45 . . . . . . **97** C4
Windsor Pl LU5 . . . . **114** D5
Windsor Rd
  Barton-le-C MK45 . . . . . . **97** C4
  Bedford MK42 . . . . **50** D4
Windsor St LU1 . . . . **123** D6
Windsor Way
  Langford SG18 . . . . **78** F6
  Sandy SG19 . . . . **54** C7
Windsor Wlk 7 LU1 . . . . . **123** D6
Winfield St LU6 . . . . **114** B1
Wingate Cl LU4 . . . . **115** F2
Wingate Dr MK45 . . . . **85** A8
Wingate Rd
  Dunstable LU5 . . . . **114** F1
  Harlington LU5 . . . . **95** F2
  Luton LU4 . . . . **115** F2
WINGFIELD **105** E1
Wingfield Ave MK45 . . . . . **74** C1
Wingfield Cl MK40 . . . . . . **49** E7
Wingfield Ct MK45 . . . . . . **84** F8
Wingfield Dr SG19 . . . . . . **56** A8
Wingfield Rd
  Bromham MK43 . . . . **36** F4
  Tebworth LU7 . . . . **105** C2
Wing Rd
  Ascott LU7 . . . . **110** B4
  Leighton Buzzard LU7 . . . . **110** D5
Winhills Prim Sch PE19 . . **22** F4
Winifred Rd MK40 . . . . . . **49** F8
Winkfield Cl LU4 . . . . **115** B1
Winsdon Ct 1 LU1 . . . . . **123** D6
WINSDON HILL **122** B7
Winsdon Rd LU1 . . . . **123** D6
Winslow Cl LU3 . . . . **116** C4
Winston Cl LU7 . . . . **103** A1
Winston Cres SG18 . . . . . **67** A7
Winton Cl LU2 . . . . **116** D6
Wintringham Rd 7 PE19 . . **22** F5
Wisdom Cl MK43 . . . . **36** D2
Wiseman Cl LU2 . . . . **116** E7
Wisteria Cl NN10 . . . .**8** B7
Wistow Ct PE19 . . . . **22** C6
Wistow Rd LU3 . . . . **116** A6
Witham Cl MK41 . . . . **38** D7
Withybrook MK45 . . . . **84** E3
Withy Cl LU4 . . . . **115** B4
Witter Ave SG5 . . . . **100** E4
WITTS END **94** B6
Wivelsfield LU6 . . . . **119** E6
Wiveton Cl LU2 . . . . **116** D7
WOBURN **92** F7
Woburn Abbey★ MK17 . . **93** D6
Woburn Cl MK45 . . . . **84** C1
Woburn Ct
  Kempston MK42 . . . . **49** D3
  Leighton Buzzard LU7 . . . . **110** E6
  Luton LU4 . . . . **115** D5
Woburn La MK17 . . . . **81** E4
Woburn Lower Sch MK17 . **92** F7
WOBURN PARK **93** D7
Woburn Pl LU7 . . . . **103** A1
Woburn Rd
  Bedford MK40 . . . . **50** A8
  Heath and Reach LU7 . . . . **103** B7
  Hockliffe LU7 . . . . **104** E3
  Kempston MK42 . . . . **49** D2
  Kempston MK43 . . . . **61** C8

Woburn Rd continued
  Marston Moretaine MK43 . . **72** C7
  Millbrook MK45 . . . . **73** B1
  Woburn Sands MK17 . . . . **81** C1
Woburn Road Ind Est
  MK42 . . . . **49** D1
Woburn Safari Pk★ MK17,
  MK43 . . . . **82** D1
WOBURN SANDS **81** A4
Woburn Sands Sta MK17 . **81** A5
Woburn St LU1 . . . . **73** D1
Wodecroft Rd LU3 . . . . . . **116** B6
Wolfsburg Ct 4 LU4 . . . . **115** C1
Wollaston Rd NN29 . . . . . . **7** A8
Wolseley Bsns Pk MK42 . . **49** E1
Wolseley Ct MK42 . . . . . . **49** E1
Wolseley Rd MK42 . . . . . . **49** E1
Wolston Cl LU1 . . . . **123** C7
Woodall Cl SG18 . . . . **66** F6
Woodbridge Cl LU4 . . . . . **115** E4
WOODBURY **43** E6
Woodbury Hill LU2 . . . . . **116** E3
Wood Cl
  Biddenham MK40 . . . . **37** C1
  Kensworth LU6 . . . . **121** E1
Woodcock Cl SG19 . . . . . . **42** B2
Woodcock Rd LU1 . . . . . . **123** A7
Woodcock Wlk MK45 . . . . **84** D1
Woodcote MK41 . . . . **39** A3
WOOD END
  MK17 . . . . **95** B5
  MK43 . . . . **48** D2
  MK43 . . . . **71** F7
  MK44 . . . .**6** D1
  MK44 . . . . **28** D3
Wood End Cl MK44 . . . . . . **16** B3
Wood End Hill AL5 . . . . . . **130** D4
Wood End JM Sch AL5 . . . **130** D3
Wood End La MK44 . . . . . . **31** C2
Wood End La MK43 . . . . . . **48** F2
Wood End Rd
  Cranfield MK43 . . . . **71** B7
  Harpenden AL5 . . . . **130** D3
  Kempston MK43 . . . . **48** D2
Woodfield Gate LU5 . . . . . **121** E6
Woodfield La MK41 . . . . . . **40** A6
Woodford Rd LU5 . . . . **114** E1
Wood Green Cl LU2 . . . . . **117** B5
Wood Green Rd LU2 . . . . . **117** C5
Woodhouse La PE19 . . . . . **21** F6
Woodhurst SG6 . . . . **101** F8
Wood La
  Aspley Guise MK17 . . . . . **81** D4
  Cotton End MK45 . . . . **63** D7
  Renhold MK41 . . . . **39** E6
  Willington MK44 . . . . **52** D7
Woodland Ave
  Leighton Buzzard LU7 . . . . **102** F2
  Luton LU3 . . . . **116** B2
Woodland Cl
  Heath and Reach LU7 . . . . **103** A5
  Potton SG19 . . . . **56** A8
Woodland Dr MK43 . . . . . . **36** F4
Woodland Mid Sch MK45 . **84** D2
Woodland Pk MK45 . . . . . . **62** F2
Woodland Rise LU6 . . . . . **127** B7
Woodlands
  Bedford MK41 . . . . **38** B6
  Caddington LU1 . . . . **122** E3
  Harpenden AL5 . . . . **130** E3
  Tebworth LU7 . . . . **105** C2
Woodlands Ave LU5 . . . . . **114** C4
Woodlands Cl MK44 . . . . . **52** A5
Woodlands Rd NN29 . . . . . .**7** A7
Woodlands The SG18 . . . . **66** C3
Woodland Way MK17 . . . . **81** B4
Woodman Cl LU1 . . . . **111** B7
Woodmer Cl SG5 . . . . **87** C2
Woodmere
  Bedford MK41 . . . . **38** F3
  Luton LU3 . . . . **108** A1
WOODMER END **87** E2
Woodpecker Way SG19 . . . **42** B2
Wood Rd MK43 . . . . **24** F7
WOODSIDE
  LU1 . . . . **123** A2
  MK41 . . . . **39** B4
Woodside
  Aspley Guise MK17 . . . . . **81** D3
  Eaton Bray LU6 . . . . **119** E6
Woodside Animal Farm &
  Leisure Park★ LU1 . . . . **129** A8
Woodside Ind Est LU5 . . . **114** D3
Woodside Mid Sch MK41 . **39** B4
Woodside Park Ind Est
  LU5 . . . . **114** C3
Woodside Rd LU1 . . . . **123** B3
Woodside Way LU7 . . . . . **110** D6
Wood St
  Dunstable LU6 . . . . **121** C8
  Luton LU1 . . . . **123** F6
  Woburn Sands MK17 . . . . **81** B4
Woodstock Rd MK40 . . . . **49** F7
Wood The LU7 . . . . **111** A8

Woodview MK45 . . . . **62** F2
Woodville Dr MK40 . . . . . **49** B6
Woolfield SG19 . . . . **54** D6
Woolgrove Ct SG4 . . . . . . **101** B1
Woolgrove Rd SG4 . . . . . . **101** B1
Woolpack Cl LU6 . . . . **121** C7
Wooton Field SG19 . . . . . **44** D4
WOOTTON **61** A7
WOOTTON BOURNE END . **48** C1
WOOTTON BROADMEAD . . **61** C3
Wootton Cl LU3 . . . . **116** B7
WOOTTON GREEN **60** D4
Wootton Lower Sch MK43 **60** F7
Wootton Rd MK43 . . . . . . **49** A1
Wootton Upper Sch MK43 **60** E7
Worboys Ct SG8 . . . . **69** F5
Worcester Rd MK42 . . . . . **50** F4
Wordsworth Ave PE19 . . . **22** D5
Wordsworth Cl SG18 . . . . **66** C8
Wordsworth Ct MK40 . . . . **37** F2
Wordsworth Rd
  Harpenden AL5 . . . . **131** A3
  Luton LU4 . . . . **115** A2
WORKHOUSE END **40** A5
Worthington Rd LU6 . . . . **120** F8
Wrayfields SG5 . . . . **91** B8
Wraysbury Cl LU4 . . . . . . **115** D3
Wren Cl
  Flitwick MK45 . . . . **84** D1
  Luton LU2 . . . . **117** C6
  Sandy SG19 . . . . **42** C1
Wren Wlk LU6 . . . . **119** E4
WRESTLINGWORTH **57** C2
Wrestlingworth CE Lower
  Sch SG19 . . . . **57** B3
Wrestlingworth Rd SG19 . **56** C6
Wrest Park Gardens★
  MK45 . . . . **86** E3
Wroxham Way
  Bedford MK40 . . . . **49** D7
  Harpenden AL5 . . . . **131** C3
Wulwards Cl LU1 . . . . **123** B6
Wulwards Cl LU1 . . . . **123** B6
Wyatt Cl SG5 . . . . **100** D4
Wyatt Rd MK42 . . . . **49** D3
WYBOSTON **32** A5
Wyboston Ct PE19 . . . . . . **22** C4
Wyboston L Pk★ MK44 . . **32** C7
Wybridge MK44 . . . . **12** B1
Wybridge Cl MK44 . . . . . . **12** B2
Wychwood Ave LU2 . . . . . **116** E3
Wychwood Rd 2 MK41 . . . **39** B4
Wycklond Cl SG5 . . . . **90** E6
Wycliffe Cl LU3 . . . . **116** C6
Wycombe Way LU3 . . . . . **116** C8
Wye Cl MK41 . . . . **38** D5
Wyken Cl LU3 . . . . **116** A7
WYMINGTON **8** B5
Wymington Rd
  Podington NN29 . . . .**7** E3
  Rushden NN10 . . . .**8** B8
Wynchwood La SG17 . . . . **77** B2
Wyndham Rd LU4 . . . . . . **115** C2
Wynd The SG6 . . . . **101** F6
Wyngates LU7 . . . . **110** E5
Wynnefield Wlk SG19 . . . **54** C8
Wysells Ct SG6 . . . . **101** D7
Wyton Cl SG17 . . . . **76** F2
Wyvern Cl LU4 . . . . **115** E3

Y

Yardley Ct 14 AL5 . . . . . . **131** B1
Yarrow Cl NN10 . . . .**8** C7
Yately Cl LU2 . . . . **116** D7
YELDEN **4** A2
Yelnow La MK44 . . . . **16** A3
Yeomans Ave AL5 . . . . . . **130** D3
Yeomans Gate MK44 . . . . **51** D4
Yeovil Ct LU2 . . . . **117** B2
Yeovil Rd LU2 . . . . **117** B2
Yew St LU5 . . . . **114** D7
Yew Tree Cl
  Eaton Bray LU6 . . . . **119** F5
  Silsoe MK45 . . . . **86** C3
Yew Tree Ct 3 LU7 . . . . . **111** A7
Yew Tree Wlk SG17 . . . . . **78** B2
York Cl
  Barton-le-C MK45 . . . . . . **97** D4
  Biggleswade SG18 . . . . . . **67** B5
York Ct LU7 . . . . **110** F7
York Rd SG5 . . . . **100** E1
York St
  Bedford MK40 . . . . **50** E8
  Luton LU2 . . . . **123** F8
Young Ind Est LU7 . . . . . **111** D6